Idiosyncratic Deals at Work

Smriti Anand · Yasin Rofcanin
Editors

Idiosyncratic Deals at Work

Exploring Individual, Organizational, and Societal Perspectives

Foreword by Denise M. Rousseau

Editors
Smriti Anand
Illinois Institute of Technology
Chicago, IL, USA

Yasin Rofcanin
University of Bath
Bath, UK

ISBN 978-3-030-88515-1   ISBN 978-3-030-88516-8 (eBook)
https://doi.org/10.1007/978-3-030-88516-8

© The Editor(s) (if applicable) and The Author(s), under exclusive license to Springer Nature Switzerland AG 2022
This work is subject to copyright. All rights are solely and exclusively licensed by the Publisher, whether the whole or part of the material is concerned, specifically the rights of translation, reprinting, reuse of illustrations, recitation, broadcasting, reproduction on microfilms or in any other physical way, and transmission or information storage and retrieval, electronic adaptation, computer software, or by similar or dissimilar methodology now known or hereafter developed.
The use of general descriptive names, registered names, trademarks, service marks, etc. in this publication does not imply, even in the absence of a specific statement, that such names are exempt from the relevant protective laws and regulations and therefore free for general use.
The publisher, the authors and the editors are safe to assume that the advice and information in this book are believed to be true and accurate at the date of publication. Neither the publisher nor the authors or the editors give a warranty, expressed or implied, with respect to the material contained herein or for any errors or omissions that may have been made. The publisher remains neutral with regard to jurisdictional claims in published maps and institutional affiliations.

This Palgrave Macmillan imprint is published by the registered company Springer Nature Switzerland AG
The registered company address is: Gewerbestrasse 11, 6330 Cham, Switzerland

Foreword

It is a pleasure to introduce this provocative compendium of the latest scholarly thinking on idiosyncratic deals. With its panoptic, multi- and cross-level, view of idiosyncratic deals, this book sheds light on overlooked facets and emergent problems, and in doing so, it highlights the multiple stakeholders these deals have inside and outside the workplace.

I-DEALS THE CONCEPT: Idiosyncratic deals (i-deals) are personalized work arrangements intended to meet those individual needs and preferences falling out outside an employer's standard offerings. Although such needs are not new, recognition of the potential of i-deals to help fulfill them has been fueled by trends toward individualization of work and more flexible bottom/up (as opposed to top/down) management practices. Employees increasingly negotiate i-deals to attain myriad goals from work life balance and career development to self-enhancement and security. Employers grant i-deals to motivate employee to join, stay, and contribute, to pilot employment innovations, and to address relational problems and conflicts on the job.

BACKGROUND: My 2005 book *I-deals: Idiosyncratic Deals Employees Bargain for Themselves* (M.E. Sharpe) introduced this workplace phenomenon to scholars and practitioners. A search in research publication databases yields 27 published articles until 2015, when Mathijs Bal and I published *Idiosyncratic Deals Between Employees and Organizations: Conceptual Issues, Applications, and the Role of Coworkers* (Routledge) to further develop the concept and stoke scholarly attention. Interest in i-deals continues to grow with a 300% increase in number of peer-reviewed articles since then, a trajectory affirming the interest in i-deals and future growth opportunities.

THIS BOOK: An i-deal's implications and repercussions depend on the perspective of the i-dealer, the manager, their coworkers, and the organization. Editors Smriti Anand and Yasin Rofcanin extend scholarship on i-deals by addressing the viewpoints of key stakeholders (i-deal recipients, granting employers, and coworkers) and expanding the theoretical lenses applied to include social influence and job demand theory among others. Anand and Rofcanin, prominent i-deal scholars themselves, have assembled an author team representing an array of perspectives, including psychology, economics, sociology, philosophy, critical management, and cross-cultural research. These perspectives encourage the reader to question assumptions often made about i-deals. Helping the reader to adopt a questioning outlook, this book offers three sets of assumption-challenging perspectives.

Expanding Views of I-deal Stakeholders: The first four chapters challenge the reader to reconsider prevailing assumptions about key stakeholders, their roles, and motives for seeking or granting i-deals. Guerrero and Bentein point out that some employees never seek out i-deals and that many i-deal requests are not granted. Yet, i-deals research has been silent on these "omissions." They make a case for expanding our focus beyond successful i-deal negotiations to examine the antecedents and consequences of absent or failed negotiations. Afacan Findikli, Las Heras, Rofcanin, and Ererdi delve into the i-deals negotiation process, introducing the notion of stakeholders coming from both work and nonwork domains. They expand conceptualization of the stakeholders of i-deals beyond work to include nonwork stakeholders including spouses, family members, friends, and others. Recognition of nonwork stakeholders introduces new i-deal forms including family and leisure i-deals. Sharma, Anand, Wagman, and Haddadian Nekah draw on economic theory to raise questions about managerial decision-making processes in granting i-deals. They note that i-deal-seeking employees have private information about their skills, working habits, and intentions, while managers often lack full information about employee performance or potential. Sharma and colleagues challenge scholars to better explicate how this information asymmetry may be reduced to better utilize i-deals as a strategic human resource practice. Finally, the dominant assumption that employees are the sole initiators of i-deal negotiations is ripe for challenge. Meuser and Cao build thought experiments to specify scenarios wherein leaders initiate i-deals for their subordinates. The authors posit that leader's offer of an i-deal triggers an appraisal process, shaped by individual and work group factors, such that the subordinate's acceptance of the deal is based on whether the leader manifests servant or exploitative leadership. In all, this first set of chapters challenges existing assumptions regarding the stakeholders of i-deals, providing direction for their more comprehensive representation.

Balancing Individual and Collective Good: The second set of chapters addresses the tricky balance that i-deals strike between individual good and collective good. The customization meted out by i-deals creates different terms of employment among members of a work unit risking disruption of group dynamics. Its three chapters focus on issues of fairness in the process of i-deals negotiation and implementation. First, Vidyarthi, Renz, Villanueva, and Anand lament cross-sectional snap shots that make up so much of i-deals research and present a framework for a more dynamic view based on the lifecycle of i-deals from employee recognition of unmet needs to negotiation, implementation, and continuation or modification of the terms of i-deals. By studying i-deals across their full life cycle in their group context, these authors argue that we can better understand how i-deals can benefit both individual employees and the collective. Second, Rofcanin, Afacan Findikli, Las Heras, and Ererdi call attention to the coworkers who observe the differentiation i-deals can create and stand to be affected by it. Taking a multi-level view from the individual, group, and organizational levels, this chapter addresses factors that shape co-worker emotional reactions to others' i-deals, including the role of social information and emotional contagion. Finally, Varma, Wang, Park, and Patel show how organizations can institutionalize i-deals as a means for effective talent management. They advocate consistent criteria for awarding individualized arrangements, clear i-deal terms to be adapted required, and transparent communication with the entire workgroup. At the same time, in a global context, they emphasize the importance of local or societal culture in implementing i-deals. In its focus on balancing the individual and collective good, this part of the book directs attention to the dynamic nature of i-deals over their full range of i-deal-related phenomena, from successfully implemented deals, the unasked for, denied, suspended and renegotiated, while calling attention to their implications for others aside from i-deal recipients and the organization. Undertaking research on balancing individual and collective goods can address key dilemmas in both strategic human resource management and organizational practice.

Critique—The Dark-Side of I-deals and Limits of Past Research: The last part of this book explores the dark side of a key force in i-deal creation, the individualization of work, with the goal of promoting i-deals research from a social justice and critical perspective. Its five chapters speculate the reasons for lower growth in i-deals research in comparison with similar conceptual areas like job crafting, despite the increasing relevance of individualization of work and individualism in contemporary society. Two key reasons for this are the tacit assumption by many i-deals scholars (N.B. not my assumption, however, as the 2005 book documents) that individualization is available and beneficial to everyone, and shortcomings in i-deals measurement instruments. First, Bal points out the ideological and practical risks in assuming egalitarian bases for i-deals whose employee-driven nature removes responsibility of employee welfare from the employers. He proposes a dignity perspective whereby instead of focusing on profit maximization employers think about enhancing employee dignity and quality of life through customization of work arrangements to fulfill their unique needs and goals. Similarly, Mughal, Wang, and Zafar draw on Michel Foucault's works to understand the implications of promoting individualization of work. They observe that i-deals may deepen power differentials, benefitting only those who are able to bargain, further disenfranchising those unable to do so. Perera and Li further expound this point by drawing on justice and diversity literatures to posit that the risk of stereotyping may dissuade marginalized or non-majority employees from pursuing i-deals. Focusing on women and older workers, this chapter explores how organizations can address these challenges, using i-deals to augment both identity blind and identity-conscious HR practices. The next two chapters critique i-deals literature for having narrow theoretical perspectives. Bakker and Ererdi propose that i-deals should be examined through the lens of job demands-resources (JD-R), for i-deals are resources that can be utilized to tackle work demands and enhance employee well-being and performance. Wasti, Erstoy, and Erdogan argue for adopting a cross-national perspective since i-deal negotiation and its processes can reflect the culture in which they are embedded. To develop a richer theory of i-deals, we must better understand what individualization of work means in different societies, labor markets, and economic conditions. In all, these five chapters prompt i-deal scholars to reconsider core assumptions and boundary conditions of i-deal theory and more deeply consider the social implications of individualization of work for power, dignity, and social justice.

Idiosyncratic deals, in my thinking, are part of the human project advancing respect for persons as both individuals and community members while creating new ways of solving emerging problems in organizations and work life. We learn by doing and reflection. It is in i-deal implementation where we can come to appreciate their benefits, repercussions, and future opportunities. In the two decades since the first book on idiosyncratic deals, our research and experience have broadened and deepened, culminating in this book, *Idiosyncratic Deals at Work: Exploring Individual, Organizational, and Societal Perspectives*. When I first wrote on i-deals I tried to make clear that their implementation is not always easy, potentially putting a sense of fairness or true equity at risk. Nor is it always desirable, since rampant one-off deals are poor substitutes for standard employment practices in which workers share. With the goal of formulating i-deals in ways that optimize their benefits and mitigate harms to their many stakeholders, the panoptic view of this book can help scholars and designers of i-deals to identify their sweet spots.

As food for thought and debate, this book provides an expansive interdisciplinary view of i-deals for a broad audience. It can stimulate scholars and graduate students in OB, strategic HRM, labor relations, sociology and critical management to drill down into the implications of i-deals for motivation, performance management, and workplace justice. At the same time, it prepares thoughtful practitioners to deploy i-deals as an essential part of a family of adaptive workplace practices, including job crafting, experiments, and innovative standard offerings, to create more satisfying and valueful work. Scholars and practitioners alike will be better informed and energized by this thoughtful book.

Denise M. Rousseau
Carnegie Mellon University
Pittsburgh, USA

Denise M. Rousseau is the H.J. Heinz II University Professor of Organizational Behavior and Public Policy at Carnegie Mellon University's Heinz College of Information Systems and Public Policy and the Tepper School of Business.

Her research focuses upon the impact workers have on the employment relationship and the firms that employ them. It advances research and practice regarding worker well-being and career development, organizational effectiveness, the management of change, firm ownership and governance, and industrial relations. Her publications include over a dozen books and over 220 articles and monographs in leading journals of management and psychology.

Contents

1 Requesting and Obtaining Development I-deals: A Career-Based Perspective — 1
Sylvie Guerrero and Kathleen Bentein

2 Does What Happen at Work, Stay at Work? Flexibility I-Deals and Employee Lives Outside of the Workplace — 21
Mine Afacan Findikli, Mireia Las Heras, Yasin Rofcanin, and Can Ererdi

3 I-deal or No I-deal? Lessons for Managers from Economic Theory — 45
Priyanka Sharma, Smriti Anand, Liad Wagman, and Pouya Haddadian Nekah

4 Servant or Sinister? A Process Model of Follower Appraisal of Leader-Initiated I-deals — 71
Jeremy D. Meuser and Xiaoyun Cao

5 Idiosyncratic Deals in Workgroups: Social Comparisons and Organizational Justice Perspectives in a Lifecycle Framework — 95
Prajya R. Vidyarthi, Franziska M. Renz, Sarah J. Villanueva, and Smriti Anand

6	Idiosyncratic Deals and Individualization of Human Resource Management Practices: The Growth of HR Differentiation Yasin Rofcanin, Mine Afacan Findikli, Mireia Las Heras, and Can Ererdi	119
7	I-deals as a Human Resource Initiative: Exciting Innovation or Passing Fad? Arup Varma, Chun-Hsiao Wang, Hyun Mi Park, and Parth Patel	143
8	A Workplace Dignity Perspective on Idiosyncratic Deals at Work P. Matthijs Bal	167
9	The Dark Side of Individualization at Work: Idiosyncratic Deal Exploitation and the Creation of Elite Workers Farooq Mughal, Siqi Wang, and Aneesa Zafar	187
10	I-deals: Not Ideal for Employee Diversity? Sanjeewa Perera and Yiqiong Li	211
11	I-deals and Employee Well-Being: Examining I-deals from JD-R Perspective Arnold B. Bakker and Can Ererdi	237
12	I-Deals in Context: A Summary and Critical Review of I-Deals Literature Around the Globe S. Arzu Wasti, Nevra Cem Ersoy, and Berrin Erdogan	257
13	I-deals and the Future of Work: A Research Agenda for the Post-pandemic Age Smriti Anand and Yasin Rofcanin	309

Index   335

Notes on Contributors

Mine Afacan Findikli, Ph.D. is Professor of Strategy and Business Administration at Istinye University where she serves as the Head of Business Department at FEAS. Her research interests include human resource differentiation and i-deals.

Smriti Anand, Ph.D. is Associate Professor of Management at Illinois Institute of Technology's Stuart School of Business in Chicago. Her research interests include leadership, diversity, and non-traditional work arrangements (i-deals) with particular focus on multi-level and cross-cultural frameworks. Her research has been published in leading journals of management, such as *Academy of Management Journal*, *Human Relations*, *Human Resource Management*, *Journal of Applied Psychology*, *Leadership Quarterly*, and *Journal of Management Studies*. Smriti is currently serving as Co-Editor for *Human Relations* journal.

Arnold B. Bakker, Ph.D. is a Professor of Work & Organizational Psychology at Erasmus University Rotterdam, Adjunct Professor at Lingnan University Hong Kong, Distinguished Visiting Professor at the University of Johannesburg, and Extraordinary Professor at North-West University, Potchefstroom, South Africa. His research interests include work engagement, JD-R theory, job crafting, work-family interface, sports psychology, and student engagement. He publishes regularly in the main journals in the field, including *Journal of Organizational Behaviour*, *Journal of Occupational Health Psychology*, and *Journal of Vocational*

Behaviour. He is Editor of *Current issues in Work and Organizational Psychology* (Psychology Press) and *Advances in Positive Organizational Psychology* (Emerald), and past President of the European Association of Work and Organizational Psychology (EAWOP).

P. Matthijs Bal, Ph.D. is a Professor of Responsible Management at the Lincoln International Business School, UK. Prior to joining Lincoln, he has been affiliated to the Universities of Bath, VU Amsterdam, and Erasmus Rotterdam, The Netherlands. His research interests concern absurdity, ideology, individualization at work, dignity at work, and imagination.

Kathleen Bentein, Ph.D. is a Professor of Organizational Behaviour at the School of Business Administration of University of Quebec at Montreal (UQAM). Her main research areas include commitment toward different foci, turnover, attitudes change across time, servant leadership, and socialization process of newcomers. Her work has been published in a variety of journals, including *Journal of Applied Psychology*, *Journal of Organizational Behavior*, *Journal of Occupational and Organizational Psychology*, *Journal of Vocational Behavior*, and *Journal of Management*.

Xiaoyun Cao, Ph.D. is a Lecturer in Business at Lake Forest College. Her research explores the mechanisms that contribute to positive experiences at work. She possesses expertise in the areas of leadership, employee work arrangements, social networks, identity and identification, and organizational culture. Her work has been published in major academic journals including the Journal of Management.

Berrin Erdogan, Ph.D. is Professor of Management at Portland State University and Distinguished Research Professor at University of Exeter. She studies leadership, person-environment fit, and how they relate to employee well-being, effectiveness, and retention. She has published over 70 articles and book chapters in journals including *Academy of Management Journal*, *Journal of Applied Psychology*, and *Personnel Psychology*. She serves as the Editor-in-Chief of Personnel Psychology (2020–2022).

Can Ererdi, Ph.D. is a Post-doctoral Fellow in Leadership at the University of Reading Henley Business School. His research focuses on the field of flexible work practices, HR differentiation, and employee well-being. His work is published in major organizational behavior and psychology journals such as the *International Journal of Human Resource Management*.

Nevra Cem Ersoy, Ph.D. is Assistant Professor at Izmir University of Economics Department of Psychology. She studies work engagement, employee well-being, and work motivation.

Sylvie Guerrero, Ph.D. is a Professor of Human Resource Management at the School of Business Administration of University of Quebec at Montreal (UQAM). Her research relates to the employment relationship (psychological contract and idiosyncratic deals), high-performance work practices, and organizational identification. She published her work in *Journal of Vocational Behavior*, *Human Resource Management Journal*, *Journal of Business*, and *Psychology and Corporate Governance: An International Journal*.

Pouya Haddadian Nekah is a Ph.D. candidate at the Illinois Institute of Technology in Chicago. His research interests focus on leadership, Top Management Team (TMT), consumer behavior, and emotional marketing. His dissertation relates to top management team structure and corporate performance.

Mireia Las Heras, Ph.D. is Professor at IESE Business School where she serves as the Research Director of the International Center for Work and Family. In 2009, she has co-edited a book on work family, A Practical Guide for Implementing Effective Work Family Policies Across Countries, and she has published other articles in work family integration, career development, and leadership.

Yiqiong Li, Ph.D. is a Senior Lecturer at the University of Queensland Business School. Her research agenda focuses upon exploring how organizational and job factors as well as HRM practices influence work-related well-being and translating this knowledge into strategies to enhance employee health and safety. Her research has been published in *Human Resource Management*, *Journal of Occupational Health and Psychology*, and *Journal of World Business*.

Jeremy D. Meuser, Ph.D. is Assistant Professor of Management at the University of Mississippi. His primary research interest is leadership—specifically leader-follower relationships (servant leadership and leader-member exchange) and the leadership construct proliferation problem.

He has published in the *Academy of Management Journal*, *The Leadership Quarterly*, the *Journal of Management*, and *The Oxford Handbook of Leadership in Organizations*. The Western Academy of Management selected him as a 2021 Ascendant Scholar recognizing excellence in research, teaching, and service.

Farooq Mughal, Ph.D. is a Senior Lecturer at the School of Management, University of Bath, UK. His research revolves around institutional, social, and culture practices that have an impact on work behaviors, leadership approaches, and learning and development activities in organizations. Farooq's work has been widely published in leading journals such as *Human Relations*, *HRMJ*, *Management Learning*, and *Business History*, among others.

Hyun Mi Park, Ph.D. is Lecturer in Business and Management in the School of Strategy and Leadership at Coventry University, UK Her research interests include human resource management and talent management, with special emphasis on talent management in Korea. Her research has appeared in several outlets including the *International Journal of Export Marketing*.

Parth Patel, Ph.D. is Senior Lecturer in Management at the Australian Institute of Business in Adelaide, Australia. He has published numerous book chapters, journal articles, and conference papers, and his area of expertise is in the disciplines of International Management-HRM and International Business.

Sanjeewa Perera, Ph.D. is a Senior Lecturer at the University of South Australia Business School. Her research focuses on demographic diversity with a special focus on age and gender. Current projects investigate the experiences of mature-age jobseekers and entrepreneurs. Her research has been published in the *Academy of Management Journal*, *The Leadership Quarterly*, and *Human Resource Management*.

Franziska M. Renz, Ph.D. earned her Ph.D. at the University of Texas at El Paso. Her research interests include leadership, organizational diversity, and psychological ownership.

Yasin Rofcanin, Ph.D. is a Professor of Organizational Psychology and Human Resources Management at University of Bath School of Management. He is also the Director of the Future of Work Research Centre in the School. His research falls in the domains of work-family management, flexible work practices, individualization of HRM practices, with focus on driving work engagement, proactivity, and well-being among employees. His research has appeared in leading journals including *Human Relations*, *Journal of Organizational Behavior*, *Journal of Vocational Behavior*, *Journal of Occupational Health Psychology*, *Journal of Occupational and Organizational Psychology*, and *Human Resource Management Journal*.

Priyanka Sharma, Ph.D. is Associate Professor of Economics at Illinois Institute of Technology's Stuart School of Business. In her research, she utilizes microeconomic theory and mathematical models to study economic questions in the areas of Industrial Organization and Information Economics. Her research interests lie in exploring how information (or lack thereof) shapes various aspects of firms' business strategies, including information acquisition, innovation, and contract design. She has presented her works at numerous conferences and published them in numerous leading academic journals.

Arup Varma, Ph.D. is Distinguished University Research Professor of Management at the Quinlan School of Business, Loyola University Chicago. His research focuses on performance appraisal, and expatriate adjustment and evaluation. His work has been published in leading OB/HR journals such as the *Academy of Management Journal*, *Human Resource Management*, *Human Resource Management Review*, *Journal of Applied Psychology*, and *Personnel Psychology*.

Prajya R. Vidyarthi, Ph.D. is Associate Professor of Management at the University of Texas at El Paso. His research interests include leadership, i-deals, workgroups, and culture. His research has been published in leading journals of management such as the *Academy of Management Journal*, *The Leadership Quarterly*, and the *Journal of Applied Psychology*.

Sarah J. Villanueva is a Ph.D. student at the University of Texas at El Paso. Her primary research interests relate to the employment experiences of individuals and groups with special emphasis on the study of military veterans in the workplace.

Liad Wagman, Ph.D. is Professor of Economics at Illinois Institute of Technology's Stuart School of Business in Chicago, and Senior Economic & Technology Advisor to the Federal Trade Commission's Office of Policy Planning. He works in the areas of Information Economics, Industrial Organization, and Law and Economics, focusing on issues at the intersection of data privacy and competition, entrepreneurship, and new venture financing.

Chun-Hsiao Wang, Ph.D. is Associate Professor at the Graduate Institute of Human Resource Management, National Central University, Taiwan. His research focuses on international assignment, organizational citizenship behavior, and strategic human resource management.

Siqi Wang is a Ph.D. candidate at the School of Management, University of Bath, UK. Her research interests center around work-family enrichment, employee proactive behaviors, and work engagement. Her dissertation focuses on family supportive supervisor behaviors, employees' job crafting and leisure crafting that shape employees' work performance, work engagement, and well-being.

S. Arzu Wasti, Ph.D. is a Professor of Management and Organization at Sabanci University. Her research is on organizational commitment, trust, and workplace aggression from a cultural perspective.

Aneesa Zafar is a part-time Teaching Fellow (VH) at the School of Management, University of Bath, UK, and a Ph.D. candidate at Lancaster University Management School, Lancaster University, UK. Her research lies at the crossroad of leadership, gender, and work from a critical perspective. For her doctoral thesis, she is endeavoring to understand women leader's narrative life experiences in illuminating the role of socio-cultural gendered practices as vessels of power in enabling and constraining women leader's identity, identity work, and work.

LIST OF FIGURES

Fig. 3.1	Information asymmetry in workplace: negative effects and mitigation strategies	51
Fig. 5.1	The i-deals lifecycle as a contextual framework for social comparisons and organizational justice perceptions in workgroups	101
Fig. 5.2	Outcomes of social comparisons and organizational justice perceptions at the recognition stage of the i-deals lifecycle	103
Fig. 5.3	Outcomes of social comparisons and organizational justice perceptions at the conduct stage of the i-deals lifecycle	109

List of Tables

Table 1.1	Avenues for future research	15
Table 3.1	Summary of employer's payoffs under various wage offers	54
Table 3.2	Payoffs under fixed wages	56
Table 7.1	Summary of key issues, proposed HR practices, and future research related to i-deals	152
Table 11.1	Summary and recommendations for future research	251
Table 12.1	Approach to cross-cultural research design	263
Table 12.2	Summary ideas for future research	268

CHAPTER 1

Requesting and Obtaining Development I-deals: A Career-Based Perspective

Sylvie Guerrero and Kathleen Bentein

REQUESTING AND OBTAINING DEVELOPMENT I-DEALS: A CAREER-BASED PERSPECTIVE

For more than a decade, the literature on i-deals has rapidly grown, providing a rich knowledge about the nature of i-deals, their antecedents and outcomes, and the group dynamics surrounding i-deals authorization (see for reviews Bal & Rousseau, 2015; Liao et al., 2014; Rosen et al., 2013). This rich literature emphasizes the benefits of development i-deals for individuals and organizations (e.g., Liao et al., 2014). Development i-deals refer to any arrangement regarding skills development that is customized to one individual, and meet personal aspirations

---

S. Guerrero (✉) · K. Bentein
University of Quebec at Montreal (UQAM), Montreal, Canada
e-mail: guerrero.sylvie@uqam.ca

K. Bentein
e-mail: bentein.kathleen@uqam.ca

© The Author(s), under exclusive license to Springer Nature Switzerland AG 2022
S. Anand and Y. Rofcanin (eds.), *Idiosyncratic Deals at Work*,
https://doi.org/10.1007/978-3-030-88516-8_1

for professional and career advancement (Hornung et al., 2009; Rousseau et al., 2006). These i-deals include therefore a myriad of activities, such as training, career fast tracks, job rotation, and opportunities for task enrichment.

Development i-deals are well aligned with the idea that the responsibility for career management has partly shifted from the organization to the individual. Driven by the notion of protean career (Hall, 2004) and boundaryless career (Arthur, 2014), recent career studies have addressed career management mostly at the individual level (e.g., Greenhaus & Kossek, 2014). This trend puts the individual at the heart of their career management, such that the individual becomes the main responsible for their career. This trend also defines careers more broadly, as any professional growth, whatever the form that growth takes (i.e., company change, vertical move, new profession, job rotation, etc.). In that perspective, development i-deals request is a tactic, among others, that employees can use to shape their career and grow professionally. Accordingly, the i-deal literature has provided solid evidence about the outcomes of development i-deals for individual careers. A positive relationship was found between these i-deals and the motivation to continue working (Bal et al., 2012), perceptions of employability (Oostrom et al., 2016) and career success measured by salary, hierarchical level and career satisfaction (Guerrero et al., 2016).

Despite the evidence that development i-deal request may be an effective tactic to shape one's career, we still lack a theoretical framework about the factors that push and inhibit development i-deal request and authorization. This chapter provides new insights in that direction. Relying on career theories and i-deals literature, it provides research avenues about the reasons why employees ask for development i-deals (Part I), are able to obtain these i-deals (Part II), and the individual outcomes of the negotiation process of developmental i-deals (Part III).

WHY DO EMPLOYEES REQUEST A DEVELOPMENTAL I-DEAL?

The i-deal literature has started to explore the individual variables that support development i-deal request. This section expands previous studies and offers a more complete framework of the individual factors that push and inhibit i-deal request.

Individual Factors that Push I-deal Request

Career goals. The individual ability to proactively manage one's career is central for requesting an i-deal. This assumption is supported by the i-deal literature, according to which being able to negotiate an i-deal, whatever its nature is, requires personal initiative by the individual (Hornung et al., 2008, 2009), that is to say, the ability to self-start and pursue personal goals. Requesting a development i-deal is thus the outcome of a personal initiative regarding career self-management, which takes the form of career proactive behaviors such as career planning—i.e., setting career goals for oneself (London, 1983). Proactive career management pushes the individual to request an i-deal, because by setting clear and explicit development goals for oneself, the individual builds a future-oriented possible self (Strauss et al., 2012) that acts as a motivational resource to control and direct one's professional development (Markus & Nurius, 1986). Requesting an i-deal is a strategy, among others, that individuals with a clear future-oriented possible self are likely to use.

Needs. Development i-deal request may also be pushed by individual needs satisfaction. For example, Ho and Kong (2015) have shown that development i-deals satisfy employees' competence need, because the skills development obtained with i-deals helps individual feel more in control of their work and environment. This result is consistent with the assumption made in the career literature that individuals shape their careers in order to satisfy some needs (e.g., need for mastery, need for power, etc.). The need for power and need for achievement (McClelland et al., 1976) have been associated with perceived promotability by Liu et al. (2010). Cabrera (2009) showed that the women she interviewed chose to adopt a protean career in order to satisfy their need for balance in their lives. Ussher et al. (2015) found a similar result, while others scholars established that growth need strength is important for individuals to be committed to their careers (Blau, 1985). These few examples show how needs satisfaction is deeply embedded in the protean career literature, and as such, may well activate the individual desire to request a development i-deal.

Motives. The i-deal literature identifies several motives for requesting an i-deal (Bal, 2017; Bal & Vossaert, 2019; Shaughnessy, 2012). We believe that some of these motives apply for development i-deals. First, i-deal request may be the response to a situation that is perceived as unfair by the individual. In that perspective, requesting an i-deal reflects a voice behavior (Ng & Fledman, 2015) enacted to compensate for a poor treatment or negative perceptions, and to satisfy injustice perceptions. Anand et al. (2010) found that i-deals compensate for poor quality exchange relationship with the leader and the team in the prediction of citizenship behaviors. In the same perspective, Guerrero et al. (2014) showed that development i-deal can serve as a buffer to the psychological breach in order to maintain high performers' organizational commitment. These findings illustrate how an individual could be motivated to use development i-deals to restore an imbalance perception (the psychological breach). In the same vein, thanks to interviews led among 31 people, Bal (2017) identified that i-deals are requested to correct an unfair situation, or a situation that did not match individuals needs and skills.

A second motive for development i-deals request is to solve a problem. Accommodative i-deals are defined as i-deals negotiated by employees with the motive to correct or solve a problem at work (e.g., when employees have difficulties in keeping up with job demands at work). For example, an employee who feel overqualified could enjoy a new challenge in their job, or an employee facing difficulties in selling products on an international market could enjoy a language or cultural training. As Bal and Vossaert (2019) developed a measure of accomodative motive, it might represent a good opportunity to start exploring how this motives influence the negotiation process.

Third, individuals may request a development i-deal because they feel entitled to. Bal (2017) interviewed supervisors and branch managers who see themselves as having a high potential or as being overperformant. These managers felt that requesting an i-deal is legitimated by their results (or status) in the firm. Interestingly, this finding is consistent with Rousseau et al. (2006)'s early definition of i-deals, according to which i-deals should be primarily granted as a reward for high performances.

Fourth and last, a development i-deal can be requested as the outcome of envy or jealousy. Rousseau et al. (2016) proposed that granting development i-deals puts the manager at risk of experiencing co-workers' jealousy. As employees compete to accede to growth opportunities, development i-deals represent a highly desirable resource. Employees compare each other and through social comparison processes, assess their i-deals relatively to those obtained by others (Vidyarthi et al., 2016). Observing a co-worker with a development i-deal may generate envy or jealousy, as suggested by Shaughnessy (2012) and evidenced by Ng (2017). Accordingly, an employee who observes co-workers with a development i-deal may want to obtain a similar arrangement for themselves.

Individual Factors that Inhibits I-deal Request

Not all employees will ask for a development i-deal. While the i-deals literature is quite talkative about what pushes individuals to request an i-deal, it remains rather silent about the individual obstacles to i-deal request. This question is important to address because the individual approach of career management promoted with development i-deal puts some individuals at risks of being excluded from development opportunities due to their tendency of not requesting development arrangements. This section identifies several avenues that future research could explore in that direction.

Inertia-enhancing mechanisms. Among the elements that prevent the individual from requesting a developmental i-deal, might be the general human tendency to delay decision-making and to avoid taking action, especially in face with difficult decision and outcome uncertainty (e.g., Verbruggen & De Vos, 2020). Based on the psychology of doing nothing (Anderson, 2003), Verbruggen and De Vos (2020) identified three inertia-enhancing mechanisms that may keep people from acting sufficiently on a desired career change. These three mechanisms, which represent unconscious processes, are built from a series of actions that over years, lead to career inertia. They might thus influence people tendency not to ask for a developmental i-deal.

First, the simple thought of acting (e.g., asking for an i-deal) might elicit fear and anxiety, and avoidance behaviors might unconsciously help people to reduce those negative feelings, at least temporarily. Second, taking action might be inhibited because people tend to concentrate more on short-term efforts and costs of the action (e.g., having a difficult conversation with the supervisor), rather than on the potential long-term gains (e.g., participating in a six-months training). Third, taking action necessitates a cognitively demanding process since people with a vague desire to change need to take additional cognitive steps to clarify what they want (e.g., which training? How could I argue to justify my request?), and eventually to compare several potential alternatives.

Self-concepts. Other important factors that might trigger avoidance behavior relate to employee self-concepts, like self-esteem and self-efficacy. Self-esteem refers to a relatively stable judgment of general self-worth (Rosenberg, 1965). High self-esteem individuals tend to be more proactive, optimistic, and have higher levels of social and civic activity relative to their lower self-esteem counterparts (Owens & McDavitt, 2006). Previous career literature has shown that individuals with high self-esteem engage in effective job search strategies when beginning their careers (Ellis & Taylor, 1983; Saks & Ashforth, 2000) or after a layoff (Kanfer & Hulin, 1985). The significant relationship between self-esteem and these employee proactive behaviors suggests that self-evaluations might be positively related to motivation to proactively request an i-deal. The main theory that supports this relationship is consistency theory, according to which individuals are motivated to believe and act in ways that are consistent with their self-image (Korman, 1970). We thus expect employees with a negative self-image to not request any specific particular developmental i-deals.

Self-efficacy, or a person's self-perceived confidence in one's abilities to successfully execute courses of action required to deal with specific situations (Bandura, 1982), might also play a role in this process. Research has shown that self-efficacy enhances several different proactive behaviors (e.g., Parker & Collins, 2010; Stevens et al., 1993). Employees who do not feel able to have an impact or who entertain serious doubts about whether they can perform a given activity are less likely to choose acting, to expand effort, and to persevere in the face of obstacles (Bandura, 2001; Bandura & Wood, 1989). So, we might expect that employees who believe that their ability to negotiate developmental i-deals is low will choose avoidance behaviors and not request any arrangements for themselves, or will exert less effort and persistence in the negotiation process.

Values. Another element that can create obstacles to requesting an i-deal is related to the individual values system. Some individuals might place more emphasis on collective gains than on individual gains, and might decide not to ask for developmental i-deals for themselves, because they see this request as contrary to their collective values. In their view, acting in their own personal specific interest goes against acting in the collective interest of the group. In an analysis of why individuals might be willing to forfeit individual gains in favor of collective interests, Brewer (1979) argued that perceived inclusion within a common social boundary reduces perceived social distance among group members, making sharp distinctions between their own and others' interests and welfare less likely. Drawing on this literature, we might expect that people with strong collective values will give greater weight to collective arrangements than to i-deals, and will be more reluctant to ask for an i-deal.

Why Do Individuals Receive a Developmental I-deal?

Without the request of a development i-deal, the i-deal negotiation process cannot start. Requesting an i-deal does not however imply that the i-deal will be authorized and obtained. The next step for the individual is to convince the employer representative, mostly the supervisor, that the i-deal request is worth being granted. The association between i-deals request and obtainment is not straightforward, and several factors may interfere in this process (Ho & Tekleab, 2017; Rofcanin et al., 2017). This second section will focus on the development i-deal negotiation process.

Manager's Perceptions Regarding the Employee

As managers mainly hold the power to authorize and implement i-deals, the leader-member exchange (LMX) quality is important for the i-deal negotiation process. As for any other types of i-deals, levels of LMX secure the negotiation process for development i-deals. This is because high LMX creates conditions conducive to negotiability and rewards given by the supervisor. Previous research established that LMX is positively related to i-deal granting (e.g., Rosen et al., 2013). Anand and Vidyarthi (2015) also propose that employees with higher levels of LMX than the average (relative LMX) are the most likely to obtain an i-deal, as they are in a position where their chance to successfully negotiate an i-deal is higher than the average.

Managers' perception of LMX is not the only perception that may explain why employees receive a development i-deal. We have identified additional managers' perceptions that should affect the specific case of development i-deals. First, supervisors' perceptions regarding the employee performances, skills and potential, might affect the i-deal negotiation outcome. The literature emphasizes that i-deals are most likely to be granted in order to reward performing employees in an organization, and to recognize the value that the individual brings to the firm (Rousseau et al., 2006). Rewarding the individual is a key feature that distinguishes i-deal from favoritism or unauthorized agreements. This assumption fully applies for development i-deals (Rousseau et al., 2006), and is consistent with the contest mobility (Turner, 1960) supported in the career literature, according to which upward mobility is the result of individual efforts, perseverance, and initiative.

Socio-demographic characteristics such as being a woman or belonging to a visible minority should also affect chances of successfully negotiate a development i-deal. All human beings do not have equal opportunities of being offered career perspectives (Ng & Feldman, 2014; Ng et al., 2005). This is explained by the sponsorship mobility (Turner, 1960), according to which those in a situation of power tend to sponsor individuals who they perceive as having a high potential. However, these perceptions are not exempt of bias and stereotypes. As decision makers are mostly white males, they tend to perceive other white males as more skilled and better fitted to organizational needs (Schein, 1975). It is likely that similar person categorization mechanisms apply when an individual negotiates development i-deal, such that personal sociodemographic characteristics affect chances of successfully negotiate a development i-deal. Unfortunately, the literature remains silent on the potential discriminatory processes occurring during i-deal negotiation, despite the fact that this point is fundamental to address if we want to ensure that i-deals are beneficial for all types of employees, and not a privileged minority of them.

Employees' Skills and Abilities

As in any negotiation process, individual skills and abilities matter to be able to convince the other party that the request is legitimate.

Ho and Tekleab (2017) investigated the role of human and social capital in i-deal negotiation. Human capital involves personal characteristics (e.g., tenure, education level, etc.) that represent an important asset to reach career success (Ng et al., 2005). It provides bargaining power to employees in that employees with a high human capital are productive and highly contribute to the organizational functioning. Human capital is thus expected to facilitate i-deal negotiation. Social capital, on the other hand, provides bargaining power to negotiate i-deals as well, because employees with a high social capital are able to build strong relationships with others. In the career-related domains, human capital and social capital have been related to objective and subjective career success (Ng & Feldman, 2014; Ng et al., 2005). However, to date, we have no empirical evidence that human and social capital affects the i-deal negotiation process.

Negotiation skills is other important individual ability for negotiating development i-deal. Organizations are political in nature, such that influence tactics and reputation affect managers' decisions. Individuals who can navigate and influence others are thus in a better position to successfully negotiate a development i-deal. Negotiation tactics like reasoning and favor rendering have proven to be positively welcome by supervisors, while tactics of self-promotion or bargaining are negatively related to supervisors' perceptions of promotability (Judge & Bretz, 1994; Wayne et al., 1997).

Political skills (Ferris et al., 2005) is a last individual characteristic that might facilitate the i-deal negotiation process. Politically skilled individuals have a deep understanding of social situations and the ability to adjust to changing situations in a way that inspires trust. This is thus not surprising that Rosen et al. (2013) found positive links between political skills and successful i-deal negotiation, including development i-deal.

Overall, employee skills and abilities should be important factors of the i-deal negotiation process because they shape the supervisors' reactions to the i-deal request. We invite future research to explore how influence tactics and negotiation skills affect supervisors' reactions to an i-deal request.

Fit with Other I-deals

Development i-deals may not be the only i-deal negotiated by the individual. If Rousseau et al. (2006)'s assumption that employees who have received an i-deal are likely to negotiate other i-deals is correct, we can expect a development i-deal to be requested within an employment relationship in which the employee has already received other i-deals, or will ask for other i-deals in the future.

First, development i-deals may enter in conflict with other types of i-deals. Gascoigne and Kelliher (2018) described how professionals working in demanding environments put their career at risk when they negotiate workload reduction i-deals. This is because requesting a flexibility i-deal is interpreted as a signal of withdrawal from the organization. The supervisor perceives a dissonance between the two requests, and may be reluctant to authorize a development i-deal to a person who benefits from a flexibility i-deal. Ho and Kong (2015) found that financial i-deals are negatively related to levels of LMX. One explanation for this result may be that salary negotiations create discomfort or negative reactions for the supervisor. It is thus likely that an employee who asks for a development i-deal will have lower chances of success if this request is done after having already obtained a financial i-deal.

Conversely, the negotiation of a development i-deal may be supported by the existence of other i-deals. Task i-deals and development i-deals are both authorized as a way to increase individual efforts and performances (Hornung et al., 2009, 2014). They share a common goal: adjusting tasks to individual needs and skills. For this reason, it is likely that these two types of i-deal interact to increase supervisor's perceptions of promotability. Rosen et al. (2013) view these two i-deals as quite identical and treated then as being of the same nature, that is, related to tasks enrichment and responsibility enhancement. Their taxonomy of i-deals support the idea that task and development i-deals form two consistent and complementary types of individual arrangements.

Fit with Organizational Culture and Career Management Practices

To finish this section, we would like to highlight that the decision to authorize an i-deal is not solely under the manager's and the employee's power. Organizational culture, support for development activities, and customized HR practices may limit or enable i-deal authorization.

First, hierarchical structures and authoritarian leadership can refrain individuals from negotiating an i-deals (Hornung et al., 2010), and refrain managers from providing an i-deal. When Bal (2017) interviewed employees about factors inhibiting i-deal negotiation success, laws that favor equal treatments, traditional human resource (HR) management, culture based on rigid hierarchy, high HR formalization, were all mentioned as inhibitors of i-deals negotiation success. The inertia mechanisms we described in the previous section to address factors that inhibits i-deal request are supposed to be stronger when outcomes are uncertain, like for example, in organizations in which developmental i-deals are not publicly known (e.g., organizations that explicitly demand workers to keep their i-deal secret), or take place in strongly top-down relationships between employees and their manager. Bal and Hornung (2019) also underlined that the possibility of successfully negotiating i-deals is dependent upon the power of an individual employee. Low-ranking employees (e.g., in a German hospital where the positions were by tradition convertible to military ranks—see Hornung et al., 2010) may not obtain any i-deal because strong hierarchy puts the employee in a low bargaining position that is unfavorable for negotiation success.

Second, the support for career and development practices (i.e., corporate training programs, visible career opportunities, etc.) may favor the granting of development i-deal. When development practices are highly supported by the organization, this support signals the importance that an organization gives to employee development (Krainer et al., 2011), and encourages managers to offer these practices and employees to request them.

The existence of an individualized or differentiated HR management (Rofcanin et al., 2019) is another organizational factor that affects the outcome of an i-deal request. With customized HR programs, organizations implement HR system in which managers have the opportunity to individually negotiate and implement HR-related agreements with their employees (Bal & Dorenbosch, 2015, p. 504). These organizations acknowledge the growing need for more flexibility in individual management and careers, and decentralize HR activities in that purpose, by opposition to the traditional standardized approach of HR management based on collective agreements and equal treatment of employees. In organizations in which HR customization is supported, employees and managers are thus more likely to negotiate development i-deals.

Outcomes of the Development I-deal Negotiation Process

Development i-deals have been associated with a variety of outcomes, related to employment relationship quality (Rosen et al., 2013; Rousseau et al., 2009), self-enhancement mechanisms (Guerrero & Chaillol-Jeanblanc, 2016; Hornung et al., 2014; Liu et al., 2013), and career prospects (Bal et al., 2012; Guerrero et al., 2016; Oostrom et al., 2016). These outcomes represent individual reactions to development i-deal *authorization* that we will explore in this section. However, the literature leaves aside the study of individual reactions to development i-deal *refusal*. In order to fill this gap, this section also explores the individual reactions for refused development i-deals.

Outcomes of not Asking for a Development I-deal

When people do not ask for a developmental i-deal that is important for them, we might expect that they experience some regrets. Literature on the experience of regret (Connolly & Zeelenberg, 2002; Pieters & Zeelenberg, 2005; Verbruggen & De Vos 2020) distinguishes between two core components of regrets, one associated with the (comparative) evaluation of the outcome, and the other with the feeling of self-blame for having made a poor choice. The overall feeling of regret at some decision is a combination of these two components: people regret both that the outcome is poorer than some standard (e.g., "If only I had participate to this training") and that the decision they made was, in retrospect, unjustified (e.g., "If only I had talked with my supervisor about my aspirations to participate to this training"). According to Verbruggen and De Vos (2020), this second component of regret is particularly challenging to the self-image of individuals, as they recognized that a once hope for future was not achieved due to their own inaction, or their own fault. Therefore regrets might be particularly painful for self-esteem, and might have a negative impact on people.

Outcomes of Development I-deal Refusal

When people asked for a developmental i-deals but did not receive it, we might expect some revision of their mental models of the employment relationship (Hornung & Rousseau, 2017). Literature on i-deals has shown that the willingness of employers to cater to individual employee needs signals to employees that they are special and worthy of the employer's special treatment (Liu et al., 2013). We might expect that denied requests of development i-deals signal employees that the organization "does not want" to take their personal needs, their competences, and ultimately their person, into consideration. Hornung et al. (2010) found that denied requests for i-deals led employees to experience work as more stressful and less controllable, two factors that undermine their well-being. Globally, these employees evaluate their work experience more negatively than peers who had either obtained or not asked for such personalized work arrangements.

Denied requests of development i-deals might also have an impact on employees' career decisions and their future work selves (Strauss et al., 2012). When employees asked for a developmental i-deal but receive a negative answer from their supervisor, they might interpret this as a negative feedback for their salient view of their future work self (Lord et al., 1999). Some employees might look for better alternatives elsewhere inside or outside the organization to find an environment that better fits the professional development needs related to their salient future work self. The denied i-deal request might precipitate a decision to leave the organization for example. Some other employees might adjust their future-oriented possible selves in terms of salience and attributes, taking this negative feedback (i.e., the denied i-deal request) into consideration.

Outcomes of Development I-deal Authorization

Outcomes of development i-deals authorization is probably the topic that has been the most investigated in the i-deal literature. Despite this, outcomes related to career prospects and career success still deserve further attention by scholars.

As by definition development i-deals provide the individual with skills development, these i-deals should have direct implications on individual career success. Negotiating a career fast track, a job rotation, or new responsibilities, is likely to lead to a new position or new effective tasks in the organization in the months following the i-deal negotiation. It is thus quite logical to observe a link between development i-deals and objective career success, measured by salary and hierarchical position (Guerrero et al., 2016).

The i-deal literature also highlights the short-term benefits of development i-deals for employees' motivation and performance. Hornung et al. (2009) showed that supervisors increase performance standards of employees to whom they authorize a development i-deal. Oostrom et al. (2016) provided evidence that older employees feel more employable when they possess development i-deals, because they feel more effective at work. As development i-deals satisfy employees needs for competence (Ho & Kong, 2015) and for self-enhancement (Liu et al., 2013), employees with such i-deal feel more in mastery of their current tasks, which fosters their motivation and should in turn increase performances.

Development i-deal are also associated with better future perspective for i-deal receivers. Professional growth is by definition a long-term process. Employees with a development i-deal possess an important resource (i.e., training, opportunity for skills development) that may lead to additional resources in the future (i.e., a career path that better fits individual needs). As employees are better able to identify future professional avenues for themselves, they feel more employable (Oostrom et al. (2016), more satisfied in their career (Guerrero et al., 2016) and in their current job (Rosen et al., 2013). Bal et al. (2012) showed that in a climate that support older employees' development, older workers are motivated to continue working when development i-deal are offered to them. These empirical findings illustrate how development i-deal foster perceptions of self-fulfillment and subjective career success.

Conclusion

The processes through which development i-deal are requested and obtained still need further investigation. This chapter tried to identify several avenues that could be explored in the future to develop knowledge on development i-deals. Table 1.1 summarizes the different propositions we suggest in this chapter. The variables we identified are not pure antecedents to be tested in a research model. They reflect individual or contextual characteristics that could help build new knowledge both for the i-deal and career literatures.

Our aim was to focus on development i-deals request and authorization as a tactic that help shape individuals' careers. In line with this assumption, we identified several individual characteristics that facilitate and inhibit i-deal request. We also listed career outcomes that represent the individual adaptation to i-deal granting or refusal, and the career paths that individual can take following decisions about i-deals. Only the factors associated with i-deal authorization are not all under the individual control, as i-deal authorization involves the organization and its representative like managers. This highlights that individuals shape their career in relationship with others and within a context that affects their career trajectories.

Table 1.1 also identifies some methodological challenges that our research suggestions raise. The adoption of in-depth qualitative research designs seems necessary to fully grasp the i-deal request inhibitors as well as the career outcomes for not asking i-deals. These designs are

Table 1.1 Avenues for future research

Areas of investigation	Topics to explore	Method challenges
Development i-deal request facilitators	Career goals Individual needs Individual motives	Creation of individual profiles
Development i-deal request inhibitors	Inertia mechanisms Poor self-concepts Collective values	Partly unconscious processes that require in depth analyses
I-deal authorization	Manager's perceptions Skills and abilities Fit with other i-deals Fit with career practices	Needs for multi-level research models, within-person designs and for adequate temporality
Career outcomes for not asking i-deals	Regrets	Need for introspective in-depth analyses
Career outcomes for not receiving an i-deal	Reassessment of the employment relationship Alternative career orientations	Longitudinal research programs
Career outcomes of i-deal granting	Career success Performance and sense of competence High career perspectives	Longitudinal research programs

barely adopted in the i-deal literature, although they are important to expand our current knowledge. More traditional but still complex research deigns (multi-level and longitudinal research designs) would help test our research propositions regarding i-deals authorization facilitators, and outcomes of i-deals authorization decision. We do hope that future research will tackle some of our suggestions.

References

Abele, A. E. (2003). The dynamics of masculine-agentic and feminine-communal traits: Findings from a prospective study. *Journal of Personality and Social Psychology*, 85, 768–777.

Anand, S., & Vidyarthi, P. (2015). Idiosyncratic deals in the context of workgroups. In P. M. Bal & D. M. Rousseau (Eds.), *Idiosyncratic deals between employees and organizations: Conceptual issues, applications, and the role of coworkers* (pp. 92–106). Psychology Press.

Anand, S., Vidyarthi, P. R., Liden, R. C., & Rousseau, D. M. (2010). Good citizens in poor-quality relationships: Idiosyncratic deals as a substitute for relationship quality. *Academy of Management Journal, 53*(5), 970–988.

Anderson, C. J. (2003). The psychology of doing nothing: Forms of decision avoidance result from reason and emotion. *Psychological Bulletin, 129*(1), 139–167.

Arthur, M. B. (2014). The boundaryless career at 20: Where do we stand and where can we go? *Career Development International, 19*, 627–640.

Bal, M. (2017). Why do employees negotiate idiosyncratic deals? An exploration of the process of i-deal negotiation. *New Zealand Journal of Employment Relations, 42*, 2–18.

Bal, P. M., & Dorenbosch, L. (2015). Age-related differences in the relations between individualised HRM and organisational performance: A large-scale employer survey. *Human Resource Management Journal, 25*, 41–61.

Bal, P. M., de Jong, S. B., Jensen, P. G. W., & Bakker, A. B. (2012). Motivating employees to work beyond retirement: A multi-level study of the role of i-deals and unit climate. *Journal of Management Studies, 49*, 306–331.

Bal, P. M., & Hornung, S. (2019). Individualization of work: from psychological contracts to ideological deals. In Y.Griep & C. Cooper, *Handbook of research on the psychological contract at work* (pp. 143–163). Edward Elgar Publishing.

Bal, M., & Rousseau, D. M. (Eds.). (2015). *Idiosyncratic deals between employees and organizations: Conceptual issues, applications and the role of co-workers.* Routledge.

Bal, M., & Vossaert, L. (2019). Development of an i-deals motivation and management measure. *Journal of Personnel Psychology, 18*, 201–215.

Bandura, A. (1982). Self-efficacy mechanism in human agency. *American Psychologist, 37*(2), 122–147.

Bandura, A. (2001). Social cognitive theory: An agentic perspective. *Annual Review of Psychology, 52*, 1–26.

Bandura, A., & Wood, R. (1989). Effect of perceived controllability and performance standards on self-regulation of complex decision making. *Journal of Personality and Social Psychology, 56*, 805–814.

Blau, G. J. (1985). The measurement and prediction of career commitment. *Journal of Occupational Psychology, 58*, 277–289.

Brewer, M. B. (1979). In-group bias in the minimal intergroup situation: A cognitive-motivational analysis. *Psychological Bulletin, 86*(2), 307–324.

Cabrera, E. F. (2009). Protean organizations: Reshaping work and careers to retain female talent. *Career Development International, 14*, 186–201.

Connolly, T., & Zeelenberg, M. (2002). Regret in decision making. *Current Directions in Psychological Science, 11*, 212–216.

De Vos, A., & Cambré, B. (2017). Career management in high-performing organizations: A set-theoretic approach. *Human Resource Management, 56*, 501–518.

Ellis, R. A., & Taylor, M. S. (1983). Role of self-esteem within the job search process. *Journal of Applied Psychology, 68*(4), 632–640.

Erdogan, B., & Bauer, T. N. (2005). Enhancing career benefits of employee proactive personality: The role of fit with jobs and organizations. *Personnel Psychology, 58*, 859–891.

Ferris, G. R., Treadway, D. C., Kolodinsky, R. W., Hochwarter, W. A., Kacmar, C. J., Douglas, C., & Frink, D. D. (2005). Development and validation of the political skill inventory. *Journal of Management, 31*, 126–152.

Gascoigne, C., & Kelliher, C. (2018). The transition to part-time: How professionals negotiate 'reduced time and workload' i-deals and craft their jobs. *Human Relations, 71*, 103–125.

Greenhaus, J. H., & Kossek, E. E. (2014). The contemporary career: A work–home perspective. *Annual Review of Organizational Psychology and Organizational Behavior, 1*, 361–388.

Guerrero, S., Bentein, K., & Lapalme, M. È. (2014). Idiosyncratic deals and high performers' organizational commitment. *Journal of Business and Psychology, 29*, 323–334.

Guerrero, S., & Challiol-Jeanblanc, H. (2016). Developmental idiosyncratic deals and helping behavior: The moderating role of i-deal opportunity for co-workers. *Journal of Business and Psychology, 31*, 433–443.

Guerrero, S., Challiol-Jeanblanc, H., & Veilleux, M. (2016). Development idiosyncratic deals and career success. *Career Development International, 21*, 19–30.

Hall, D. T. (2004). The protean career: A quarter-century journey. *Journal of Vocational Behavior, 65*, 1–13.

Ho, V. T., & Kong, D. T. (2015). Exploring the signaling function of idiosyncratic deals and their interaction. *Organizational Behavior and Human Decision Processes, 131*, 149–161.

Ho, V. T., & Tekleab, A. G. (2017). A model of idiosyncratic deal-making and attitudinal outcomes. *Journal of Managerial Psychology, 31*, 642–656.

Hoobler, J. M., Wayne, S. J., & Lemmon, G. (2009). Bosses' perceptions of family-work conflict and women's promotability: Glass ceiling effects. *Academy of Management Journal, 52*, 939–957.

Hornung, S., & Rousseau, D. M. (2017). Psychological contracts and idiosyncratic deals: Mapping conceptual boundaries, common ground, and future research paths. In P. Bhatt, P. Jaiswal, B. Majumdar, & S. Verma (Eds.), *Riding the new tides: Navigating the future through effective people management* (pp. 81–91). Emerald.

Hornung, S., Rousseau, D. M., & Glaser, J. (2009). Why supervisors make idiosyncratic deals: Antecedents and outcomes of i-deals from a managerial perspective. *Journal of Managerial Psychology, 24*, 738–764.

Hornung, S., Rousseau, D. M., & Glaser, J. (2008). Creating flexible work arrangements through idiosyncratic deals. *Journal of Applied Psychology, 93*, 655–664.

Hornung, S., Rousseau, D. M., Glaser, J., Angerer, P., & Weigl, M. (2010). Beyond top-down and bottom-up work redesign: Customizing job content through idiosyncratic deals. *Journal of Organizational Behavior, 31*(2–3), 187–215.

Hornung, S., Rousseau, D. M., Weigl, M., Mueller, A., & Glaser, J. (2014). Redesigning work through idiosyncratic deals. *European Journal of Work and Organizational Psychology, 23*, 608–626.

Judge, T. A., & Bretz, R. D., Jr. (1994). Political influence behavior and career success. *Journal of Management, 20*, 43–65.

Kanfer, R., & Hulin, C. L. (1985). Individual differences in successful job searches following lay-off. *Personnel Psychology, 38*(4), 835–847.

Korman, A. K. (1970). Toward an hypothesis of work behavior. *Journal of Applied Psychology, 54*, 31–41.

Kraimer, M. L., Seibert, S. E., Wayne, S. J., Liden, R. C., & Bravo, J. (2011). Antecedents and outcomes of organizational support for development: The critical role of career opportunities. *Journal of Applied Psychology, 96*, 485–500.

Liao, C., Wayne, S. J., & Rousseau, D. M. (2014). Idiosyncratic deals in contemporary organizations: A qualitative and meta-analytical review. *Journal of Organizational Behavior, 37*, S9–S29.

Liu, J., Lee, C., Hui, C., Kwong Kwan, H., & Wu, L.-Z. (2013). Idiosyncratic deals and employee outcomes: The mediating roles of social exchange and self-enhancement and the moderating role of individualism. *Journal of Applied Psychology, 98*, 832–840.

Liu, Y., Liu, J., & Wu, L. (2010). Are you willing and able? Roles of motivation, power, and politics in career growth. *Journal of Management, 36*, 1432–1460.

London, M. (1983). Toward a theory of career motivation. *Academy of Management Review, 8*(4), 620–630.

Lord, R. G., Brown, D. J., & Freiberg, S. J. (1999). Understanding the dynamics of leadership: The role of follower self-concepts in the leader/follower relationship. *Organizational behavior and Human Decision Processes, 78*(3), 167–203.

Luksyte, A., & Spitzmueller, C. (2016). When are overqualified employees creative? It depends on contextual factors. *Journal of Organizational Behavior, 37*, 635–653.

Markus, H., & Nurius, P. (1986). Possible selves. *American Psychologist, 41*, 954–969.
McClelland, D. C., Atkinson, J. W., Clark, R. A., & Lowell, E. L. (1976). *The achievement motive*. Irvington.
Ng, T. W. (2017). Can idiosyncratic deals promote perceptions of competitive climate, felt ostracism, and turnover? *Journal of Vocational Behavior, 99*, 118–131.
Ng, T. W., Eby, L. T., Sorensen, K. L., & Feldman, D. C. (2005). Predictors of objective and subjective career success: A meta-analysis. *Personnel Psychology, 58*, 367–408.
Ng, T. W., & Feldman, D. C. (2014). Subjective career success: A meta-analytic review. *Journal of Vocational Behavior, 85*, 169–179.
Ng, T. W., & Feldman, D. C. (2015). Idiosyncratic deals and voice behavior. *Journal of Management, 41*, 893–928.
Ng, T. W., & Lucianetti, L. (2016). Goal striving, idiosyncratic deals, and job behavior. *Journal of Organizational Behavior, 37*, 41–60.
Oostrom, J. K., Pennings, M., & Bal, P. M. (2016). How do idiosyncratic deals contribute to the employability of older workers? *Career Development International, 21*, 176–192.
Owens, T. J., & McDavitt, A. R. (2006). The self-esteem motive: Positive and negative consequences for self and society. *Self-esteem issues and answers: A sourcebook of current perspectives*, 398–406.
Parker, S. K., & Collins, C. G. (2010). Taking stock: Integrating and differentiating multiple proactive behaviors. *Journal of Management, 36*(3), 633–662.
Pieters, R., & Zeelenberg, M. (2005). On bad decisions and deciding badly: When intention–behavior inconsistency is regrettable. *Organizational Behavior & Human Decision Processes, 97*, 18–30.
Rofcanin, Y., Berber, A., Marescaux, E., Bal, P. M., Mughal, F., & Afacan Findikli, M. (2019). Human resource differentiation: A theoretical paper integrating co-workers' perspective and context. *Human Resource Management Journal, 29*, 270–286.
Rofcanin, Y., Kiefer, T., & Strauss, K. (2017). What seals the I-deal? Exploring the role of employees' behaviours and managers' emotions. *Journal of Occupational and Organizational Psychology, 90*, 203–224.
Rosen, C. C., Slater, D. J., Chang, C. H., & Johnson, R. E. (2013). Let's make a deal: Development and validation of the ex post i-deals scale. *Journal of Management, 39*, 709–742.
Rosenberg, M. (1965). *Society and the adolescent self-image*. Princeton University Press.
Rousseau, D. M., Ho, V. T., & Greenberg, J. (2006). I-deals: Idiosyncratic terms in employment relationships. *Academy of Management Review, 31*, 977–994.

Rousseau, D. M., Hornung, S., & Kim, T. G. (2009). Idiosyncratic deals: Testing propositions on timing, content, and the employment relationship. *Journal of Vocational Behavior, 74*, 338–348.

Rousseau, D. M., Tomprou, M., & Simosi, M. (2016). Negotiating flexible and fair idiosyncratic deals (i-deals). *Organizational Dynamics, 45*, 185–196.

Saks, A. M., & Ashforth, B. E. (2000). The role of dispositions, entry stressors, and behavioral plasticity theory in predicting newcomers' adjustment to work. *Journal of Organizational Behavior, 21*, 43–62.

Schein, V. E. (1975). Relationships between sex role stereotypes and requisite management characteristics among female managers. *Journal of Applied Psychology, 60*, 340–344.

Shaughnessy, B. A. (2012). *The negotiation of i-deals in organizations: A process model incorporating individual and relational motivations, political skills, and employee outcomes (unpublished doctoral dissertation)*. State University of New York.

Stevens, C. K., Bavetta, A. G., & Gist, M. E. (1993). Gender differences in the acquisition of salary negotiation skills: The role of goals, self-efficacy, and perceived control. *Journal of Applied Psychology, 78*(5), 723–735.

Strauss, K., Griffin, M. A., & Parker, S. K. (2012). Future work selves: How salient hoped-for identities motivate proactive career behaviors. *Journal of Applied Psychology, 97*, 580–598.

Turner, R. H. (1960). Sponsored and contest mobility and the school system. *American Sociological Review*, 855–867.

Ussher, S., Roche, M., & Cable, D. (2015). Women and careers: New Zealand women's engagement in career and family planning. *New Zealand Journal of Employment Relations, 40*, 24–43.

Verbruggen, M., & De Vos, A. (2020). When people don't realize their career desires: Toward a theory of career inaction. *Academy of Management Review, 45*, 376–394.

Vidyarthi, P. R., Singh, S., Erdogan, B., Chaudhry, A., Posthuma, R., & Anand, S. (2016). Individual deals within teams: Investigating the role of relative i-deals for employee performance. *Journal of Applied Psychology, 101*(11), 1536–1552.

Wayne, S. J., Liden, R. C., Graf, I. K., & Ferris, G. R. (1997). The role of upward influence tactics in human resource decisions. *Personnel Psychology, 50*, 979–1006.

CHAPTER 2

Does What Happen at Work, Stay at Work? Flexibility I-Deals and Employee Lives Outside of the Workplace

Mine Afacan Findikli, Mireia Las Heras, Yasin Rofcanin, and Can Ererdi

INTRODUCTION

Working flexibly is a new trend in today's ever-changing and competitive work settings. In the face of the kind of difficulties faced to keep talented employees happy and productive, organizations are beginning

---

Mine Afacan Findikli is funded by the Scientific and Technological Research Council of Turkey under the scheme "2219".

M. Afacan Findikli (✉)
Istinye University, Istanbul, Turkey
e-mail: mine.findikli@istinye.edu.tr

M. L. Heras
University of Navarra IESE Business School, Barcelona, Spain
e-mail: mlasheras@iese.edu

© The Author(s), under exclusive license to Springer Nature Switzerland AG 2022
S. Anand and Y. Rofcanin (eds.), *Idiosyncratic Deals at Work*,
https://doi.org/10.1007/978-3-030-88516-8_2

to offer highly flexible work arrangements to maintain their engagement (Hornung et al., 2009). Such work arrangements can be tailored to address employees' specific work needs and preferences and take the form of the flexibility to choose where and when one works (Rousseau et al., 2006). Referred to as flexibility i-deals, a growing body of research has shown that such i-deals are beneficial to both organizations and their employees. For example, it has been shown that the provision of flexibility i-deals is positively related to the motivation to continue working after retirement (Bal et al., 2012) and work performance (Las Heras, Rofcanin, et al., 2017), as well as potential gains for one's family life (Hornung et al., 2013). Despite these positive gains, there are also studies showing that working flexibly may harm one's mental and physical health. These contradictory findings emphasize the importance of looking at a more nuanced model to understand how flexibility i-deals operate and impact on work outcomes. Furthermore, in the growing body of research on i-deals, there has been relatively less attention paid to flexibility i-deals. Most of the associated research to date has focused on task, career, and developmental i-deals (Liao et al., 2016), with less attention on how and under which conditions flexibility i-deals are most effective and sustainable. A less-explored yet a highly important area of inquiry is how flexibility i-deals are related to and operate within the context of one's family and non-work domain. In a few exceptional studies (i.e., Las Heras, Rofcanin, et al., 2017), it has been shown that flexibility i-deals can drive one's engagement in the family domain.

The primary goal of this chapter is to explore flexibility i-deals in the context of one's family and non-work life. We first describe and define flexibility i-deals. Following this, we describe and discuss the roles of various parties in how flexibility i-deals are negotiated and, subsequently, unfold. As such, we describe the role of spouse, friends, family, community, and broader organizational support in ensuring flexibility i-deals are

---

Y. Rofcanin
University of Bath, Bath, UK
e-mail: Y.Rofcanin@bath.ac.uk

C. Ererdi
Bogazici University, Istanbul, Turkey

University of Bath School of Management, Bath, UK

obtained. Under each of these sections and sources of support, we delineate future research suggestions. We conclude our chapter with a roadmap of research on flexibility i-deals.

The Rise of Flexibility in Work-Family Domain and Flexibility I-Deals

"The early bird catches the worm." But early birds still get the same twenty-four hours in their day as everyone else, no matter how early they rise. In these twenty-four hours, we all have to fit our work, family life, personal interests, and social commitments. And it is not easy, in a time in which work has become much faster (Jarvis, 2011), global (Rainnie & Dean, 2020) and all-encompassing (Gawlik, 2017), putting more demands on employees (Bakker & Demerouti, 2013), creating stress (Parker & DeCotiis, 1983), requiring their undivided attention, while offering numerous distractions and demands (Bakker & Demerouti, 2013). Employees often try to solve this puzzle by sleeping less, ignoring personal care, and neglecting significant others, which are the very sources of recovery people need.

Lacking the resources and the time to achieve all we want to in a given day is not a new problem. Sure enough, many professionals felt this way in the 50s, 60s, and 70s. Nonetheless, there seems to be a consensus that the problem is more acute now than ever (Lloyd & Harris, 2007). Technology has blurred the boundaries between work and non-work. Globalization has led to 24/7 demands on many employees. More women in the workforce mean less backup for a child at home and no-one to care for the elderly.

Rapid changes in competition (Balboa, 2017), unrest in social and legal structures (Ponticelli & Voth, 2020), and volatility in market valuation (Ballinari et al., 2020) all require that companies and individuals be agile and adaptable. While these changes create new work and business opportunities, as well as new career structures, they also pose tough questions and create stress for managers, organizations, employees, and society with regard to how to manage the work/non-work interface. Managers attempt to attract and retain human capital and, to do so effectively, must be simultaneously developing their potential and fostering engagement (Aguenza & Som, 2018). Organizations have to adapt their structures and get the best out of their employees. Employees struggle in their attempts to live purposeful lives both within and outside the work sphere.

Society wrestles to maintain the well-being that has been achieved in years past while at the same time maintaining a demographic balance (Bakker & van Wingarden, 2020; Coyle-Shapiro & Shore, 2007). As a result of the changes discussed above, employees seek to receive various flexibilities from their employers and this situation will render flexibility i-deals relevant and dominating subject in the field of organizational behavior.

FLEXIBILITY I-DEALS

In light of these changes, employees are increasingly negotiating for flexibility i-deals to gain a work-family balance and achieve a certain cohesion in the intersection of these domains. However, what exactly are flexibility i-deals? These i-deals provide employees with flexibility in terms of the timing and location of their work, that is, where and when employees conduct their work and the new forms of employment they undertake (Rofcanin, Kiefer, et al., 2017; Rousseau et al., 2006).

Following the definition of flexibility i-deals, the question that immediately occurs is: Why are flexibility i-deals becoming common tools? I-deals have a potential to become a prominent HRM strategy to attract and retain talent who seek to obtain work conditions that allow these employees to meet their individual needs (Anand et al., 2010; Call et al., 2015; Rousseau et al., 2006). First of all, younger generations have lower levels of work centrality than previous generations (Campbell et al., 2017) and also have a greater interest in achieving work-life balance. Second, more women are entering the labor market, which results in an increase in the number of single working mothers and dual-earner families. Third, changes in workplace demographic have resulted in more men and women in managerial positions who have primary (or shared) elder and childcare responsibilities. Overall, when employees consider work-family balance, the most important needs of the employee are shaped within the framework of their responsibilities at home and the needs related to home. Thanks to the benefits of flexibility i-deals, they can generate further resources at home and in appropriate societal environments, such as spending more time with family or taking care of children during the day, with the associated implications for improved family- and social relations (Las Heras, Rofcanin, et al., 2017; Rousseau et al., 2016). For this reason, flexible i-deals might be the most appropriate and generally applicable form of employment contract.

The Role of Key Parties in Flexibility I-Deals Process

The Role of the Supervisor in I-Deal Granting and Work-Life Balance

In the course of the i-deal negotiation process, supervisors play the important role of the liaison between employees and the organization to facilitate the realization of i-deals in practice (Las Heras, Rofcanin, et al., 2017; Lee & Hui, 2011). In this role, they need to know the expectations and the needs of their employees so that they can effectively realize the exchange of resources between the two parties (employer and employee). This is because i-deals are context-dependent, and individual-level factors have the potential to influence whether and how they are obtained and implemented effectively (Liao et al., 2016). Supervisors are key organizational agents whose legitimate power is highly influential with regard to the rights granted to their workers (Stinglhamber & Vandenberghe, 2003). Supervisors are the primary bargaining partners for negotiating i-deals (*cf.*, "Ideal-granter"), as the latter is only possible in case of both employees who are willing to negotiate and supervisors who Rhoades and Eisenberger (2002) carefully and fairly accommodate employees' needs (Hornung et al., 2009). Focusing on the broader type of i-deals, i.e., integrating and combining all types of i-deals, it is revealed that when supervisors are perceived as considerate, they are more likely to grant i-deals (Hornung et al., 2011). We also know that high-quality exchange relationships between supervisors and employees positively relate to i-deal negotiation (Hornung et al., 2014; Rosen et al., 2013) be an antecedent of i-deal formation.

When the manager side is examined, they should be willing to provide i-deals to their subordinates as long as these contribute to employee motivation and to observe employees' performance (Hornung et al., 2009; Las Heras, Van der Heijden et al., 2017). From this perspective, the perspective of supervisors who authorize i-deals and manage their consequences is also important. This favorable perception of i-deals by the employer/supervisor has been shown to be related to positive outcomes such as an increase of employee proactive behavior and motivation on the part of the employee.

However, research on flexibility i-deals is just beginning to gain momentum. In only a few of the studies that focused on the role of supervisors has their important role been underpinned: Las Heras and colleagues (2017) studied a family-related characteristic of the supervisor that serves as an antecedent of i-deal granting. Specifically, they explored the extent to which care for the elderly and children relates to the supervisors' capacity to grant flexibility i-deals. They found that elder's caregiving relates to flexibility i-deal granting, while childcare does not (Las Heras, Rofcanin, et al., 2017). The key finding of this study is that supervisors with responsibilities to care for elders are more likely to grant such types of i-deals to their subordinates. Rofcanin, Kiefer, et al. (2017) found that supervisors grant flexibility i-deals to those subordinates who demonstrate socially connecting behaviors toward their colleagues. The main finding of this study is that supervisors, as discussed above, hold the key power to grant i-deals and subordinate prosocial behaviors are key triggers in the decision whether to grant i-deals or otherwise. Finally, in a recent study, Kelly and colleagues (2020) revealed the role of schedule flexibility i-deals as a mechanism to explain how and why supervisor emotional support leads to desirable employee behaviors. Their findings demonstrated that when supervisors show emotional support for their subordinates, they are more likely to obtain schedule flexibility i-deals, and subordinates in receipt of such deals are likely to devote these resources to their work (work performance) and family domains (family performance).

The Role of Spouse Support in I-Deals

The sustainability and effect of i-deals depend on the various sources of support available at work. One of the key resources relates to spouses, who are the significant partners of i-dealers (Ten Brummelhuis & Bakker, 2012). Spouses contribute to the well-being of their partners through the moral and emotional support they offer, as well as through sharing skills and knowledge to help with their partner's work (Amin et al., 2017). Currently, to the best of our knowledge, there is no research that has explored the role of spouses in terms of how and when flexibility i-deals unfold and how their effects are seen on the spouses. In a study by the co-authors of this chapter, Las Heras et al. (in press) have developed a construct called Work Supportive Spouse Behaviours (WSSB). WSSB mirrors Family Supportive Supervisor Behaviours (FSSB) but originates in the work-life sphere. That is, while FSSB originates in the work domain and aims to foster effective family functioning, WSSB originates at home and aims to facilitate effective functioning at work. The impact of WSSBs is likely to be sustainable and positive, leading to the successful transitioning of the benefits of flexibility i-deals into the work domain, for example, work performance and productivity.

WSSB is a resource in that spouses (partners) offer emotional and instrumental support, act as role models, and show creativity in terms of implementing actions that benefit the work-family balance of their spouses. For instance, we expect WSSB to allow for work-family enrichment and offer satisfaction with the work-family balance, and reduce work-family conflict, stress, and depression. That is, we expect that WSSB will serve to enforce similar outcomes to those produced by FSSB; more specifically, we expect it to foster the successful negotiation of i-deals.

We posit that WSSB will attract research interest in the near future since it is our firm belief that resources should originate in both domains, at work *and* at home, and indeed that they should benefit both the work and home domains. Yet to our knowledge, most of the research in the work-family field has investigated how resources in the work domain might benefit the family domain, but not the opposite. It is only fair to think that while we expect a supervisor to support their subordinates at work with regard to family matters, we should also expect a partner to support the focal person's work as well. We expect that when both sources of support are proportional, the focal person might be able to function effectively and without excessive strain.

In addition to WSSBs, a second and important source of support is Family Supportive Supervisor Behaviours (FSSBs): These are resources in which supervisors offer emotional and instrumental support, act as role models, and show creativity in the implementation of actions that benefit the work-family balances of their subordinates (Hammer et al., 2009). FSSBs have shown to enrich the work-family balance (Bagger & Li, 2014) and reduce work-family conflict (Odle-Dusseau et al., 2012). A recent review study on FSSBs reveals that they are positively associated with work and non-work outcomes and enable employees to generate further resources in these domains. Further research is needed to integrate and draw on WSSBs and FSSBs to explore and identify how flexibility i-deals relate to these sources of support and under which conditions the outcomes are optimized for both the employee and the organization.

The Role of Friendship and Wider Community Support in I-Deals

As also mentioned above, the interchange of certain resources during i-deals actualizes the mutual relationship between the recipient and the giver. However, apart from these two sources of support, other social relationships and stakeholders are important in the i-deals process and can be considered important parties in the associated negotiations. Parties in this relationship are also indirectly affected by the agreement between i-dealer and manager. The most important of these resources is family and friend support in which socio-emotional support is provided. Therefore, the employee always wants to keep the balance between work-family and work-private life within the requirements of the job (Rousseau, 2005). Social resources of the employees (family and close friends) also give support to them socially and emotionally.

Social support contains three basic perspectives, the structural, functional, and contextual. In this sense, support that comes from friends may be accepted as a valuable resource from both the functional and contextual perspectives (Awang et al., 2014; Garcia-Martin et al., 2016). The functional perspective addresses the type of support received. For example, while emotional support practices encompass affection, empathy, love, and trust, instrumental support may be equivalent to help in the form of money or time invested, informational support indicates advice and suggestions, or guidance to help the person deal with challenges. The contextual perspective addresses the specific settings or networks in which social support is given or received (House, 1983). These kinds of resources have been shown to promote mental health and act as a buffer against stressful life events (Cohen & Wills, 1985; Steese et al., 2006). On the other hand, a scarcity of social support may result in mental health problems, which have a negative impact on the quality of life (Alsubaie et al., 2019).

From the standpoint of the manager, the fact that an employee cares about their family and social life has certain benefits to the company. As mentioned above, family and close friends are indirectly affected by the agreement between the i-dealer and manager. Therefore, they are the most closely affected by the recipient's happiness and their ability to maintain a work-private life balance. Managers are aware that social support, in the form of friendship, is of consequence to the outcomes of i-deals, and are in the best position to keep this mutual relationship fair and open so that all parties involved in i-deals benefit from it (e.g., Liao et al., 2016).

When the friends and co-workers of the i-dealer notice that these arrangements have been made in fair and transparent ways, they signal the value of the company to the market. In this regard, the company becomes increasingly likely to attract and keep talented employees motivated and productive. An interesting area of work that can be linked to i-deals is brand identity and how it maintains employee morale and motivation. Furthermore, the provision of i-deals in fair and transparent ways could lead to important outcomes for the organization, including "Employer of Choice" and how this is likely to keep a perfect balance for employees between their work and family lives (O'Donohue & Wickham, 2008).

The Role of Organizational Support in Flexibility I-Deals

The role of organizational support can manifest itself in two ways: perceived organization support (POS) and family-friendly work environment perceptions. POS refers to the degree to which employees perceive that their employer and the broader organization in which they are working consider their needs and demands as important (Eisenberger et al., 2002). POS shows that the organization values the well-being and work outcomes of employees and that it is likely to invest in their proper functioning (Kossek et al., 2011). As a form of support emanating from the organizational resources, limited studies exist that show how and why POS matters for i-deals: Focusing on flexibility i-deals, Las Heras, Rofcanin, et al. (2017) showed that in organizations where they felt greater POS, employees were better able to make use of and translate the benefits of flexibility i-deals into family performance in the form of showing enhanced family performance. In addition to the role of POS, other studies focus on a more specific form of organizational culture or climate about family friendliness. A recent study on schedule flexibility i-deals (Kelly et al., 2020) demonstrated that employees working in family-friendly organizations are better able to seek and make use of the emotional support of their supervisors and obtain schedule flexibility i-deals. This study exhibits the role of working for family-friendly organizations to obtain and benefit from such types of arrangements.

In a conceptual study of human resource management differentiation, Rofcanin et al. (2019) revealed the importance of perceived mastery and competitive climate as boundary conditions to the discussion of the consequences and effectiveness of i-deals. In a work context defined by perceived mastery climate, employees are likely to share the benefits of i-deals with other co-workers, whereas in a climate characterized by competitive climate, employees are less likely to do so. The common element of these studies is that they underline the role of organizations; overall, i-deals are granted in organizations that are supportive and resourceful. Future research is suggested to consider the role of team climate at a more micro-level to explore and understand the dynamics of how i-deals unfold and lead to various employee consequences. Examples of further research that can focus on new forms of climates include family- and flexibility-oriented climates.

Non-work Leisure Resources and I-Deals

The current theory on i-deals refers to the fact that these arrangements are aimed at addressing employees' specific work needs and preferences, which suggests that i-deals do not have to unfold in one's work and family domain. However, they can also relate to an employee's leisure and non-work times. In this regard, leisure refers to free time in which an individual does not work or carry out activities to sustain life, which may include physical activities that allow an individual to improve certain skills or to build social relationships (Leitner & Leitner, 2012). According to Ragheb and Tate (1993), leisure encompasses activities like hobbies, as well as sports, outdoor, and social activities. Recent research shows that leisure activities can generate resources that then spill over into the work domain. Resources generated in non-work domains, such as hobbies, can create positive interactions between work and personal life and are characteristic of sustainable careers (Valcour, 2015).

From the perspective of resource theories, engagement in leisure activities generates personal resources for the employee, leading to better work outcomes of engagement, commitment, and satisfaction. However, if employees can have i-deals about their leisure pursuits, they are likely to feel more valued by the organization and, as a result, more committed and productive. While there are still no studies into this nascent field, the authors of this project have collected interview data in which the importance of leisure and leisure i-deals is apparently revealed. For example, one of the interviewees discussed the idea that by taking part in a photography class, which was her hobby, she was more motivated and felt cared for. From the manager's perspective, granting this employee leisure i-deals meant that this focal employee felt motivated, and there were no additional costs associated with the implementation of these deals for the focal employee. In other words, managers and organization, as the grantors of i-deals, were able to create a platform where the recipients acknowledged the personalized touch they were offered and transformed into informal advocates of the organization. In a similar field to i-deals, research into job crafting has explored the concept of leisure crafting and empirically revealed that such a form of leisure crafting is likely to lead to desirable employee behaviors and attitudes, both inside and outside the organization. Yet, i-deals research has been silent in this regard, which lays out an important opportunity to define and deconstruct the construct of leisure i-deals and explore how and under which conditions it is likely to lead to various employee results. Furthermore, these deals are supposed to be mutually beneficial; hence, they are also expected to contribute to financial return and productivity at the organizational level.

Future Research

As summarized above, little knowledge exists regarding the role of the supervisor in i-deal granting and how it relates to work-life outcomes. To date, most research into i-deals and work life have focused on gaining an understanding of what types of work-life outcomes i-deals generate. While it makes sense that the field started by studying outcomes (who would be willing to offer i-deals if these do not lead to positive results?), future research should pursue a more nuanced understanding of the relationship between i-deals and work-family. In light of the above discussions, we raise some possible questions below regarding the role of supervisors and employee outcomes in the context of flexibility i-deals.

(A) Are there family-related characteristics (or experiences) of supervisors that make them more likely to offer i-deals? What are the underlying processes that foster those relationships?

Addressing this research question is important as the family-related characteristics and experiences have to date remained an unknown and will be an important addition to the current literature, as well as a linking point integrating supervisor characteristics with the role and consequences of flexibility i-deals. Other (work) family characteristics, such as supervisors' motivation to work (i.e., family motivation), their preference for home-schooling or homecare for the elderly, or a religious meaning to life and work, for instance, might affect their willingness to grant—or, indeed, even promote—i-deals among their employees. Finally, it can be the case that supervisors may be forced to adopt flexible work schedules (i.e., coronavirus situation), and their adoption of such work practices may be seen as role models and trickle down to how their subordinates work and adopt similar flexibility i-deals. Such role-modeling and trickle-down perspectives have recently been considered in other i-deals research (e.g., Rofcanin et al., 2018) and can similarly be extended to this type.

(B) What are the family consequences, for the supervisor and employees, of granting flexibility i-deals?

Among the most relevant work-life consequences of flexibility i-deals, we know that task and career i-deals positively relate to work-family conflict and to working unpaid overtime, as well as to increased performance expectations and affective organizational commitment (Hornung et al., 2009). On the other hand, we know that schedule flexibility i-deals, those that result in customizing work hours, negatively relate to work-family conflict and working unpaid overtime (Hornung et al., 2009, 2011). Thus, it cannot be simply concluded that greater levels of flexibility i-deals lead to enhanced employee work-life outcomes, as such an impact is influenced by various contextual conditions including organizational support, co-worker reactions and, possibly, personal and organizational characteristics.

In extending the consequences of flexibility i-deals, research should consider the work-family consequences of for both of the parties in an i-deal negotiation process: the i-dealer and the recipient of i-deals. This could be achieved by adopting a new methodological perspective, the APIM (Actor Partner Interdependence) model, which can help to understand how the granting of i-deals affects the outcomes of both parties, and how the granting will ultimately affect the supervisor him- or herself. The core premise of APIM is that because members of the dyads share the environment, any data obtained from them are not independent; a person's outcome is affected both by their characteristics (actor effect) and by the characteristics of their partner (partner effect).

To illustrate our point about the adoption of the APIM models, we propose a model in which supervisors and employees occupy the central position. Here, we suggest that various co-worker, team, and organizational characteristics have an effect on supervisors' and employees' receipt of i-deals, and consequently influences their work and home outcomes. Further, since both work in the same organization and thus experience a similar environment and culture, the perception of the work-family culture (co-worker support and spousal support) by the employee and their supervisor will not be independent.

(C) (Mis)fit of perceptions relating to flexibility i-deals and consequences for employees

I-deals occur in a dyadic relationship and it is crucial that both the employee and the employer see eye-to-eye when it comes to negotiating them. It is crucial to their sustainability and to realize their future gains that a balance between demands and expectations is met. However, it is also apparent that it is not always easy to gain agreement on the two parties' obligations in the employment relationship, generally due to employees' tendency to overestimate their contributions and underestimate those of the other party (Vidyarthi et al., 2014: 248).

Research on i-deals has been mainly dominated by a social exchange perspective. According to this perspective, achieving balance in what is a give-and-take relationship is crucial; specifically, employers, as the providers of i-deals, and employees, as the recipients, define and shape the norm of reciprocity (Vidyarthi et al., 2014). Therefore, for successful i-deal negotiations, whether both sides meet the conditions and the fit of their expectations is important (Rofcanin, Kiefer, et al., 2017). These studies emphasize that employees and employers have to see eye-to-eye with regard to the conditions and content of i-deals, and similarly have to understand the associated implications. While, to the best of our knowledge, there are no previous studies on this topic available in the literature, the interview findings of the authors of this chapter (currently unpublished) reveal some interesting findings. As such, accounts of two HR managers working for one of the largest media companies in Turkey emphasize the importance of misfit when it comes to the requests associated with i-deals. In their negotiation with their HR managers, the accounts given by managers and employees showed that when both parties understood the purpose and aim of granting an i-deal, their outcomes are the most effective. This is an important finding that underlines the fact that when negotiating i-deals, the conditions, goals, and purposes of these arrangements should be made clear and outlined openly to both the HR manager and recipient. A common expectation was that both the manager and the employee would be expected to show an increase in work performance, demonstrating how the perceptions of congruence between an i-deal request and that request being granted are of particular importance.

Yet, we are blind to the effect of the misfit of perceptions. We think this is problematic because we do not know whether misalignment between the perception of i-deals given (by the supervisor) and received (by the employee) substantially affect (or potentially even thwart) the beneficial effect of i-deals on employee outcomes (such as work-family conflict, family performance, and family engagement). The majority of research on i-deals has implicitly assumed that subordinates' and supervisors' perceptions of i-deals are accurate and aligned (e.g., Bagger & Li, 2014; Rofcanin, Las Heras, et al., 2017). However, we know that perceptions are socially constructed, and often do not reflect an objective reality; moreover, we know that perceptions are relevant to individuals and their functioning. For instance, we know from research into the effects of subjective age (Montepare, 2019) that there are organizational-level antecedents (i.e., high work-related meaning) and consequences (i.e., individual goal accomplishment and performance) to feeling younger than one's objective chronological age. An example of a misalignment of perceptions between supervisors and employees regarding i-deals granted could occur when a supervisor perceives that he or she granted a micro-i-deal to an employee because they allowed them to leave work earlier to pick up a sick child from school, while the focal person might feel that this is not a micro-i-deal since the employer is obliged by the national labor laws to do so. In another example, a supervisor might think they have granted an employee an ideal because they are working a shift that is more convenient to them, while the focal employee might perceive that such an arrangement is not an i-deal because it is part of the firm's policy to allow employees with young children to do so.

Any disagreement in perceptions has a potentially important impact on employees, as well as on supervisors. When the perception of the supervisor is higher than that of the employee, the employee might feel frustrated by the supervisor's apparently inflated expectations with regard to reciprocation, leading to increased stress, lower sleep quality, and family performance, for instance. Similarly, such misalignment might lead the supervisor to feel unhappy by the apparent lack of gratitude and commitment on the part of the employee. The opposite situation might occur when the employee has a higher perception than that of the supervisor, the low demands posed by the supervisor, plus the feeling of enjoying an i-deal might lead to increased commitment, and a "flow" at work and home. Thus, future work in the field should explore these dynamics, and make appropriate recommendations as to how to capitalize on the value of i-deals.

Potential Theoretical Perspectives on Flexibility I-Deals

Action Regulation Theory Approach to Flexibility I-Deals

Potentially, researchers could use the action regulation theory to scrutinize i-deals from a work-family interface perspective. The action aspect of action regulation theory argues that the proactive action on part of the employee should be encouraged (Seibert et al., 1999). Additionally, the operationalization of action regulation theory in the shape of career self-management behavior argues that employees should take proactive action that would be beneficial to the employee career in the longer term (Godat & Brigham, 1999). Although the idea that an employee's proactive pursuit of an i-deal with their supervisors could increase the likelihood of obtaining the i-deal has been empirically proven, calls for further research into "proactive behaviours as they are driven by the focal employee and are aimed at modifying one's work conditions" (Hacker, 2003) remain. Thus, future research could potentially examine the nomological network in terms of how the proactive pursuit of such i-deals would result on part of the employee, basing their hypotheses on the action aspect of action regulation theory.

Effort Recovery Approach to Flexibility I-Deals

Future studies are recommended to conceptualize i-deals as a tool in response to the stress endured by the employee during work. Employees who negotiate these kinds of deals, especially flexibility i-deals, could strategically arrange these agreements so that they improve or increase the time allocated to recovery from stress. Demerouti et al. (2009) argued that there has been little emphasis on the role of recovery from the associated strain during non-work time, and future research could benefit from scrutinizing how the recovery process proceeds during non-work hours. Future researchers interested in i-deals could use the work-family interface to consider how i-deals obtained in the organization in response to stress could affect the family life of the focal employee. Additionally, although recovery may occur in the context of work and non-work (Ganster & Schaubroek, 1991; Geurts & Sonnentag, 2006), the effects of non-work recovery on family members of the focal employee who received the i-deal could lead to an interesting stream of research.

Spillover/Crossover Approach to Flexibility I-Deals

A key development regarding flexibility i-deals (and i-deals in general) relates to the crossover and spillover perspective. I-deals offer and provide personalized resources to the recipients and, understandably, the benefits of flexibility i-deals transfers between domains, or from one domain to another. This is referred to as spillover (Bakker & Demerouti, 2013). Where resources are transmitted between partners and individuals in a close and dependent relationship, this is referred to as crossover (Bakker & Demerouti, 2013). In the context of latest research and developments in the field, it is suggested that future research should explore the dynamic and reverse of resource transitions from work to home and possibly the opposite. Important questions that can be explored include the understanding and exploration of the mechanisms and boundary conditions of how resources of flexibility i-deals are shared between domains and between parties. In this regard, the field will benefit from further research using diary studies. Diary studies are specifically useful when studying the everyday experiences of working individuals. We know from our own experience, and that of others, that work and family experiences can vary over relatively short periods. While your colleagues might be supportive this week because they have the time and feel in the mood to do so, they might not be so supportive next week when they have to care for a sick elderly dependent or just because they feel very tired. Diaries allow the analysis of the effects of such fluctuations. Diaries will allow the thoughts, feelings, and behaviors within the work and family contexts, as well as characteristics of the work and family where a situation that may fluctuate on a daily/weekly basis, to be studied. In these studies, data should be collected on many different occasions from the same individual, thus allowing the capture of the short-term dynamics of experiences within and between individuals in the work context.

Time-Spatial Approach to Flexibility I-Deals

Time-spatial job crafting can be conceptualized as employees' ability to decide where, when, and for how long to work daily (Jeffrey Hill et al., 2008). At its core, time-spatial job crafting consists of components such as reflection, selection, and adaptation. Reflection is referred to as a deep consideration of past behavior to align future behavior (Schön, 1983). Selection in the case of time-spatial job crafting refers to the actual process in which employees select where, when, and for how long they want to work depending on their personal preferences. Finally, adaptation in the context of time-spatial job crafting refers to the adaptive behavior on the part of the employee in response to changing conditions, in this case, adaptation to the hindrances that may affect their selection criteria (Wessels et al., 2019).

From an i-deals and work-home perspective, the reflection and selection aspects of time-spatial job crafting could be conceptualized as antecedents to the i-deal negotiation process. Future researchers could use these concepts to examine how the process that leads to flexibility i-deals could occur in terms of how employees reflect and select the type of i-deal that they are going to negotiate. Additionally, there is a bidirectional process of time-spatial job crafting close to i-deals where the antecedents of reflection and selection could then become consequences in the future, as this job crafting initiative takes a looped form whenever the focal employee attempts to "adapt" to their environment. In this context, we believe further research into flexibility i-deals and time-spatial job crafting could use intervention and longitudinal studies to capture the effects of this "loop."

Conclusion

This chapter has attempted to explore a specific type of i-deals, flexibility i-deals, and how this relates to the work and non-work domains. Given the nature of these deals, that they are intended to offer flexibility in terms of when and where one works, they clearly have potential implications for one's work and family lives. It was noted that there are relatively few studies on flexibility i-deals compared to task and career i-deals. Important questions that emerged from this chapter and that needs further exploration are as follows:

1. Why and under which conditions do managers grant flexibility i-deals? Relatively more is known regarding the consequences of flexibility i-deals, and a perspective on the antecedents from the manager's and co-worker's side is needed to understand the triggers.
2. The types of flexibility i-deals and how they relate to certain employee outcomes need to be disentangled. Flexibility i-deals have elements of location and timing to them. Understanding how they relate to certain work as well as family outcomes and discussing their key characteristics suggest future research plans.
3. Extending flexibility to family and non-work domains. Understanding the exact mechanisms and boundary conditions of how flexibility i-deals relate to family and defining family i-deals will constitute an important area of work for future research.
4. Spillover-crossover perspectives on flexibility i-deals. Given the nature of these deals, namely that they are intended to benefit the non-work domain of the recipient, the spillover-crossover perspective should be novel and interesting. How are these resources transmitted between partners and between domains? This question remains unexplored, yet is clearly important to future research.

REFERENCES

Aguenza, B. B., & Som, A. P. M. (2018). Motivational factors of employee retention and engagement in organizations. *International Journal of Advances in Agriculture Sciences, 1*(6), 88–95.

Alsubaie, M., Stain, H. J., & Webster, L. A. (2019). The role of sources of social support on depression and quality of life for university students. *International Journal of Adolescence and Youth, 24*(4), 484–496.

Amin, S., Arshad, R., & Ghani, R. (2017). Spousal support and subjective career success: The role of work-family balance and career commitment as mediator. *Jurnal Pengurusan (UKM Journal of Management), 50*, 133–142.

Anand, S., Vidyarthi, P. R., Liden, R. C., & Rousseau, D. M. (2010). Good citizens in poor-quality relationships: Idiosyncratic deals as a substitute for relationship quality. *Academy of Management Journal, 53*(5), 970–988.

Awang, M., Kutty, F. M., & Ahmad, A. R. (2014). Perceived social support and well being: First-year student experience in university. *International Education Studies, 7*(13), 261–270. https://doi.org/10.5539/ies.v7n13p261

Bagger, L., & Li, A. (2014). How does supervisory family support influence employees' attitudes and behaviors? A social exchange perspective. *Journal of Management, 40*(4), 1123–1150.

Bakker, A. B., & Demerouti, E. (2013). The Spillover-Crossover model. In J. Grzywacs & E. Demerouti (Eds.), *New Frontiers in Work and Family Research* (pp. 54–70). Psychology Press.

Bakker, A. B., & van Wingerden, J. (2020). Do personal resources and strengths use increase work engagement? The effects of a training intervention. *Journal of Occupational Health Psychology, 21*(1), 20–30.

Bal, P. M., De Jong, S. B., Jansen, P. G., & Bakker, A. B. (2012). Motivating employees to work beyond retirement: A multi-level study of the role of I-deals and unit climate. *Journal of Management Studies, 49*(2), 306–331.

Balboa, C. M. (2017). Mission interference: How competition confounds accountability for environmental nongovernmental organizations. *Review of Policy Research, 34*(1), 110–131.

Ballinari, D., Audrino, F., & Sigrist, F. (2020, November 9). When does attention matter? The effect of investor attention on stock market volatility around news releases. *The Effect of Investor Attention on Stock Market Volatility Around News Releases.*

Call, M. L., Nyberg, A. J., & Thatcher, S. M. B. (2015). Stargazing: An integrative conceptual review, theoretical reconciliation, and extension for star employee research and extension for star employee research. *Journal of Applied Psychology, 100*(3), 623–640. https://doi.org/10.1037/a0039100

Campbell, S. M., Twenge, J. M., & Campbell, W. K. (2017). Fuzzy but useful constructs: Making sense of the differences between generations. *Work, Aging and Retirement, 3*(2), 130–139.

Cohen, S., & Wills, T. (1985). Stress, social support, and the buffering hypothesis. *Psychological Bulletin, 98*(2), 310–357.

Coyle-Shapiro, J. A., & Shore, L. M. (2007). The employee–organization relationship: Where do we go from here? *Human Resource Management Review, 17*(2), 166–179.

Demerouti, E., Bakker, A. B., Geurts, S. A., & Taris, T. W. (2009). Daily recovery from work-related effort during non-work time. *Current perspectives on job-stress recovery.*

Eisenberger, R., Singlhamber, F., Vandenberghe, C., Sucharski, I., & Rhoades, L. (2002). Perceived supervisor support: Contributions to perceived support and employee retention. *Journal of Applied Psychology, 87*(3), 565–573.

Ganster, D. C., & Schaubroeck, J. (1991). Work stress and employee health. *Journal of Management, 17*, 235–271. https://doi.org/10.1177/014920 639101700202

Garcia-Martin, M. A., Hombrados-Mendieta, I., & Gomez-Jacinto, L. (2016). A multidimensional approach to social support: The questionnaire on the frequency of and satisfaction with social support (QFSSS). *Anales De Psicoligia, 32*(2), 501–515. https://doi.org/10.6018/analesps.32.2.201941

Gawlik, R. (2017, July). Encompassing the work-life balance into early career decision-making of future employees through the Analytic Hierarchy Process. In *International Conference on Applied Human Factors and Ergonomics* (pp. 137–147). Springer.

Geurts, S. A., & Sonnentag, S. (2006). Recovery as an explanatory mechanism in the relation between acute stress reactions and chronic health impairment. *Scandinavian Journal of Work, Environment & Health, 32*, 482–492. https://doi.org/10.5271/sjweh.1053

Godat, L. M., & Brigham, T. A. (1999). The effect of a self-management training program on employees of a mid-sized organization. *Journal of Organizational Behavior Management, 19*(1), 65–83. https://doi.org/10.1300/J075v19n0 1_06

Hacker, W. (2003). Action Regulation Theory: A practical tool for the design of modern work processes? *European Journal of Work and Organizational Psychology, 12*(2), 105–130. https://doi.org/10.1080/13594320344000075

Hammer, L. B., Kossek, E. E., Yragui, N. L., Bodner, T. E., & Hanson, G. C. (2009). Development and validation of a multidimensional measure of family supportive supervisor behaviors (FSSB). *Journal of Management, 35*(4), 837–856.

Hornung, S., Rousseau, D., & Glaser, J. (2009). Why supervisors make idiosyncratic deals: Antecedents and outcomes of i-deals from a managerial perspective. *Journal of Managerial Psychology, 24*(8). https://doi.org/ 10.1108/02683940910996770

Hornung, S., Rouseau, D. M., Glaser, J., Angerer, P., & Weigl, M. (2011). Employee-oriented leadership and quality of working life: Mediating roles of idiosyncratic deals. *Psychological Reports, 108*(1), 59–74.

Hornung, S., Rousseau, D. M., Weigl, M., Mueller, A., & Glaser, J. (2014). Redesigning work through idiosyncratic deals. *European Journal of Work and Organizational Psychology, 23*(4), 608–626.

Hornung, S., Weigl, M., Glaser, J., & Angerer, P. (2013). Is it so bad or am I so tired? Cross-lagged relationships between job stressors and emotional exhaustion of hospital physicians. *Journal of Personnel Psychology, 12*(3), 124–131.

House, J. S. (1983). *Work stress and social support*. Addison-Wesley.

Jarvis, J. (2011). *Public parts: How sharing in the digital age improves the way we work and live*. Simon and Schuster.

Jeffrey Hill, E., Grzywacz, J. G., Allen, S., Blanchard, V. L., Matz-Costa, C., Shulkin, S., & Pitt-Catsouphes, M. (2008). Defining and conceptualizing workplace flexibility. *Community, Work & Family, 11*(2), 149–163. https://doi.org/10.1080/13668800802024678

Kelly, C. M., Rofcanin, Y., Las Heras, M., Ogbonnaya, C., Marescaux, E., & Bosch, M. (2020). Seeking an "i-deal" balance: Schedule-flexibility i-deals as mediating mechanisms between supervisor emotional support and employee work and home performance. *Journal of Vocational Behavior, 118*. https://doi.org/10.1016/j.jvb.2019.103369

Kossek, E. E., Pichler, S., Bodner, T., & Hammer, L. B. (2011). Workplace social support and work–family conflict: A meta-analysis clarifying the influence of general work–family-specific supervisor and organizational support. *Personnel Psychology, 64*(2), 289–313.

Las Heras, M., Rofcanin, Y., Bal, P., & Strollberg, J. (2017). How do flexibility i-deals relate to work performance? Exploring the roles of family performance and organizational context. *Journal of Organizational Behavior, 38*(8). https://doi.org/10.1002/job.2203

Las Heras, M., Van der Heijden, B., De Jong, J., & Rofcanin, Y. (2017). "Handle with care": The mediating role of schedule i-deals in the relationship between supervisors' own caregiving responsibilities and employee outcomes. *Human Resource Management Journal, 27*(3), 335–349. https://doi.org/10.1111/1748-8583.12160

Lee, C., & Hui, C. (2011). Antecedents and consequences of idiosyncratic deals: A frame of resource exchange. *Frontiers of Business Research in China, 5*(3), 380–401.

Leitner, M. J., & Leitner, S. F. (2012). *Leisure in after life* (4th ed., pp. 1–464). Sagamore Publishing.

Liao, C., Wayne, S. J., & Rousseau, D. M. (2016). Idiosyncratic deals in contemporary organizations: A qualitative and meta-metaanalytical review. *Journal of Organizational Behavior, 37*(S1), S9–S29.

Lloyd, J., & Harris, R. (2007). The truth about Gen Y. *Marketing Magazine, 112*(19), 12–22.

Montepare, J. M. (2019). An exploration of subjective age, actual age, age awareness, and engagement in everyday behaviors. *European Journal of Ageing*, 1–9.

Odle-Dusseau, H. N., Britt, T. W., & Greene-Shortridge, T. M. (2012). Organizational work–family resources as predictors of job performance and attitudes: The process of work–family conflict and enrichment. *Journal of Occupational Health Psychology, 17*(1), 28–40. https://doi.org/10.1037/a0026428

O'Donohue, W., & Wickham, M. (2008). Managing the psychological contract in competitive labor-market conditions. *Journal of Global Business Issues*. https://eprints.utas.edu.au/8093/1/ODonohue_and_Wickham.pdf

Parker, D. F., & DeCotiis, T. A. (1983). Organizational determinants of job stress. *Organizational Behavior and Human Performance*, 32(2), 160–177. https://doi.org/10.1016/0030-5073(83)90145-9

Ponticelli, J., & Voth, H. J. (2020). Austerity and anarchy: Budget cuts and social unrest in Europe, 1919–2008. *Journal of Comparative Economics*, 48(1), 1–19.

Ragheb, M., &. Tate, M. (1993). A behavioural model of leisure participation, based on leisure attitude, motivation and satisfaction. *Leisure Studies*, 12, 61–70.

Rainnie, A., & Dean, M. (2020). Industry 4.0 and the future of quality work in the global digital economy. *Labour & Industry: A Journal of The Social and Economic Relations of Work*, 30(1), 16–33.

Rhoades, L., & Eisenberger, R. (2002). Perceived organizational support: A review of the literature. *Journal of Applied Psychology*, 87(4), 698–714.

Rofcanin, Y., Berber, A., Marescaux, E., Bal, P., Mughal, F., & Afacan Findikli, M. (2019). Human resource differentiation: A theoretical paper integrating co-workers' perspective and context. *Human Resource Management Journal*, 29(2), 270–286.

Rofcanin, Y., Kiefer, T., & Strauss, K. (2017). What seals the I-deal? Exploring the role of employees' behaviours and managers' emotions. *Journal of Occupational and Organizational Psychology*, 90(2), 203–224. https://doi.org/10.1111/joop.12168

Rofcanin, Y., Las Heras, M., & Bakker, A. B. (2017). Family supportive supervisor behaviors and organizational culture: Effects on work engagement and performance. *Journal of Occupational Health Psychology*, 22(2), 207.

Rofcanin, Y., Las Heras, M., Bal, P. M., Heijden, B., & Erdoğan, D. T. (2018). A trickle-down model of task and development i-deals. *Human Relations*. https://doi.org/10.1177/0018726717751613

Rosen, C. C., Slater, D. J., Chang, D., & Johnson, R. E. (2013). Let's make a deal: Development and validation of the ex post i-deals scale. *Journal of Management*, 39(3), 709–742. https://doi.org/10.1177/0149206310394865

Rousseau, D. M. (2005). *I-deals: Idiosyncratic deals employees bargain for themselves*. M.E. Sharpe.

Rousseau, D. M., Ho, V. T., & Greenberg, J. (2006). I-deals: Idiosyncratic terms in employment relationships. *Academy of Management Review*, 31(4), 977–994.

Rousseau, D. M., Tomprou, M., & Simosi, M. (2016). Negotiating flexible and fair idiosyncratic deals (i-deals). *Organizational Dynamics, 45*(3), 185–196. https://doi.org/10.1016/j.orgdyn.2016.07.004

Schön, D. A. (1983). *The reflective practitioner: How professionals think in action.* Basic Books.

Seibert, S. E., Crant, J. M., & Kraimer, M. L. (1999). Proactive personality and career success. *Journal of Applied Psychology, 84*(3), 416–427. https://doi.org/10.1037/0021-9010.84.3.416

Steese, S., Dollette, M., Phillips, W., & Hossfeld, E. (2006). Understanding girls' circle as an intervention on perceived social support, body image, self-efficacy, locus of control, and self-esteem. *Adolescence, 41*(161), 55.

Stinglhamber, F., & Vandenberghe, C. (2003). Organizations and supervisors as sources of as sources of support and targets of commitment: A longitudinal study. *Journal of Organizational Behavior: The International Journal of Industrial, Occupational and Organizational Psychology and Behavior, 24*(3), 251–270. https://doi.org/10.1002/job.192

Ten Brummelhuis, L. L., & Bakker, A. B. (2012). A resource perspective on the work–home interface: The work–home resources model. *American Psychologist, 67*(7), 545–556. https://doi.org/10.1037/a0027974

Valcour, M. (2015). Facilitating the crafting of sustainable careers in organizations. In A. De Vos & B. Van der Heijden (Eds.), *Handbook of Research on Sustainable Careers* (pp. 20–34). Edward Elgar.

Vidyarthi, P. R., Chaudhry, A., Anand, S., & Liden, R. C. (2014). Flexibility i-deals: How much is ideal? *Journal of Managerial Psychology, 29*(3). 246–265. https://doi.org/10.1108/JMP-07-2012-0225

Wessels, C., Schippers, M. C., Stegmann, S., Bakker, A. B., van Baalen, P. J., & Proper, K. I. (2019). Fostering flexibility in the new world of work: A model of time-spatial job crafting. *Frontiers in Psychology, 10*, 505. https://doi.org/10.3389/fpsyg.2019.00505

CHAPTER 3

I-deal or No I-deal? Lessons for Managers from Economic Theory

Priyanka Sharma[ID], Smriti Anand[ID], Liad Wagman[ID], and Pouya Haddadian Nekah

IDIOSYNCRATIC DEALS AND INFORMATION ASYMMETRY

Ash has a long commute to work that is beginning to cause her stress. She also has a young child, which aggravates the challenges raised by the commute. Ash's employer does not offer work location or schedule flexibility as part of its standard policies. Ash decides to reach out to her boss to request the ability to work from home on at least two days a

P. Sharma (✉) · S. Anand · L. Wagman · P. Haddadian Nekah
Stuart School of Business, Illinois Institute of Technology, Chicago, IL, USA
e-mail: priyanka.sharma@stuart.iit.edu

S. Anand
e-mail: sanand12@stuart.iit.edu

L. Wagman
e-mail: lwagman@stuart.iit.edu

P. Haddadian Nekah
e-mail: phaddadiannekah@hawk.iit.edu

© The Author(s), under exclusive license to Springer Nature Switzerland AG 2022
S. Anand and Y. Rofcanin (eds.), *Idiosyncratic Deals at Work*,
https://doi.org/10.1007/978-3-030-88516-8_3

week. She has a good relationship with her boss, and he agrees to this idiosyncratic arrangement. Ash is thus able to achieve a better balance between the responsibilities of her work and her family roles.

Six months later, Ash's boss ends up leaving after a significant reorganization effort at the firm. The new boss, Jack, immediately asks everyone to come to work every day and follow the standard schedule. Ash tries this arrangement for a couple of weeks, and then decides to approach Jack to seek the ability to work from home. During the meeting, Jack makes several derogatory comments about working from home (e.g., "when I work from home, I just watch TV or babysit my kids"). Shortly after the meeting, Ash receives an email from Jack in which he refuses her request. Two months later Ash leaves the firm.

The situation above demonstrates an idiosyncratic deal (i-deal) where an employee wishes to fulfill a unique need, desire, or goal by negotiating one or more non-standard arrangements with the employer (Anand & Mitra, 2021; Rousseau et al., 2006). I-deals serve as informal contracts that help fill gaps left by formal job contracts and organizational policies. Substantial research attests to the win-win nature of i-deals through an array of benefits such as work-family balance and career growth to the seeking employees, and enhancements in employee loyalty and performance to the granting employers (Anand et al., 2010; Hornung et al., 2008). However, i-deals also pose considerable challenges to both parties (Greenberg et al., 2004; Marescaux et al., 2021).

Many of these challenges arise because of information asymmetries between employees and employers. I-deals are informal arrangements that lie outside of organizational policies and are usually not written down (Rofcanin et al., 2017). I-deals are meant to create value for both parties, so a manager may not grant an i-deal unless convinced that it is going to benefit the organization. The manager has to consider the possibility of undesirable behaviors such as a decline in the employee's performance after receiving the i-deal. In the aforementioned example, if Jack were completely aware of Ash's performance abilities, and/or could monitor all of her actions while working from home, he may have made a different decision about whether or not grant the i-deal requested by Ash. In addition to his ignorance about Ash's performance potential and work ethics, Jack is also ignorant about the exact extent to which Ash will benefit from the i-deal and reciprocate to the organization. Unfortunately, the private information held by Ash hinders Jack from making a mutually beneficial decision.

I-deals are not the only scenario rife with information asymmetries. Most interactions that take place within an organization are associated with information asymmetries in that one side is often more informed than the other. For example, skills and resources that affect an employee's ability to perform and succeed at the assigned task may be known only to the employee. She/he may also possess private information about the time and effort expended toward completing an assigned task. On the other hand, the employer/manager/supervisor[1] may know more about the value, profitability, and significance of the project assigned to the employee to the organization. As employer-employee interactions often take place in situations where one party is more informed than the other regarding some payoff-relevant variables, such information asymmetries may play into the self-interested tendencies of the informed party— encouraging them to behave in a manner that may conflict with the objectives of the other, and potentially result in inefficient outcomes (Akerlof, 1970; Grossman & Hart, 1983a; Hart & Holmström, 1987). For instance, when an employee's effort is not observable by the manager, the manager cannot tie employee compensation to effort. Knowing this, the employee may have an incentive to neglect or avoid job-related duties, and the manager, in turn, may be inclined to offer less compensation than what she/he would if the effort were directly observable.

Beginning with the seminal work of Akerlof (1970), economists have long been studying the topic of information asymmetry across numerous economic interactions, while also highlighting its associated undesirable effects. These studies have led to a concomitant growth in the literature on the role of various contracts in eliminating market inefficiencies in insurance, banking, and other industries (Grossman & Hart, 1983b; Holmström, 1999; Laffont & Martimort, 2009; Riley, 2001; Spence, 2002; Stiglitz, 1974, 1975). For example, firms that sell car insurance need to understand the risk of accidents associated with insurance buyers in order to offer them appropriate premiums. This situation has information asymmetry because only the buyers have full information about their risks. If the insurers offer a single "average" premium with the aim of attracting both low and high-risk buyers, the low-risk buyers will choose not to purchase insurance and the insurers will end up incurring losses in

---

[1] We use manager and employer/organization/firm/supervisor interchangeably.

serving only the high-risk buyers. In addition, insurance itself may incentivize buyers to engage in riskier driving patterns than uninsured drivers. Insurers may aim to gain more information about drivers by offering insurance buyers the option to install a driving tracking device in their car and/or a tracking app on their smartphone, which tracks and assesses their driving behaviors, in exchange for a discount on their insurance premiums. A buyer's decision of whether or not to opt into this program may allow the insurance company to deduce some information about their driving behavior (Stiglitz, 1975). The tools of economic theory are not only useful in foreseeing these potential inefficiencies and complexities but also provide ways to resolve them in a way that increases profitability.

Economic models of information asymmetry can also augment our understanding of i-deals—informal contracts operating in tandem with asymmetric information in the workplace. We note that employees can negotiate i-deals (before or after entering an organization) with various organizational representatives such as human-resources staff, hiring managers, business unit heads, and direct supervisors. However, even when an i-deal is negotiated elsewhere in the organization's chain of command, an employee's direct supervisor plays a key role in implementing the deal (Anand et al., 2018; Rosen et al., 2013). Thus, in our model, we assume that the manager and the employee are the two relevant parties to an i-deal.[2] In our analysis, we utilize the well-known principal-agent framework (Holmström, 1979; Laffont & Martimort, 2009; Mirrlees, 1976; Ross, 1973). In this framework, the manager, referred to as the principal, offers a contract[3] to the employee, referred to as the agent, who acts under the terms of the contract. As is standard in rational actor models of economic theory (Mas-Colell et al., 1995; Samuelson, 1947), it is assumed that both parties will maximize their own expected payoffs. Further, both parties hold private information that may lead to inefficient outcomes at the workplace. In this chapter, we focus on a managerial perspective and assume that the employee seeking an i-deal has private information about her skills, working habits, and/or

---

[2] Rousseau and other scholars maintain that co-workers are important third parties to any i-deals in the workgroup (Marescaux et al., 2021; Rousseau et al., 2006); however, in keeping with our focus on managerial perspectives, our analysis restricts attention to a manager and an employee.

[3] In our context, the term contract refers to any verbal or written agreement between the two parties that is enforceable by a court of law.

intent to exert effort, while the manager is the less informed party who has to decide whether to grant or continue an i-deal. We make this choice to facilitate a comparison between the two strands of literature: the economic theory of contracts, or "contract theory," and i-deals. The analysis and discussion in this chapter can be easily extended to contexts where the employer also has private information that is unknown to the employee.

As mentioned earlier, information asymmetries in employer-employee interactions may arise either due to hidden information known to the employee or due to private, unobservable actions and decisions taken by the employee (Laffont & Martimort, 2009). Information asymmetry due to hidden information arises when one party has information to which the other party is not privy. When this information transpires prior to the beginning of a transaction between two parties, the informed party has incentives to make false, misleading claims about their private information to convince the uninformed party to trade with them. This phenomenon is formally known as adverse selection (Akerlof, 1970). It arises when the informed party has an incentive to hide information that can adversely affect the uninformed party. On the other hand, information asymmetry due to hidden action arises when one party takes a private or hidden action that is non-verifiable by the other party. In such a scenario, the party taking the action automatically becomes informed, with the other party being uninformed. One can envision scenarios where the informed party may take actions that serve their personal interests and not those of the uninformed party. When such behavior transpires during an ongoing transaction after the two parties have agreed to contract with one another, it has the potential to reduce the overall value of the transaction. This phenomenon is known as "moral hazard" in economics and is highlighted in Holmström (1979).

The inefficiencies associated with asymmetric information have led to the development of several economic mechanisms that strive to prevent, or at least circumvent, these issues. In this chapter, we provide a description of two such popular mechanisms, namely screening and signaling (Akerlof, 1970; Riley, 2001; Spence, 1973). Screening mechanisms are applicable in scenarios where prior to starting a transaction the uninformed party can incentivize information revelation by the informed party. Signaling mechanisms, on the other hand, are applicable when the informed party reveals her private information by sending some signal, at some cost, to the uninformed party. For example, the success of a project may depend on the employee's hidden information such as personality fit with the work team, or the employee's hidden actions such as the amount of effort being exerted.

In an effort to obtain a job or preserve their job security, an employee may claim great fit with a team, regardless of the actual situation. Since an employee who is a poor fit can be detrimental to the team's productivity, the manager has an interest in learning about the employee's true fit, while the employee has an interest in hiding this information. Adverse selection arises in this case as employees make choices that can lead to adverse outcomes for the manager. The manager may foresee the issue of adverse selection and offer the employee choices, such as: (1) stay permanently with the current team or (2) participate in a rotation program to work with a different team every quarter. A low person-team fit employee recognizes that the job requires close interactions with other team members, which is going to be difficult in the current team. Therefore, the employee may opt for the rotation program to find a more suitable team. On the other hand, if the employee has a great fit with the current team, she may refuse participation in the rotation program. In either case, the employee's choice reveals hidden information about her person-team fit to the manager.

The models of information asymmetry assume that both parties are aware of the asymmetry itself as well as its potential consequences. Thus, while the uninformed party (manager) chooses a screening strategy, the informed party (employee) may utilize a signaling strategy by proactively committing to a year-long assignment with the team with the aim of sending a costly signal to the manager about her person-team fit. The signal is costly for the employee because she is committing to working with a team that may not be ideally suited to her work style. Further, the manager may preemptively address the issue of moral hazard by offering variable pay-for-performance bonuses to motivate employee effort and improve the alignment between both parties' incentives. The employee, for her own part, may offer to send daily progress reports to the manager, to mitigate some of the information asymmetry by sharing information about her private actions relevant to the work assignment.

To summarize, in this chapter, we explore idiosyncratic deals through the lens of theories of economics. Figure 3.1 provides a glance at the economic concepts discussed in this work. The remainder of this chapter is organized as follows. First, we develop models of adverse selection and moral hazard in the context of employee-employer interactions. After

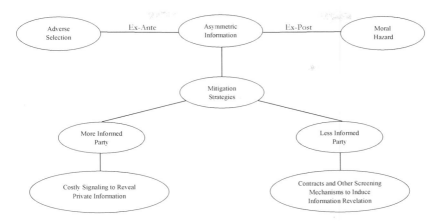

Fig. 3.1 Information asymmetry in workplace: negative effects and mitigation strategies

highlighting the inefficiencies associated with information asymmetry, we proceed to discuss screening and signaling mechanisms that can at least partially mitigate these asymmetries. We conclude the chapter by discussing implications for i-deals theory and by making suggestions for future research.

Adverse Selection

Adverse selection is one of the most discussed manifestations of information asymmetry. This phenomenon arises because the decisions of one party in a transaction (e.g., the agent) are dependent on some information that is not readily available to another party (e.g., the principal), who may be adversely affected by the decisions of the former (Akerlof, 1970; Laffont & Martimort, 2009; Mas-Colell et al., 1995). An example of this phenomenon in the labor market is employers offering low wage/compensation with the end result of primarily hiring lower-skilled employees.[4] Knowing they do not have full information about job applicants' skills and abilities, employers are induced to offer compensation suited to the average skilled applicant. In making such a decision, the

---

[4] We use the terms wage and compensation interchangeably.

implicit assumption is that, on average, some high quality and some low quality applicants in terms of performance and overall work ethics will be hired. However, the average compensation attracts only the applicants who cannot attract other higher offers, whereas high quality applicants may have better outside options. Altogether, the firm may end up losing productivity due to its inability to attract a reasonable proportion of high quality employees. This example draws on Akerlof's (1970) pioneering work on information asymmetry, which is the foundation of our next characterization.

Consider an applicant who faces the decision of whether or not to accept a job offer from a firm for a compensation w. Depending upon her skills, training, education, experience, etc., the applicant can be labeled as one of two types: High Performer (H) or Low Performer (L). We denote the type of the applicant with $\theta \in \{H, L\}$ and refer to her as a θ-applicant. We assume that the applicant seeks to maximize the return from her labor and can choose to either work for the firm or pursue another option such as working for a rival firm or setting up her own business. Suppose that these alternative options guarantee a compensation R_H to the high performer and $R_L < R_H$ to the low performer. Therefore, the lowest compensation that a θ-applicant would accept for employment with the firm is R_θ (known as her reservation wage). Hence, the lowest compensation with which the firm can expect to hire any applicant is R_L.[5] From the perspective of the manager, a type H applicant is more valuable than L, and when hired creates value V_H versus $V_L < V_H$, where V_L is the value created by an L applicant. V_H thus represents the maximum compensation that the firm would be willing to offer any applicant. Combining this observation with the reservation wage of each type of applicant, it follows that the compensation offered by the firm should be between R_L and V_H. As long as $R_L < V_H$, the firm would be able to offer a compensation that is acceptable to at least type L applicants.

As a benchmark case, we consider a symmetric information scenario where an applicant's potential is known to both herself and the firm. In

---

[5] For modeling ease, we assume that an applicant accepts employment with the firm whenever she is indifferent between her choices. Mathematically, in a rational actor model, this is readily the case, since the firm can hire the employee by offering a wage of $R_\theta + \epsilon$ with ϵ arbitrarily close to 0. That is, whenever the employee is indifferent between the two options, the employer can incentivize the applicant to break this difference in favor of accepting the offer by offering compensation slightly above the applicant's reservation wage.

this case, the firm will hire a θ-applicant by offering R_θ (or a slightly higher amount) as the compensation, earning, in net, $V_\theta - R_\theta$ from the employee. As long as $R_\theta < V_\theta$, this decision is optimal for both the firm and the applicant. Henceforth, we assume that this condition is met for each $\theta \in \{H, L\}$, such that, in an overall sense, it is beneficial if both types of applicants worked for the firm.

Consider now the scenario where an applicant's type $\theta \in \{H, L\}$ is her private information. This private information brings a degree of uncertainty to the manager's hiring decision, as the applicant's future performance on the job is unclear. Since the applicant's type (H or L) is no longer observable, the manager cannot effectively wage discriminate, and thus has to offer a single compensation to all types of applicants. This makes the question of optimal compensation less straightforward than the benchmark case with no hidden information. Assume the firm places some probability α on the applicant being a high performer. Then the firm's net expected payoff from hiring the applicant is $\alpha V_H + (1-\alpha)V_L - w$, where w is the offered compensation. If the firm chooses to offer compensation R_H, it will be acceptable to both types of applicants. However, this higher compensation reduces the firm's earnings from hiring the L-type performer from $V_L - R_L$ to $V_L - R_H$. This reduction in earnings hints at the first undesirable effect of asymmetric information.

If $V_L < R_H$, the firm ends up incurring losses whenever the hired applicant turns out to be a low performer. In this case, the firm's expected payoff from hiring the applicant may become negative and the firm may choose not to hire any applicant at all. Such a scenario will arise whenever either V_L is very low in comparison to R_H or the firm places a very low probability on the employee being a high performer. Given this possibility of losses, one may ask: What if the firm offers a compensation that equals the applicant's expected reservation wage, that is, $w = \alpha R_H + (1-\alpha)R_L$? Will that safeguard the firm against potential losses from hiring type L performers? The answer to this question is: No. Because, as $R_H > R_L$, this lower compensation will be acceptable only to low performers; the high-performing applicants will not be attracted to the firm. Therefore, the firm's expected payoff from hiring the applicant will always reduce to V_L. Table 3.1 depicts the firm's payoffs under various scenarios.

This phenomenon, where the informed applicants are using their private information to make decisions that can have an adverse consequences for the uninformed employer, is known as adverse selection. Faced with this situation, the optimal choice for the firm is to offer

Table 3.1 Summary of employer's payoffs under various wage offers

		Employee's type	
		High performer ($\theta = H$) Value to employer: V_H	Low performer ($\theta = L$) Value to employer: V_L
Salary offers	R_H	$V_H - R_H$	$V_L - R_H$
	R_L	0 (employee rejects employer's offer)	$V_L - R_H$

a compensation R_L, which will be acceptable only to type L applicants, whereas type H applicants will choose to pursue other options outside of the firm. While this lowered wage safeguards the firm against the losses from adverse selection, the problem highlighted above makes the firm miss out on boosting its productivity and profits from hiring high-performing applicants.

We note that these dynamics may also arise when multiple firms compete to hire an individual, or the individual is assumed to have all the bargaining power in salary negotiations. In such cases, if wages ultimately track an employee's expected productivity or type, a similar situation as far as adverse selection may arise. It is also a possibility that the firm offers $\alpha V_H + (1 - \alpha) V_L$, which is accepted by both types of applicants as long as $\alpha V_H + (1 - \alpha) V_L \geq R_H$. This last condition will be met only as long as the likelihood that the employee is a high performer is sufficiently high and/or if the output of a low performer V_L is not too low relative to the high performer's outside option R_H. If these conditions are not met, then an offer made by any firm that tracks an employee's expected type, $\alpha V_H + (1 - \alpha) V_L$, will be lower than the best outside option R_H available to high performers. Consequently, the offered compensation remains attractive only to low performers, leading to adverse selection and necessitating further adjustments in firms' compensation offers to reflect the lower output level V_L that is expected from new employees. Adverse selection may thus have detrimental effects on markets overall, if firms lower their wages and exhibit lower productivities.

Moral Hazard

The concept of moral hazard is another important building block in the study of asymmetric information. The problem of moral hazard arises because, even after entering into a contract with one another, one party in the transaction does not have access to full information regarding all of the actions of the other party (Arrow, 1984; Holmström, 1979; Jensen & Meckling, 1976). An example of this phenomenon in the labor market is employees engaging in undesirable behaviors such as shirking on their job duties (Dye, 1986). Employees know that their employers cannot monitor all of their actions or use performance metrics to precisely assess their levels of effort. Employers, on the other hand, may design position responsibilities, reporting duties, and compensation plans to reflect the likelihood that employees will act to maximize their own rather than the employer's payoffs. Altogether, the firm may end up with lower productivity and revenues by poorly designing compensation structures that motivate employees to shirk or engage in other unwanted behaviors.

To formalize, we consider the decision facing an employee who has already been hired by an employer in exchange for a wage w, where the employee is working on a specific project. Given the employee's ability to perform, their employer/manager/supervisor now needs to ensure that the employee works in a manner aligned with the firm's interests. We assume that the firm's payoff is V if the project is successful, and 0 otherwise. The likelihood that the project succeeds is dependent on the actions taken by the employee. The employee has two options: working hard (H) or being lazy (L). The option that is chosen by the employee is unobservable to the employer. If she chooses option L, then the project succeeds with a probability $0 < p_L < 1$ and yields an expected payoff of $p_L V - w$ to the firm. While this option, being lazy, is associated with no effort costs for the employee, working hard incurs an effort cost c for the employee. However, by working hard, the employee can increase the likelihood of the project's success from p_L to p_H, where $p_L < p_H < 1$. By choosing to work hard (the action H that comes at an effort cost), the employee can increase the employer's expected payoff from $p_L V - w$ to $p_H V - w$. The employer will certainly want the employee to choose action H instead of L, but for the employee, choosing H is costly, and unless this cost is compensated in some way, self-interest may drive her away from incurring this cost. Specifically, the employee's net payoff from choosing to exert effort and take action H is $w - c$, and w otherwise, so the employee may not choose H without some incentive. This situation illustrates the issue of moral hazard. Table 3.2 depicts the firm's payoffs under the fixed-wage compensation scheme delineated above.

Table 3.2 Payoffs under fixed wages

	Employee's action	
	Work hard (H)	Stay lazy (L)
	Cost to employee: c Project success probability: p_H Value of project: V	Cost to employee: 0 Project success probability: $p_L < p_H$ Value of project: V
Employee's payoff	$w - c$	w
Employer's payoff	$p_H V - w$	$p_L V - w$

Moral hazard arises because employees knowingly make choices or take actions that do not serve the best interests of the employer. Employers can neither monitor nor perfectly evaluate all employee actions (Dye, 1986). Outcomes of task assignments are imperfect indicators of the choices made by employees. For instance, a project may succeed by sheer chance, or because the employee had exerted exceedingly high effort. When employee choices have no consequences for their individual payoffs, there is a mismatch between their objectives and those of the employer's. This raises the question: How can an employer incentivize an employee to choose hard work over shirking? The answer to this question lies in the structure of the employee's compensation scheme, utilizing the information embedded in the relative likelihood of project success under low and high employee effort. In particular, by giving the employee "skin in the game" and tying her compensation to the project's outcome, the employee may be induced to take actions that benefit the firm. To this end, we assume that the firm benefits from offering some added compensation to the employee should the project succeed; that is, the employee's cost of choosing hard work H is below the expected benefit to the firm, $c < (p_H - p_L)V$. If this condition is met, the employee's high effort leads to the creation of positive gains that can be split between the employee and the employer.

As a benchmark case, consider the scenario where an employee's choice is perfectly observable and verifiable by the employer. In this case, the employer can tie the employee's compensation directly to her effort by offering her the following contract: earn w if you work hard, and 0 otherwise. Upon choosing effort H, the employee's payoff is $w - c$, whereas it is 0 if effort L is chosen. The employee can thus be incentivized to choose

H as long as the offered compensation w is at least as high as the cost of exerting high effort, c. Knowing this, the employer will offer compensation that is just slightly higher than (and can be arbitrarily close to) c. Therefore, the employer's expected payoff when the employee's effort is perfectly observable is given by $p_H V - c$.

Moving from this case to one where an employee's choice is not observable, consider an extreme scenario where the employer "sells the project" to the employee in return for a fixed payment φ. In contrast to the previous discussion, now the employee bears the full consequences of her actions because her payoff is dependent on the success of the project. If the project is successful, she now receives a gross amount of V, and 0 otherwise; she has to pay the employer φ under both scenarios. Therefore, the employee's expected payoff from choosing effort H is $p_H V - \varphi - c$, and $p_L V - \varphi$ from choosing effort L. As long as $\varphi \leq p_H V - c$, the employee will accept such a contract and will end up exerting high effort. Thus, appropriate contract design can enable the employer to circumvent at least some moral hazard-related inefficiencies. The key lies in establishing a close association between the employee's effort and compensation (Laffont & Martimort, 2009; Myerson, 1982; Ross, 1973; Stiglitz, 1974). This example also highlights that moral hazard may not even arise, or not arise to the same extent, provided the employer preemptively considers and identifies ways to address of all hidden actions possible for the employee and ensures alignment between the interests of the two parties under the possible scenarios.

Next, we consider a contract that is more common in the workplace: a two-part compensation, denoted by (w, b) where w corresponds to a fixed base compensation and b indicates a performance bonus that is paid contingent upon observing a successful project outcome. The employee's total expected compensation is now given by: $w + pb$ where p, which denotes the probability of project success, equals either p_H or p_L, depending upon the employee's chosen action. In designing the contract (w, b), the employer factors in the following: (i) Upon accepting (w, b), the employee should find it optimal to choose effort H over L. This is called the employee's incentive compatibility constraint and translates to the following condition: $p_H b + w - c \geq p_L b + w$. (ii) Upon accepting (w, b) and choosing H, the employee receives a payoff that is at least as high as her reservation payoff. This is called an employee's participation constraint and translates to the following condition: $p_H b + w - c \geq p_L b - c \geq 0$. Keeping in mind that a profit-maximizing employer will choose the lowest possible (w, b) that will satisfy both incentive compatibility and participation constraints, it follows that the optimal performance bonus equals $b = \frac{c}{p_H - p_L}$ and the fixed compensation equals $w = -\frac{cp_L}{p_H - p_L}$. The employer's expected payoff under this compensation scheme is given by: $p_H V - p_H b - w$, which equals $p_H V - c$ once we substitute for w and simplify. Note that this alternative compensation scheme makes the employer's expected payoff when employee effort is under unobservable identical to that when employee effort is observable, and thus addresses the issue of moral hazard. However, it is contingent on offering the employee a base wage that is negative, which often is unrealistic. As a result, in practice, given that wages are often bounded below by zero or a minimum wage, the employer is forced to settle for an outcome that is worse than that when effort is observable, but is the best the employer can achieve under asymmetric information and moral hazard.

SIGNALING

The inefficiencies highlighted earlier such as adverse selection and moral hazard have led to the development of mechanisms that are aimed at ameliorating the negative effects, whereby the informed party, for instance, takes steps to reveal or "signal" her private information to the uninformed party. High performers (H) likely have an incentive to distinguish themselves from low performers (L), so they may take costly actions or send costly signals to employers to identify and distinguish themselves (Riley, 1979; Spence, 1973). An effective signal for a high performer is one that low performers would not choose to imitate. Some of the most common examples of such signals in the labor market include academic credentials (e.g., by way of diplomas and grade transcripts), recommendation letters, and professional certifications. Individuals often spend a great deal of time, money, and effort in acquiring and disseminating these signals to employers with the intent of credibly communicating their higher performance potential to secure better positions and higher compensations. Interestingly, despite their widespread usage, there are times when these credentials do not translate to enhanced on-the-job performance by the signaling individual, which raises questions about the usefulness of these signals. To put this into context and to highlight the underpinnings of this mechanism, we next elaborate on the job-signaling model of Spence (1973).

We consider the same model as in section "Adverse Selection" with the following modification. Before applying for a job, an applicant may acquire education. The role of education in the present scenario is limited only to its signaling value by assuming that more education does not change the value V_θ created by a θ-applicant. First, we consider the scenario where neither high- nor low-performing applicants incur any costs for obtaining education. That education is costless makes it straightforward for the L-type applicants to mimic the education levels of the H types, thereby limiting the usefulness of education as a credible signal of potential on-the-job performance. This suggests that a credible signal must be costly for it to allow the informed party to meaningfully reveal her private information. Therefore, we assume that education, even though it may not be associated with any productivity gains, can be acquired at a cost c_θ borne by each θ-applicant that chooses to pursue it, where $0 \leq c_H < c_L$. This assumption implies that the acquisition of education is costlier for L applicants versus H applicants. Further, for modeling ease, we assume that $c_H = 0$; that is, H applicants incur no cost in acquiring education. If education credibly conveys that an applicant is an H type, since an H applicant can costlessly acquire education, she will always choose to do so. On the other hand, an L applicant incurs a cost for acquiring education, which forces her to be more strategic about whether or not to use education as a signal of her ability. We note that the value generated by a costly signal is still dependent on how it is interpreted by the employer; that is, for education to credibly signal that an applicant is an H type, it should be pursued by H types but not by L types—a condition that will be formalized.

Let us consider a situation where an employer does view an educated applicant as a high-performing employee. The employer consequently offers a high compensation R_H to an educated applicant and R_L to the others. Then, a type L applicant's payoff from acquiring education is $R_H - c_L$, and R_L otherwise. The L applicant will thus acquire education whenever $R_H - c_L > R_L$ or equivalently, $c_L < R_H - R_L$. In other words, whenever acquiring education is not too costly for the L applicant, she will also acquire it, as doing so enables her to receive a level of compensation that is higher than what she would have received otherwise. In this scenario, as both types of applicants end up sending the education signal, it is no longer optimal for the employer to interpret education as a signal of employee ability. Similar dynamics will occur as long as (a) the compensation differential arising from a signal is higher than its acquisition cost to an applicant, and (b) the lack of a signal is interpreted as conclusive evidence of an applicant's low performance potential.

The above discussion illustrates that for a signal to be meaningful, it is not enough that it is costly to acquire and send such a signal—the associated costs should be high enough to justify the ensuing compensation differentials. For a signal to be credible in information disclosure, it should not be easily imitable by all types of the informed side. In summary, only when costly signaling remains elusive to some of the applicants does it have any value for the employer and for the high performance applicants. We note that this point is valid even when education is not just a signal but actually improves employee performance on-the-job (Spence, 1973). This is because intelligence, conscientiousness, and other traits associated with acquisition of higher education are strongly associated with an individual's job performance (Barrick & Mount, 2009). These highly desired traits are difficult to assess accurately during any firm's recruitment process; however, applicants' education level can serve as a proxy for their personality traits. For instance, a graduate degree indicates career ambitions and perseverance beyond that required for acquiring an undergraduate degree. Therefore, employers can use employees' precise education levels as meaningful signals of their underlying traits relevant to job performance and design appropriate compensation mechanisms to retain them.

Another closely related strategy that can be employed by an informed party is signal jamming (Fudenberg & Tirole, 1986; Holmström, 1999), where informed players may intentionally limit the availability of information. For instance, the L performers of both sections "Adverse Selection" and "Moral Hazard" will have incentives to be confused with H performers. Accordingly, they may take actions that prevent the employers from correctly identifying them. This is why job applicants often request recommendation letters to be solicited from individuals who will provide favorable information on their capabilities. Students with low GPA often omit that information from their resumes. By a similar reasoning as before, it can be seen that if signal jamming is not too costly, informed players will engage in it. At the same time, it is important to bear in mind that signal jamming may not be perfect—omitting a GPA from one's resume in itself sends a signal.

Screening

Screening is a strategy employed by the less informed party to reduce information asymmetry by getting the more informed party to reveal their private information truthfully (Rothschild & Stiglitz, 1976; Wilson, 1977). For example, an employer may offer different compensation options to employees, such that an employee's choice of a compensation option may reveal whether she is a high or low performer. Screening design thus often has the aim of separating employee types; for instance, so that the choice that benefits a high performer should not benefit the low performer. Next, we describe an adaptation of Rothschild and Stiglitz's (1976) screening model to a labor market example where uninformed employers take steps to screen employees that have relevant private information.

We consider the same setup as in section "Adverse Selection" with the following change. Alongside the compensation offered to job applicants, the employer now also specifies an additional aspect of the employment relationship, referred to as task level, and aims to use it to screen the different applicant types. Task level can be any secondary aspect of employment that is readily quantifiable and verifiable by the employer, such as expected hourly output, weekly project deliverables, daily working hours, sales targets. The applicants are now presented with a choice between two contract options: (w_H, t_H) and (w_L, t_L), where $w_H > w_L$ and $t_H > t_L$. Each option specifies a compensation level and a corresponding task level, such that applicants can receive high compensation by undertaking higher task levels. The employer can successfully distinguish between high and low performers only if they each choose different options.

First, we consider the scenario where the higher task level t_H does not impose any additional costs on either applicant type. Then an applicant, irrespective of her underlying type, will choose the option with w_H, thereby limiting the usefulness of the associated task level as an effective screening mechanism. This suggests that an effective screening mechanism must include some deterrent that reduces the attractiveness of the high compensation option to the low types and induces them to reveal their private information through their choice of a contract option.

To that end, we assume that t_H is associated with a positive incremental cost c that is incurred by type L applicants. In contrast, type H applicants can perform both t_H and t_L without any such costs. Therefore, by offering $w_H = R_H$, the employer can incentivize H applicants to choose the contract option (w_H, t_H). On the other hand, the positive cost associated with t_H forces L applicants to be more strategic about their choice of a contract. Their payoff equals $w_H - c$ from choosing (w_H, t_H), and w_L otherwise. The employer will be able to successfully screen between H and L types whenever $c \geq w_H - w_L$. Given the differential compensation that the employer would like to offer to the two types of applicants, any task level can be utilized for screening purposes as long as it imposes sufficient costs on the low types to deter them from choosing the contract option with high compensation. A firm that is able to successfully screen between the two applicant types will then maximize its profit by offering $w_H = R_H$ and $w_L = R_L$, an outcome identical to the benchmark situation where the employer could directly observe applicants' types.

While our discussion in this section has been limited to the contracts that tie compensation to task levels, it can be further extended to other contracts as well. For example, for a sales job, an employer might ask employees to choose between (low target, low salary) and (high target, high salary) contract options. For screening to be effective in this case, the high target/salary combination should be set to only induce high types to choose it.

We also note the similarities between effective signaling and screening mechanisms. If successful, they both enable employers to perfectly learn employees' private information and behave as they would have in the absence of any information asymmetry. However, any signaling or screening mechanism is effective only when it is costly enough to justify the compensation differential between the two types of employees. Otherwise, the low performers will easily be able to imitate the high performers and render the screening or signaling mechanism useless. We also note that many of the aforementioned examples pertain to contracts that are associated with employee recruitment; however, information asymmetry can occur both before and after organizational entry. Employers and employees alike should recognize the potential for information asymmetry in any transaction and preemptively address the associated inefficiencies (Riley, 2001). For example, prior to beginning a transaction, employers can design effective contracts to screen desirable employees and align their interests with those of the organization. Employees, on their part, can signal their performance potential and alignment with the organization's objectives both during recruitment and after joining the organization.

Discussion

Going back to the story of Ash and Jack with which we began the chapter, we can see that there is information asymmetry between the two parties. Ash, the i-deal seeking employee, is the only one with full information about her skills, work ethic, and work methods, whereas Jack, the granting manager, is the uninformed party. Ash's private information is creating issues of adverse selection and moral hazard. First, Jack knows neither Ash's true performance potential nor the effect of an i-deal on her life in work and personal domains. On Ash's end, she has the incentive to inflate her skillset and performance so as to obtain her desired i-deal. Second, it is difficult for Jack to assume that Ash's behavior will not change after receiving the i-deal. Not only does Jack not know Ash well, but he is also unable to monitor or assess all of her actions, to the same extent as at the office, while she is working from home. For instance, Ash may take multiple breaks, perform her job duties at a slower pace, have distractions near her work space, or reduce the overall quality of her work in imperceptible ways because no one is monitoring her actions. Finally, Jack has to consider the possibility that granting Ash's i-deal will open the door to other team members requesting their own unique arrangements, further multiplying these issues. He may hesitate to make an exception for Ash, and then say no to everyone else. In following standardized HR policies and procedures designed to take care of majority employee needs, Jack may also be trying to be a fair manager who does not give preferential treatment to any employee. I-deals create different arrangements for members of the same team, which creates concerns about unfairness (Greenberg et al., 2004).

In Jack's shoes, many managers will make similar suboptimal choices and refuse employee requests for i-deals. Drawing on the concepts of economic theory, we suggest that Jack should utilize one or more screening strategies to improve his decision-making. First, right after joining his team, Jack should have announced his wish to establish close relationships with all team members. A face-to-face setting is more conducive to relationship building, so Jack could have mandated that during his initial period (e.g., first 3 months) with the team, all team members must work in the office. This announcement would have set a positive tone for the team and closed the door on any work from home requests. Jack should be able to establish one-on-one relationships with his subordinates within a short time. Our assertion is in line with leader-member exchange (LMX) literature, which maintains that the quality of leader-follower relationships tend to be established within a short period after the dyad formation and remains stable afterward (Liden et al., 1993). Managers offer roles/assignments to new followers, who may choose to accept those, such that after a few interactions the LMX quality is established. High LMX employees are part of the leader's trusted in-group, with access to benefits such as socio-emotional support, promotions, and an expanded negotiation latitude (Dulebohn et al., 2012; Graen & Scandura, 1987). Other employees, in contrast, tend to have low to medium quality relationships with the leader, defined by the terms of the formal job contract. Leader-follower relationships can thus serve as a screening mechanism.

Even in the present scenario, Jack can utilize a screening strategy by offering a richer menu of contract options to Ash. One choice may be to accept goals that are more challenging for the next 3 months and receive the deal to work from home, while another choice may be to stay with her current goals and work in the office. Furthermore, to mitigate the issue of moral hazard, Jack can tie Ash's performance to increments in her vacation time, bonus, or promotion. As far as the specifics of Jack's discussion with Ash, we note that Jack should not have made derogatory remarks about work from home during their meeting. Those remarks may make him seem biased against individualized work arrangements, with the potential of making Ash feel unfairly treated. Had Jack preemptively planned and explained his screening strategies, Ash's reactions may have been less extreme. These assertion draw on empirical evidence attesting to the fact that negative outcomes are more palatable in the presence of fair treatment (Colquitt et al., 2001).

On Ash's part, she could have considered using a signaling strategy to reveal her performance potential to Jack. One obvious signal is mentioning her past performance and declaring her intent to maintain or enhance her performance level after receiving the i-deal. However, this signal does not cost her anything, and thus is not credible, unless Jack can identify evidence to attest to her past performance. Even in the presence of this evidence, Jack may not be confident about Ash's behavior remaining the same under work from home arrangement. These doubts could be allayed by Ash offering to take on more challenging tasks and maintain daily logs of her work, both of which would cost her time and effort. Moreover, at the outset, Ash may have been presumptive to believe that her i-deal would continue with the new manager. She could have first tried to build a stronger work relationship with Jack, and used the relationship quality, and the information Jack may have gleaned as part of the relationship, to signal her true performance potential and work ethic.

More broadly, the situation faced by Ash and Jack is likely to be increasingly common across organizations globally as the demand for i-deals escalates with increase in workforce diversity (Anand & Mitra, 2021). Worldwide, the workforce is becoming more diverse in terms of age, gender, sexual orientation, cultural values, and a host of other factors (Catalyst, 2021; Ortiz-Ospina et al., 2018). Workforce diversity comes with a plethora of unique needs that may not all be fulfilled through standard organizational policies. For instance, single parents or employees with multigenerational households may need work schedule or location flexibility to balance their family needs with those of their jobs. Millennials and Gen Z employees may need developmental training and assignments to grow in their current careers or to switch to new ones (Schroth, 2019; Twenge et al., 2010). Individualization of work can be a great talent management tool without incurring additional monetary costs to the employers. It is therefore critical to understand how to deal with information asymmetries in the context of i-deals, so that managers can make optimal decisions for their firms.

By creating different terms of employment for employees at the same hierarchical level, i-deals create wage differentials and afford managers the ability to wage discriminate in order to attract, retain, and motivate desired employees. I-deals can be received both pre- and post-organizational entry, as individuals can negotiate i-deals during recruitment prior to signing their formal employment contract (ex-ante i-deals), or later, while on the job (ex-post i-deals). In the case of an ex-ante i-deal, the individual's hidden information (e.g., skillset, personality) may cause the problem of adverse selection, since the hiring manager may not know the applicant's true performance potential and consequently fail to grant appropriate i-deals to meet his/her compensation and performance criteria. For ex-post i-deals, due to their occurrence in the context of an existing manager-subordinate relationship, there is a lesser concern about hidden information about the employee. That is, over multiple interactions, the manager may be able to gauge the subordinate's true skills and abilities. However, even in this scenario, we cannot ignore the potential for employee behavior changes after receiving an i-deal, and thus the room for moral hazard concerns.

For both ex-ante and ex-post i-deals, managers face the possibility of moral hazard after granting a deal, because they cannot observe all of the actions taken by employees. The potential inefficiencies that may result from information asymmetries can be addressed, at least in part, by the manager utilizing effective screening, monitoring, and contract design, and the employee utilizing appropriate costly signaling strategies. Information asymmetries, if not adequately addressed, can lead to large costs for employees, employers, and the broader market and society. Employers may not offer adequate i-deals to attract or retain the desired talent, and thus lose potential productivity. Many employees may not be able to stay in the workforce without receiving their requisite i-deals (for instance, single parents may be unable to work in their desired positions without receiving sufficient schedule and/or location flexibilities). In such cases, the value that these individuals could add to their organizations is never realized.

Conclusion

Our conceptual models point to a gap in i-deals research. This literature has largely grown under the assumption that i-deals benefit both the seeking employee and the granting employer. Scholars have utilized social exchange-based reciprocity, competence need satisfaction, and self-enhancement motives to explain the mutually beneficial outcomes of i-deals (Anand et al., 2010; Ho & Kong, 2015; Liu et al., 2013). Research has also established a number of other reasons for which managers grant i-deals, such as managers' personal caregiving responsibilities and own use of i-deals, employee rehabilitation, and compensating for prior broken promises (Hornung et al., 2009; Las Heras et al., 2017; Laulié, Tekleab, & Lee, 2019). Research also exists on the conditions that favor i-deals, such as leader fairness, high quality leader-follower relationships, and an organizational culture of flexibility (Anand et al., 2017; Hornung et al., 2008; Rosen et al., 2013). However, the effects of information asymmetries between i-deal seekers and grantors are yet to be examined. And, in particular, the reasons underlying managers' refusal to grant or continue i-deals remain largely unexplored.

The interface between these two untapped strands of the literature offers a promising direction for future work. It behooves i-deal scholars to study the extent to which issues of adverse selection and moral hazard permeate these individualized arrangements and may or may not lead to managers' (rational) refusal to grant or continue i-deals. In the same vein, future scholars can also investigate from both employee and employer perspectives the different ways in which issues of adverse selection and moral hazard manifest while creating new i-deals or continuing existing i-deals. Empirical research can uncover the conditions that promote or discourage issues of adverse selection and moral hazard for different types of i-deals. For instance, moral hazard may be a larger issue with work schedule or location flexibility i-deals, wherein offsite employee actions are difficult to monitor. On the other hand, adverse selection may be more prevalent with developmental i-deals, whereby an employee who is assumed to be a team player refuses to share knowledge—acquired on an employer's time—to enhance the team's productivity. The findings of such research will help management practitioners design, evaluate, and implement i-deals that maximize value for different stakeholders.

REFERENCES

Akerlof, G. A. (1970). The market for lemons: Quality uncertainty and the market mechanism. *Quarterly Journal of Economics, 84*(3), 488–500.

Anand, S., Hu, J., Vidyarthi, P., & Liden, R. C. (2018). Leader-member exchange as a linking pin in the idiosyncratic deals-Performance relationship in workgroups. *The Leadership Quarterly, 29*(6), 698–708.

Anand, S., Meuser, J. D., Vidyarthi, P. R., Rousseau, D. M., & Ekkirala, S. (2017). *I-deal makers in workgroups: Multi-level effects of leader fairness and i-deal distribution.* Annual Meeting of the Academy of Management in Atlanta, GA.

Anand, S., & Mitra, A. (2021). No family left behind: Flexibility i-deals for employees with stigmatized family identities. *Human Relations.* https://doi.org/10.1177/0018726721999708

Anand, S., Vidyarthi, P. R., Liden, R. C., & Rousseau, D. M. (2010). Good citizens in poor-quality relationships: Idiosyncratic deals as a substitute for relationship quality. *Academy of Management Journal, 53*(5), 970–988.

Arrow, K. J. (1984). *The economics of agency.* Stanford University.

Barrick, M. R., & Mount, M. K. (2009). Select on conscientiousness and emotional stability. In *Handbook of principles of organizational behavior* (pp. 19–40). Blackwell Publishers.

Catalyst. (2021). *Generations—Demographic trends in population and workforce: Quick take.* https://www.catalyst.org/research/generations-demographic-trends-in-population-and-workforce/. Accessed May 24, 2021.

Colquitt, J. A., Conlon, D. E., Wesson, M. J., Porter, C. O., & Ng, K. Y. (2001). Justice at the millennium: A meta-analytic review of 25 years of organizational justice research. *Journal of Applied Psychology, 86*(3), 425–445.

Dulebohn, J. H., Bommer, W. H., Liden, R. C., Brouer, R. L., & Ferris, G. R. (2012). A meta-analysis of antecedents and consequences of leader-member exchange: Integrating the past with an eye toward the future. *Journal of Management, 38*, 1715–1759.

Dye, R. A. (1986). Optimal monitoring policies in agencies. *Rand Journal of Economics, 17*, 339–350.

Fudenberg, D., & Tirole, J. (1986). A "signal-jamming" theory of predation. *Rand Journal of Economics, 17*, 366–376.

Graen. G. B., & Scandura. T. A. (1987). Toward a psychology of dyadic organizing. In L. L. Cummings & B. M. Staw (Eds.). *Research in organizational behavior, 9*, 175–208.

Greenberg, J., Roberge, M. É., Ho, V. T., & Rousseau, D. M. (2004). Fairness in idiosyncratic work arrangements: Justice as an i-deal. *Research in Personnel and Human Resources Management, 23*, 1–34.

Grossman, S. J., & Hart, O. D. (1983). An analysis of the principal-agent problem. *Econometrica, 51*, 7–45.

Grossman, S. J., & Hart, O. D. (1983b). Implicit contracts under asymmetric information. *Quarterly Journal of Economics, 98*, 123–156.

Hart, O., & Holmström, B. (1987). *The theory of contracts. Advances in economic theory: Fifth world congress* (Vol. 1). Cambridge University Press.

Ho, V. T., & Kong, D. T. (2015). Exploring the signaling function of idiosyncratic deals and their interaction. *Organizational Behavior and Human Decision Processes, 131*, 149–161.

Holmström, B. (1979). Moral hazard and observability. *Bell Journal of Economics, 10*, 74–91.

Holmström, B. (1999). Managerial incentive problems: A dynamic perspective. *Review of Economic Studies, 66*(1), 169–182.

Hornung, S., Rousseau, D. M., & Glaser, J. (2008). Creating flexible work arrangements through idiosyncratic deals. *Journal of Applied Psychology, 93*(3), 655–664.

Hornung, S., Rousseau, D. M., & Glaser, J. (2009). Why supervisors make idiosyncratic deals: Antecedents and outcomes of i-deals from a managerial perspective. *Journal of Managerial Psychology, 24*, 738–764.

Jensen, M. C., & Meckling, W. H. (1976). Theory of the firm: Managerial behavior, agency costs and ownership structure. *Journal of Financial Economics, 3*(4), 305–360.

Laffont, J. J., & Martimort, D. (2009). *The theory of incentives: The principal-agent model.* Princeton University Press.

Las Heras, M., Van der Heijden, B. I., De Jong, J., & Rofcanin, Y. (2017). "Handle with care": The mediating role of schedule i-deals in the relationship between supervisors' own caregiving responsibilities and employee outcomes. *Human Resource Management Journal, 27*(3), 335–349.

Laulié, L., Tekleab, A. G., & Lee, J. J. (2019). Why grant i-deals? Supervisors' prior i-deals, exchange ideology, and justice sensitivity. *Journal of Business and Psychology, 36*, 1–15.

Liden, R. C., Wayne, S. J., & Stilwell, D. (1993). A longitudinal study on the early development of leader-member exchanges. *Journal of Applied Psychology, 78*(4), 662–674.

Liu, J., Lee, C., Hui, C., Kwan, H. K., & Wu, L. Z. (2013). Idiosyncratic deals and employee outcomes: The mediating roles of social exchange and self-enhancement and the moderating role of individualism. *Journal of Applied Psychology, 98*(5), 832–840.

Marescaux, E., De Winne, S., & Rofcanin, Y. (2021). Co-worker reactions to i-deals through the lens of social comparison: The role of fairness and emotions. *Human Relations, 74*(3), 329–353.

Mas-Colell, A., Whinston, M. D., & Green, J. R. (1995). *Microeconomic theory* (Vol. 1). Oxford University Press.

Mirrlees, J. A. (1976). The optimal structure of incentives and authority within an organization. *Bell Journal of Economics, 7*, 105–131.

Myerson, R. B. (1982). Optimal coordination mechanisms in generalized principal–agent problems. *Journal of Mathematical Economics, 10*(1), 67–81.

Ortiz-Ospina, E., Tzvetkova, S., & Roser, M. (2018). Women's employment. https://ourworldindata.org/female-labor-supply. Accessed May 24, 2021.

Riley, J. G. (1979). Informational equilibrium. *Econometrica, 47*, 331–359.

Riley, J. G. (2001). Silver signals: Twenty-five years of screening and signaling. *Journal of Economic Literature, 39*(2), 432–478.

Rofcanin, Y., Kiefer, T., & Strauss, K. (2017). What seals the I-deal? Exploring the role of employees' behaviours and managers' emotions. *Journal of Occupational and Organizational Psychology, 90*(2), 203–224.

Rosen, C. C., Slater, D. J., Chang, C. H., & Johnson, R. E. (2013). Let's make a deal: Development and validation of the ex post i-deals scale. *Journal of Management, 39*(3), 709–742.

Ross, S. A. (1973). The economic theory of agency: The principal's problem. *American Economic Review, 63*(2), 134–139.

Rothschild, M., & Stiglitz, J. (1976). Equilibrium in competitive insurance markets: An essay on the economics of imperfect information. *Quarterly Journal of Economics, 80*, 629–649.

Rousseau, D. M., Ho, V. T., & Greenberg, J. (2006). I-deals: idiosyncratic terms in employment relationships. *Academy of Management Review, 31*(4), 977–994.

Schroth, H. (2019). Are you ready for gen Z in the workplace? *California Management Review, 61*(3), 5–18.

Samuelson, P. A. (1947). *Foundations of economic analysis.* Harvard University Press.

Spence, M. (1973). Job market signaling. *Quarterly Journal of Economics, 87,* 355–374.

Spence, M. (2002). Signaling in retrospect and the informational structure of markets. *American Economic Review, 92*(3), 434–459.

Stiglitz, J. E. (1974). Incentives and risk sharing in sharecropping. *Review of Economic Studies, 41*(2), 219–255.

Stiglitz, J. E. (1975). The theory of "screening", education, and the distribution of income. *American Economic Review, 65*(3), 283–300.

Twenge, J. M., Campbell, S. M., Hoffman, B. J., & Lance, C. E. (2010). Generational differences in work values: Leisure and extrinsic values increasing, social and intrinsic values decreasing. *Journal of Management, 36*(5), 1117–1142.

Wilson, C. (1977). A model of insurance markets with incomplete information. *Journal of Economic Theory, 16*(2), 167–207.

CHAPTER 4

Servant or Sinister? A Process Model of Follower Appraisal of Leader-Initiated I-deals

Jeremy D. Meuser and Xiaoyun Cao

> Someday, and that day may never come, I'll call upon you to do a service for me. But uh, until that day -- accept this justice as a gift....
> —Vito Corleone, *The Godfather*

In *The Godfather* classic, Don Corleone, before offering a favor to a man says, "You never wanted my friendship. And uh, you were afraid to be in my debt." This classic scene reminds us that people in positions of

---

J. D. Meuser (✉)
School of Business Administration, The University of Mississippi (Ole Miss), Oxford, MS, USA
e-mail: jmeuser@bus.olemiss.edu

X. Cao
Lake Forest, IL, USA
e-mail: xcao@mx.lakeforest.edu

© The Author(s), under exclusive license to Springer Nature Switzerland AG 2022
S. Anand and Y. Rofcanin (eds.), *Idiosyncratic Deals at Work*, https://doi.org/10.1007/978-3-030-88516-8_4

power can offer favors and that "some favors come with too high a price" (Straczynski, 1995).

Organizational scholars have a term for special treatments that are often negotiated with and granted by leaders: Idiosyncratic deals (i-deals; Rousseau et al., 2006). By definition, whether it be working from home, shorter workdays or weeks, or other forms of idiosyncratic arrangements, i-deals *should* benefit not only the employee but also the employer. As other chapters in this volume explicate the nature and definition of i-deals, we now turn our attention to leadership vis a vis i-deals and propose that when a formal leader initiates i-deals, the position of power from which the leader operates adds a complex aspect to the process. Leaders may offer an i-deal for any number of reasons. For example, leaders may offer special training, mentoring, or other developmental opportunities customized to the follower's needs, offer a modified work schedule to an employee who frequently arrives late to accommodate day care schedules, or time off to enhance well-being and improve productivity at a later date. Yet, we argue that not all leaders offer or grant i-deals to benefit both parties, but rather can do so in a self-serving exploitative way. For example, employees offered work-at-home arrangements may be expected to be available constantly; alternatively leaders may want a productive employee at home so that the leader can take credit for the employee's work; special training opportunities might come with the price tag of extraordinarily and unhealthily long workdays. In this chapter, we introduce a lens of leadership appraisals and provide explanations to a previously unexplored mechanism of creating i-deals.

The theoretical assumption of the leader's role as a simple Boolean "grant / no grant" decision leaves the leader by the wayside of i-deals exploration. Even though theory specifies that the leader is a critical perhaps even necessary component in the i-deals negotiation and granting process, little i-deals research has focused on the leader as an object of study, preferring rather the mechanisms and outcomes of i-deals in the workplace (Liao et al., 2017). When researchers have considered the leader in i-deals research, leader-member exchange (LMX; Gottfredson et al., 2020) is the dominate operationalization. Researchers have taken a variety of perspectives on its influence. First, it seems that the relationship with the leader influences the reception of i-deals. For example, Hornung et al. (2014) viewed LMX as an antecedent to i-deals. Similarly, Ho and Tekleab (2016) found that employees who request i-deals and have higher LMX receive them more often. Second, LMX may be a contextual factor such that i-deals may impact outcomes more strongly in the presence of low quality LMX relationships. For example, Anand et al. (2010) found that LMX moderates the relationship between i-deals and OCB, finding a stronger relationship when LMX was low. I-deals may also affect the LMX relationship, which serves as a conduit for the influence of i-deals on employee outcomes. For example, Anand et al. (2018) found that i-deals granted to a follower by a leader enhance the LMX relationship between them. Similarly, Singh and Vidyarthi 2018 found that receiving i-deals improves one's sense of LMX. These scholars, noting that i-deals and LMX do not occur in a vacuum, but rather in the context of a team with members sensitive to social comparison issues, also show that i-deal reception improves a sense of relative standing on LMX within the workgroup. Likewise, Vidyarthi et al. (2016) provide evidence that the perception of receiving i-deals to a greater extent than other members of the work group improves the recipient's performance. It also improves the recipient's sense of relative standing with the leader when the culture of the team is not team oriented. Clearly, the relationship with the leader is a critical and complex component of why i-deals exist and how they impact employee and workgroup functioning.

The sheer almost dizzying plethora of leadership constructs (Meuser et al., 2016) is perhaps a reason why i-deals scholars have largely not investigated leadership vis a vis i-deals. Fundamentally, there are so many leader constructs that it can be difficult to choose, especially given how similar many of them are (e.g., Lemonie et al., 2019) and the mounting criticisms of long-standing theories such as transformational (van Knippenberg & Sitkin, 2013) and leader-member exchange (Gottfredson et al., 2020). The present chapter identifies two leadership constructs particularly relevant to i-deals: servant leadership and exploitative leadership. Leaders employing one of these styles may offer i-deals, but do so for opposite (follower vs leader focused) reasons. Exceptions of any nature, i-deals, can be given to either reward and develop as an expression of servant leadership, or to manipulate and exploit a follower as an expression of exploitative leadership.

Servant leaders (Greenleaf, 1977; Liden et al., 2008), because of the priority they place on growing, developing, and supporting followers, theoretically employ i-deals (developmental, flexibility, and task) as a mechanism by which they can serve their followers. Conversely, from the perspective of exploitative leadership, i-deals could be a form of power and influence applied as a manipulation tactic. The fundamental social dilemma (Lind, 2001; Lind et al., 2001) highlights one critical question a follower must address when accepting an i-deal: "why do I think the leader is offering/granting the i-deal?" From the perspective of appraisal theory (Lazarus, 1991; Lazarus & Smith, 1988; Smith & Lazarus, 1990), leader and follower make appraisals (that is, causal explanations) for each other's behavior and performance, which impact subsequent motivation, affect, expectations, and behavior. We therefore build a theory of leadership and i-deals integrating and building on appraisal theory, servant leadership, and exploitative leadership. We explain why follower attachment style, trust propensity, leadership prototypes, schemas from experience with current and prior leaders, and social information impact the appraisal of the leaders' offer of an i-deal as either servant or exploitative leadership.

THEORY AND PROPOSITIONS

The i-deals literature focuses on follower-initiated arrangements perhaps because researchers interpreted the definition "Idiosyncratic employment arrangements are special terms of employment negotiated between individual workers and their employers" (Rousseau et al., 2006, p. 977) to imply workers initiated the negotiation. Yet these same researchers also say, "Either *an employer* or a worker can initiate an i-deal" (p. 978, emphasis ours). On one hand, the concept of i-deals as an idiosyncratic arrangement particular to a follower or a proportionally small set of followers within a workgroup remains constant whether a leader versus a follower initiates the negotiation and subsequent deal. On the other hand, because of the leader's positional power, leader-initiated deals deserve a special attention—attention lacking in the literature. When a *follower* chooses to initiate a deal negotiation toward potential subsequent acceptance, the follower has negotiated a labyrinth of social, psychological, and logistical details, such as how the i-deal will help the follower and team achieve their respective goals and potential social pressures that might emerge due to the i-deal. When the *leader* initiates an i-deal offer, those same details are potentially nebulous to the follower offered the i-deal. Further, the position of power from which the leader operates adds a complex aspect to the i-deal process, which deserves more attention (Liao et al., 2016). I-deals requested by the follower are, we hold, ontologically distinct from i-deals offered by the leader. In the former case, they can be a means of increasing a follower's own work-reward ratio. In the latter case, they are an influence tactic and the acceptance or rejection of such an offer comes with both a complex appraisal process and potential social consequences.

Do Followers Accept All I-deals Offered by Leaders?

Research directly linking power and influence tactics to other theories of leadership in a coherent model are rare (Meuser et al., 2016). Research on influencing tactics has illustrated 11 different tactics that leaders can employ (Yukl & Seifert, 2002; Yukl et al., 1992, 2005). Among them, i-deals relate most strongly to exchange tactics and collaboration, ideas compatible with the dominate framing of i-deals as a social and/or economic exchange process (Liao et al., 2016). *Exchange tactics* "involve explicit or implicit offer to provide something the target persons wants in exchange for carrying out a request" (Yukl, 2010, p. 175). I-deals are often given to encourage or maintain high performance. *Collaboration tactics* are similar to exchange tactics with the main difference being the relevance of the exchange to the current tasks. Leaders offering i-deals that relate to the present task, such as training, are employing collaboration tactics. Leaders offering i-deals that are ancillary to the present task, such as work-at-home privileges, are employing exchange tactics.

At first glance, one might expect that followers would always accept special arrangements offered by leaders because they single out the employee as special in some way and benefit the employee. We suggest that this is not always the case. We know that followers do not uniformly respond to influence tactics (Yukl, 2010). Followers express a range of responses from commitment (an enthusiastic response), to compliance (a willing albeit indifferent apathetic response), to resistance (opposition). This corresponds to a follower either enthusiastically accepting, accepting potentially with reservation or even under protest, or rejecting the i-deal. Employees may resist i-deals for a variety of reasons. We offer three examples: (1) growth needs strength (Hackman & Oldham, 1975) research suggests that followers differ on their willingness to expand their skillsets and responsibilities at work; (2) people are sensitive to influences from teammates with respect to i-deals (e.g., Vidyarthi et al., 2016); (3) recall, "some favors come with too high a price" (Straczynski, 1995). A fundamental reason to accept or reject an i-deal offered by a leader arises from the fundamental social dilemma (Lind, 2001). This dilemma springs from a need to balance the control one has arising from autonomy versus the safety, security, and other benefits that arise from membership in a social collective. In order to benefit from membership in such a collective, one must adhere to and subsume under the authority accepted by the social structure of the collective. The social structures' leadership and the motives and goals the follower ascribes to it are a critical determinate of which side of the dilemma the follower falls on—acceptance or rejection.

Proposition 1: *Followers will differ on their response to a leader offering an i-deal. Some followers will accept the i-deal (commitment or compliance) whereas some will reject the i-deal, choosing a resistance stance.*

Leader behaviors run a gambit between developmental and destructive. On one hand, servant leadership (Liden et al., 2008) is a constructive, developmental leader behavior that contributes to other productive and prosocial work behaviors even to the point of building a serving culture (Liden et al., 2014). These leaders experience a trusting and developmental dynamic with their followers consistent with high quality relationships. On the other hand, as exemplified in Niccolo Machiavelli's *The Prince*, leaders can serve their own needs first, even to the detriment of their followers. Self-interested exploitative leaders leverage their influence to benefit their own goals in contrast to the other-focus of servant leaders. These exploitive leaders often employ pressure, even in friendly ways, such as offering an i-deal even if it overburdens the followers (Schmid et al., 2019).

A key point: followers respond not to the leader's intent, but rather what the followers believe the leaders' intent to be (Caprara & Cervone, 2000). It is therefore possible that one follower, when faced with the same i-deal opportunity on a work team, would see their leader enacting servant behaviors designed to facilitate that follower reaching his or her potential. Another follower could view the exact same scenario as an attempt to exploit and manipulate the follower. Personality and appraisal research shows that how a person evaluates and responds to a critical situation in the present depends a great deal on their past experiences. "Concepts that are strongly interrelated for one person may be unrelated for another" (Caprara & Cervone, 2000, p. 260). This "eye of the beholder" effect complicates the leader's offering of i-deals.

Proposition 2: *When a leader offers an i-deal, the follower considers the offering leader's stance as servant or exploitative.*

A Framework for Understanding Follower Reactions to Leader-Initiated I-Deals: The Knowledge and Appraisal Personality Architecture (KAPA)

There are many reasons followers will differ on their appraisal and response to a leader offering an i-deal. The knowledge and appraisal personality architecture (KAPA; Cervone, 2004) can serve as a framework to integrate the multifaceted information and experience available to the follower during their appraisal process. KAPA suggests that present attitudes and behaviors emerge out of appraisal of present situations. Appraisal processes are at the heart of modern personality psychology, which recognizes human behavior is not driven by a taxonomy of immutable "traits" (e.g., Big Five; Costa & McCrae, 1992) but rather by an ongoing socio-cognitive process (Caprara & Cervone, 2000; Cervone, 2004), especially about those situations that focal individuals perceive to be relevant to their well-being (Lazarus & Smith, 1988). Appraisals are affected, informed, and influenced by cognitive and affective memories, conscious and unconscious, of psychologically similar or relevant events. Appraisals are fundamentally relational in that they include evaluation of present environmental conditions and relevant components of prior experience. Our cognitive and affective memories influence our present cognitive and affective realities, which in turn impact our attitudes and behaviors. Appraisals are dyadic in that they are specific to the person and the situation.

Over time, we habituate to common environmental stimuli, forming "if-then" profiles. If in situation X then do Y; if in situation A then do B. The KAPA approach explains why some students are vocal with friends but not in class or why some people feel comfortable giving a presentation at work or school but not being the focus of attention at karaoke or a sporting event. Recently, management scholars have recognized the KAPA framework, showing the value of contextualized behavioral assessments (Pathki et al., in press).

While familiar situations are processed automatically from habituated "if-then" profiles, uncertain, unfamiliar situations are not. By definition, idiosyncratic deals are special, valuable, unfamiliar, and rare events (Rousseau et al., 2006) that can easily impact a follower's well-being (Hornung et al., 2014). Appraisal processes involve assessing situations that are perceived to have a potential impact on one's own well-being.

A leader's offer of an i-deal to a follower represents an unfamiliar situation for that follower. Unfamiliar situations generally prime controlled processing of events, where environmental factors are weighed against prior experience more consciously than the automatic processing of familiar situations requires (Schneider & Shiffrin, 1977).

Proposition 3: *A leader's offer of an i-deal triggers an appraisal process in the follower pertaining to the i-deal.*

The KAPA architecture also incorporates packages of expectations known as schemas. These are derived from prior experience and influence reactions to present stimuli. KAPA suggests that prior experience with authority figures can influence cognitive and affective structures toward them. Attachment theory (Bartholomew, 1990; Bowlby, 1969) describes this process in more detail. Followers' caregivers/parents represent first socialization with authority figures and are particularly powerful because of a *tabula rasa* lack of preexisting cognitive and affective structures. Early experiences with authority figures are encoded in the cognitive and affective memory structures, which inform later expectations for how these relationships unfold. The notion that early life experiences are profoundly influential on behavior is well-established with a long history (e.g., Jung's work).

Attachment theory specifies that because of prior relationship experience, we develop schemas (Platts et al., 2002) and habituate to a comfort level with close relationships that extends to the leader–follower relationship (Harms, 2011; Hazen & Shaver, 1990; Keller, 2003; Yip et al., 2017). Attachment needs serve as a lens through which followers evaluate their leaders (Yip et al., 2017). Ainsworth et al. (1978), building on Bowlby's (1973) work, specify three kinds of attachment styles. *Anxious attachment* describes "the extent to which a person worries that others will not be available in times of need and anxiously seeks… their love and care" (Mikulincer & Shaver, 2015, p. 18). These individuals are overly sensitive to feedback and are potentially prone to see leaders as more supportive than they actually are (Hansbrough, 2012). These individuals are likely to ignore the potential risk associated with a leader-offered i-deal, optimistically viewing it as service behavior.

Avoidant attachment describes "the extent to which a person distrusts others' good will and defensively strives to maintain behavioral and emotional independence" (Mikulincer & Shaver, 2015, p. 18). These individuals avoid their leaders, resist them (Keller, 2003), and are unlikely to trust them (Harms et al., 2016) and therefore avoid the risk associated with potentially exploitative leader-initiated i-deals, as they could compromise the independence they value so strongly.

Secure attachment describes those who suffer from neither of the above issues, but rather believe others will be responsive and supportive to their needs (Mikulincer & Shaver, 2015). These individuals are likely to trust their leaders and see their offer of an i-deal as a benevolent serving behavior (Frazier et al., 2015).

Proposition 4a: *Followers with an anxious attachment style view i-deals offered by a supervisor as serving behaviors.*

Proposition 4b: *Followers with an avoidant attachment style view their supervisor offered i-deals as manipulative behaviors.*

Proposition 4c: *Followers with a secure attachment style view i-deals offered by a supervisor as serving behaviors.*

The KAPA framework also suggests that prior experiences will influence trust propensity (Colquitt et al., 2007), that is, the extent to which a follower is prone to trust people, including their leader. Those who have had positive experiences with gifts and offers in the past, especially from authority figures, possess schemas that enable trust (Govier, 1994; Lewis & Weigert, 1985). Consequently, these individuals are prone to trust that an i-deal offered by a supervisor is a supportive, developmental opportunity. Conversely, those who have been wronged in social exchange relationships are more likely to possess schemas that promote a cautious outlook and these individuals are not prone to trust, especially in unfamiliar situations with a new supervisor (Bigley & Pearce, 1998). These individuals are likely to appraise the offer of an i-deal from a supervisor with suspicion and as a dangerous, potentially exploitative social situation with likely negative future consequences.

Proposition 5: *Trust propensity is related to the appraisal of an i-deal such that an i-deal is appraised as more supportive and less exploitative as trust propensity increases; conversely, as trust propensity decreases, i-deals are appraised as less supportive and more exploitative.*

Implicit theories or leadership prototypes are another kind of schema accounted for in the KAPA framework. These are derived from prior experience with leaders and authority figures, and influence reactions to present leaders. Put simply, through experience, we have built our own idiosyncratic image of "right" and "wrong" or "good" and "bad" with respect to leaders. We use these images of the way things "should" be to help us interpret the behavior of others (Wofford et al., 1996) and more efficiently process environmental demands (Caprara & Cervone, 2000). Scholars have applied this concept to leadership (Lord et al., 2020) as a relational schema similar to those prescribed by attachment theory. Followers have images of "right" and "wrong" for leader behaviors and attributes. While there are general social expectations for a leader (Epitropaki & Martin, 2005; Offermann & Coats, 2018), components of these schemas are idiosyncratic (Markus et al., 1987; Meuser, 2018; Meuser et al., 2011). Leader divergence from the follower's leadership prototype has negative relationship and performance consequences. Conversely, to the extent a leader adheres to his or her follower's prototype for "leader," that follower will be disposed to rate their leader favorably, and this has positive consequences for their relationship and the follower's performance. For example, congruence yields higher quality leader-member exchange relationships (Engle & Lord, 1997; Epitropaki & Martin, 2005), follow trust in leader (Sy, 2010), and follower acceptance of leader decisions (Lord, 1985)—all key features that positively influence the appraisal of an i-deal as beneficial, serving behaviors. Therefore, comfort with an i-deal offering will increase as the leader's attributes and behaviors are congruent with the follower's leadership prototype. Conversely, we tend to view those who violate our norms and expectations with suspicion. Therefore, in this case, followers appraise an i-deal offering as exploitative, manipulative behaviors.

Proposition 6: *As congruence between follower's leadership prototypes and perceptions of his/her actual leader behaviors and attributes increases, the offer of an i-deal will be more likely appraised as serving and less likely exploitive. Conversely, as congruence decreases, the offer of an i-deal will be more likely appraised as exploitive and less likely serving.*

While in some aspects of life, "past results are not indicative of future returns," we tend to have a sharper view that the past actions of an individual are strong predictors of their future actions. Prior experience with the particular supervisor offering the i-deal is an important knowledge component of the appraisal process according to the KAPA framework (Caprara & Cervone, 2000). Prior experience influences the follower's appraisal of the leader's trustworthiness and the more recent and the more frequent the experiences, the more they influence current appraisal processes (Srull & Wyer, 1979). Of the three aspects of trustworthiness (ability, benevolence, and integrity; Mayer et al., 1995), two are relevant. Benevolence (Mayer et al., 1995) involves the appraisal that the leader is operating in the follower's best interest (serving behaviors) vs the leader's own (exploitative behaviors). Integrity involves the view that the leader engages in consistently fair behaviors and fulfills promises. Followers who have been wronged by their supervisors in the past, either through overt exploitive treatment, unethical behavior, or promise violation are less likely to expose themselves to risk again (Colquitt et al., 2007). These followers hold the belief that their current leader is also an exploitative leader. Such people follow the motto, "fool me once, shame on you; fool me twice, shame on me." Conversely, those who have had experiences with their leader that suggest them to be benevolent and persons of integrity will see these leaders as trustworthy servant leaders.

Proposition 7: *Prior experience with the current leader influences the appraisal of an i-deal offer. If the prior experience was exploitative, followers will appraise the present offer as exploitative. If the prior experience was serving, followers will appraise the present offer as serving.*

The KAPA framework also accounts for knowledge accumulated from experience with prior supervisors. Especially when current leaders are similar to prior leaders, followers tend to engage in leader transference—a process whereby followers employ cognitive schemas developed under the old supervisor to appraise current leaders (Ritter & Lord, 2007). Therefore, positive (negative) experiences with a prior leader offering an i-deal will dispose the follower to assume positive (negative) experiences will likely follow with the current supervisor.

Proposition 8: *Similarity between current and former leaders increases the likelihood of leader transference. Prior experience with former leaders influences the appraisal of an i-deal offer when transference occurs. If the prior supervisor was exploitative, followers will appraise the present offer as exploitative. If the prior supervisor was serving, followers will appraise the present offer as serving.*

As a social-cognitive framework, KAPA also includes social learning processes (Bandura et al., 1986) as part of knowledge acquisition. Social information derived from peers is a critical component of knowledge in a socio-cognitive appraisal. Followers are aware of their peers' fairness perceptions of their supervisor (Colquitt, 2004) and coworkers' beliefs and experiences can provide both key information regarding the fairness of a leader and a reality check against one's own beliefs (Carver & Scheier, 2001). Should followers derive information from peers that their leader is untrustworthy, exploitative, and manipulative, followers will be reticent to accept an i-deal (Anand et al., 2017), as they likewise appraise the leader as exploitative. Conversely, if information derived from peers suggests the leader is trustworthy and supportive, followers are more likely to appraise the i-deal as supportive serving behavior and accept it.

Proposition 9: *Social information derived from peers influences the i-deal appraisal process. If peer information indicates the leader is exploitative, followers will believe likewise. If peer information indicates the leader is a servant leader, followers will believe likewise.*

Core to the appraisal process is an evaluation of a situation with respect to the appraiser's well-being (Caprara & Cervone, 2000). People develop schemas of what they expect from their supervisors (Lord et al., 2020) and these schemas inescapably influence our thoughts, emotions, and subsequent inferences, expectations, and actions (Caprara & Cervone, 2000). These schemas are to some extent idiosyncratic (Markus et al., 1987). Idiosyncratic too are the standards by which an employee evaluates the "goodness" or the safety versus risk of situations determined by the employee to be significant. These standards are constructed cognitively in part from environmental stimuli (Miller & Prentice, 1996). When approached by a leader and offered an i-deal, followers consider a range of personal, leader, and environmental factors (e.g., those mentioned in Propositions 4–9) when engaging in an appraisal process to determine the risk associated with accepting an i-deal. KAPA theory suggests that followers accept an i-deal when the appraisal process yields a *safe* decision—one that associates the i-deal with servant leadership. When the appraisal process yields a sense of *risk* associated with exploitative leadership, followers resist the i-deal offer as they appraise it to be an exploitative influence attempt.

Proposition 10: *Followers appraise the offering of an i-deal as safe servant leadership or risky exploitative leadership. Followers accept i-deals appraised as serving leadership behaviors and shun i-deals appraised as exploitative leadership behaviors.*

DISCUSSION

The present chapter makes several theoretical contributions. First, we expand the usual framing of i-deals as a follower-initiated concept to recognize leaders can offer i-deals on their own initiative. We believe that, while there may be aspects of the negotiation process that are common with follower-initiated i-deals, leader-initiated i-deals have important distinctions that arise from the position of power from which the offer arises. We encourage a more comprehensive dyadic theorization and investigation of i-deals. I-deals researchers can learn from the lacunae in the study of leadership. (1) In the study of leadership, there has been an over emphasis on a top-down approach (Uhl-bien et al., 2014). Similarly, there has been an overemphasis on an i-deals bottom-up process. (2) There has been an underemphasis on the various ways followers experience and prefer leadership. Similarly, how followers experience leader-initiated i-deals is a largely uncharted territory. (3) There has been an under appreciation for the dyadic (Gardner et al., 2020; Gooty & Yammarino, 2011) and relational nature of leadership (Scandura & Meuser, 2022; Uhl-Bien, 2006). I-deals are negotiated and maintained within this relational dyad. We hope that as researchers continue to explore the i-deals phenomena, these lacuna will be closed.

Second, we employ a socio-cognitive framework of personality (KAPA) to integrate in an overall appraisal process several aspects of knowledge schemas of self, leader, and coworker environment salient and relevant to an employee when a leader makes an i-deal offer. KAPA, an ideographic view of a person accounting for idiosyncratic knowledge and appraisal processes, is appropriate to describe the idiosyncratic nature of i-deals.

In many ways, a KAPA approach to the individual is vastly superior to the more traditional approach in management of the Big Five (McCrae & Costa, 1996) or other nomothetic approaches (e.g., HEXACO; Ashton & Lee, 2007). Research shows that such static, monolithic, and strictly nomothetic views of the person are theoretically challenged (Cervone, 2004; Mischel & Shoda, 1995) whereas person in situation approaches (e.g., Pathki et al., in press) offer improved prediction capacity. Individuals are not static. They evolve over time in response to stimuli and adapt to common stimuli patterns encountered in the environment. While recognizing biological underpinnings of these processes, the KAPA model resists reduction of the person (Polanyi, 1959) to biologically defined traits. Rather it emphasizes the roles of "nurture" and autocratic will-based processes in defining the source of human attitudes and behavior.

Third, we highlight a challenge for leadership researchers. Most leadership research is cross sectional and obtains average leader behavior reports from a leader's followers (Dinh et al., 2014; Gardner et al., 2020). These reports are really amalgamations of appraisals of individual experiences involving the leader. By capturing individual appraisal events, leadership researchers may move beyond the average labeling of supervisors as servant, transformational, abusive, or any of the plethora of labels available to researchers (see Meuser et al., 2016, for a list) to understand the idiosyncratically evaluated interaction events that create these overall impressions. This will allow researchers to investigate beyond average styles and account for leaders who themselves do not operate consistently from day to day, some days offering more servant behaviors and others destructive (Schyns & Schilling, 2013). Whereas in the common overall approach, followers may excuse these occasional negative behaviors and therefore not include them in ratings of their leaders, such events likely have impact on the relationship and subsequent follower variables (e.g., satisfaction, performance, well-being) and team processes at least in the short term (Lewicki & Brinsfield, 2017). Study of event-level leader–follower phenomena is largely absent, eclipsed by individual level studies (Dinh et al., 2014; Gardner et al., 2020). Our chapter is an example of event-level theory applied to a research question important for understanding the nuances of the leader–follower relationship.

Future Research

We have focused our theorizing on a critical and under-researched aspect of i-deals: leader-initiated i-deals. There are many research questions related to leadership and i-deals that are of theoretical and practical import. Here we discuss the i-deal phenomena with respect to the leader's role in i-deals for which present research provides little to no guidance.

Previous i-deals research focuses on follower-initiated deals and assumes followers will accept the i-deal. While *prima facie*, that may seem a logical conclusion, it fails to account for changes that may occur to the i-deal or other facts that may change or become salient though the negotiation process that may end with the follower abandoning the negotiation. The i-deal may be granted, but only contingent on additional tasks or responsibilities for which the requesting follower may have no desire or ability to complete. The i-deal may be available, but to a lesser degree such that it is no longer adequate to meet the needs of the requesting follower. The leader may be willing to grant the request, but point out potential social or career consequences that may arise that discourage the requesting follower. The KAPA idiosyncratic view can be expanded to appreciate nuances of follower-initiated i-deal requests. Likewise, the KAPA architecture can also be employed to explain both sides of the leader–follower dyad so essential to i-deals.

While many workplaces have a documented and enforced chain of command, many others are more informal with "open door" policies at any level of management. Smaller organizations tend to be more dynamic and informal, offering the opportunity for i-deals from more than the immediate supervisor. For example, sometimes followers negotiate or are offered i-deals by their supervisor's supervisor, the location director vs their team lead, or the business owner vs the business manager. The human resources department may even offer i-deals that depart with standard operating procedure to perhaps compensate for some prior wrong done by the organization or to coincide the treatment of the employee with expectations from other organizations, their native country, or that arose from a hiring, transfer, or promotion negotiation. In these cases, immediate managers must permit the i-deal and in many cases, the responsibility of "selling" the fairness of the deal to the rest of the employee's workgroup falls to them. This stream of research would contribute to the paucity of research on multiple leaders and leader level interactions and contribute to more robust leadership theory in context of a leadership hierarchy.

Follower experience with a prior supervisor can impact experience with the present supervisor (Ritter & Lord, 2007). Practically, this can mean a newly appointed supervisor may be in the awkward place of navigating several complex i-deal related questions. First, the newly appointed supervisor must learn about i-deals made by a predecessor and do so in a way that is accurate without followers taking advantage of the leader by falsely indicating that i-deals were instituted that were in fact not. Second, the newly appointed supervisor must discern, often without much prior knowledge of the team dynamics, which i-deals to maintain and which to disrupt or terminate. Leadership research has tended to focus on the present team leader without awareness of the prior leader. We therefore do not know much about this "to kill the grandfather" question. Third, ancient wisdom reminds us "a pharaoh rose up who knew not Joseph," (Ex 1:8) which is to say disruptions in operating procedures and team dynamics are not uncommon when a new supervisor takes over. Newly appointed supervisors must navigate the complex political and emotional realities involved in the perception of potential loss or actual loss of an i-deal important to (a) follower(s). This stream of research would contribute to more robust theory about the leader–follower relationship.

I-deals do not exist in a vacuum. While some research has investigated i-deals in context of the team (e.g., Anand & Vidyarthi, 2015; Anand et al., 2017; Liao et al., 2017), research can offer little guidance to supervisors about what happens when new organizational policies make existing i-deals verboten or otherwise disrupt them. I-deals already represent a departure from the norms of a workplace or group. Followers that have been treated in a special way may believe that new policy does not apply to them. Leaders must then make decisions to dismantle the i-deal or advocate for why an i-deal should persist in spite of new organizational realities. This is complex if a type of i-deals common to many employees had been abused by those employees. This stream of research would contribute to more robust theory regarding team processes.

Relatedly, we know little about the ongoing maintenance of the i-deal. Research tends to focus on the antecedents and outcomes of i-deals and often in a cross sectional way (Liao et al., 2016). Yet i-deals are a component of a relationship and we know that relationships are not static entities but rather evolve over time. Changing needs and circumstances of employees, teams, and organizational goals may force one or the other party to reconsider the i-deal or even cancel it. We know little about the i-deals re-negotiation or cancelation process. Similarly, we also know little about the abuse of i-deals, which can have negative relational consequences. The old proverb "give them an inch and they will take a mile" (Heywood, 1546) reminds us that followers granted exceptions may abuse those exceptions. For example, employees allowed to work from home may do only six instead of eight hours of work, justifying it by believing that they are more productive at home or otherwise deserve it. Fundamentally, we know little about the lifespan of an i-deal and this stream of research would contribute to more robust i-deals theory.

Practical Implications

Leaders must guard their reputations regarding fairness and motives to enact i-deals effectively (Anand et al., 2017; Liao et al., 2017). Just as leaders create and guard climates within their teams for good or ill (e.g., Koene et al., 2002; Liden et al., 2014; Mayer et al., 2012; Offermann & Malamut, 2002), they also cultivate a reputation that can be inseparable from the team identity (Hogg, 2001). We recommend that leaders remember their words and actions carry particular import and followers are employing appraisal processes to understand their intent. We recommend that leaders choose their words carefully, actively watch for signs of miscommunication, and address those proactively and immediately.

Our theoretical model suggests that the reputation of a leader impacts how his or her actions are interpreted. While leaders viewed as fair, ethical, and trustworthy may offer supportive i-deals designed to serve their followers' needs, the exact same behaviors enacted by leaders viewed as unethical and untrustworthy are likely interpreted with skepticism and viewed as manipulative or exploitive. This highlights the importance and difficulty of relationship repair—leaders with bad reputations may be shunned while attempting relationship repair, which is far from a trivial task. Research suggests short-term strategies may be ineffective; for example, the followers may be tired of hearing excuses and apologies and disregard denials. Longer-term strategies, such as refraining from committing additional relationship damage and putting the terms of an i-deal in writing to waylay fears of later exploitation may be effective in rehabilitating a leader with a poor reputation (Lewicki & Brinsfield, 2017).

Leaders have many aspects of the follower of which to be aware in order to enact i-deals effectively. Some followers are simply less trusting for a variety of reasons. Some of these are challenging to overcome, such as attachment issues arising from relational schemas learned during childhood. Leaders can be sensitive to these issues and, should the company offer mental health benefits, recommend to employees struggling with trust to explore their use. A passive approach is to simply be aware of followers' attachment issues during a negotiation and address them on a case by case basis. Another source of mis- or distrust can arise from experience with prior leaders. Here, leaders can openly encourage and engage in conversation about past wrongs endured from prior leaders, and do so without names so that the experiences rather than the perpetrators remain the central focus of the discussion. This way residual issues from prior leaders that might impact the current leader–follower relationship will be salient to both parties. The leader can thereby be aware of followers' areas of particular sensitivity. Also, followers often benefit psychologically from discussing prior wrongs, allowing for closure (Caprara & Cervone, 2004). While it is beyond the scope of the present research, leaders should remember that employees differ in their level of commitment to work and in their career goals (Hackman & Oldham, 1975), and this can impact their willingness to accept an i-deal. It is also important that leaders directly inquire about career goals and values rather than assuming them, as leaders can often hold incorrect assumptions regarding them (Eagly & Carli, 2004).

Followers have expectations for their leaders and violation of those expectations comes at a cost for the relationship. While some aspects of the leader (e.g., gender and height) are static, decades of thought suggest that leaders can adjust their behaviors to meet follower needs. For example, the leader-member exchange and servant leader models are predicated on the ability to differentially relate to and serve followers according to needs. Leaders can reduce the impact of prototype violation by asking followers about their expectations for the leader–follower relationship. In theory, this will enable leaders to employ i-deals more effectively in their work teams.

Conclusion

I-deals research recognizes the critical role of exchange in the leader–follower relationship. The present theory calls for a greater appreciation of the status of the evolving leader–follower relationship at the time of i-deal offering. We also argue that offering i-deals may have a heretofore underappreciated impact on the leader–follower relationship. Leaders that are not aware of their position of power when offering an i-deal may unknowingly and unwittingly force a follower into a position of discomfort when intending to provide the opposite. The balance between challenging followers to growth and overburdening them is a fine line for the leader to walk.

References

Ainsworth, M. D. S., Blehar, M. C., Waters, E., & Wall, S. (1978). *Patterns of Attachment: A psychological study of the strange situation*. Erlbaum.

Anand, S., & Vidyarthi, P. (2015). Idiosyncratic deals in the context of workgroups. In *Idiosyncratic deals between employees and organizations: Conceptual issues, applications, and the role of coworkers* (pp. 92–106). Psychology Press.

Anand, S., Meuser, J. D., Vidyarthi, P. R., Rousseau, D. M., & Ekkirala, S. (2017, August). *I-deal makers in workgroups: Multi-level effects of leader fairness and i-deal distribution*. Paper presented at the annual meeting of the Academy of Management, Atlanta, GA.

Anand, S., Hu, J., Vidyarthi, P., & Liden, R. C. (2018). Leader-member exchange as a linking pin in the idiosyncratic deals-Performance relationship in workgroups. *The Leadership Quarterly, 29*(6), 698–708.

Anand, S., Vidyarthi, P. R., Liden, R. C., & Rousseau, D. M. (2010). Good citizens in poor-quality relationships: Idiosyncratic deals as a substitute for relationship quality. *Academy of Management Journal, 53*(5), 970–988.

Ashton, M. C., & Lee, K. (2007). Empirical, theoretical, and practical advantages of the HEXACO model of personality structure. *Personality and Social Psychology Review, 11*, 150–166.

Bandura, A., & National Inst of Mental Health. (1986). *Prentice-Hall series in social learning theory. Social foundations of thought and action: A social cognitive theory*. Prentice-Hall, Inc.

Bartholomew, K. (1990). Avoidance of intimacy: An attachment perspective. *Journal of Social and Personal Relationships, 7*, 147–178.

Bigley, G. A., & Pearce, J. L. (1998). Straining for shared meaning in organizational science: Problems of trust and distrust. *Academy of Management Review, 23*, 405–421.

Bowlby, J. (1969). *Attachment and loss: Attachment. V*. Basic Books.

Bowlby, J. (1973). *Attachment and loss: Volume II: Separation, anxiety and anger* (pp. 1–429). The Hogarth press and the institute of psycho-analysis.

Caprara, G. V., & Cervone, D. (2000). *Personality: Determinants, dynamics, and potentials*. Cambridge.

Carver, C. S., & Scheier, M. F. (2001). *On the self-regulation of Behavior*. Cambridge University Press.

Cervone, D. (2004). The architecture of personality. *Psychological Review, 111*(1), 183–204.

Colquitt, J. A. (2004). Does the justice of the one interact with the justice of the many? Reactions to procedural justice in teams. *Journal of Applied Psychology, 89*, 633–646.

Colquitt, J. A., Scott, B. A., & Lepine, J. A. (2007). Trust, trustworthiness, and trust propensity: A meta-analytic test of their unique relationships with risk taking and job performance. *Journal of Applied Psychology, 92*(4), 909–927.

Costa, P. T., & McCrae, R. R. (1992). Four ways five factors are basic. *Personality and Individual Differences, 13*, 653–665.

Dinh, J. E., Lord, R. G., Gardner, W., Meuser, J. D., Liden, R. C., & Hu, J. (2014). Leadership theory and research in the new millennium: Current theoretical trends and changing perspectives. *The Leadership Quarterly, 25*, 36–62.

Eagly, A. H., & Carli, L. L. (2004). Women and men as leaders. In J. Antonakis, R. J. Sternberg, & A. T. Cianciolo (Eds.), *The nature of leadership* (pp. 279–301). Sage.

Engle, E. M., & Lord, R. G. (1997). Implicit theories, self-schemas, and leader-member exchange. *Academy of Management Journal, 40*, 988–1010.

Epitropaki, O., & Martin, R. (2005). From ideal to real: A longitudinal study of the role of implicit leadership theories on leader-member exchanges and employee outcomes. *Journal of Applied Psychology, 90*(4), 659–676.

Frazier, M., Gooty, J., Little, L., & Nelson, D. (2015). Employee attachment: Implications for supervisor trustworthiness and trust. *Journal of Business and Psychology, 30*, 373–386.

Gardner, W. L., Lowe, K. B., Meuser, J. D., Noghani, F., Gullifor, D. P., & Cogliser, C. C. (2020). The leadership trilogy: A review of the third decade of The Leadership Quarterly. *The Leadership Quarterly, 31*, 1–26.

Gooty, J., & Yammarino, F. J. (2011). Dyads in organizational research: Conceptual issues and multilevel analyses. *Organizational Research Methods, 14*, 456–483.

Gottfredson, R. K., Wright, S. L., & Heaphy, E. D. (2020). A critique of the Leader-Member Exchange construct: Back to square one. *The Leadership Quarterly, 31*, 1–17. https://doi.org/10.1016/j.leaqua.2020.101385

Govier, T. (1994). Is it a jungle out there? Trust, distrust and the construction of social reality. *Dialogue, 33*, 237–252.

Greenleaf, R. K. (1977). *Servant leadership: A journey into the nature of legitimate power and greatness*. Paulist Press.

Hackman, J. A., & Oldham, G. R. (1975). Development of the job diagnostic survey. *Journal of Applied Psychology, 60*(2), 159–170.

Hansbrough, T. (2012). The construction of a transformational leader: Follower attachment and leadership perceptions. *Journal of Applied Social Psychology, 42*, 1533–1549.

Harms, P. D. (2011). Adult attachment styles in the workplace. *Human Resource Management Review, 21*, 285–296.

Harms, P. D., Bai, Y., & Han, G. (2016). How leader and follower attachment styles are mediated by trust. *Human Relations; Studies towards the Integration of the Social Sciences, 69*, 1853–1876.

Hazan, C., & Shaver, P. (1990). Love and work: An attachment-theoretical perspective. *Journal of Personality and Social Psychology, 59*, 270–280.

Heywood, J. (1546). *Fletestrete by Thomas Berthelet*.
Ho, V. T., & Tekleab, A. G. (2016). A model of idiosyncratic deal-making and attitudinal outcomes. *Journal of Managerial Psychology, 31*(3), 642–656.
Hogg, M. A. (2001). A social identity theory of leadership. *Personality and Social Psychology Review, 5*(3), 184–200.
Hornung, S., Rousseau, D. M., Weigl, M., Mueller, A., & Glaser, J. (2014). Redesigning work through idiosyncratic deals. *European Journal of Work and Organizational Psychology, 23*(4), 608–626.
Keller, T. (2003). Parental images as a guide to leadership sensemaking: An attachment perspective on implicit leadership theories. *The Leadership Quarterly, 14*, 141–160.
Koene, B. A. S., Bogelaar, A. L. W., & Soeters, J. L. (2002). Leadership effects on organizational climate and financial performance: Local leadership effect in chain organizations. *The Leadership Quarterly, 13*, 193–215.
Lazarus, R. S. (1991). *Emotion and adaptation*. Oxford University Press.
Lazarus, R. S., & Smith, C. A. (1988). Knowledge and appraisal in the cognition-emotion relationship. *Cognition and Emotion, 2*, 281–300.
Lemoine, G. J., Hartnell, C. A., & Leory, H. (2019). Taking stock of moral approaches to leadership: An integrative review of ethical, authentic, and servant leadership. *Academy of Management Annals, 13*(1), 148–187.
Lewicki, R. J., & Brinsfield, C. (2017). Trust repair. *Annual Review of Organizational Psychology and Organizational Behavior, 4*, 287–313.
Lewis, J. D., & Weigert, A. (1985). Trust as a social reality. *Social Forces, 63*, 967–985.
Liao, C., Wayne, S. J., & Rousseau, D. M. (2016). Idiosyncratic deals in contemporary organizations: A qualitative and meta-analytical review. *Journal of Organizational Behavior, 37*, S9–S29.
Liao, C., Wayne, S. J., Liden, R. C., & Meuser, J. D. (2017). Idiosyncratic deals and individual effectiveness: The moderating role of leader-member exchange differentiation. *The Leadership Quarterly, 28*, 438–450.
Liden, R. C., Wayne, S. J., Zhao, H., & Henderson, D. (2008). Servant leadership: Development of a multidimensional measure and multi-level assessment. *The Leadership Quarterly, 19*(2), 161–177.
Liden, R. C., Wayne, S. J., Liao, C., & Meuser, J. D. (2014). Servant leadership and serving culture: Influence on individual and unit performance. *Academy of Management Journal, 57*, 1434–1452.
Lind, E. A. (2001). Fairness heuristic theory: Justice judgments as pivotal cognitions in organizational relations. In J. Greenberg & R. Cropanzano (Eds.), *Advances in Organizational Justice, 56*(8).
Lind, E. A., Kray, L., & Thompson, L. (2001). Primacy effects in justice judgments: Testing predictions from fairness heuristic theory. *Organizational Behavior and Human Decision Processes, 85*(2), 189–210.

Lord, R. G. (1985). An information processing approach to social perceptions, leadership perceptions and behavioral measurement on organizational settings. In B. M. Staw & L. Cummings (Eds.), *Research in organizational behavior* (pp. 87–128). JAI Press.

Lord, R. G., Epitropaki, O., Foti, R. J., & Hansbrough, T. K. (2020). Implicit leadership theories, implicit followership theories, and dynamic processing of leadership information. *Annual Review of Organizational Psychology and Organizational Behavior, 7*, 49–74.

Markus, H. R., Hamill, R., & Sentis, K. P. (1987). Thinking fat: Self-schemas for body weight and the processing of weight relevant information. *Journal of Applied Social Psychology, 17*, 50–71.

Mayer, R. C., Davis, J. H., & Schoorman, F. D. (1995). An integrative model of organizational trust. *Academy of Management Review, 20*, 709–734.

Mayer, R. C., Aquino, K., Greenbaum, R. L., & Kuenzi, M. (2012). Who displays ethical leadership and why does it matter? An examination of antecedents and consequences of ethical leadership. *Academy of Management Journal, 55*(1), 151–171.

McCrae, R. R., & Costa, P. T., Jr. (1996). Toward a new generation of personality theories: Theoretical contexts for the five-factor model. In J. S. Wiggins (Ed.), *The five-factor model of personality* (pp. 51–87). Guilford Press.

Meuser, J. D. (2018, August). *Current developments in leader-member exchange (LMX): A research incubator: LMX Prototype*. Session held at the annual meeting of the Academy of Management, Chicago, IL.

Meuser, J. D., Liden, R. C., Wayne, S. J., & Henderson, D. J. (2011, August). *Is servant leadership always a good thing? The moderating influence of servant leadership prototype*. Paper presented at the annual meeting of the Academy of Management, San Antonio, TX.

Meuser, J. D., Gardner, W. L., Dinh, J. E., Hu, J., Liden, R. C., & Lord, R. G. (2016). A network analysis of leadership theory: The infancy of integration. *Journal of Management, 42*(5), 1374–1403.

Mikulincer, M., & Shaver, P. (2015). The psychological effects of the contextual activation of security-enhancing mental representations in adulthood. *Current Opinion in Psychology, 1*, 18–21.

Miller, S. M., & Prentice, D. A. (1996). The construction of social norms and standards. In E. T. Higgins & A. W. Kruglanski (Eds.), *Social Psychology: Handbook of basic principles* (pp. 3–38). Gulliford.

Mischel, W., & Shoda, Y. (1995). A cognitive-affective system theory of personality: Reconceptualizing situations, dispositions, dynamics, and invariance in personality structure. *Psychological Review, 102*(2), 246–268. https://doi.org/10.1037/0033-295X.102.2.246

Offermann, L. R., & Malamut, A. B. (2002). When leaders harass: The impact of target perceptions of organizational leadership and climate on harassment reporting and outcomes. *Journal of Applied Psychology, 87*(5), 885–893.

Offermann, L. R., & Coats, M. R. (2018). Implicit theories of leadership: Stability and change over two decades. *The Leadership Quarterly, 29*, 513–522.

Pathki, C. S., Kluemper, D. H., Meuser, J. D, & McLarty, B. D. (in press). The Org-B5: Development of a short work frame-of-reference measure of the Big Five. *Journal of Management.* https://journals-sagepub-com.umiss.idm.oclc.org/doi/10.1177/01492063211002627

Platts, H., Tyson, M., & Mason, O. (2002). Adult attachment styles and core beliefs: Are they linked? *Clinical Psychology & Psychotherapy, 9*, 332–348.

Polanyi, M. (1959). *The study of man.* Routledge and Kegan Paul.

Ritter, B. A., & Lord, R. G. (2007). The impact of previous leaders on the evaluation of new leaders: An alternative to prototype matching. *Journal of Applied Psychology, 92*(6), 1683–1695.

Rousseau, D. M., Ho, V. T., & Greenberg, J. (2006). I-deals: Idiosyncratic terms in employment relationships. *Academy of Management Review, 31*(4), 977–994.

Scandura, T. A., & Meuser, J. D. (2022). Relational dynamics of leadership: Problems and prospects. *Annual Review of Organizational Psychology and Organizational Behavior.* https://www.annualreviews.org/doi/abs/10.1146/annurev-orgpsych-012420-091249

Schmid, E. A., Verdorfer, A. P., & Peus, C. (2019). Shedding light on leaders' self-interest: Theory and measurement of exploitative leadership. *Journal of Management, 45*(4), 1401–1433.

Schneider, W., & Shiffrin, R. M. (1977). Controlled and automatic human information processing. I. Detection, search, and attention. *Psychological Review, 84*(1), 1–66.

Schyns, B., & Schilling, J. (2013). How bad are the effects of bad leaders? A meta-analysis of destructive leadership and its outcomes. *The Leadership Quarterly, 24*, 138–158.

Srull, T. K., & Wyer, R. S. (1979). The role of category accessibility in the interpretation of information about persons: Some determinates and implications. *Journal of Personality and Social Psychology, 70*, 127–140.

Smith, C. A., & Lazarus, R. S. (1990). Emotion and adaptation. In L. A. Pervin (Ed.), *Handbook of personality: Theory and research* (pp. 609–637). Gulliford.

Singh, S., & Vidyarthi, P. R. (2018). Idiosyncratic deals to employee outcomes: Mediating role of social exchange relationships. *Journal of Leadership & Organizational Studies, 25*(4), 443–455.

Straczynski, J. M. (Writer), & Eagle, D. J. (Director). (1995). In the shadow of Z'ha'dum. In J. M. Straczynski & D. Netter (Executive producers), *Babylon 5*. Los Angeles: Warner Bros.

Sy, T. (2010). What do you think of followers? Examining the content, structure and consequences of implicit followership theories. *Organizational Behavior and Human Decision Processes, 113*, 73–84.

Uhl, M. (2006). Relational leadership theory: Exploring the social processes of leadership and organizing. *The Leadership Quarterly, 17*, 654–676.

Uhl, M., Riggio, R. E., Lowe, K. B., & Carsten, M. K. (2014). Followership theory: A review and research agenda. *The Leadership Quarterly, 25*, 83–104.

Van Knippenberg, D., & Sitkin, S. B. (2013). A critical assessment of charismatic – transformational leadership research: Back to the drawing board?". *Academy of Management Annals, 7*(1), 1–60.

Vidyarthi, P. R., Singh, S., Erdogan, B., Chaudhry, A., Posthuma, R., & Anand, S. (2016). Individual deals within teams: Investigating the role of relative i-deals for employee performance. *Journal of Applied Psychology, 101*(11), 1536.

Wofford, J. C., Joplin, J. R., & Cornforth, B. (1996). Use of simultaneous verbal protocols in analysis of group leaders' cognitions. *Psychological Reports, 79*, 847–858.

Yip, J., Ehrhardt, K., Black, H., & Walker, D. O. (2017). Attachment theory at work: A review and directions for future research. *Journal of Organizational Behavior, 39*, 185–198.

Yukl, G. A., Lepsinger, R., & Luca, A. (1992). Preliminary report on development and validation of the influence behavior questionnaire. In K. Clark, M. B. Clark, & D. P. Campbell (Eds.) *Impact of leadership* (pp. pp. 417–427). Center for Creative Leadership.

Yukl, G. A., Seifert, C. (2002). *Preliminary validation research on the extended version of the influence behavior questionnaire.* Poster at the Society for Industrial and Organizational Psychology meeting, Toronto, CA.

Yukl, G. A., Chavez, C., & Seifert, C. F. (2005). Assessing the construct validity and utility of two new influence tactics. *Journal of Organizational Behavior, 26*(6), 705–725.

Yukl, G. A. (2010). *Leadership in organizations* (7th ed.). Pearson Education.

CHAPTER 5

Idiosyncratic Deals in Workgroups: Social Comparisons and Organizational Justice Perspectives in a Lifecycle Framework

*Prajya R. Vidyarthi, Franziska M. Renz,
Sarah J. Villanueva, and Smriti Anand*

INTRODUCTION

Individualized work arrangements (i.e., idiosyncratic deals or i-deals) are increasingly used to attract and retain employees with desirable skills and abilities, support differing needs and preferences of workers, and enhance work-life balance within an organization (Liao et al., 2016). I-deals have been empirically related to a variety of desired individual-level outcomes, including increased job performance, affective commitment,

---

P. R. Vidyarthi (✉) · F. M. Renz · S. J. Villanueva
The University of Texas, El Paso, TX, USA
e-mail: prvidyarthi@utep.edu

F. M. Renz
e-mail: fmrenz@utep.edu

S. J. Villanueva
e-mail: sjvillanueva@utep.edu

© The Author(s), under exclusive license to Springer Nature Switzerland AG 2022
S. Anand and Y. Rofcanin (eds.), *Idiosyncratic Deals at Work*,
https://doi.org/10.1007/978-3-030-88516-8_5

organizational citizenship behaviors, and reduced turnover (Anand et al., 2010; Ho & Tekleab, 2016; Hornung et al., 2008; Vidyarthi et al., 2016). Theoretical work has consistently argued that i-deals can affect and are affected by, workgroup and organizational characteristics, climates, and perceptions (Anand & Vidyarthi, 2015; Rousseau et al., 2006). A growing body of literature has examined the relationships between employees seeking or having received i-deals (i.e., i-dealers) and the workgroups in which they are embedded. These studies of i-deals in workgroups may be broadly categorized into two streams. The first stream considers how group contextual factors influence i-deals' formation, while the second stream examines how i-deals affect group and organizational contexts and outcomes.

The relationships between i-deals, group context, group outcomes, and individual outcomes arise from complex social relations at individual, dyadic, triadic, and group levels. In this chapter, we focus on how social comparisons (Festinger, 1954; Wood, 1996) and organizational justice perceptions (Adams, 1965; Colquitt et al., 2001) influence group- and meso-level relationships between i-deals, their antecedents, and outcomes. Our focus on social comparison and organizational justice theories does not necessarily preclude considerations of social exchange theory as a viable explanatory mechanism for outcomes of i-deals. However, since we consider group context, we primarily focus on social comparisons and organizational justice perceptions. The dynamic nature of i-deals as negotiated arrangements (Rousseau et al., 2016) poses a challenge to static theoretical models and empirical examination. To address the dynamic nature of i-deals, we introduce an i-deals lifecycle framework that includes four distinct but highly related stages: recognition, negotiation, execution, and renegotiation. We use the lifecycle as a conceptual framework to integrate and extend the discussion of within-group social comparisons and organizational justice perceptions of i-deals and their outcomes at each stage.

In the following sections, we first outline the theoretical underpinnings (i.e., social comparison theory and organizational justice theory). Next, we review the extant research on i-deals in workgroups. Then, we derive

---

S. Anand
Stuart School of Business, Illinois Institute of Technology, Chicago, IL, USA
e-mail: smriti.anand@stuart.iit.edu; sanand12@stuart.iit.edu

the i-deals lifecycle framework from existing literature. Finally, we discuss theoretical and practical implications and directions for future research. In doing so, we draw upon research from other streams. We specifically consider the similarities and parallels of leader-member exchange (i.e., LMX) to i-deals which can inform i-deals research.

Theoretical Underpinnings of I-deals in Workgroups

Social Comparison Theory

Social comparison theory describes individuals' innate need to assess themselves (e.g., ideas, skills, abilities) in relation to other individuals who are like them in some characteristics. These comparisons take place when objective standards to evaluate themselves are missing (Festinger, 1954; Wood, 1996). Social comparison theory is foundational in understanding i-deals in group contexts because i-deals collaborate in workgroups with similar others. Although i-deals are individually negotiated between the i-dealer and manager (Anand et al., 2018; Rosen et al., 2013), all members of the workgroup can and do compare their work arrangements with each other's. Members of one's own workgroup are likely referents for these comparisons because all workgroup members share a manager who represents the organization in the i-deals negotiation. Workgroup members also have similar professional backgrounds, are each other's most frequent contacts in the organization, and are privy to work-related information about one another (Vidyarthi et al., 2016). Social comparisons in the workgroup involve employees' conscious and unconscious mental processes. While they compare themselves with other group members, they avoid senseless competition within the group to ensure the survival of the group (Spence et al., 2011).

Social comparisons in the context of i-deals are inevitable and parallel to the comparisons and differentiation taking place in LMX relationships. LMX differentiation describes how managers form relationships of different quality with their subordinates that lead to within-group social comparisons. Differentiated relationships between managers and subordinates described in LMX literature (e.g., Vidyarthi et al., 2010) must be considered in the examination of i-deals because the manager-employee and manager-coworker dyads are key to the negotiation and execution of i-deals (Anand et al., 2010). Social comparisons in the context of LMX are also based on similarity in various characteristics including skills, abilities, and background. They inform subordinates about their relative standing in the workgroup (Anand et al., 2015). I-deals are used by employees to evaluate their standing and worth to the organization (Rousseau, 2005). Even in a workgroup context, the purpose of i-deals is not only to benefit the i-dealers but also the organization (Anand et al., 2010). Social comparisons allow the i-dealers to assess whether both parties, vis-à-vis other relationships, meet their obligations on a day-to-day basis (Goodman, 1977; Greenberg et al., 2007). I-dealers can develop a desire to improve their job performance or renegotiate the work arrangement if they perceive an unequal distribution of benefits. The distribution of benefits, execution of workplace procedures, and interpersonal interactions within the workgroup give rise to various organizational justice perceptions.

Organizational Justice Theory

Employees want their inputs to match their outputs in the organization. They compare their input–output ratio to the ratio of similar workgroup members (Adams, 1965). For i-dealers, i-deal terms are outputs that are granted by the organization to benefit employees. In exchange, i-dealers tend to increase their inputs into the organization, such as organizational citizenship behaviors (Anand et al., 2010). We draw on organizational justice theory to assert that if employees' inputs do not match their current work arrangements, they are likely to recognize the potential for an i-deal and negotiate or renegotiate their work arrangements. Consequently, i-deal recognition, negotiation, and renegotiation can be explained by the principal of equity (Adams, 1965).

In a workgroup, the individual-level input–output ratio is embedded in a constellation of such assessments. Organizational justice perceptions are highly relevant in the group context because they predict work attitudes and behaviors (Li & Cropanzano, 2009), including group-level outcomes of i-deals. Since i-deals are individualized work arrangements, each workgroup member may not get an i-deal. Even if everyone has an i-deal, these deals are unlikely to be perceived as equally valuable. This unequal distribution of i-deals may follow the principal of equity but likely violates the norm of equality at the group-level. Thus, the norm of equality as well as principal of equity needs to be considered to determine implications for employees' attitudes and behaviors at different stages of i-deals formation and execution (Marescaux et al., 2019).

Extant Research on I-deals in Workgroups

I-deals research has considered the i-dealer as well as the i-dealer's coworkers as important stakeholders in i-deal negotiation and conduct (e.g., Kong et al., 2020; Lai et al., 2009). The i-dealer, coworkers, and manager form a tripartite system of dyads (Rousseau et al., 2006). In this system, the i-dealer individually negotiates with the manager, while relationships between coworkers and the manager and coworkers and the i-dealer influence the workgroup's acceptance of the i-deal and its subsequent outcomes. The group- and meso-level outcomes of i-deals are fueled by justice perceptions based on social comparisons between i-dealers and coworkers. Unique, dyadic exchange relationships between manager and i-dealer as well as similar exchanges between manager and coworkers, such as those entailed in LMX, also affect these multi-level outcomes (Anand et al., 2010; Vidyarthi et al., 2016). Recent multi-level examinations of i-deals consider group characteristics, climates, and processes as important influences on the formation of i-deals as well as individual-level and group-level outcomes of i-deals (Anand et al., 2017, 2018).

Given the theoretical importance of coworker and within-group relationships in organizations, it is not surprising that research has examined how group context (i.e., the environment and circumstances in which the group exists) and employee perceptions of group context influence i-deal formation, acceptance, and subsequent outcomes for both individuals and their workgroups. Studies using individual perceptions of workgroup context provide evidence of the complex social interactions that arise when i-deals occur within workgroups. For example, the perceived availability of i-deals in a workgroup not only enhances coworker acceptance of another's i-deal (Lai et al., 2009), but also enhances an individual's evaluation of own i-deals (Ng & Lucianetti, 2016). However, i-deals can also arouse feelings of envy and competitive climate in the workgroup leading to negative outcomes like felt ostracism and employee turnover (Ng, 2017). Comparison of one's i-deals with those of the coworkers' may engender emotional exhaustion and deviant behaviors (Kong et al., 2020). I-deals can violate coworkers' distributive justice perceptions and motivate them to complain and demand their own i-deals (Marescaux et al., 2019).

Research has shown that i-deals can influence group processes, perceptions, and outcomes. Theoretical models indicate that group norms and characteristics related to i-deals affect group processes like cohesion, collaboration, and climate, which lead to group-level outcomes, including group performance, citizenship behavior, and creativity (Anand & Vidyarthi, 2015; Liao et al., 2016). Empirical work has shown that i-deals are related to increased collective commitment within the workgroup and improved client satisfaction (Bal & Boehm, 2019) as well as socially connecting behaviors among team members (Rofcanin et al., 2018). The relationship between i-deals and group attributes is reciprocal, as evidenced by studies showing moderation of i-deals to individual employee performance, job satisfaction, helping and citizenship behaviors relationships by group attributes like team orientation, task interdependence, value congruence, and LMX differentiation (Anand et al., 2018; Liao et al., 2017; Vidyarthi et al., 2016). Altogether, research supports multi-level theories of reciprocal relationships between i-deals, group contextual factors, and group outcomes (Anand & Vidyarthi, 2015; Liao et al., 2016).

Understanding the relationships between i-deals, group context, and group outcomes is important, because managers must carefully weigh the benefits of i-deals against their potentially undesirable effects on group processes and outcomes when allocating scarce organizational resources. Social comparison theory and organizational justice theory provide insights into the mechanisms that underlie group- and meso-level relationships with i-deals and explain positive and negative outcomes of i-deals. Although i-deals are often studied as static entities, they are dynamic arrangements, responding to changing needs of the i-dealer and organization as well as changing social context of the workgroup in which they occur. Scholars note implications for employees, managers, and coworkers at various points in i-deals formation and execution (Rofcanin et al., 2017; Rofcanin, Las Heras, Bosch, Stollberger & Mayer, 2020; Rousseau et al., 2006, 2016). We therefore propose a dynamic life-cycle framework of i-deals and consider the implications of within-group comparisons and justice perceptions at each stage.

I-DEALS LIFECYLE IN WORKGROUPS

Group-level and meso-level constructs such as workgroup climate and leader-member exchange social comparison (i.e., LMXSC) affect the decision to seek i-deals and i-deals negotiation (Anand & Vidyarthi, 2015; Anand et al., 2017). By theorizing or testing relationships which distinctly influence the negotiation, formation, or execution of i-deals, the existence of an i-deals lifecycle is implied. In this lifecycle, various constructs and contextual factors may differentially influence the creation, execution, and conclusion of i-deals. Despite some discussion of stage-based considerations for i-deals (Rofcanin et al., 2017; Rousseau et al., 2016), no explicit lifecycle framework from i-deal formation through conclusion has been advanced. We depict the i-deals lifecycle framework in Fig. 5.1. The i-deals lifecycle is not conceptualized as a group-level or meso-level model, rather, it provides an intuitive way to integrate group-level and meso-level

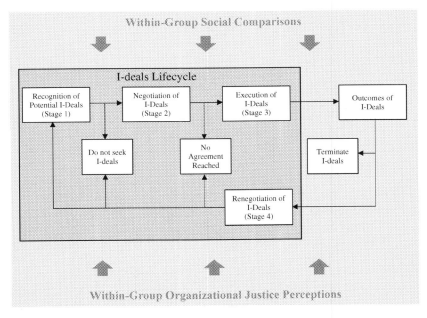

Fig. 5.1 The i-deals lifecycle as a contextual framework for social comparisons and organizational justice perceptions in workgroups

implications of i-deals and contributes to future longitudinal research of i-deals in workgroups.

First Stage: Recognition of Potential I-deals

The recognition stage begins when a current or prospective employee or the organization, typically represented by a manager, identify unmet individual or organizational needs. Either or both of the parties can decide to seek or advance an i-deal. They can either proactively or reactively assess the employment relationship and capitalize on its characteristics (Hornung et al., 2010; Rousseau et al., 2006). The recognition stage concludes with the decision to proceed or stop i-deal negotiations. Both outcomes of this stage are affected by social comparisons.

Social comparisons allow the employee to assess the benefits of i-deals, like being able to satisfy one's individual needs, while being able to maintain positive social relationships. This need is a motivator to participate in the negotiation process (Rofcanin et al., 2020). Social comparisons also let the employee evaluate i-deal availability (Anand & Vidyarthi, 2015; Vidyarthi et al., 2016) and generate perceptions of fairness (Marescaux et al., 2019). Manager is the primary contact to negotiate an i-deal, so the employee's within-group relative standing with the manager (Singh & Vidyarthi, 2018; Vidyarthi et al., 2010) matters to i-deals. Having a relatively high-quality LMX relationship with the manager increases the employee's scope to negotiate about a work arrangement. Thus, employees with a higher quality LMX relationship perceive an enhanced availability of i-deals (Anand & Vidyarthi, 2015).

Similarly, organizational justice perceptions allow employees to assess the fairness of the prospective i-deal negotiation process, including whether they are likely to obtain an i-deal in the organization (Lai et al., 2009). This assessment is influenced by perceptions in some or all four dimensions of organizational justice: distributive, procedural, interpersonal, and informational (Anand et al., 2017; Greenberg, 1993). Employees who perceive that they are likely to receive an i-deal are more willing to accept a coworkers' i-deal (Lai et al., 2009). However, because i-deals confer a unique benefit to an individual, they can carry a "stigma of unfairness" (Anand & Vidyarthi, 2015: 97) within the workgroup. The stigma can be avoided if the workgroup's manager is regarded as fair (Anand & Vidyarthi, 2015). This is especially true when existing work arrangements within the organization foster the individualization of employment relationships (e.g., part-time work, telecommuting), support employee personal initiative, and develop firm-specific human capital. In that case, the fair manager is perceived to have equitably distributed organizational resources among group members. Employees believe that they will have the opportunity to fairly negotiate scarce resources in the future (Hornung et al., 2008; Lee et al., 2015). In contrast, if the manager is regarded as unfair, workgroup members do not perceive that i-deals will be fairly negotiated. Then, i-deals are seen as favoritism and a mechanism to undermine the workgroup justice climate which may prevent employees from recognizing the potential for an i-deal (Anand & Vidyarthi, 2015).

We describe the outcomes of social comparisons and organizational justice perceptions at the recognition stage in Fig. 5.2. When social comparisons and organizational justice perceptions are both high, employees perceive that they are relatively deserving of i-deals (i.e., high availability) and that their negotiation will be handled fairly. In this case, employees likely recognize opportunities and will negotiate for i-deals. When social comparisons and organizational justice perceptions are both low, employees will perceive that they are rather ineligible for i-deals (i.e., low availability), and, even if they pursued an i-deal, the negotiation would be unfair. In this case, employees are unlikely to recognize

		Organizational Justice Perceptions	
		High	*Low*
Social Comparisons	**High**	*Proposition 1a:* • High availability, high fairness • Pursue negotiation	*Proposition 1c:* • High availability, low fairness • Consider negotiation
	Low	*Proposition 1c:* • Low availability, high fairness • Consider negotiation	*Proposition 1b:* • Low availability, low fairness • Forego negotiation

Fig. 5.2 Outcomes of social comparisons and organizational justice perceptions at the recognition stage of the i-deals lifecycle

opportunities and negotiate for i-deals. When social comparisons are high but organizational justice perceptions are low, employees will perceive that they are relatively deserving of i-deals (i.e., high availability), but that the negotiations may not be conducted fairly. In contrast, when social comparisons are low and organizational justice perceptions are high, employees will perceive that they are rather ineligible for i-deals (i.e., low availability), but if they pursued i-deals, the i-deals would be fairly negotiated. In these scenarios, the employee will weigh the potential benefit of an i-deal against the potential loss in relative standing within the workgroup if the negotiation is unsuccessful.

Proposition 1a *When employees' social comparisons are high and organizational justice perceptions are high, employees will pursue i-deals negotiation.*

Proposition 1b *When employees' social comparisons are low and organizational justice perceptions are low, employees will forego i-deal negotiation.*

Proposition 1c *When employees' social comparisons and organizational justice perceptions are opposed (high/low or low/high), employees will pursue i-deals negotiation if the potential benefit of the i-deal outweighs the potential loss in relative standing within the workgroup.*

Second Stage: Negotiation of I-deals

Once the employee has recognized the potential for an i-deal and chooses to pursue it, the employee enters the second stage, negotiation of i-deals. This stage includes all bargaining activities between employee and the manager. The i-dealers content is the focus of the negotiations and provides some benefit to both the employee and organization (Rofcanin et al., 2020). The negotiation stage concludes when an idiosyncratic agreement is reached or when negotiations cease without an agreement.

I-deals are negotiated based on a number of factors, including merit, individual performance, turn-taking, allocation of scarce resources such as training, or work-unrelated bases such as the accommodation of individual needs (Lai et al., 2009). The perceived bases for granted i-deals influence organizational justice perceptions because i-deals respond to various circumstances where standardized employment arrangements are unlikely to be perceived as equitable, fair, or just. Because of their unique, individualized value to employees, i-deals have been theorized as alternate forms of compensation (Greenberg, 1982; Rousseau, 2004, 2006; Scholl, 1981). A promotion or pay raise, for instance, could be substituted with an i-deal that fulfills an employee's individual needs or goals, like a developmental assignment, flexible schedule, or work content customization. Regardless of the complexity and combination of factors behind i-deals negotiation, social comparison and organizational justice perspectives inform the i-deals negotiation process.

Social comparisons provide i-dealers with information about their relative standing within the workgroup which can be used as leverage in the negotiations (Vidyarthi et al., 2016). When organizations offer i-deals to employees or show readiness to engage in negotiations, employees feel valued by the organization (Hornung et al., 2010). However, i-dealers tend to attribute the negotiation of an i-deal to the manager who personifies the organization (Shore et al., 2004). Employees may draw upon the quality of their LMX relationship with this manager during the negotiation process. Yet, high within-group value congruence among coworkers hinders this process because differentiation is less appreciated within a workgroup when the workgroup is highly interdependent or members' values are highly similar to each other's (Anand & Vidyarthi, 2015; Anand et al., 2018). Social comparisons are the basis for i-dealers' negotiation (i.e., deservingness, fairness, need) and define negotiation boundaries (i.e., collaborative versus adversarial) and intensity (i.e., low versus high). Coworkers who are privy to the i-dealers negotiation similarly interpret the negotiation as a signal of the i-dealer's and their own relative standing in the workgroup (Rofcanin et al., 2020). These interpretations can be flawed if coworkers and i-dealers make erroneous assumptions about how the manager allocates resources.

The negotiation stage is also affected by organizational justice perceptions. Employees' organizational justice perceptions are determined by the negotiation context, including the point in the employment relationship when an i-deal is negotiated (i.e., ex ante—before the individual is hired by the organization, or ex post—after the individual is hired by the organization). Ex ante i-dealers may have little knowledge about other workgroup members' i-deals, relative standing in the workgroup, and organizational justice climate. Likewise, ex post i-dealers may lack knowledge of external market or competitive forces. Both ex ante and ex post i-dealers may over- or under-estimate their bargaining position and select an ineffective negotiation strategy, form, and intensity.

The point in the employment relationship additionally affects the group context. Coworkers are more likely to accept market factors as the justification for an i-deal if the i-deal is negotiated ex ante than if the i-deal is negotiated ex post (Rousseau et al., 2006). By attributing ex ante i-deals to external forces, potential coworker perceptions of favoritism and distributive inequity are decreased. Employees' organizational justice perceptions and acceptance of a coworker's i-deal also depend on the exchange relationship the employees have with the manager (i.e., LMX) or the organization (i.e., POS). An economic exchange relationship has a negative effect while a social exchange relationship shows a positive effect on coworkers' i-deal acceptance (Lai et al., 2009).

Overall, organizational justice perceptions and social comparisons affect i-deals negotiations since they inform employees about their relative contributions to the workgroup and relationship quality with the manager and coworkers (Anand et al., 2018; Hornung et al., 2010; Vidyarthi et al., 2016). These cues indicate the strength of the i-dealer's bargaining position, which establishes the i-dealer's negotiation strategy (i.e., individual deservingness, group norms of equity, and personal need), and sets the tone for the negotiation form (i.e., collaborative or adversarial) and intensity (i.e., high or low). I-deals negotiations also affect organizational justice perceptions and social comparisons if the workgroup can accurately observe the negotiation and its outcomes (Marescaux et al., 2019).

Proposition 2a *Employees' organizational justice perceptions inform their i-deal negotiation strategy, form, and intensity.*

Proposition 2b *Employees' social comparisons inform their i-deal negotiation strategy, form, and intensity.*

Proposition 2c *I-deals negotiations affect coworkers' organizational justice perceptions if the workgroup can accurately observe the negotiation and its outcomes.*

Proposition 2d *I-deals negotiations affect coworkers' social comparisons if the workgroup can accurately observe the negotiation and its outcomes.*

Third Stage: Execution of Agreed-Upon I-deals

The execution stage begins after the employee and manager have agreed upon the terms of an i-deal and the individualized arrangement is put in place. The conduct stage concludes when agreed-upon terms have been fulfilled, either party ceases to perform in the agreed-upon manner, or renegotiation begins. In a close-ended i-deal (e.g., flexible scheduling for a parent to care for children during school breaks), the i-dealer returns to the standard work arrangement once the defined end of the i-deal is reached (e.g., school break ends). In an open-ended i-deal (e.g., the assignment of a developmental responsibility outside of the i-dealer's job description), the individualized work arrangement may continue indefinitely. The possible outcomes of the execution stage are i-deals renegotiation or return to the standard work arrangement.

Social comparisons allow employees to evaluate their own i-deals relative to their coworkers' (Marescaux et al., 2019; Vidyarthi et al., 2016). The i-dealers value to an i-dealer is not only determined by the extent the i-deal benefits the i-dealer but also by the value of i-deals the other employees in the workgroup have negotiated with the organization. If employees experience an economic exchange relationship with the organization (i.e., low POS) or its representative (i.e., low-quality LMX relationship) instead of a social exchange relationship (i.e., high POS, high-quality LMX relationship), the employees draw rather negative social comparisons to their coworkers with social exchange relationships (Lai et al., 2009). An i-dealer's standing in the i-deals distribution of a workgroup (i.e., relative i-deals) predicts the i-dealer's performance. This relationship is mediated by the i-dealer's relative standing with the manager (i.e., LMXSC) when team orientation and task interdependence are low in the workgroup (Vidyarthi et al., 2016).

The execution stage is also affected by organizational justice perceptions. I-deals can create perceptions of unfairness among coworkers (Lai et al., 2009; Marescaux et al., 2019; Rofcanin et al., 2020) when i-deals cause workgroup members to perform different tasks and receive different rewards (Anand et al., 2010). Justifying an employee's i-deal to coworkers in the same workgroup can become problematic for managers (Rousseau, 2005). However, i-deals are distinct from favoritism, cronyism, and unauthorized arrangements since i-deals are intended to benefit the employee as well as the organization. Whether group members can discern the benefit that the organization derives from i-deals, however, is highly dependent upon the group context.

The group context includes the structure and size of the workgroup, effect of the i-deal on coworkers, and coworker relationships (Hornung et al., 2010). An i-dealer's standing in the workgroup and relationship quality with the manager influences the i-deal conduct. Employees in high-quality LMX relationships have greater leeway and zones of acceptance with their managers (Hornung et al., 2010; Simon, 1997). I-dealers in such relationships may have wide latitude to perform within their negotiated i-deals, whereas employees in low-quality LMX relationships may be bound more tightly to the terms of their arrangements. These differences may increase perceptions of inequity or unfairness.

Another contextual factor which impacts organizational justice perceptions is the effect of an employee's i-deal on coworkers. Coworkers may gain or lose through the focal employee's i-deal. The benefit of one employee likely causes loss to another employee since organizational resources are limited (Lai et al., 2009; Rousseau et al., 2006). For instance, one employee's pay raise limits the availability of funds and pay raises for coworkers. Similarly, a reduced workload for one employee increases the workload of coworkers. To compensate for potential losses, i-dealers engage in organizational citizenship behavior toward the organization and individuals within the organization (Anand et al., 2010). This way, i-dealers minimize or make up for the inconveniences that their i-deals may cause to their coworkers. I-deals that incur costs with coworkers are perceived as rather unfair compared to cost-neutral i-deals. I-deals that benefit coworkers are perceived as rather fair compared to i-deals that carry no benefits for coworkers (Rousseau et al., 2006). Not surprisingly, i-deals that are neutral or beneficial to coworkers are more likely to be supported by coworkers than i-deals that incur costs with the i-dealer's coworkers (Lai et al., 2009).

An additional contextual factor that affects organizational justice perceptions in the execution stage is the relationships coworkers have with the organization. As in the negotiation stage, if the coworkers have an economic exchange relationship with the organization, they tend not to accept the i-deal granted to the focal employee and perceive it as unfair, but if the coworkers have a social exchange relationship, they likely accept the i-deal and perceive it as fair. Similarly, the interpersonal relationships the coworkers have with the i-dealer affect their organizational justice perceptions. Friendship, including personal affinity, care, and liking, between the i-dealer and coworkers fosters the coworkers' acceptance of an i-deal (Lai et al., 2009). Employees may also show positive and negative emotions regarding coworkers' i-deals. If coworkers perceive that the i-dealer deserves the i-deal, they may feel positive emotions toward the organization like admiration or gratitude. In contrast, if the coworkers perceive that the i-dealer does not deserve an i-deal, they may experience ingratitude, envy, guilt, anger, and resentment toward the focal employee and the organization (Kong et al., 2020; Ng, 2017).

Overall, organizational justice perceptions and social comparisons considerably affect the conduct of the agreed-upon i-deal. Employees ascribe value to i-deals depending on LMX differentiation in the workgroup (Anand & Vidyarthi, 2015; Vidyarthi et al., 2016), and coworkers react emotionally to granted i-deals (Kong et al., 2020; Ng, 2017). Contextual factors such as the structure and size of the workgroup (Hornung et al., 2010), effect of i-deals on coworkers, and coworkers' relationships with the organization and i-dealer (Lai et al., 2009) determine perceived fairness. We describe the outcomes of social comparisons and organizational justice perceptions at the conduct stage in Fig. 5.3. When social comparisons and organizational justice perceptions are both high, the i-dealer will be perceived as highly deserving, the i-deal will be regarded as fair, and retention of the i-deal is likely. When social comparisons and organizational justice perceptions are both low, the i-dealer will be perceived as undeserving, the i-deal will be regarded as unfair, and premature termination of the i-deal is likely. When social comparisons and organizational justice perceptions are opposed (i.e., high/low or low/high), the i-deal will be regarded undeserved or unfair, and it

		Organizational Justice Perceptions	
		High	*Low*
Social Comparisons	*High*	*Proposition 3a:* • High deservingness, high fairness • High retention	*Proposition 3c:* • High deservingness, low fairness • Renegotiation
	Low	*Proposition 3c:* • Low deservingness high fairness • Renegotiation	*Proposition 3b:* • Low deservingness, low fairness • Low retention

Fig. 5.3 Outcomes of social comparisons and organizational justice perceptions at the conduct stage of the i-deals lifecycle

will be considered for renegotiation to align with social comparisons and restore perceived fairness.

Proposition 3a : *When social comparisons are high and organizational justice perceptions are high, i-deals will be retained.*

Proposition 3b *When social comparisons are low and organizational justice perceptions are low, i-deals will be terminated prematurely.*

Proposition 3c *When social comparisons and organizational justice perceptions are opposed (i.e., high/low or low/high), i-deals will be considered for renegotiation.*

Fourth Stage: Renegotiation of I-deals

The final stage of the lifecycle, renegotiation, encompasses the end of an i-deal and may start while execution of the i-deal is ongoing or in temporal proximity to the conclusion of an i-deal. The renegotiation stage begins when the employee and manager re-assess the i-deal and find that the outcomes of the i-deal are no longer beneficial for either or both of the parties. This includes scenarios in which an i-deal reaches its defined conclusion, the outcomes of the i-deal cease to be needed by the employee or organization, or one party identifies potential changes to the i-deals terms which would lead to more beneficial outcomes for the employee, organization, or both. This stage is recursive and can initiate an entirely new lifecycle of recognition-negotiation-execution or prompt an abbreviated lifecycle of negotiation-execution. The renegotiation stage ends when the execution of a modified i-deal begins. Until then, the execution of the former i-deal continues without modification. If no agreement is reached, the employee returns to a standard work arrangement. These are also the outcomes of the renegotiation stage.

Renegotiation results from social comparisons assessing the relative value of i-dealers within a workgroup (Anand & Vidyarthi, 2015; Lai et al., 2009) that make i-dealers and managers re-evaluate agreed-upon terms and seek a more beneficial work arrangement. However, i-deals can also become dysfunctional when employees use them to bargain for status and repeatedly attempt to renegotiate within a short period of time (Rofcanin et al., 2020). In these cases, i-dealers seek intrinsic or extrinsic rewards to demonstrate their relative status and value to the organization, but the organization does not receive any performance from the i-dealers beyond existing contributions. The i-dealer's status pursuit and resource demands will continue. However, no work arrangement will be adequate to satisfy the i-dealer's demands. Repeated bargaining is associated with diminishing marginal returns for the organization and changes the meaning of i-deals for i-dealers, coworkers, and managers (Rousseau, 2005). These dysfunctional attempts at renegotiation may result in a stalemate where i-deal terms are unmodified, or the employee returns to a standard work arrangement.

Renegotiation including dysfunctional renegotiation also influences organizational justice perceptions. Frequent and escalating requests by one employee shape workgroup beliefs and behavior (Marescaux et al., 2019; Rousseau, 2005). Specifically, if i-dealers violate distributive justice perceptions, coworkers can be expected to engage in voice behavior (i.e., actively and constructively trying to enhance working conditions; Rusbult et al., 1988) to reestablish equity which otherwise undermines the effectiveness of an i-deal. The more interdependent the workgroup is, the more employees may perceive that distributive justice perceptions are violated, and the more employees show voice behavior. Similarly, idiosyncrasies in financial incentives (e.g., bonuses) likely violate distributive justice perceptions and lead to the highest occurrence of voice behavior (Marescaux et al., 2019).

Overall, organizational justice perceptions and social comparisons affect the renegotiation of i-deals by coworkers' evaluations of i-deals (Anand & Vidyarthi, 2015; Lai et al., 2009), dysfunctional i-dealing (Rousseau, 2005), and voice behavior (Marescaux et al., 2019). Coworkers' behavior may also shape value perceptions of an i-deal. Employees can directly learn from their coworkers how valuable their i-deals are. This information may determine the employees' perception of equity and equality within the workgroup. Organizational justice perceptions and social comparisons may redirect or mutually reinforce each other. Consequently, employees and managers may want to renegotiate, prolong, or terminate an i-deal.

High social comparisons and low organizational justice perceptions likely lead i-dealers to repeated (dysfunctional) renegotiations because they perceive that they are entitled to greater rewards. Workgroup norms for fairness are not applied by organizations and managers. In contrast, when social comparisons are low and organizational justice perceptions are high, i-dealers likely renegotiate if the potential benefit of the new i-deal outweighs the potential loss of workgroup standing. I-dealers believe that workgroup norms for fairness are applied. In both scenarios, renegotiation is successful when the value of subsequent i-deals is greater than the potential loss of standing within the workgroup to the i-dealer and disruption of the workgroup to the manager.

Proposition 4a *When social comparisons are high and organizational justice perceptions are low, i-dealers pursue repeated (dysfunctional) renegotiations.*

Proposition 4b *When social comparisons are low and organizational justice perceptions are high, i-dealers pursue functional renegotiation.*

Proposition 4c *I-deal renegotiation is successful when the value of the i-deal is greater than the potential loss of standing within the workgroup to the i-dealer and the disruption of the workgroup to the manager.*

Discussion

Although we have separately discussed the four stages i-deals in a lifecycle framework, i-dealers as well as their managers and coworkers are continuously transitioning between these stages. Examining the effects of social comparisons and organizational justice perceptions at each stage offers a parsimonious way to predict how group characteristics promote or inhibit i-deals and how i-deals are likely to align with existing or desired group climates. The lifecycle framework allows to derive implications of how i-deals may evolve within a group over time and may be a useful tool to organize future theory development, empirical research, and practical considerations of i-deals.

Theoretical and Practical Implications

There are several theoretical and practical considerations for organizations, managers, and employees resulting from the i-deals lifecycle. From a strategic HRM perspective, the alignment of idiosyncrasy in work arrangements with organizational culture and climate may describe boundary conditions for the formation of i-deals and related group- and meso-level outcomes. For example, in organizations with low LMX differentiation and low distributive justice perceptions, employees may not seek i-deals, even if they are explicitly available. Similarly, the implications of climate and culture at various stages in the i-deals lifecycle could offer considerable insight into the mechanisms by which multi-level outcomes of i-deals are observed. For example, coworkers' acceptance of an i-deal at the negotiation stage may differ from and have differentiated effects upon individual, meso-, and group-level outcomes than their acceptance of an i-deal at the execution or renegotiation stages, based upon social comparisons and organizational justice perceptions. The development of stage-specific theory about i-deals within a group context offers a clear framework to refine our understanding of complex social processes and interactions.

In practice, managers need to understand the role of social comparisons and organizational justice perceptions at each stage of the lifecycle: recognition, negotiation, execution, and renegotiation. The considerations we have discussed support managers in effectively negotiating i-deals that promote desirable outcomes of i-deals and minimize workgroup conflict. By understanding the impact of i-deals for the group and its members, managers are able to determine how to successfully allocate scarce resources and create desired group climate perceptions. Similarly, employees can benefit from understanding group-level implications of i-deals. Our discussion allows those who desire an i-deal to determine which organizations and managers likely support idiosyncrasy and how an i-deal may influence their standing with the manager and workgroup members.

Implications for Future Research

The lifecycle framework offers a useful structure upon which future research can be built to understand the group-level implications of i-deals. Focusing future research on outcomes by lifecycle stage will serve to clarify the mechanism by which these outcomes are achieved. Future research at the recognition stage should empirically test relationships between group-level factors, including social comparisons and justice climates, and the employee's decision to seek an i-deal. How these factors differ in their influence upon ex ante and ex post negotiations is also of significant theoretical importance.

At the negotiation stage, future research should give greater consideration to how group climates influence managers' negotiations and decisions to accept or reject i-deals. The influence of the workgroup on the employee has been widely researched, but little is theorized about the managers' considerations regarding group factors, including the weight that they place on potential disruptions to the workgroup, concerns for equity and equality perceptions, and managers' relative assessments of group members' standing within the workgroup during i-deal negotiation.

At the execution stage, future research should assess the characteristics of social comparisons and justice climates within the workgroup related to i-deals. Little is known about the relative stability of these judgments, nor the factors which promote or inhibit the dynamism of these perceptions. Also, the accuracy and reliability of these comparisons are unclear. Understanding whether employees accurately identify the bases for i-deals within a workgroup (e.g., employee standing with manager, employee need, organizational need, seniority) would be theoretically meaningful and of great practical significance.

Finally, at the renegotiation stage, research is needed to understand how group-level context influences employees to alter an existing i-deal, and how repeated renegotiations impact group perceptions and outcomes. Scholars may want to examine whether the negotiation of a new i-deal causes all group members to re-evaluate the fairness, equity, and equality of their employment terms, leading to renegotiation of existing i-deals. Investigating how group transparency in individualized work arrangements promotes or inhibits the renegotiation process may allow to identify critical boundaries within the theory of i-deals.

Conclusion

The i-deals lifecycle is a valuable framework to analyze how social comparisons and organizational justice perceptions interact with i-deals and their outcomes. Theoretical examination of group- and meso-level boundary conditions of i-deal recognition, negotiation, execution, and renegotiation are facilitated. The lifecycle framework also addresses the dynamic nature of i-deals within workgroups and promotes thorough understanding of the multi-level implications of i-deals. By examining each of the four stages in a logical sequence, existing research is integrated and expanded to derive implications for future research.

References

Adams, J. S. (1965). Inequity in social exchange. In L. Berkowitz (Ed.), *Advances in experimental psychology* (Vol. 2, pp. 267–299). Academic Press.

Anand, S., & Vidyarthi, P. R. (2015). I-deals in the group context. In P. M. Bal & D. M. Rousseau (Eds.), *Idiosyncratic deals between employees and organizations: Conceptual issues, applications, and the role of coworkers* (pp. 92–106). Routledge—Taylor & Francis Group.

Anand, S., Hu, J., Vidyarthi, P., & Liden, R. C. (2018). Leader-member exchange as a linking pin in the idiosyncratic deals—Performance relationship in workgroups. *The Leadership Quarterly, 29*(6), 698–708.

Anand, S., Meuser, J. D., Vidyarthi, P. R., Rousseau, D. M., & Ekkirala, S. (2017). *I-deal makers in workgroups: Multi-level effects of leader fairness and i-deal distribution.* Annual Meeting of the Academy of Management in Atlanta, GA.

Anand, S., Vidyarthi, P. R., & Park, H. S. (2015). LMX differentiation: Understanding relational leadership at individual and group levels. In T. N. Bauer & B. Erdogan (Eds.), *Oxford handbook of leader-member exchange* (pp. 263–291). Oxford University Press.

Anand, S., Vidyarthi, P. R., Liden, R. C., & Rousseau, D. M. (2010). Good citizens in poor-quality relationships: Idiosyncratic deals as a substitute for relationship quality. *Academy of Management Journal, 53*(5), 970–988.

Bal, P. M., & Boehm, S. A. (2019). How do i-deals influence client satisfaction? The role of exhaustion, collective commitment, and age diversity. *Journal of Management, 45*(4), 1461–1487.

Colquitt, J. A., Conlon, D. E., Wesson, M. J., Porter, C. O., & Ng, K. Y. (2001). Justice at the millennium: A meta-analytic review of 25 years of organizational justice research. *Journal of Applied Psychology, 86*(3), 425–445.

Festinger, L. (1954). A theory of social comparison processes. *Human Relations, 7*(2), 117–140.

Goodman, P. S. (1977). Social comparison process in organizations. In G. Salancik & B. Staw (Eds.), *New directions in organizational behavior* (pp. 97–132). St. Clair Press.

Greenberg, J. (1982). Approaching equity and avoiding inequity in groups and organizations. In J. Greenberg & R. L. Cohen (Eds.), *Equity and justice in social behavior* (pp. 389–435). Academic Press.

Greenberg, J. (1993). The social side of fairness: Interpersonal and informational classes of organizational justice. In R. Cropanzano (Ed.), *Justice in the workplace: Approaching fairness in human resource management* (pp. 79–103). Erlbaum.

Greenberg, J., Ashton-James, C. E., & Ashkanasy, N. M. (2007). Social comparison process in organizations. *Organizational Behavior and Human Decision Processes, 102*, 22–41.

Ho, V. T., & Tekleab, A. G. (2016). A model of idiosyncratic deal-making and attitudinal outcomes. *Journal of Managerial Psychology, 31*(3), 642–656.

Hornung, S., Rousseau, D. M., & Glaser, J. (2008). Creating flexible work arrangements through idiosyncratic deals. *Journal of Applied Psychology, 93*(3), 655–664.

Hornung, S., Rousseau, D. M., Glaser, J., Angerer, P., & Weigl, M. (2010). Beyond top-down and bottom-up work redesign: Customizing job content through idiosyncratic deals. *Journal of Organizational Behavior, 31*(2–3), 187–215.

Kong, D. T., Ho, V. T., & Garg, S. (2020). Employee and coworker idiosyncratic deals: Implications for emotional exhaustion and deviant behaviors. *Journal of Business Ethics, 164*(3), 593–609.

Lai, L., Rousseau, D. M., & Chang, K. T. T. (2009). Idiosyncratic deals: Coworkers as interested third parties. *Journal of Applied Psychology, 94*(2), 547–556.

Las Heras, M., Rofcanin, Y., Bal, M. P., & Stollberger, J. (2017). How do flexibility i-deals relate to work performance? Exploring the roles of family performance and organizational context. *Journal of Organizational Behavior, 38*(8), 1280–1294.

Lee, J. Y., Bachrach, D. G., & Rousseau, D. M. (2015). Internal labor markets, firm-specific human capital, and heterogeneity antecedents of employee idiosyncratic deal requests. *Organization Science, 26*(3), 794–810.

Li, A., & Cropanzano, R. (2009). Fairness at the group level: Justice climate and intraunit justice climate. *Journal of Management, 35*(3), 564–599.

Liao, C., Wayne, S. J., & Rousseau, D. M. (2016). Idiosyncratic deals in contemporary organizations: A qualitative and meta-analytical review. *Journal of Organizational Behavior, 37*, S9–S29.

Liao, C., Wayne, S. J., Liden, R. C., & Meuser, J. D. (2017). Idiosyncratic deals and individual effectiveness: The moderating role of leader-member exchange differentiation. *The Leadership Quarterly, 28*(3), 438–450.

Liden, R. C., & Maslyn, J. M. (1998). Multidimensionality of leader-member exchange: An empirical assessment through scale development. *Journal of Management, 24*(1), 43–72.

Marescaux, E., De Winne, S., & Sels, L. (2019). Idiosyncratic deals from a distributive justice perspective: Examining co-workers' voice behavior. *Journal of Business Ethics, 154*(1), 263–281.

Ng, T. W. (2017). Can idiosyncratic deals promote perceptions of competitive climate, felt ostracism, and turnover? *Journal of Vocational Behavior, 99*, 118–131.

Ng, T. W., & Lucianetti, L. (2016). Goal striving, idiosyncratic deals, and job behavior. *Journal of Organizational Behavior, 37*(1), 41–60.

Rofcanin, Y., Kiefer, T., & Strauss, K. (2017). What seals the i-deal? Exploring the role of employees' behaviours and managers' emotions. *Journal of Occupational and Organizational Psychology*, 90(2), 203–224.

Rofcanin, Y., Las Heras, M., Bal, P. M., Van der Heijden, B. I., & Erdogan, D. (2018). A trickle-down model of task and development i-deals. *Human Relations*, 71(11), 1508–1534.

Rofcanin, Y., Las Heras, M., Bosch, M., Stollberger, J., & Mayer, M. (2020). How do weekly obtained task i-deals improve work performance? The role of relational context and structural job resources. *European Journal of Work and Organizational Psychology*, 30(4), 555–565.

Rosen, C. C., Slater, D. J., Chang, C. H., & Johnson, R. E. (2013). Let's make a deal: Development and validation of the ex post i-deals scale. *Journal of Management*, 39(3), 709–742.

Rousseau, D. M. (2004). Under the table deals: Preferential, unauthorized or idiosyncratic. In R. W. Griffin & A. M. O'Leary-Kelly (Eds.), *The dark side of organizational behavior* (pp. 262–290). Wiley.

Rousseau, D. M. (2005). *I-deals: Idiosyncratic deals employees bargain for themselves*. M. E. Sharpe.

Rousseau, D. M. (2006). The shift in risk from employers to workers in the new employment relationship. In E. E. Lawler III & J. O'Toole (Eds.), *America at work: Choices and challenges* (pp. 153–172). Palgrave Macmillan.

Rousseau, D. M., Ho, V. T., & Greenberg, J. (2006). I-deals: Idiosyncratic terms in employment relationships. *Academy of Management Review*, 31, 977–994.

Rousseau, D. M., Tomprou, M., & Simosi, M. (2016). Negotiating flexible and fair idiosyncratic deals (i-deals). *Organizational Dynamics*, 45(3), 185–196.

Rusbult, C. E., Farrell, D., Rogers, G., & Mainous III, A. G. (1988). Impact of exchange variables on exit, voice, loyalty, and neglect: An integrative model of responses to declining job satisfaction. *Academy of Management Journal*, 31(3), 599–627.

Scholl, R. W. (1981). Differentiating organizational commitment from expectancy as a motivating force. *Academy of Management Review*, 6(4), 589–599.

Shore, L. M., Tetrick, L. E., Taylor, M. S., Jaqueline, A. M., Liden, R. C., Parks, J. M., et al. (2004). The employeeorganization relationship: A timely concept in a period of transition. In *Research in personnel and human resources management*. Emerald Group Publishing Limited.

Simon, H. A. (1997). *Administrative behavior: A study of decision-making processes in administrative organizations* (4th ed.). The Free Press.

Singh, S., & Vidyarthi, P. R. (2018). Idiosyncratic deals to employee outcomes: Mediating role of social exchange relationships. *Journal of Leadership & Organizational Studies*, 24(4), 443–455.

Spence, J. R., Ferris, L., Brown, D. J., & Heller, D. (2011). Understanding daily citizenship behaviors: A social comparison perspective. *Journal of Organizational Behavior, 32*, 547–571.

Vidyarthi, P. R., Liden, R. C., Anand, S., Erdogan, B., & Ghosh, S. (2010). Where do I stand? Examining the effects of leader–member exchange social comparison on employee work behaviors. *Journal of Applied Psychology, 95*(5), 849–861.

Vidyarthi, P. R., Singh, S., Erdogan, B., Chaudhry, A., Posthuma, R., & Anand, S. (2016). Individual deals within teams: Investigating the role of relative i-deals for employee performance. *Journal of Applied Psychology, 101*(11), 1536–1552.

Wood, J. V. (1996). What is social comparison and how should we study it? *Personality and Social Psychology Bulletin, 22*, 520–537.

CHAPTER 6

Idiosyncratic Deals and Individualization of Human Resource Management Practices: The Growth of HR Differentiation

Yasin Rofcanin, Mine Afacan Findikli, Mireia Las Heras, and Can Ererdi

INTRODUCTION

The world of work has experienced radical transformations in which hierarchical and bureaucratic structures have turned into contexts where individualized human values and preferences have gained considerable importance (Hughes, 2017). The demise of bureaucratic organizations and the growth of entrepreneurial-corporate institutions have placed individualized human needs and value at the center of human resource practices (Bal & Rousseau, 2016). Inspired by and drawing on the roots of social contracts in which a legitimate political authority was sought

---

Y. Rofcanin (✉)
University of Bath, Bath, UK
e-mail: Y.Rofcanin@bath.ac.uk; yr308@bath.ac.uk

M. Afacan Findikli
Istinye University, Istanbul, Turkey
e-mail: mine.findikli@istinye.edu.tr

© The Author(s), under exclusive license to Springer Nature Switzerland AG 2022
S. Anand and Y. Rofcanin (eds.), *Idiosyncratic Deals at Work*,
https://doi.org/10.1007/978-3-030-88516-8_6

to regulate interactions at the societal level, the term "psychological contract" was developed by Denise Rousseau to refer to the mutuality of expectations and perceptions of employees and their employers. This was one of the foundational works to inspire employee expectations and requests from their employers, giving rise to fulfillment (vs. breach of) psychological contracts. Following this stream of research, a growing body of studies have started focusing on individualized work needs and preferences, referred to as idiosyncratic deals (i-deals; Rousseau, 2005). These deals emphasize the unique work needs, preferences, and values of employees and are based on the premise that individualized HR practices work better, above and beyond the impact of individualized personalized deals (Marescaux et al., 2019; Rofcanin et al., 2019).

Considering the above point, a growing body of research seems to show that providing employees with i-deals improves their well-being, productivity, and functioning at work, leading to desirable employee work behaviors and attitudes (see Liao et al., 2016, for a recent review of research on i-deals). Yet, at the same time, an important aspect remains unexplored that affects the sustainability of these deals: those co-workers who are the key parties of i-deal negotiations. Co-workers are important parties in an i-deal negotiation process because by the i-deals of a focal employee, working conditions (including demand and schedules) of co-workers change who, as a result, have to adapt to the privileged situation of recipients (Marescaux et al., 2019). This situation raises concerns about fairness and various behavioral as well as attitudinal responses by co-workers. Integrating recent research into the role of co-workers as excluded parties to i-deals and underscoring the importance of individualized HR practices in this context, this chapter aims to delineate and reveal a broader picture of how i-deals are struck from the perspective of co-workers and the related theoretical perspectives. This chapter contributes to recent debates on the importance of co-workers who are important

---

M. L. Heras
University of Navarra IESE Business School, Barcelona, Spain
e-mail: mlasheras@iese.edu

C. Ererdi
Bogazici University, Istanbul, Turkey

University of Bath School of Management, Bath, UK

facilitators and enablers of i-deals. More broadly speaking, in considering the adoption of individualized HR practices, this chapter outlines the idea that the rights and conditions of co-workers who do not obtain similar privileges need to be considered in rendering these deals effective and sustainable. In a world where individualized needs have become the cornerstone of effective functioning, it is key to ensure fairness and equality among the various HR practices provided to employees.

The Political Context and the Drivers of Individualism at the Societal Level

Hierarchical and bureaucratic structures that had been developed from the social welfare perspective after the 1929 Economic Crisis and the Second World War have been found incapable of addressing the needs of today's modern society. Furthermore, political and economic developments such as an increasing focus on competitive labor markets, capitalism, and rising concerns about inequality have changed the dynamics among individual employees. Thus, societal changes have contributed to the changes in individual-level relations. These periods, especially since the 1920s, were mainly characterized by a bureaucratic management approach that was appropriate to ensure the success of business management. Although the standardization of the work and the hierarchical structure of organizations provided certainty in work, it was not suitable for social relations, creativity, and activities that required innovation within the business (Hughes, 2017). The period commencing the 1980s was marked with neoliberal and essentially antisocial doctrine and policies, surrounding and impacting the world in general. Neoliberalism, which is based on the principles of liberalism but with the intention to be applied on a wider scale, has refused old management habits, divisions of labor, social relations, and has reestablished the functioning of the market by elevating individualism. It is the core element of liberalism that has seeded the growth of the individualized approach to human resource management practices and that has trigged employees to seek individualized deals at work (Bal, 2017).

With regard to a neoliberal policy and context, employees increasingly (would like to) feel they are the owners of their jobs, and who become proactive in terms of seeking personalized deals and preferences. This leads to an environment where the individual's reflexivity increases and allows individuals a certain creative capacity to shape themselves

(Houston, 2014). Neoliberalism underlines the need for individuals to support their intellectual capital and reduce the extent to which employees are dependent on others for their existence and social relations at work. These developments, in the form of the individual defense against society in terms of the freedom regarding one's beliefs and preferences, the individual's uniqueness, as well as their self-sufficiency have culminated in the concept of idiosyncrasies in work arrangements. As a follow-up step, and as a consequence of the efforts taken place in the society during this time, employees have started to believe that instead of creating benefits for their organizations and society as a whole, these two stakeholders (namely companies and organizations) may serve as tools to serve individual interests (Watt, 1989). Concordantly, individualism has flourished since the nineteenth century (Realo et al., 2002).

Individualism values the sense and being of individuals within the framework of their singularity, including the independence of the individual within organizations. Moreover, individualism asserts the value of the individual's private life and property, and the value of their intellectual capital, and the potential of self-development as well (Foucault, 2007). Thus, individualism, which stems from a neoliberal perspective, refers to the rights, freedoms, and overall prominence of the individual in modern society. It is also emphasizes that people, as agents, are no longer bound by traditional, cultural mores, immutable relationships, and predictable, solid routines (Houston, 2014). The foundation of individualism has emerged by virtue of the individual's awareness of their autonomy, self-responsibility, and their uniqueness, underpinning the need to seek and negotiate certain work arrangements. Autonomy describes how one individual stands alone, without the need to co-depend on and exist with the help and relations of others. Autonomous individuals prioritize their own goals, perspectives, and aims in life, separating them the rest of the team/organizational members and thus creating a cycle of individual needs. The autonomy plays a central role in workplace-related individualism (e.g., Hofstede, 1980). The second component of individualism is mature self-responsibility, which means that a person accepts responsibility for their self and their actions. The result is a heightened and observed sense of self-confidence in one's actions. The last component of individualism, uniqueness, is related to the assumption of being different to others (Realo et al., 2002). Being unique is reflected in the form of possessing different work needs, preferences, and values in comparison to others in a work context.

Thus far, individualism has been discussed within a positive frame. However, one should also acknowledge that it comes with a "dark" side. As emphasized in recent research (e.g., Bauman, 2006), individualism has certain issues that can be damaging to the sustainability and long-term visions of both companies and individuals. A primary concern is that employees with individualistic pursuits are known to privatize their identities, goals, and agendas at work, usually at the cost of benefit to both the company and wider society. Reflecting on this phenomenon, employees might be driven to perform in accordance with only short-term goals. The commonly observed experience of the "do-it-yourself" challenge brings challenges that fit a linear, homogeneous experience at the organizational and societal levels (Houston, 2014).

The Rise of Individualism in the Context of Human Resource Management Practices

Organizations operate in societies, and the structures of these societies shape how they respond to the challenges presented by their employees. These organizations are not more than the sum of their employees. In order to create a more productive and competitive organizational structure, which constitute the core goals of their existence, organizations seek to protect the values of autonomy and commitment of employees. From the employees' point of view, with the growing concerns of individualism in society (Greene, 2008), they feel a pressure to shape, direct, and maneuver their personal career goals (Dardot & Laval, 2010). Competition has permeated in every aspect of work-life and to stand against the key dynamics of hyperactive work settings, employees have grasped the need to invest in their skills, competencies, and work abilities to thrive and achieve their best in the work environment. From a neoliberalist perspective, social and economic relations are based on flexible and short-term contracts; furthermore, individual relations such as friendships and work-life have been integrated into one's working life. The increasing predominance of this understanding has caused a decline in the long-term unity and solidarity of employees at work. Thus, one can observe that society has become hyper-individualized, trapped by the lure of material success, and stripped of any obligation to the other (Giroux, 2014).

In light of these gradual changes and structural developments, organizations have devised new approaches to the management of their human resources. One prominent and influential way through which these changes are observed is via psychological contracts: These contracts are based on the premise that mutual expectations between an employee and an agent of the organization (e.g., manager, HR unit) determine the dynamics of dyadic social relations (Robinson & Morrison, 1995). Interactions are dynamic, open to change, and are grounded in the perceptions of both parties (Shore & Tetrick, 1994). A key feature of these contracts, as the name suggests, is that they exist in the perceptions of the beholder and are open to breach as well as a violation when expectations are not met by the agent of the organization (Robinson & Rousseau, 1994). Bal and Hornung stated that (2019) the rise of the psychological contract cannot be perceived separately from the societal trends in which the rise has been embedded. They also emphasized the role of critically assessing the roots of the concept in terms of sociological and macro-perspectives and the context of contemporary societal trends. They stated that until the 1980s, employment relations could be defined as "social contracts", emphasizing the common nature in a collective system where their mutual obligation perceptions were based on a lesser, but more powerful, hierarchical position. Social contracts and their collective results have created an implicit understanding of the shift in employment toward psychological contracts, the employment relationship in individualist terminology. These developments discussed above, and the changing needs of employees have transformed the concept of psychological contracts into idiosyncratic deals, where the individual sits in the central limelight and attention of ongoing employee-employer relations.

I-DEALS IN A RELATIONAL CONTEXT: THE ROLE OF CO-WORKERS

As discussed above, i-deals emanate from the consequences of a neoliberal society and the changing dynamics of psychological contracts, where the individual occupies a central stage. The foundations of i-deals rest on the dyadic relational dynamic of employees and their managers in which one party is the negotiator and the other is the grantor (Rousseau, 2005). The difference between i-deals and a psychological contract is that the former are based on concrete and written principles of give-and-take relationships, and hence are likely to deviate from the perception-driven idea of psychological contracts (Liao et al., 2016). I-deals are intended to be "win–win" for both the focal employee and the employer (i-dealer and the employer). Emerging research reveals that i-deals can vary in content as they contain the frame of employment terms that i-dealers bargain for themselves. Mostly, they can take advantage of flexibility i-deals (Las Heras et al., 2017), developmental i-deals (i.e., training and career development and task i-deals) (Rosen et al., 2013). The various characteristics of i-deals and their various types have the potential to benefit both the employee and the employer. The main focus of i-deals theory has been on the recipients and their benefits, including motivation, productivity, and work performance, while allowing employers to attract, retain, or motivate talents (Bal & Hornung, 2019).

In research into i-deals to date, the assumption has been that they are granted to employees who are "star performers" or "good citizens" (Liao et al., 2016). This is built on the assumption that the benefits of i-deals are likely to accrue for the grantor and the recipient in mutually win–win ways when granted to star performers (Rousseau et al., 2006). This means organizations, or the agents of the organizations, do not grant i-deals to employees unless they are likely to be beneficial to themselves as well. However, as stated above, organizations do not only consist of only talented employees (Rofcanin et al., 2019). Thus, the effectiveness of an i-deal is dependent on a relationship triangle that includes not only the i-dealer and the employer, but also the co-workers (Marescaux et al., 2019). This means that without the co-workers' acceptance, the company would not be able to gain any effective benefit from i-deals regardless (Greenberg et al., 2004).

The features of i-deals raise some concerns about the fairness of their implementation that are likely to hamper the trust and commitment of employees toward their organization. I-deals are always realized between the individual and the employer. Moreover, if the i-dealer is a more successful negotiator, they may well be able to acquire more favorable deals than others, which puts the co-workers in an unfair situation because they are deprived of similar conditions and advantages. For this reason, i-deals are likely to lead to within-group differences in conditions of employment; such differences can easily jeopardize group fairness among co-workers (Liao et al., 2016).

Moreover, Vidyarthi et al. (2014) revealed that based on social cognition and the "better than average" perspective in the context of i-deals, the i-dealer may believe that they deserve much more resources (Vidyarthi et al., 2014). However, the perspective of co-workers is also significant to determine the consequences of i-deals. So, the co-worker may assert that they deserve individualized resources in a similar manner to the i-dealer.

Considering this, co-worker's responses are indicative of how effectively an i-deal process be managed in terms of co-worker's acceptance. In this respect, emotions, which are the primary reactions to unfairness, are likely to be inflamed and therefore should be considered a primary element of discussion in this body of research (Marescaux et al., 2019).

I-deals and Emotions in the Eyes of Co-workers

I-deals occur in a dyadic relationship between employees and their managers. However, co-workers are part and parcel of this relationship (Lai et al., 2009). An immediate reaction that is observed in co-workers is perceptions of unfairness regarding i-deals; when co-workers feel that they are left out of i-deals offered to focal employees, they are likely to consider this to be unfair and react by engaging in positive and negative emotions (Barclay & Kiefer, 2014). Indeed, research on justice and emotions reveal that emotions are the most proximal and expected reactions to the unfairness of i-deals (Barclay et al., 2005). Thus, emotions are key to exploring the reactions of co-workers.

Emotions are described as one's affective states, directed at a specific cause or target, which is related to the individual's perspective (Rofcanin et al., 2017). In other means, emotions are associated with thoughts, feelings, behaviors, and a degree of pleasure or displeasure whenever a person has perceived or indeed faced a positive or negative experience. Positive emotions occur as a result of events that facilitate one's goal achievement while negative emotions emerge after events that are likely to hinder the same (Lazarus, 1991). Previous research shows that emotions are very much related to the behavioral regulation and action management of employees (Gross, 1998; Weiss & Cropanzano, 1996) and facilitate or impede their goal achievement.

A key tenet of these theories is that emotions are at the center of events at work. A key theoretical framework that influences the emergence of emotions is affective events theory (Weiss & Cropanzano, 1996), which describes emotions as emanating from key work events and that links employees' work goals to their emotions. In this regard, i-deals, which are individually negotiated work arrangements between employees and their supervisors, are likely to be considered important work events. These deals are initiated by the focal employee but help both the employee as well as the organization to achieve their goals and purposes (Liao et al., 2016). Furthermore, they are personalized and valuable, meaning that other co-workers will not have access to similar deals. In this context, co-workers are likely to feel various emotions in response to i-deals and, in the sections below, we will review this body of research briefly and discuss possible research avenues.

In a limited body of research focusing on co-worker reactions to i-deals, it has been found that certain key emotions that come to the surface; in particular, envy. Focusing on co-workers of employees who receive i-deals, Ng (2017) showed that the recipients of i-deals are generally envied. Furthermore, co-workers also feel envious of the recipients. These feelings lead to perceptions of a competitive climate that, as a result, lead to feelings of ostracism and increased turnover intentions. Integrating social comparison theory and focusing on co-workers, Marescaux et al. (2019) deconstructed the role of envy into two components, the malicious and the benign. The propositions of their conceptual model point out that in an environment characterized by high organizational fairness, co-workers are likely to develop benign envy, whereas in a context characterized by low organizational fairness, malicious envy is more likely. Finally, Rofcanin et al. (2017) revealed that managers reacted negatively (i.e., developed such negative emotions as anger, betrayal, disappointment, dissatisfaction, and unhappiness) when focal employees engaged in socially disconnecting behaviors toward their colleagues. These studies are the only ones, to date, that focus on the darker side of emotions. Focusing on positive emotions, Marescaux et al. (2019) discussed the role of sympathy and schadenfreude that co-workers feel when a focal employee obtains i-deals. They argued that if the organization adopts and implements fair procedures and if the context is supportive, co-workers are likely to develop these emotional reactions toward them.

As can be seen, there is only a limited number of studies that have explored the role of emotions relating to this process. Guilt and pride are examples of discrete emotions which can be explored in the context of i-deals. Interesting research questions that can be explored in relation to further studies are:

R1: Do the recipients of i-deals feel proud or guilty? What are the mediating and moderating mechanisms that can explain these expressed emotions?
R2: What types of discrete emotions, and under what conditions, do managers feel about the i-deals of a focal employee?
R3: Can we talk about team-level emotions and emotional reactions?

R4: Can we talk about the resistance of emotions at the team level and do the contagion of emotions explain this process?

R5: Can the consequences of emotions of the recipient's and/or the co-worker's crossover to partners or other significant parties (e.g., family members) at home?

POSSIBLE CONTEXTUAL VARIABLES THAT SHAPE THE IMPACT OF CO-WORKER REACTIONS

Friendship

An important moderator is the nature and quality of relationships employees have with others. Friendship here is key and is an important identifier of how and why your i-deals are likely to be effective or otherwise. As such, friendships play a central role both in people's private and work lives where the quantity and quality of the interpersonal relationship are found to be prominent indicators of employee satisfaction, creativity, and career advancement (Sias et al., 2012). Workplace friendship is defined as "nonexclusive voluntary workplace relations that involve mutual trust, commitment, reciprocal liking and shared interests and values" (Berman, 2002). It has been revealed that they are not imposed by organizational requirements, but are rather initiated and developed voluntarily. They are personalistic beyond their organizational roles (Sias et al., 2012). They are also found to be impactful resources that facilitate employees' ability to reduce work stress, and can even provide them with a certain energy (Buunk & Hoorens, 1992). Socially structured workplace friendships allow important changes in the communication between partners, including increased communication frequency, and increased intimacy. The friendships AMONG peer co-workers have a significant effect on employee outcomes by providing instrumental and emotional support by way of social exchanges.

Individuals are found to be subjective and biased self-evaluators (Dijkstra, 2010) because they are influenced by social emotions (Blader, 2010) and may also react emotionally.

As stated above, individuals generally do not interpret facts and situations objectively or, indeed, rationally. They perceive the environment in terms of their own values, needs, goals, and usually tend to compare themselves with others. In other words, they react through both emotional and cognitive processing (Garg & Fulmer, 2017). Thus, co-workers, as individuals, are likely to have a range of different reactions to i-deals because they are not likely to be informed to the same extent as the i-dealers in any given social exchange, where co-workers are likely to have different perspectives than the i-dealers (Rousseau et al., 2006). However, here, the type of friendship may be an important element by which to judge the effectiveness of i-deals.

Friendships in organizations can be formed at two levels: surface-level friendships—friendships in which interactions progress due to existing roles in organizations but may not include meaningful conversations—and deep friendships. Moreover, it has been revealed that the increased cohesion between workgroup friendships allows people to more easily share ideas, improve communication, and provide emotionally and socially supportive work environment (Jones et al., 2020). Furthermore, building confidence, trust, and respect within the workgroup lead to increased enthusiasm and a more positive attitude within the group (Jehn & Shah, 1997). An interesting line of inquiry could be to explore how different types of friendships affect the receipt and success of i-deals (surface-level versus deep-level friendships). Based on the i-deal theory, when co-workers perceive a workgroup friendship exists in their organization, they may find i-deals acceptable (Lai et al., 2009), which would be the antecedent of positive emotions. In contrast, if i-deals have been realized between employer and non-friends, these exchanges are more likely to spark the perception of unfairness and the negative emotions that diminish acceptance of such among co-workers. Moreover, based on social comparison theory (Festinger, 1954), employees tend to compare their behaviors and attitudes to these of others. To be more precise, when lacking objective means for appraisal of their opinions and capabilities, people compare their opinions and capabilities to those of others that are similar to them. They then attempt to correct any differences found (Fridman & Kaminka, 2007). This means, as a consequence of the social comparison process, co-workers are in a position to have a significant impact on the effectiveness of the focal employee's i-deals.

It is stated that while a colleague's i-deal may be perceived as beneficial by some co-workers, for others, some i-deals (e.g., a flexibility i-deal that allows the employee to leave early from work) can soon increase negative emotions, regardless of whether they believe the recipient deserved the i-deal (Garg & Fulmer, 2017). However, as stated above, if the friendship between co-workers and i-dealers is strong, co-workers may well feel that i-dealer deserved their arrangement and will be happy for the recipient (Lai et al., 2009; Rousseau et al., 2016). Because friendships are conducted by socio-emotional goals, their primary purpose is to foster affective and relational well-being (Pillemer & Rorthbard, 2018).

The Nature of the Employment Relationship and Perception of Workplace Justice

Facing increasing competition and blurred, dynamic environments, HR professionals struggle to attract, motivate, and retain talents and qualified employees. For this reason, over the last three decades, the nature of the employment relationship is accepted as being central to a wide range of HRM activities. A report summarizing the Inter-Council Meeting on Employer Contracts revealed that to understand the "new deal" between employers and employees is one of the greatest challenges to HRM activities (Roehling et al., 2000).

One key element that impacts these patterns of relationships is the quality of the employee-manager relationship (Rousseau et al., 2016). Studies show that when the recipients of i-deals enjoy good quality relationships with their managers, co-workers notice and are likely to attribute this to the differentiated nature of the relationship between a focal employee and their manager (Anand et al., 2010). However, to date, there are no studies available in the literature that explore this relationship pattern in a triadic context, that is, employees, their managers, and co-workers. In a conceptual study by Marescaux et al. (2019), the triadic relationship quality between employees, their managers and co-workers are underlined to affect and shape the effectiveness of i-deals.

A second aspect that impacts the effectiveness of i-deals is the quality of the relationships employees have and share with their managers. Referred to as psychological contract, these deals are perceptual, unwritten, and shared by the mutual experiences and expectations of the parties in this relationship. The extent to which employees consider their psychological contacts relational- and transactional-based influences the expectations and meaning-making of the i-deals (Coyle-Shapiro & Kessler, 2000). Relational psychological contracts, as they are based on informal and intangible cues of the mutual relationships between two parties, are less likely to be observed and noticed by co-workers. On the other hand, transactional contracts are based on visible and tangible give-and-take relationships; thus, they are more likely to be noticed and observed by co-workers. An important message for HR managers is that they must manage the psychological contract and i-deals of employees in an inherently fair and just manner in the eyes of their co-workers (Peck, 1994).

As being aware of i-dealers' employment arrangements, after the comparison and the sense-making process, co-workers may feel certain emotions such as anger, happiness, admiration, gratitude, or resentment. According to appraisal theory, emotions are associated with a set of appraisals that reflect the situation eliciting the emotions (Smith & Ellsworth, 1985). Considering this, co-workers react with the scope of their other-oriented and self-oriented cognitions. In other words, co-workers become aware of another's i-deal and begin to react according to both emotional and cognitive processing. Co-workers' perceptions of deservingness of the i-dealers' employment arrangement may be high or low, and they may react negatively, neutrally, or positively (Garg & Fulmer, 2017).

The Impact of Perceived Organizational Climate (e.g., Performance-Oriented Versus Mastery Climate)

Workplace climate refers to the extent to which employees perceive and feel part of their organization (Muchinsky, 2000). Perceptions of climate have the potential to influence relationships among employees and how various co-workers react as a result. The climate of the organization enables favorable member interactions by way of sharing each other's ideas as well as using morale-building communication. Few studies have been conducted on how workplace climate shapes and influences employee reactions to a focal employee's i-deals. In their conceptual study, Rofcanin et al. (2019) revealed that in a work unit characterized by learning and collaboration, employees are likely to trust each other and work together to achieve shared goals. As a common fate of looking into the future develops, members of such teams take care of each other and learn how to deal with the i-deals of focal employees. For these employees, working in a mastery climate and benefiting from the i-deals of a focal employee is an advantage as they approach such arrangements as opportunities for self-development and growth (Beersma et al., 2003). This assumes that the insights gained and experiences learned by one team member are shared with other team members so that they can learn from and develop themselves according to the existing opportunities and capabilities (Johnson et al., 2006).

In the event that an employee receives a more advantageous outcome, a mastery climate will lead to more positive reactions from co-workers for several reasons. In such a climate, knowledge and self-development are key skills that lead to development at the team level. Furthermore, knowledge-sharing is supported between hierarchies, making it less of a problem when employees and managers or others hide knowledge or do not share it with others (Nerstad et al., 2013). Contrary to the impact of mastery climate, in a performance climate the relationships among employees, co-workers, and their managers are based on knowledge-hiding and individual performance of information-hiding. In such a context, receiving i-deal arrangements is important and recipients are likely to hide this knowledge from others in the hope that they will be better off. Thus, in the context of i-deals, we expect the negative impact of a performance-oriented climate to be more negative and pronounced with regard to co-worker reactions to the i-deals of a focal employee compared to a climate characterized by mastery-oriented characteristics of knowledge sharing and mutual understanding and growth.

The combination of these contextual factors suggests important future research avenues. Co-workers are key parties to the effectiveness of i-deals and how, as well as under which conditions, they become sufficiently effective to require further elements. Some possible research questions that we raise are as follows:

R1: Do unit and organizational climate impact on co-worker reactions differentially and in what ways?

R2: Do different elements of heterogeneity in teams, such as race, gender, ethnicity, etc., have an impact on co-worker reactions to i-deals, and if so, how?

R3: Finally, can different approaches be adopted to analyze co-worker reactions to i-deals? One such possible approach is network analysis and considering how the centrality and position of employees can impact on employee outcomes.

Potential Theoretical Perspectives to Integrate into I-deals Research

Although research into emotions is historically and contemporarily very popular within the OB/HRM literature, its potential impact and theoretical cross-section with the i-deals literature is, in our opinion, underscrutinized. In this context, one of our aims in this chapter is to expand on the limited research using affective theories in exploring i-deals by bringing emotional theories to the i-deals literature. In this section, we will examine five affective based theories (i.e., affective events theory, affect theory of social exchange, emotional contagion theory, appraisal theory of emotion, and emotions as social information theory) and their potential uses in expanding research on i-deals.

As introduced to the literature by Weiss and Cropanzano (1996), affective events theory explains the shift in certain affective states of employees in response to the events occurring in the organizational environment. Further conceptualization of the theory has produced positive and negative affective states as a result of these responses. Affective events theory suggests that, over time, these positive or negative affect states accumulate and lead to certain attitudes and behaviors on the part of the employee regarding the organization (Weiss & Cropanzano, 1996). The affective events view on i-deals starts at this point. Conceptualizing the negotiation process of i-deals as an antecedent of an affective event would then position the granting of the i-deal as the affective event itself. In accordance with affective events theory, employees then are expected to shift between negative and positive states depending on the outcome of the i-deals negotiation. Finally, touching on the accumulation of positive and negative affect states tenet of the theory, we would assume that continuous rejection or acceptance of the i-deal granting process by the organization could lead to positive or negative attitudes and behaviors on the part of the employee. Future research on i-deals could then use affective events theory to examine the longitudinal effects of the i-deal negotiation process on the attitudes and behaviors of the focal employee.

Although the affect theory of social exchange is usually used in the context of leader-member exchange relationships, the central tenet of the theory explains how and why an effect is produced within a social exchange relationship (Tse et al., 2018). According to affect theory of social exchange, certain positive and negative affect states appear as a result of the social exchange between the leader and the follower. If this social exchange produces a positive effect as a result, both the employee and the leader experience a certain "uplift"; conversely, if the social exchange produces negative affect as a result, both the employee and the leader experience difficulties (Lawler, 2001). In linking the affect theory of social exchange and i-deals, future research can conceptualize the i-deal negotiation process as a social exchange between the focal employee and the manager who grants the i-deals. The positive consequence version of this exchange also supports the tenet of i-deals which argues that they should be beneficial for both the employee and the organization. Conclusively, future research could explore how the i-deal negotiation process could be conceptualized as a social exchange, and whether the results of the negotiation process produce positive or negative affect states for the parties involved.

The third main affect theory that could potentially be used in future research in relation to i-deals is emotional contagion theory. Introduced by Hatfield et al. (1992), emotional contagion theory explains the unconscious and unintentional transfer of emotions (Tse et al., 2018) between certain parties, whether it be leader-member dyads or groups. Emotional contagion susceptibility, on the other hand, refers to the extent to which a person is vulnerable to this unconscious transfer of emotions (Doherty, 1997). Looking at i-deals from an emotional contagion perspective, future research could examine the emotional contagion present in the i-deal granting process. During the negotiation phase of i-deals in particular, the reciprocity between the focal employee and the manager increases, and thus could be an area of potential interest as this reciprocity is bound to create an emotional contagion effect on the part of the employee; accordingly, future research could look into the amount of emotional contagion that occurs in the negotiation and granting process.

According to the appraisal theory of emotion, emotions arise as a result of individual perception and evaluation of specific events (Scherer et al., 2001). Immediately relating this tenet of appraisal theory of emotion to i-deals, we could argue that the focal employees involved in the i-deal process would then individually assess and evaluate the i-deal granting process as an event which would produce emotions as a result. Delving deeper into appraisal theory, the perspectives from which the focal employee evaluates the event are 1) relational, 2) motivational, and 3) cognitive. The relational evaluation of events argues that the employee evaluates the interaction and the situational environment that is present within the event (Tse et al., 2018). In this context, we could argue that the focal employee could appraise the event (i.e., i-deal process) from the perspective of the interaction that occurs between themselves and the manager. If the focal employee evaluates the interaction during the i-deal process as being positive, positive emotions could well arise. On the other hand, if the focal employee evaluates the interaction during the i-deal process to be negative, the resulting emotions could be negative. Secondly, the motivational perspective argues that the focal employee evaluates the situation according to its relationship with the individual's goals. In the context of i-deals, a failed i-deals process could be evaluated as a roadblock in the path to the set goals, thus negative emotions could arise. Alternatively, the successful granting of i-deals could be evaluated as a facilitator for part of the organization, and positive emotions could arise on the part of the focal employee.

Finally, the cognitive appraisal of an event is related to how relevant the event is to the goal attainment of the focal employee. In the context of i-deals, if the employee perceives the process to be relevant to their goals, the resulting intensity of emotions, depending on whether the process is successful or not, will be increased. Future researchers on i-deals from an appraisal of emotions theory perspective could thus should examine how the perspective of appraisal affects the intensity and direction of the emotions resulting from the i-deals process.

Emotions social information theory, as developed by van Kleef (2009), relates to how people regulate their emotional states according to their perceptions of others' emotional states. Emotion regulation as an effort to influence our responses to certain events precedes emotions as social information theory. Westen (1994) argued that in order to influence our responses we use (1) coping, (2) emotion regulation, and (3) mood regulation. Emotion regulation in this context refers to attempts to influence which emotions one has, when one has them, and how one experiences these emotions (Gross, 1998). In examining strategies that allow emotional regulation, the process model of emotion regulation is essential since it not only contains intrinsic emotion regulation which refers to the modification (or regulation) of one's own emotions, but to the modification of the situation and the cognitive self as well. Situation modification refers to attempts to alter the situation (e.g., i-deals) to also modify its emotional impact on the person. In the context of i-deals, we can think of a focal employee who attempts to modify the situational factors present in the i-deal negotiation process in order to alter the positive or negative affect that will arise from the situation (I-deal process) and thus effect the focal employee. Cognitive change, on the other hand, refers to the changes in the employee's emotional attachment to the situation (Gross, 1998). Relating the cognitive change aspect of emotional regulation to i-deals, the focal employee could regulate the consequential emotions of the i-deals granting process by attaching more or fewer emotions to the i-deal granting process itself. Future research could potentially examine how cognitive change would alter the end emotions as a result of the i-deal process. The situation selection aspect of the emotion regulation process, on the other hand, refers to the selection of events by the focal employee in which they select to participate in the events depending on the emotional consequences they expect the event to bring back to them.

In the context of i-deals, if the focal employee perceives the i-deal negotiation process to end in an unwanted emotional consequence, they could opt not to participate in the process from the beginning. On the other hand, if the focal employee perceives the i-deals process to end in a desirable emotional consequence, they would be more inclined to participate in such a process. Finally, the attentional development aspect of emotion regulation refers to the change in the direction of attention with the goal of influencing emotional response (Gross, 1998). In the context of i-deals, future researchers could explore how the focal employee in the i-deal-granting process uses distraction as a method of regulating their emotions in the pursuit of altering the emotional consequence of the process.

Discussion and Conclusion

This chapter is driven by the goal of exploring the role of co-workers and their emotions in the process of i-deal negotiation and how i-deals are run. Rooted in the foundational work of Rousseau (2005) and drawing from the studies of Greenberg et al. (2004) and Lai et al. (2009), our chapter has taken this stream of research one step further to emphasize how and when co-workers may react the way they do. Our chapter underscored the role of co-worker emotions and, in contrast to previous research where the main emphasis was on negative emotions and reactions, our chapter underscored the role of positive as well as negative co-worker emotions.

Understanding the big picture in which both negative and positive emotions are elicited is important because, by its nature, i-deals may not always lead to negative emotions and understanding this is important for various reasons: first of all, when the i-deals of a focal employee are elicited positively, this means that HR managers and practitioners can design and implement such policies in a way to motivate and keep the workforce productive and committed.

With respect to the role of positive emotions, our study emphasized the importance of climate, culture, and perceived support among co-workers. Central to our discussions was the idea that when an organization cares for the well-being of its employees and provides them with individualized HR practices, co-workers take this as a positive message, implement this in their lives, and adopt their lives according to the impact of i-deals. Hence, as purported in previous research, i-deals are not likely to lead to negative reactions under all conditions and, sometimes, depending on the context and role of others—as well as the situation and the environment—co-workers may react positively and hence the sustainability of i-deals can be maintained for a long time. Our chapter identified key elements as to when and how co-workers react positively:

1. Are there any other positive emotional and behavioral reactions other than the satisfaction and happiness of employees? How can research elicit and explore these reactions?
2. Are there other contextual and boundary conditions, such as teamwork and climate, that lead to positive emotions and acceptance of co-workers?
3. Are positive emotions and reactions of co-workers sustainable and on-going? To understand the sustainability of co-worker reactions, emotions and contextual conditions need to be explored in the long term.
4. To elucidate the short-term and dynamic reactions to a focal employee's i-deals, what types of data collection methods can be used? Future possible research includes diary studies and other experiential methods of data collection.

In addition to the positive reactions, as research has more generally underlined, co-workers are also likely to react negatively. Among these reactions, research has revealed these reflections: envy (Ng, 2017), unfairness (Marescaux et al., 2019), counter-productive work behaviors (Vidyarthi et al., 2016), exclusion within teams (Anand et al., 2010), and lack of support from co-workers when the differential implementation of

HR practices becomes a policy (Marescaux et al., 2019). These reactions are likely to be negative and reactive in the circumstance where the organization is not supportive, and co-workers are less likely to be accepting and appreciative of the focal employee's conditions. Some further research questions that can be explored in studies are listed below:

1. From the perspective of the organization and the HR departments; what are the consequences of engaging in negative reactions and do the benefits of providing i-deals outweigh the costs of co-worker reactions to the recipients of i-deals?
2. Similar to the context of co-workers, how can research capture the negative reactions of a co-worker in a sustainable manner? To explore this research question, longitudinal studies will be helpful to understand the process of how i-deals unfold.
3. In addition to exploring the negative reactions of co-workers in a longitudinal setting, future research could attempt to understand and test for negative reactions using diary and experiential methods.

Funding Mine Afacan Findikli is funded by the Scientific and Technological Research Council of Turkey under the scheme "2219".

Mirea Las Heras is funded by Universidad de Navarra, PIUNA. This chapter is part of the project "Project Spousal positive crossover and spillover of emotions, experiences and cognitions" (POS-SPOUSE).

REFERENCES

Anand, S., Vidyarthi, P. R., Liden, R. C., & Rousseau, D. M. (2010). Good citizens in poor-quality relationships: Idiosyncratic deals as a substitute for relationship quality. *Academy of Management Journal, 53,* 970–988. https://doi.org/10.5465/AMJ.2010.54533176

Bal, P. (2017). *Dignity in the workplace: New theoretical perspectives.* Palgrave Macmillan.

Bal, P. M., & Hornung, S. (2019). Individualization of work: From psychological contracts to idiosyncratic deals. In Y. Griep & C. Cooper (Eds.), *Handbook of research on psychological contracts* (pp. 143–163). Edward Elgar. https://doi.org/10.4337/9781788115681

Bal, M., & Rousseau, D. M. (2016). *Idiosyncratic deals between employees and organizations: Conceptual issues.* Routledge.

Bauman, Z. (2006). *Küreselleşme.* Ayrıntı Publications.

Barclay, L. J., Skarlicki, D. P., & Pugh, S. D. (2005). Exploring the role of emotions in injustice perceptions and retaliation. *Journal of Applied Psychology, 90*, 629–643.

Barclay, L. J., & Kiefer, T. (2014). Approach or avoid? Exploring overall justice and the differential effects of positive and negative emotions. *Journal of Management, 40*(7), 1857–1898.

Beersma, B., Hollenbeck, J. R., Humphrey, S. E., Moon, H., Conlon, D. E., & Ilgen, D. R. (2003). Cooperation, competition, and team performance: Toward a contingency approach. *Academy of Management Journal, 46*, 572–590.

Berman, E. W. (2002). Workplace relations: Friendship patterns and consequences (according to managers). *Public Administration Review, 62*, 217–230.

Blader, S. L. (2010). Social emotions and justice: How the emotional fabric of groups determines justice enactment and reactions. In M. A. A. Mannix (Ed.), *Research on managing groups and teams: Fairness & groups* (pp. 13:29–62). Emerald Publishing. https://doi.org/10.1108/S1534-0856(2010)0000013005

Buunk, B., & Hoorens, V. (1992). Social support and stress—The role of social-comparison and social-exchange processes. *British Journal of Clinical Psychology, 31*, 445–457. https://doi.org/10.1111/j.2044-8260.1992.tb01018.x

Coyle-Shapiro, J., & Kessler, I. (2000). Consequences of the psychological contract for the employment relationship: A large-scale survey. *Journal of Management Studies, 37*(7), 903–930.

Dardot, P., & Laval, C. (2010). *La nouvelle raison du monde: Essai sur la société néolibérale*. La Decouverte Poche.

Dijkstra, P. G. (2010). Social comparison theory. In J. E. Tangney (Eds.), *Social psychological foundations of clinical psychology* (pp. 195–211). The Guilford Press.

Doherty, R. W. (1997). The emotional contagion scale: A measure of individual differences. *Journal of Nonverbal Behavior, 21*(2), 131–154.

Fridman, N., & Kaminka, G. A. (2007). *Towards a cognitive model of crowd behavior based on social comparison theory* (pp. 731–737). www.aaai.org/Papers/AAAI/2007/AAAI07-116.pdf

Festinger, L. (1954). A theory of social comparison processes. *Human Relations, 7*(2), 117–140. https://doi.org/10.1177/001872675400700202

Foucault, M. (2007). *Security, territory, population*. Palgrave.

Garg, S., & Fulmer, I. (2017). Ideal or ordeal organizations? The spectrum of co-worker reactions to idiosyncratic deals. *Organizational Psychology Review, 7*(4), 281–305.

Giroux, H. A. (2014). Neoliberalism and the death of the social state: Remembering Walter Benjamin's Angel of History. *Social Identities: Journal for the Study of Race, Nation and Culture, 17*(4), 587–601. https://doi.org/10.1080/13504630.2011.587310

Greenberg, J., Roberge, M. É., Ho, V. T., & Rousseau, D. M. (2004). Fairness in idiosyncratic work arrangements: Justice as an i-deal. *Research in personnel and human re-sources management* (pp. 1–34). Emerald Publishing.

Greene, T. W. (2008). Three ideologies of individualism: Toward assimilating a theory of individualisms and their consequences. *Critical Sociology, 34*, 117–137.

Gross, J. (1998). The emerging field of emotion regulation: An integrative review. *Review General Psychology, 2*, 271–299.

Hatfield, E., Cacioppo, J. T., & Rapson, R. L. (1992). Primitive emotional contagion. *Review of Personality and Social Psychology, 14*, 151–177.

Hofstede, G. (1980). *Culture's consequences: International differences in work-related values.* Sage.

Houston, S. (2014). Beyond individualism: Social work and social identity. *British Journal of Social Work, 46*(2), 532–548. https://doi.org/10.1093/bjsw/bcu097

Hughes, O. E. (2017). *Public management and administration* (5th ed.). Red Globe Press.

Jehn, K., & Shah, P. (1997). Interpersonal relationships and task performance: An examination of mediating processes in friendship and acquaintance groups. *Journal of Personality and Social Psychology, 72*, 775–790.

Johnson, M. D., Hollenbeck, J. R., Humphrey, S. E., Ilgen, D. R., Jundt, D., & Meyer, C. J. (2006). Cutthroat cooperation: Asymmetrical adaptation to changes in team reward structures. *Academy of Management Journal, 49*(1), 103–119. https://doi.org/10.5465/amj.2006.20785533

Jones, M., Stromberger, M., Pape, E., Chapman, K., & Borremans, A. (2020, January 10). *Workplace friendships: Examining friendships at work and their impact on job satisfaction and perceived productivity.* https://minds.wisconsin.edu/bitstream/handle/1793/70485/JonesSpr14.pdf?sequence=1

Lai, L., Rousseau, D. M., & Chang, K. T. (2009). Idiosyncratic deals: Co-workers as Interested Third Parties. *Journal of Applied Psychology, 94*(2), 547–556. https://doi.org/10.1037/a0013506

Las Heras, M. R., Rofcanin, Y., Bal, P., & Strollberg, J. (2017). How do flexibility i-deals relate to work performance? Exploring the roles of family performance and organizational context. *Journal of Organizational Behavior, 38*(8), 1280–1294. https://doi.org/10.1002/job.2203

Lawler, E. J. (2001). An affect theory of social exchange. *American Journal of Sociology, 107*(2), 321–352.

Lazarus, R. S. (1991). *Emotion and adaptation.* Oxford University Press.

Liao, C., Wayne, S. J., & Rousseau, D. M. (2016). Idiosyncratic deals in contemporary organizations: A qualitative and meta-analytical review. *Journal of Organizational Behavior, 37*, 9–29. https://doi.org/10.1002/job.1959

Marescaux, E., Winne, S. D., & Sels, L. (2019). Idiosyncratic deals from a distributive justice perspective examining co-workers' voice behaviour. *Journal of Business Ethics, 154*(1), 263–281.

Muchinsky, M. (2000). Emotions in the workplace: The neglect of organizational behavior. *Journal of Organizational Behavior, 21*(7), 801–805.

Nerstad, C. G. L., Roberts, G. C., & Richardsen, A. M. (2013). Achieving success at work: The development and validation of the motivational climate at work questionnaire (MCWQ). *Journal of Applied Social Psychology, 43*(11), 2231–2250. https://doi.org/10.1111/jasp.12174

Ng, T. W. (2017). Can idiosyncratic deals promote perceptions of competitive climate, felt ostracism, and turnover? *Journal of Vocational Behavior, 99*, 118–131.

Peck, S. R. (1994). Exploring the link between organizational strategy and the employment relationship the role of human resources policies. *Journal of Management Studies, 31*(5), 716–736.

Pillemer, J., & Rorthbard, N. (2018). Friends without benefits: Understanding the dark sides of workplace friendship. *Academy of Management Review, 43*(4), 1–26.

Realo, A., Koid, K., Cuelemans, E., & Allık, J. (2002). Three components of individualism. *European Journal of Personality, 16*, 163–184.

Robinson, S. L., & Rousseau, D. M. (1994). Violating the psychological contract: Not the exception but the norm. *Journal of Organizational Behavior, 15*, 245–259.

Robinson, S. L., & Morrison, E. W. (1995). Psychological contracts and OCB: The effect of unfulfilled obligations on civic virtue behavior. *Journal of Organizational Behavior, 16*(3), 289–298.

Roehling, M., Cavanaugh, M., Moynihan, L., & Boswell, W. (2000). The nature of the new employment relationship: A content analysis of the practitioner and academic literatures. *Human Resource Management, 39*(4), 305–320.

Rofcanin, Y., Kiefer, T., & Strauss, K. (2017). What seals the i-deal? Exploring the role of employees' behaviours and managers' emotions. *Journal of Occupational and Organizational Psychology, 90*(2), 203–224.

Rofcanin, Y., Berber, A., Marescaux, E., Bal, P., Mughal, F., & Afacan Findikli, M. (2019). Human resource differentiation: A theoretical paper integrating co-workers' perspective and context. *Human Resource Management Journal, 29*(2), 270–286.

Rosen, C. C., Slater, D.J., Chang, C.-H., & Johnson, R.E. (2013). Let's make a deal: Development and validation of the ex-post i-deals scale. *Journal of Management, 39*(3), 709–742. https://doi.org/10.1177/0149206310394865

Rousseau, D. M. (2005). *I-deals: Idiosyncratic deals employees bargain for themselves*. M.E. Sharpe.

Rousseau, D. M., Ho, V., & Greenberg, J. (2006). I-deals: Idiosyncratic terms in employment relationship. *Academy of Management Review, 31*(4), 977–994.

Rousseau, D., Tomprou, M., & Simosi, M. (2016). Negotiating flexible and fair idiosyncratic deals (i-deals). *Organizational Dynamics, 45*, 185–196.

Scherer, K. R., Schorr, A., & Johnstone, T. (Eds.). (2001). *Appraisal processes in emotion: Theory, methods, research*. Oxford University Press.

Sias, P. M., Gallagher, E. B., Kopaneva, I., & Pedersen, H. (2012). Attaining workplace friendships: Perceived politeness and predictors of maintenance tactic choice. *Communication Research, 39*(2), 239–268. https://doi.org/10.1177/0093650210396869

Shore, L. M., & Tetrick, L. E. (1994). The psychological contract as an explanatory framework in the employment relationship. In C. L. Cooper & D. M. Rousseau (Eds.), *Trends in organizational behavior* (pp. 91–109). Wiley.

Smith, C. A., & Ellsworth, P. C. (1985). Patterns of cognitive appraisal in emotion. *Journal of Personality and Social Psychology, 48*, 813–838.

Tse, H. H., Lam, C. K., Gu, J., & Lin, X. S. (2018). Examining the interpersonal process and consequence of leader–member exchange comparison: The role of procedural justice climate. *Journal of Organizational Behavior, 39*(8), 922–940.

Van Kleef, G. A. (2009). How emotions regulate social life: The emotions as social information (EASI) model. *Current Directions in Psychological Science, 18*(3), 184–188.

Vidyarthi, P. R., Chaudhry, A., Anand, S., & Liden, R. C. (2014). Flexibility i-deals: How much is ideal? *Journal of Managerial Psychology, 29*(3), 246–265. https://doi.org/10.1108/JMP-07-2012-0225

Vidyarthi, P. R., Singh, S., Erdogan, B., Chaudhry, A., Posthuma, R., & Anand, S. (2016). Individual deals within workgroups: Investigating the role of relative i-deals for employee performance. *Journal of Applied Psychology, 101*, 1536–1552.

Watt, J. (1989). *Individualism and educational theory*. Kluwer Academic.

Weiss, H., & Cropanzano, R. (1996). Affective events theory: A theoretical discussion of affective experiences at work. In B. M. Staw & L. L. Cummings (Eds.), *Research in organizational behavior* (pp. 1–74). Greenwich CT: JAI Press.

Westen, D. (1994). Toward an integrative model of affect regulation: Applications to social-psychological research. *Journal of Personality, 62*(4), 641–667.

CHAPTER 7

I-deals as a Human Resource Initiative: Exciting Innovation or Passing Fad?

Arup Varma, Chun-Hsiao Wang, Hyun Mi Park, and Parth Patel

INTRODUCTION

Rapid advancements in technology and changes in society have made idiosyncratic deals (i-deals hereon) increasingly critical for organizations around the globe. When we add unprecedented events such as COVID-19 to this mix, it becomes clear that organizations need to be agile and flexible to effectively meet the fast-changing needs of both employees and employers (see, e.g., Zhang & Varma, 2020). I-deals are customized

A. Varma (✉)
Loyola University Chicago, Chicago, IL, USA
e-mail: avarma@luc.edu

C.-H. Wang
National Central University, Taoyuan City, Taiwan
e-mail: wangch@cc.ncu.edu.tw

H. M. Park
Coventry University, Coventry, UK
e-mail: ad0042@coventry.ac.uk

© The Author(s), under exclusive license to Springer Nature Switzerland AG 2022
S. Anand and Y. Rofcanin (eds.), *Idiosyncratic Deals at Work*,
https://doi.org/10.1007/978-3-030-88516-8_7

employment arrangements negotiated between individual employees and employers, which are intended to benefit both sides, as opposed to arrangements made via favoritism (Rousseau, 2001). Next, various forms of i-deals have been identified, such as the three types discussed by Rousseau et al. (2009)—namely developmental (e.g., special training), flexibility (e.g., flexible working hours), and reduced workload i-deals (e.g., less strenuous tasks).

A great deal of research on i-deals has appeared in the literature over the past two decades (please see Liao et al., 2016 for a meta-analytic review). Much of this research has focused on how i-deals could be utilized by organizations as a means to promote positive organizational functioning. In this connection, Anand and colleagues have conducted important studies that shed light on how i-deals enhance employee outcomes such as LMX quality, and improve organizational effectiveness (see, e.g., Anand et al., 2010, 2018). Relatedly, Ng and Lucianetti (2016) found that developmental & flexibility i-deals led to higher levels of supervisors' assessments of employee in-role job performance, voice behavior, and interpersonal citizenship behavior. Hornung et al. (2010) found that task i-deals were negatively related to work stressors. Similarly, Wang et al. (2018) found that developmental & flexibility i-deals were positively related to employee creativity across three study sites. Based on data from a large sample, Bal and Boehm (2019) also found that developmental & flexibility i-deals were negatively related to employee emotional exhaustion. As for the underlying mechanisms connecting i-deals and positive employee behaviors and attitudes, Liu et al. (2013) found that both social exchange and self-enhancement mediated the relationships between flexibility & developmental i-deals and affective commitment and proactive behavior. Vidyarthi and colleagues (2016), on the other hand, found social comparison to be the link between i-deals and employee performance in workgroup settings.

Furthermore, Rofcanin et al. (2018) have observed that managers' task & developmental i-deals lead to higher levels of subordinates' task & developmental i-deals, and most importantly, the authors proposed and found that managers' task & developmental i-deals were positively

---

P. Patel
Australian Institute of Business, Adelaide, SA, Australia
e-mail: Parth.Patel@aib.edu.au

related to positive employee outcomes (e.g., job performance, career promotability, and socially connecting behaviors) via subordinates' task & developmental i-deals. Similarly, Anand and colleagues (2018) found that developmental i-deals enhanced the quality of leader-subordinate relationship, which led to better employee performance. Thus, it is evident that i-deals can be mutually beneficially for all the parties involved (e.g., managers, subordinates, and the organization). In other words, if implemented effectively, i-deals can create a win-win situation for all.

It is clear that i-deals are becoming more common in the contemporary workplace. However, given that i-deals are individually negotiated employment arrangements, an increasing number of studies have begun to examine some of the issues associated with i-deals, especially around the non-standard nature of i-deals (Greenberg et al., 2004). Of course, on the one hand, there are some positive outcomes associated with the non-standard nature of i-deals. For example, drawing upon social comparison theory, Vidyarthi et al. (2016) argued that in reality, i-deals are rare to receive and i-deals recipients simply do not exist in vacuum. Further, the authors noted that relative developmental & flexibility i-deals motivated individual team members to work harder; more specifically, the paired sample shows that relative i-deals led to higher levels of supervisor-assessed job performance and organizational citizenship behaviors. On the other hand, considerably more studies have focused on how the non-standard nature of i-deals might cause some problems for the coworkers of i-deal recipients and their work environment, in general. For instance, drawing on equity theory, Ng (2017) found that receiving developmental i-deals and witnessing coworkers' developmental i-deals were positively related to being envied and to envy, respectively. Similarly, drawing on conservation of resources theory, Kong et al. (2020) found that upward comparison of coworker's task i-deals led to higher levels of one's emotional exhaustion and subsequent coworker-rated deviant behaviors. In a similar vein, using deontic justice theory, Rofcanin et al. (2019) proposed a conceptual framework to argue that i-deals might be a double-edged sword if they are not implemented appropriately. The authors proposed that when coworkers do not perceive i-deals to meet the conditions of procedural and interactional justice, they are more likely to display anger and avoidance behaviors toward the i-deal recipients.

In this connection, it should be noted that differentiated HR practices, such as i-deals, are often seen as unique motivators that allow organizations to tailor their motivation techniques and stimuli to individual needs (see, e.g., Hu & Varma, 2020) with positive outcomes. However, as Marescaux et al. (2013) have cautioned, differentiated incentives/motivators may be a "double-edged sword" (p. 329) as these can have negative impact on many employees and the subsequent reactions of these employees may negatively impact overall organizational morale and productivity.

Given the pros and cons of i-deals, as noted above, we argue that it is imperative for future researchers and practitioners to explore the concepts of i-deals through the HR lens. Indeed, we believe that organizations should keep track of the deals being individually negotiated. Once a specific type of deal reaches a certain threshold, it can become part of HR policy. Indeed, this is how HR innovations like flex time have gone on to become part of HR policy for many organizations.

In this chapter, we discuss how organizations can most effectively institutionalize i-deals as individualized and fair HR practices. Next, we discuss how practicing supervisors can endeavor to make i-deals fair and effective. And, last but not the least, we explore where i-deals fit in the international human resource management (IHRM) context. In addition, in each of the following sections, we also propose future research directions in the area.

How Do Organizations Institutionalize I-deals Effectively?

Setting up the Needed HR Policies

If organizations aspire to institutionalize individualized i-deals as effective HR practices, they will need to first set up the relevant and requisite HR policies surrounding the use of i-deals, in order to make it fair and transparent to all employees. Please note that here we refer to the both i-deals that are negotiated during recruitment (ex-ante i-deals) and i-deals that are negotiated during existing employment relationships (ex-post i-deals; Rousseau et al., 2006). In other words, organizations need to set up the terms of i-deals clearly, so that i-deals are awarded in a fair and consistent manner. This is especially important so that employees do not perceive i-deals as dysfunctional personalized employment arrangements that smack of favoritism, given that there can be identical i-deals serving different purposes/needs for completely different employee groups. As an example, organizations might provide certain i-deals such as developmental and workload i-deals to reward/retain good performers or to address performance problems. Thus, it is important for organizations to be transparent about the terms of the i-deals with the recipients and other coworkers. This is likely to be very crucial for whether the organization is able to institutionalize i-deals successfully because researchers have found that coworkers' beliefs regarding their own likelihood of comparable i-deals in the future were positively related to their acceptance of others' i-deals (e.g., Lai et al., 2009).

Next, it is extremely important for organizations to set up guidelines to determine who is most suitable to receive i-deals and equally important, to be able to change the terms of i-deals as and when required (e.g., to suspend an existing developmental i-deal from a recipient). Further, organizations also need to establish eligibility rules for employees requesting i-deals. More specifically, organizations need to put in writing the obligations (e.g., performance expectations) and commitments (e.g., time limits) they have agreed with the i-deal recipients (Rousseau et al., 2016). To do so, organizations require an effective performance management system in place (DeNisi & Smith, 2014; Varma & Budhwar, 2020a). Performance management practices like performance appraisal and feedback allow employees to know how well they are performing in the organization and how do their performance evaluations stand as compared to other employees (see, e.g., Varma & Budhwar, 2020b). Organizations should be clear about the expected performance levels (e.g., above 90% targets achieved over the past two years) to be eligible to request certain special arrangements like developmental and flexibility i-deals. Given that prior studies (e.g., Hornung et al., 2010) have noticed that denied task i-deals had distinctive independent effects (in addition to successful task i-deals) on work control and stressors, future research should take into account the eligibility to request i-deals with the success of i-deals negotiation itself.

Organizations should also connect performance management with fair employee differentiation practices such as talent management (Cappelli & Keller, 2014). By doing so, organizations will be able to distinguish employees into different potential levels: senior high potentials, junior high potentials, and non-high potentials (e.g., Gelens et al., 2014). In Gelens et al. (2014), the study site (a large financial institution) identified two levels of high potentials in the organization: senior high potentials and junior high potentials, which account for 0.4 and 0.7% of the organization's workforce, and most importantly, the two groups of high potential employees were explicitly informed about their status by the HR department and given information about the procedures for applying for i-deals. Such differentiation allows organizations to make more strategic/fair judgements related to entitlement to ask for i-deals and who should be granted with i-deals. Future research can explore whether such employee differentiation can make supervisor authorization of i-deals lead to higher levels of talent development (Hornung et al., 2009). It is also critical for organizations to be clear about the terms of i-deals after the i-deals have been granted to employees. For example, if the i-deals recipients consistently fail to meet performance expectations, organizations should reserve the right to suspend the existing i-deals. This is especially critical, given that some i-deals recipients might engage in socially disconnecting behaviors following their i-deals negotiations and keep the benefits of i-deals only for themselves and not share with the team (Rofcanin et al., 2017). Furthermore, applicants might sometimes negotiate special employment arrangements with organizations prior to joining, and organizations often provide i-deals to applicants who have high labor market value (e.g., unique skills or experiences) or during highly competitive labor periods. In this case, organizations need to clearly communicate with the applicants in the employment contract about the conditions of their i-deals (e.g., the time limit of i-deals and the expected performance levels upon employment). It should be noted here that our current knowledge about the effects on suspended i-deals on employees is empirically underdeveloped, and future research should investigate the above-mentioned issues accordingly. For instance, it is possible that the suspension of i-deals could lead to higher perceived inducement breach (Mossison & Robinson, 1997), but what is not clear is whether a clear prior HR policy could mitigate this effect.

Setting up the Supporting Organizational Climate

After setting up the needed HR policies associated with i-deals, in order to institutionalize i-deals effectively, organizations should also use HR practices to create and facilitate an organizational climate that can support the effective practice of i-deals. Organizational climate refers to a "set of perceptions that reflect our work environments, including organizational attributes, are cognitively appraised and represented in terms of their meaning to and significance for individuals" (James et al., 1988, p. 129).

Prior studies have provided indirect evidence that organizations should intend to foster organizational climates that could eventually support the institutionalization of i-deals. For instance, Lai et al. (2009) found that the extent to which an employee perceives his or her employment relationship with the organization as a social exchange was positively related to his or her acceptance of coworkers' i-deals. Indeed, the authors argue that it is important for organizations that wish to use i-deals to ensure that the use of i-deals does not create too much backlash from coworkers, as otherwise they could have difficulty retaining valuable employees.

An important related construct is perceived organizational support (POS; Eisenberger et al., 2020), which is the extent to employees perceive that the organization values their contributions and cares about their well-being (see, e.g., Varma & Russell, 2016). In a meta-analysis, Kurtessis et al. (2017) found that a number of HR practices were positively related to employees' POS, which included developmental opportunities, job security, flexible work schedule, employee benefits, job enrichment, autonomy, and participation in decision-making. Some HR practices were found to be highly associated with POS, such as job enrichment and developmental opportunities. These meta-analytic results from Kurtessis et al. (2017) provide an evidence-based framework for organizations to use HR practices to foster a supportive organizational climate that increases the likelihood of coworkers accepting others' i-deals. Future research could examine whether HR practices like developmental opportunities and job security could lead to the creation of a climate of social exchange, thus increasing employees' acceptance of others' i-deals (i.e., decreases negative social comparisons among employees).

Further, Las Heras et al. (2017) found that supervisors' caregiving responsibilities for elders were positively related to successful flexibility i-deals offered to subordinates. As suggested by the results, the authors argued that organizations need to develop a family supportive organizational climate by investing in and implementing periodic interventions aimed at evaluating employees' family responsibilities outside of work, such as the need for elder care. In particular, a number of studies have examined how a family supportive organizational climate can be developed through HR policies and practices. For instance, in a meta-analytic examination, drawing on signaling theory, Butts et al. (2013) argued that family supportive practices can be communicated as a symbol of organizational concern for family well-being and found that family supportive policy availability was positively related to family supportive organization perceptions. Subsequently, the authors found that family supportive organization perceptions led to lower levels of work-to-family conflict and higher levels of positive work attitudes (e.g., job satisfaction and intentions to stay). Of course, certain i-deals are more likely to be influenced by family supportive organization perceptions, such as flexibility and task i-deals. We urge scholars to explore whether family supportive practices would lead to higher numbers of supervisors granting, and employees requesting, flexibility i-deals and accepting others' flexibility i-deals via a family supportive organizational climate.

Lastly, some i-deals researchers (e.g., Anand & Vidyarthi, 2015; Bal & Boehm, 2019) have noticed that the i-deal literature has mostly examined the issues of i-deals at the individual level, and not at the team level. In particular, Vidyarthi et al. (2016) found that the positive relationships between relative developmental & flexibility i-deals and employee performance were lower when groups had higher levels of team orientation and task interdependence. Building on their findings and taking into the account that prior studies have consistently observed the positive effects of team orientation and task interdependence on positive team outcomes (e.g., Bachrach et al., 2006; Mohammed & Angell, 2004; Somech et al., 2009), we argue that organizations should foster a strong teamwork climate where team members share a common identity and most importantly, organizations should utilize the benefits of having effective teams (i.e., high team orientation, task interdependence, and team performance) and design i-deals at the team level. In other words, i-deals like flexibility and developmental should be designed for the whole team. For instance, the specialized work schedules and special opportunities for skill acquisition should be made available for all the members in the team. Such team-based i-deals can be used to reward/motivate good team behaviors (e.g., performance, trust, communication, cooperation, and cohesiveness). On the other hand, team members can also collectively request certain i-deals that meet their collective needs as zone team, for example, task i-deals. Future researchers are encouraged to explore the issues of team-based i-deals, such as the extent to which self-managed teams are likely to apply for some i-deals as a team, and how self-managed teams might benefit from team-based i-deals (c.f., Edmondson, 1999).

To create a strong teamwork climate, organizations need to carry out team-building practices that promote a common team identity. Future researchers can borrow some of the insights from the team-building literature on designing effective team-building practices/interventions, and their influences on team-based i-deals. In this connection, Salas and his colleagues (1999, 2005) identified four components of team-building practices/interventions: goal setting, role clarification, interpersonal relations, and problem solving. Subsequently, a meta-analysis by Klein et al. (2001) showed that goal setting and role clarification had the strongest effects on team performance. Thus, it would be useful to replicate such findings in the context of team-based i-deals. Perhaps, future i-deals researchers could also examine the effects of team-oriented HR practices (e.g., Bouwmans et al., 2019) on the effectiveness of team-based i-deals (Table 7.1).

How to Ensure Supervisors Authorize I-deals Effectively?

Since i-deals are usually negotiated between employees and their supervisors (e.g., Rousseau et al., 2006, 2016), it is important that supervisors are empowered to offer and authorize i-deals effectively, if organizations want to be able to draw upon the benefits of i-deals. Across two hospitals in Germany and US, Hornung et al. (2009) found that employees were most likely to negotiate task i-deals when they had higher quality relationships with their supervisors (see, e.g., Martin et al., 2016; Varma & Stroh, 2001), and task i-deals led to higher levels of job complexity and control, which then predicted greater employee personal initiative and work engagement. When it comes to i-deals, supervisors need to be fully aware of the crucial role they play: Employees often first start negotiating (or even start assessing the possibility to negotiate) customized employment terms with their supervisors, and the behaviors of supervisors will greatly influence the effects of i-deals on employee perceptions and behaviors. Given that i-deals are typically initiated by employees, negotiated between employees and supervisors, and authorized by supervisors (with HR approval), supervisors need to understand that i-deals are different from favoritism and nepotism, and the primary objective of i-deals is to benefit both the employee and organization.

Next, we discuss how to use HR practices to increase supervisors' fairness and perspective taking, which in turn can lead to greater effectiveness in supervisory authorization of i-deals.

First, supervisors' overall fairness can be achieved through justice training that is carefully designed (e.g., Skarlicki & Latham, 2005). In this connection, prior studies have demonstrated that supervisors can be

Table 7.1 Summary of key issues, proposed HR practices, and future research related to i-deals

HR Practices	Future Research
Setting up the Needed HR Policies • Setting up a clear *definition* of i-deals • Indicating agreed and communicated performance expectations, commitments (e.g., time limit of i-deals) in the employment contract • Establishing clear *rules*: for example, who is entitled to ask for i-deals, and who should be granted i-deals - Performance management (e.g., appraisal and feedback). For example, to apply i-deal programs, an employee should have met 90% of his/her performance targets in the past two years is required	1. Eligibility to request i-deals through successful negotiations (Hornung et al., 2010) 2. The effects on suspended i-deals on employees: - The suspension of i-deals could lead to higher perceived inducement breach (Mossison & Robinson, 1997) - A clear prior HR policy on the suspension of i-deals minimizes the impact of i-deals suspension on perceived inducement breach 3. Whether such employee differentiation can through supervisor authorization of i-deals to better talent development (Hornung et al., 2009)
Setting up the Supporting Organizational Climates • Using evidence-based HR framework to increase the likelihood of coworkers accepting others' i-deals (Kurtessis et al., 2017) • A family supportive organizational climate (e.g., lower levels of work-family conflict) can be developed through HR policies and practices	4. Whether HR practices (e.g., developmental opportunities and job security) could lead to the creation of a climate of social exchange, and then increases employees' acceptance of others' i-deals - Whether appropriate HR practices can decrease negative social comparisons among employees 5. Whether family supportive organizational climate and practices would lead to more supervisors granting/employees requesting flexibility i-deals and accepting others' i-deals

HR Practices	Future Research
• Team-based i-deals can be used to reward and motivate good team behaviors • Team-building practices can help to promote a common team identity	6. To what extent are self-managed teams likely to apply for i-deals as a team? 7. How will self-managed teams benefit from team-based i-deals (Edmondson, 1999)? 8. Relationship between effective team-building practices and interventions (e.g., goal setting, role clarification, etc.), and their influences on team-based i-deals 9. The effects of team-oriented HR practices (e.g., Bouwmans et al., 2019) on the effectiveness of team-based i-deals
How to Ensure Supervisors Authorize I-deals Effectively • Supervisors' fairness and perspective taking lead to greater effectiveness in supervisory authorization of i-deals • Supervisors should be trained to be fair/just in their dealings with subordinates • Organizations should promote supervisor contacts with subordinates	10. How the six elements of supervisory fair behaviors (Gonzalez-Morales et al., 2018) could possibly influence the ways employees come to perceive the authorization of i-deals 11. Address a model examining whether providing supervisor with repeated/continuous contacts with their subordinates could lead to greater perspective taking, thus impacting their tendency to make more favorable decision to grant i-deals for their subordinates proactively
I-deals in the IHRM Context • Individualism in Western cultures vs. Collectivism in Eastern cultures impact acceptance of coworkers' i-deals • The relationship of i-deals with expatriate issues needs to be better understood • Family issues can be a unique phenomenon in expatriate assignments	12. Team-based i-deals in the IHRM context (e.g., Eastern versus Western) 13. To explore the effects of various i-deals types on employee willingness to expatriate (Konopaske et al., 2005) 14. To investigate the effects of flexibility i-deals the adjustment and performance of expatriate/spouse, and also the willingness of expatriate/spouse to expatriate

trained to be fair—indeed, Gonzalez-Morales et al. (2018) argued that supervisors' overall fairness can be increased by training supervisors on six elements of fair behaviors: procedures based on accurate information, rules and policies applied uniformly, procedures neutral and unbiased, opportunity for employee voice, opportunity for correction and appeal, and explain reasons for decisions using social accounts. In future research, it would be critical to look at how these six elements of supervisory fair behaviors could possibly influence the ways employees perceive the authorization of i-deals. We previously mentioned that organizations need to set up clear HR policies regarding i-deals—more specifically, how existing i-deals could be suspended. If that is the case, per the voice effect perspective (e.g., Lind & Tyler, 1988), it is likely that opportunities for employee voice and correction, as well as appeal are going to minimize the likely negative impacts on the attitudes and behaviors of i-deals recipients. Furthermore, given that supervisors cannot authorize i-deals to all the employees who request such deals, it is also very important for supervisors to deal with employees who have had their requests for i-deals denied in a fair and equitable fashion. In this regard, Greenberg (2006) has provided evidence that before giving the news of pay cut, supervisors should be trained in interpersonal and informational justice behaviors, which in turn predicted lower levels of reported employee insomnia. Specific contents of interpersonal justice (e.g., treating employees with politeness, dignity, and respect: Bies & Moag, 1986) and informational justice (e.g., communicating details in a timely and individualized manner; Shapiro et al., 1994) should be able to promote better and airer experiences to those employees who have had their i-deal requests denied.

Second, perspective taking refers to one's tendency to be aware of and adopt the perspective of the other (Davis et al., 1996). We argue that this individual difference is likely to increase supervisors' authorization and implementation of i-deals to subordinates, especially in a proactive fashion (i.e., top-down i-deals initiation by management, as opposed to the usual bottom-up initiation by employee; Hornung et al., 2010). Perspective taking is critical because supervisors often have more knowledge of their subordinates' performance and needs. As such, in order to be able to approach i-deals proactively, supervisors need to be able to adopt another's viewpoint—in this case, the subordinate's viewpoint. In this connection, Grant and Berry (2011) have suggested that one's perspective taking allows him or her to determine the best ideas and to elaborate them in useful and creative ways. Similarly, prior studies of i-deals have consistently found supervisors' i-deals to be positively related to their subordinates' i-deals (e.g., Laulié et al., 2020; Rofcanin et al., 2018). Specifically, Las Heras et al. (2017, p. 338) argued that "experience of a certain need increases empathy for another person currently experiencing the same need" and found that supervisors' caregiving responsibilities for elders were positively related to successful flexibility i-deals granting to subordinates. Relatedly, Kelly et al. (2020) also found that supervisors who understood the work-life balance needs of their subordinates were more likely to grant flexibility i-deals for their subordinates. As for the HR practices that increase supervisors' perspective taking of their subordinates, we argue that insights can be drawn from the intergroup contact literature (e.g., Aberson & Haag, 2007).

Indeed, the intergroup contact researchers have argued, and found evidence, that increased contacts with another group led to higher degree of perspective taking of that group. Similar results can also be found in the management studies (e.g., interactions with suppliers led to greater supplier perspective taking: Parker & Axtell, 2001). In the context of i-deals, opportunities for perspective taking between supervisors and their subordinates enable two things: supervisors understand more about their subordinates' needs and at the same time subordinates communicate the urgency of their concerns. Thus, future examinations might address a model examining whether providing supervisors with repeated/continuous contacts with their subordinates could lead to greater perspective taking, thus impacting their tendency to make more favorable decision to grant i-deals for their subordinates proactively.

I-DEALS IN THE IHRM CONTEXT

Given that contemporary organizations are increasingly operating in a global context, across various cultural environments, and sending high potential employees on international assignments, organizations should also be aware of the potential issues surrounding i-deals in the IHRM context.

First, in the past two decades, researchers have conducted numerous examinations regarding i-deals in different cultural environments. In their study of 53 work groups in India, Anand et al. (2010) found that the relationship between i-deals and organizational citizenship behavior was stronger for employees with lower quality relationships with their supervisors or team members. In a meta-analysis of 23 empirical studies, Liao et al. (2016) separated the studies into two cultural groups: Eastern cultures (e.g., China, India, and South Korea) and Western cultures (e.g., Germany, US, and Netherlands). While finding some similarities in both Eastern and Western cultures, the authors (Liao et al., 2016) also noted some interesting differences. We argue that these differences help to open up new and potentially fruitful areas for further investigation. For example, the positive effects of leader-member exchange (i.e., supervisor-subordinate relationships) and proactive personality were smaller in Eastern cultures than in Western cultures. It is possible that, in general, individuals in Eastern cultures tend to be more collectivistic (Hofstede, 1980; House et al., 2004) and more attuned to the attitudes of others in the group (e.g., one's acceptance of coworkers' i-deals; Lai et al., 2009). This ability to understand others might become one of the critical factors (e.g., positively moderates the effects between leader-member exchange/proactive personality when other workers' perceived acceptance is high) when employees in Eastern cultures are negotiating for i-deals. Similarly, Eastern cultures are also characterized by high power distance (Hofstede, 1980; House et al., 2004) whereby employees accept a high degree of authority and status difference between themselves and their supervisors. In such cultures, employees are less likely to voice their need for a negotiated work arrangement (i-deal), so it is critical that investigations of i-deals in the international arena take into account the impact of local cultural practices.

In this connection, Chen and Miller (2011) report that the Eastern perspective emphasizes the group, group harmony, and shared accomplishment, whereas Western perspective emphasizes individual and personal achievement. In other words, it would be useful in future research to explore a greater degree of coworker issues (e.g., the interpersonal relationships between i-dealers and coworkers) when examining i-deals in Eastern cultures. Future researchers can also explore the previously mentioned concept of team-based i-deals in the IHRM context (e.g., Eastern versus Western). Here, Liao et al. (2016) observed that older employees had lower chance to obtain i-deals in Western cultures as opposed to Eastern cultures. It would be informative to include other closely associated elements in the organizational settings, like one's organizational rank and seniority (c.f., the different moderating effects of rank and seniority between the Korean and US samples: Hong et al., 2016), into the effects of age in i-deals related studies.

Second, as the global economy continues to develop, more organizations will continue to globalize their operations and expatriates play an important role in this process of globalization (Caligiuri & Bonache, 2016; Varma & Tung, 2020b). However, a search of the literature reveals that studies on i-deals and expatriates are still in the early stage of development (for an exception, see Tornikoski, 2011). We argue that future researchers should explicitly tap into the concepts of i-deals in connection with expatriate assignments, as expatriate assignments are often based on special agreements between the expatriate and his/her organization. As such, future research can explore the effects of various i-deals types on employee willingness to accept expatriate assignments (Konopaske et al., 2005). In this connection, Wang (2018) applied social informational processing theory and found that the degree to which an expatriate perceives international assignment experience to be valuable to his or her career and also perceives that his/her international assignment experience is valued by the organization, is positively associated with higher levels of employee willingness to expatriate. Building on this foundation, organizations would be more successful in enhancing employee willingness to expatriate when they present the expatriate request as a personalized opportunity to expand one's competencies and pursue career advancement that is going to be valued highly by the organization and supervisors (i.e., developmental i-deals). However, in order to closely link expatriate assignment and career development, organizations must first, strategically design the expatriate assignment with repatriation in the mind (see Baruch et al., 2016; Varma & Tung, 2020a, for discussions on expatriation and repatriation); and second, include the use of expatriate assignment into their long-term talent management (see Cerdin & Brester, 2014 for a detailed discussion on talent management and expatriation).

Next, family issues present a unique perspective to expatriate assignments that is worthy of mention in i-deals research. For example, researchers have argued and confirmed that expatriates' family members (e.g., spouse) can be both a demand on, and an important resource for, the functioning of expatriates (e.g., adjustment and performance: Lazarova et al., 2010; Takeuchi et al., 2002). Building on this logic, organizations would be more successful in increasing the adjustment and performance of expatriate/spouse when expatriates or spouses are provided with certain special arrangements for work schedules (i.e., flexibility I-deals). In particular, based on the needs of expatriates (e.g., children's schooling needs) and long-term, mutually beneficial relationships between expatriates and organizations, organizations could provide special holiday arrangements (e.g., paid travels) for the expatriate and family members to take as a family or for the family members to visit the expatriate in the host country. Further studies can investigate the effects of these flexibility i-deals on not only the adjustment and performance of expatriate/spouse, but also the willingness of expatriate/spouse to expatriate (e.g., as ex-ante i-deals; negotiated prior to accepting an assignment request).

Conclusions and Discussion

It has been almost two decades since Rousseau and colleagues (Rousseau, 2001, 2005; Rousseau et al., 2006) introduced the concept of "i-deals" and, since then, research on i-deals has been able to inform scholars and practitioners of the impact of i-deals on HR activities and outcomes (Bal & lub, 2016; Liao et al., 2016). There is no doubt that HR practices designed based on a traditional standard workplace arrangement cannot fit in contemporary organizational conditions, where employees are increasingly self-reliant to take care of their careers (Feldman & Pentland, 2003; Olson, 2013) and where unexpected events like COVID-19 can force organizations to re-think their processes and structures. As Kniffin et al. (2021, p. 74) note, "Covid-19 will be recognized for changing the ways people work in fundamental ways." Indeed, organizations have had to resort to asking/allowing employees to work from home, and many organizations plan to continue with this (or a hybrid model) even after the pandemic is over. In order to get some employees to come back to work, while others continue to work from home and yet others work on mixed model (work part of the week from home, part in the office), organizations will need to negotiate with individual employees, depending on the nature of their job content and personal situations. In other words, organizations will need to employ i-deals more frequently going forward.

Clearly, i-deals are often adopted as part of the HR practices, in order to respond to today's labor market requirements and maintain sustainable strategic HR systems. This practice also helps deal with increased talent mobility, decentralized employment relationships and rapid technological change in the current challenging economic climate (e.g., online platform and gig economy) (Cappelli, 2000; Cascio & Boudreau, 2016).

Although we are now witnessing rapidly expanding interest in i-deals among HRM scholars, we need to learn much more about the effective application of i-deal related HR practices in the global workplaces. It is often assumed that i-deals are strategic HRM choices within organizations (Kroon et al., 2019), however, literature found not only positive outcomes, but also negative consequences associated with the non-standard nature of i-deals, even though i-deals are typically beneficial for all the parties involved.

In response, this chapter has elucidated how organizations most effectively institutionalize i-deals as individualized and fair HR practices, how supervisors make i-deals fair and effective, and where i-deals fit in the IHRM field, in order to increase our understanding of the benefits of i-deals, and to allow us to explore the concepts of i-deals through the HR lens. We have also offered several specific suggestions for future research and practice.

First, in terms of HR policies, it is critical that organizations spell out their policies related to i-deals in clear terms, with a view to providing fair and transparent treatment to all employees. In order to do this, organizations should elaborate on the application process for i-deals, employee obligations, and other related terms, such as the conditions under which either party can terminate the i-deal. Relatedly, the organization's performance and talent management systems should incorporate i-deals, so that these become part of the organization's fabric. This is critical as these evidence-based HR practices help organizations create and foster appropriate climates (e.g., supportive of employees' development, their well-being and family care, as well as collective teamwork climate) that can enhance organization's effective i-deals institutionalization.

Second, as noted above, it is critical that supervisors recognize that their own behaviors should reflect fairness and perspective taking, as this would positively influence their subordinates' appropriate perception and attitudes in an i-deal negotiation, and support supervisors' effective authorization of i-deals. Practical HR guidance for supervisors (e.g., justice training, caregiving responsibilities, etc.) are discussed in the previous section and summarized in Table 7.1.

Third, we provide scholarly insights through integrating the concepts of i-deals and IHRM issues. Studies on i-deals that compare countries have found that i-deals approaches and practices are different between

Eastern and Western countries. This implies that i-deals are context-specific (not a context-free universal concept) and, as such, it is important that the practice of i-deals is adapted to the local context of the country and the culture.

In sum, this chapter has discussed how i-deals impact HR philosophy and practices and how HR departments may lead the effort to institutionalize such deals. It is critical that academics and practitioners alike understand the i-deal contexts as a means to promote positive organizational functioning. We hope that our discussion here can advance the study of i-deals in the HR context and help HR professionals determine the sustainability of i-deals as an HR initiative.

REFERENCES

Anand, S., Hu, J., Vidyarthi, P., & Liden, R. C. (2018). Leader-member exchange as a linking pin in the idiosyncratic deals-performance relationship in workgroups. *The Leadership Quarterly, 29*(6), 698–708.

Anand, S., & Vidyarthi, P. (2015). Idiosyncratic deals in the context of workgroups. *Idiosyncratic deals between employees and organizations: Conceptual issues, applications, and the role of coworkers*, 92–106.

Anand, S., Vidyarthi, P. R., Liden, R. C., & Rousseau, D. M. (2010). Good citizens in poor-quality relationships: Idiosyncratic deals as a substitute for relationship quality. *Academy of Management Journal, 53*(5), 970–988.

Aberson, C. L., & Haag, S. C. (2007). Contact, perspective taking, and anxiety as predictors of stereotype endorsement, explicit attitudes, and implicit attitudes. *Group Processes & Intergroup Relations, 10*(2), 179–201.

Bachrach, D. G., Powell, B. C., Collins, B. J., & Richey, R. G. (2006). Effects of task interdependence on the relationship between helping behavior and group performance. *Journal of Applied Psychology, 91*(6), 1396–1405.

Bal, P. M., & Boehm, S. A. (2019). How do I-deals influence client satisfaction? The role of exhaustion, collective commitment, and age diversity. *Journal of Management, 45*(4), 1461–1487.

Bal, P. M., & Lub, X. D. (2016). Individualization of work arrangements: A contextualized perspective on the rise and use of I-deals. In P. M. Bal & D. M. Rousseau (Eds.), *Current issues in work and organizational psychology. Idiosyncratic deals between employees and organizations: Conceptual issues, applications, and the role of co-workers* (pp. 9–23). Routledge/Taylor & Francis Group.

Baruch, Y., Altman, Y., & Tung, R. L. (2016). Career mobility in a global era: Advances in managing expatriation and repatriation. *The Academy of Management Annals, 10*(1), 841–889.

Bies, R. J., & Moag, J. F. (1986). Interactional justice: Communication criteria of fairness. In R. J. Lewicki, B. H. Sheppard, & M. H. Bazerman (Eds.), *Research on negotiation in organizations* (Vol. 1, pp. 43–55). JAI Press.

Bouwmans, M., Runhaar, P., Wesselink, R., & Mulder, M. (2019). Stimulating teachers' team performance through team-oriented HR practices: The roles of affective team commitment and information processing. *The International Journal of Human Resource Management, 30*(5), 856–878.

Butts, M. M., Casper, W. J., & Yang, T. S. (2013). How important are work–family support policies? A meta-analytic investigation of their effects on employee outcomes. *Journal of Applied Psychology, 98*(1), 1–25.

Caligiuri, P., & Bonache, J. (2016). Evolving and enduring challenges in global mobility. *Journal of World Business, 51*(1), 127–141.

Cappelli, P. (2000). A market-driven approach to retaining talent. *Harvard Business Review, 78,* 103–111.

Cappelli, P., & Keller, J. R. (2014). Talent management: Conceptual approaches and practical challenges. *Annual Review of Organizational Psychology and Organizational Behavior, 1*(1), 305–331.

Cascio, W. F., & Boudreau, J. W. (2016). The search for global competence: From international HR to talent management. *Journal of World Business, 51*(1), 103–114.

Cerdin, J. L., & Brewster, C. (2014). Talent management and expatriation: Bridging two streams of research and practice. *Journal of World Business, 49*(2), 245–252.

Chen, M. J., & Miller, D. (2011). The relational perspective as a business mindset: Managerial implications for East and West. *Academy of Management Perspectives, 25*(3), 6–18.

Davis, M. H., Conklin, L., Smith, A., & Luce, C. (1996). Effect of perspective taking on the cognitive representation of persons: A merging of self and other. *Journal of Personality and Social Psychology, 70*(4), 713–726.

DeNisi, A., & Smith, C. E. (2014). Performance appraisal, performance management, and firm-level performance: A review, a proposed model, and new directions for future research. *Academy of Management Annals, 8*(1), 127–179.

Edmondson, A. (1999). Psychological safety and learning behavior in work teams. *Administrative Science Quarterly, 44*(2), 350–383.

Eisenberger, R., Rhoades Shanock, L., & Wen, X. (2020). Perceived organizational support: Why caring about employees counts. *Annual Review of Organizational Psychology and Organizational Behavior, 7,* 101–124.

Feldman, M. S., & Pentland, B. (2003). Reconceptualizing organizational routines as a source of flexibility and change. *Administrative Science Quarterly, 48,* 94–120.

Gelens, J., Hofmans, J., Dries, N., & Pepermans, R. (2014). Talent management and organisational justice: Employee reactions to high potential identification. *Human Resource Management Journal, 24*(2), 159–175.

Gonzalez-Morales, M. G., Kernan, M. C., Becker, T. E., & Eisenberger, R. (2018). Defeating abusive supervision: Training supervisors to support subordinates. *Journal of Occupational Health Psychology, 23*(2), 151–162.

Grant, A. M., & Berry, J. W. (2011). The necessity of others is the mother of invention: Intrinsic and prosocial motivations, perspective taking, and creativity. *Academy of Management Journal, 54*(1), 73–96.

Greenberg, J. (2006). Losing sleep over organizational injustice: Attenuating insomniac reactions to underpayment inequity with supervisory training in interactional justice. *Journal of Applied Psychology, 91*(1), 58–69.

Greenberg, J., Roberge, M. E., Ho, V. T., & Rousseau, D. M. (2004). Fairness in idiosyncratic work arrangements: Justice as an i-deal. *Research in Personnel and Human Resources Management, 23*, 1–34.

Hofstede, G. (1980). *Culture consequences: International differences in work-related values.* Sage.

Hong, G., Cho, Y., Froese, F. J., & Shin, M. (2016). The effect of leadership styles, rank, and seniority on affective organizational commitment. *Cross Cultural & Strategic Management, 23*(2), 340–362.

Hornung, S., Rousseau, D. M., & Glaser, J. (2009). Why supervisors make idiosyncratic deals: Antecedents and outcomes of I-deals from a managerial perspective. *Journal of Managerial Psychology, 24*(8), 738–764.

Hornung, S., Rousseau, D. M., Glaser, J., Angerer, P., & Weigl, M. (2010). Beyond top-down and bottom-up work redesign: Customizing job content through idiosyncratic deals. *Journal of Organizational Behavior, 31*(2–3), 187–215.

House, R. J., Hanges, P. J., Javidan, M., Dorfman, P. W., & Gupta, V., & GLOBE Associates. (2004). *Culture, leadership, and organizations: The GLOBE study of 62 societies.* Sage.

Hu, B., & Varma, A. (2020). Motivation and feedback. In A. Varma & P. Budhwar (Eds.), *Performance management systems: An experiential approach* (pp. 111–134). Sage.

James, L. R., Joyce, W. F., & Slocum, J. W., Jr. (1988). Comment: Organizations do not cognize. *Academy of Management Review, 13*(1), 129–132.

Kelly, C. M., Rofcanin, Y., Las Heras, M., Ogbonnaya, C., Marescaux, E., & Bosch, M. J. (2020). Seeking an "i-deal" balance: Schedule-flexibility I-deals as mediating mechanisms between supervisor emotional support and employee work and home performance. *Journal of Vocational Behavior, 118*, 103369.

Klein, H. J., Wesson, M. J., Hollenbeck, J. R., Wright, P. M., & DeShon, R. P. (2001). The assessment of goal commitment: A measurement model meta-analysis. *Organizational Behavior and Human Decision Processes*, 85(1), 32–55.

Kniffin, K. M., Narayanan, J., Anseel, F., Antonakis, J., Ashford, S. P., Bakker, A. B., Bamberger, P., Bapuji, H., Bhave, D. P., Choi, V. K., Creary, S. J., Demerouti, E., Flynn, F. J., Gelfand, M. J., Greer, L. L., Johns, G., Kesebir, S., Klein, P. G., Lee, S. Y., ... Vugt, M. V. (2021). COVID-19 and the workplace: Implications, issues, and insights for future research and action. *American Psychologist*, 76(1), 63.

Kong, D. T., Ho, V. T., & Garg, S. (2020). Employee and coworker idiosyncratic deals: Implications for emotional exhaustion and deviant behaviors. *Journal of Business Ethics*, 164(3), 593–609.

Konopaske, R., Robie, C., & Ivancevich, J. M. (2005). A preliminary model of spouse influence on managerial global assignment willingness. *The International Journal of Human Resource Management*, 16(3), 405–426.

Kroon, B., Freese, C., & Schalk, R. (2019). A strategic HRM perspective on I-deals. In C. Cooper (Ed.), *Current issues in work and organizational psychology* (pp. 371–385). Routledge.

Kurtessis, J. N., Eisenberger, R., Ford, M. T., Buffardi, L. C., Stewart, K. A., & Adis, C. S. (2017). Perceived organizational support: A meta-analytic evaluation of organizational support theory. *Journal of Management*, 43(6), 1854–1884.

Lai, L., Rousseau, D. M., & Chang, K. T. T. (2009). Idiosyncratic deals: Coworkers as interested third parties. *Journal of Applied Psychology*, 94(2), 547–556.

Las Heras, M., Van der Heijden, B. I., De Jong, J., & Rofcanin, Y. (2017). "Handle with care": The mediating role of schedule i-deals in the relationship between supervisors' own caregiving responsibilities and employee outcomes. *Human Resource Management Journal*, 27(3), 335–349.

Laulié, L., Tekleab, A. G., & Lee, J. J. (2020). Why grant I-deals? supervisors' prior i-deals, exchange ideology, and justice sensitivity. *Journal of Business and Psychology*, 36(1), 17–31.

Lazarova, M., Westman, M., & Shaffer, M. A. (2010). Elucidating the positive side of the work-family interface on international assignments: A model of expatriate work and family performance. *Academy of Management Review*, 35(1), 93–117.

Liao, C., Wayne, S. J., & Rousseau, D. M. (2016). Idiosyncratic deals in contemporary organizations: A qualitative and meta-analytical review. *Journal of Organizational Behavior*, 37(S1), S9–S29.

Lind, E. A., & Tyler, T. R. (1988). *The social psychology of procedural justice*. Plenum Press.

Liu, J., Lee, C., Hui, C., Kwan, H. K., & Wu, L. Z. (2013). Idiosyncratic deals and employee outcomes: The mediating roles of social exchange and self-enhancement and the moderating role of individualism. *Journal of Applied Psychology, 98*(5), 832–840.

Marescaux, E., De Winne, S., & Sels, L. (2013). HR practices and affective organisational commitment: (When) does HR differentiation pay off? *Human Resource Management Journal, 23*(4), 329–345.

Martin, R., Guillaume, Y., Thomas, G., Lee, A., & Epitropaki, O. (2016). Leader–member exchange (LMX) and performance: A meta-analytic review. *Personnel Psychology, 69*(1), 67–121.

Mohammed, S., & Angell, L. C. (2004). Surface- and deep-level diversity in workgroups: Examining the moderating effects of team orientation and team process on relationship conflict. *Journal of Organizational Behavior, 25*(8), 1015–1039.

Morrison, E. W., & Robinson, S. L. (1997). When employees feel betrayed: A model of how psychological contract violation occurs. *Academy of Management Review, 22*(1), 226–256.

Ng, T. W. (2017). Can idiosyncratic deals promote perceptions of competitive climate, felt ostracism, and turnover? *Journal of Vocational Behavior, 99*, 118–131.

Ng, T. W., & Lucianetti, L. (2016). Goal striving, idiosyncratic deals, and job behavior. *Journal of Organizational Behavior, 37*(1), 41–60.

Olson, G. (2013). *Empathy imperiled: Capitalism, culture, and the brain*. Springer.

Parker, S. K., & Axtell, C. M. (2001). Seeing another viewpoint: Antecedents and outcomes of employee perspective taking. *Academy of Management Journal, 44*(6), 1085–1100.

Rofcanin, Y., Berber, A., Marescaux, E., Bal, P. M., Mughal, F., & Afacan Findikli, M. (2019). Human resource differentiation: A theoretical paper integrating co-workers' perspective and context. *Human Resource Management Journal, 29*(2), 270–286.

Rofcanin, Y., Kiefer, T., & Strauss, K. (2017). What seals the I-deal? Exploring the role of employees' behaviours and managers' emotions. *Journal of Occupational and Organizational Psychology, 90*(2), 203–224.

Rofcanin, Y., Las Heras, M., Bal, P. M., Van der Heijden, B. I., & Taser Erdogan, D. (2018). A trickle-down model of task and development I-deals. *Human Relations, 71*(11), 1508–1534.

Rousseau, D. M. (2001). The idiosyncratic deal: Flexibility versus fairness? *Organizational Dynamic, 29*(4), 260–273.

Rousseau, D. M. (2005). *I-deals: Idiosyncratic deals employees bargain for themselves*. M. E. Sharpe.

Rousseau, D. M., Ho, V. T., & Greenberg, J. (2006). I-deals: Idiosyncratic terms in employment relationships. *Academy of Management Review, 31*(4), 977–994.

Rousseau, D. M., Hornung, S., & Kim, T. G. (2009). Idiosyncratic deals: Testing propositions on timing, content, and the employment relationship. *Journal of Vocational Behavior, 74*(3), 338–348.

Rousseau, D. M., Tomprou, M., & Simosi, M. (2016). Negotiating flexible and fair idiosyncratic deals (I-deals). *Organizational Dynamics, 45*(3), 185–196.

Salas, E., Priest, H. A., & DeRouin, R. E. (2005). Team building. In N. Stanton, H. Hendrick, S. Konz, K. Parsons, & E. Salas (Eds.), *Handbook of human factors and ergonomics methods* (pp. 465–470). Taylor & Francis.

Salas, E., Rozell, D., Mullen, B., & Driskell, J. E. (1999). The effect of team building on performance: An integration. *Small Group Research, 30*(3), 309–329.

Shapiro, D. L., Buttner, E. H., & Barry, B. (1994). Explanations: What factors enhance their perceived adequacy? *Organizational Behavior and Human Decision Processes, 58*(3), 346–368.

Skarlicki, D. P., & Latham, G. P. (2005). How can training be used to foster organizational justice? In J. Greenberg & J. A. Colquitt (Eds.), *Handbook of organizational justice* (pp. 499–522). Erlbaum.

Somech, A., Desivilya, H. S., & Lidogoster, H. (2009). Team conflict management and team effectiveness: The effects of task interdependence and team identification. *Journal of Organizational Behavior, 30*(3), 359–378.

Takeuchi, R., Yun, S., & Tesluk, P. E. (2002). An examination of crossover and spillover effects of spousal and expatriate cross-cultural adjustment on expatriate outcomes. *Journal of Applied Psychology, 87*(4), 655–666.

Tornikoski, C. (2011). Fostering expatriate affective commitment: A total reward perspective. *Cross Cultural Management: An International Journal, 18*(2), 214–235.

Varma, A., & Budhwar, P. (2020a). Introduction—Performance management in context. In A. Varma & P. Budhwar. (Eds.), *Performance management systems: An experiential approach* (pp. 1–14). Sage.

Varma, A., & Budhwar. P. (2020b). *Implementing a performance management system*. In A. Varma & P. Budhwar. (Eds.), *Performance management systems: An experiential approach* (pp. 165–180). Sage.

Varma, A., & Russell, L. (2016). Women and expatriate assignments: Exploring the role of perceived organizational support. *Employee Relations, 38*(2), 200–223.

Varma, A., & Stroh, L. K. (2001). The impact of same-sex LMX dyads on performance evaluations. *Human Resource Management, 40*(4), 309–320.

Varma, A., & Tung, R. (2020a). Performance management for expatriates. In A. Varma & P. Budhwar (Eds.), *Performance management systems: An experiential approach* (pp. 153–164). Sage.

Varma, A., & Tung, R. (2020b). Lure of country of origin: An exploratory study of ex-host country nationals in India. *Personnel Review, 49*(7), 1487–1501.

Vidyarthi, P. R., Singh, S., Erdogan, B., Chaudhry, A., Posthuma, R., & Anand, S. (2016). Individual deals within teams: Investigating the role of relative I-deals for employee performance. *Journal of Applied Psychology, 101*(11), 1536–1552.

Wang, C.-H. (2018). To relocate internationally or not to relocate internationally: A Taiwanese case study. *Journal of Global Mobility, 6*(2), 226–240.

Wang, S., Liu, Y., & Shalley, C. E. (2018). Idiosyncratic deals and employee creativity: The mediating role of creative self-efficacy. *Human Resource Management, 57*(6), 1443–1453.

Zhang, Y., & Varma, A. (2020, September–October). Organizational preparedness with COVID-19: Strategic planning and human creativity. *The European Business Review*, 22–33.

CHAPTER 8

A Workplace Dignity Perspective on Idiosyncratic Deals at Work

P. Matthijs Bal

INTRODUCTION

The literature on idiosyncratic deals has gained some popularity over the last 15–20 years since it was coined by Denise Rousseau (2001, 2005; Rousseau et al., 2006). However, it is also relevant to mention that idiosyncratic deals have never seen the popularity of the concept of the psychological contract, its predecessor both in terms of scholarship of Rousseau and more conceptually in terms of description of the contemporary employment relationship. While the psychological contract has been successfully translated into a measurable concept that can be easily implemented in a variety of moderation and mediation models (primarily focused on breach of the contract; Zhao et al., 2007), the topic of idiosyncratic deals remains more elusive. It is still largely restricted to a small number of people globally who investigate i-deals, and the number of publications on i-deals remains somewhat low. This is surprising given

P. M. Bal (✉)
University of Lincoln, Lincoln, UK
e-mail: mbal@lincoln.ac.uk

the enormous relevance of individualization and individualism in contemporary society and workplaces (Bal & Dóci, 2018) and deserves some further thought. The purpose of this chapter, therefore, is to understand the concept of i-deals better from a societal perspective, and in particular that of rising individualism (Santos et al., 2017). It does so through offering a dignity perspective on i-deals, the reason for which is twofold: (1) this chapter explicitly aims to build on previous work around individualization and i-deals (see, e.g., Bal & Hornung, 2019; Bal & Lub, 2015; Hornung & Höge, 2019), and (2) the chapter aims to deepen the conceptual depth of understanding of the role of individualization and i-deals.

Because it can be observed how (Western) societies are currently developing into post-neoliberal societies, manifesting both in the rise of authoritarian populism and marginalization of dissonant voices (Norris & Inglehart, 2019; Žižek, 2018), it is imperative to contextualize contemporary work arrangements in light of such societal changes. While research and theory on i-deals has traditionally refrained from incorporating critical perspectives, this is needed however for two reasons. On the one hand, i-deal theorization follows dominant discourse in society, and thereby reproduces hegemonic beliefs in society about the employment relationship and in particular the ways through which employees and workers should feel and behave in the workplace. Hence, research and theory on i-deals have a *performative* function in reproduction of what can be considered 'normal' in society, such as the need for workers to individually arrange and negotiate their working conditions. On the other hand, research and theory on i-deals have a *constative* function, as they deliberately take a perspective of the contemporary workplace and structure it. Thereby, research projects a particular meaning upon that what is currently taking place in workplaces, and contributes to understanding of the workplace as where one *should* individually negotiate one's working conditions and be self-managing and self-reliant (Hornung and Höge, 2019). It is this double meaning of i-deals, which is far from uncommon in contemporary scientific research (Bal & Dóci, 2018), that elucidates the nature of i-deals as ideological (Bal & Hornung, 2019). The implications of which will be discussed in this chapter, including the implications for further research and theory on i-deals. The chapter will finish with a presentation of a dignity perspective on i-deals through which its conceptual richness may be enhanced.

Individualization and Idiosyncratic Deals

While previous reviews and conceptual work have conceptualized and discussed i-deals extensively (e.g., Bal & Rousseau, 2015; Greenberg et al., 2004; Liao et al., 2016; Rousseau, 2001, 2005; Rousseau et al., 2006), there is no need to repeat such arguments. More important, though, is the discussion of why i-deals have not reached the popularity of job crafting research. Job crafting and i-deals can be differentiated on the basis of two main differences: (1) while i-deals refer to specific agreements or deals that are negotiated between two parties, job crafting refers to 'behavior' without any reference to an agreement (i.e., between employee and organization). The implicitness of benefit of job crafting for organizational outcome is not just coincidental, but designed on purpose. (2) I-deals refer to explicit agreements between employee and employer resulting from a negotiation, whereby the assumption is of explicit exchange. Job crafting, in contrast, refers to unauthorized behavior in the workplace that may enrich one's work experience, and is assumed to contribute to organizational goals as well (Rofcanin et al., 2016). It is interesting to observe how job crafting research has skyrocketed (Rudolph et al., 2017), whereas i-deals research has lagged behind. As the two concepts can be seen as competing within the same conceptual space, one has to ask why i-deals research has never really received the same interest as the psychological contract did (the concept Rousseau popularized earlier, with an enormous impact on research, and possibly as well on practice), as well as job crafting research.

There are some superficial arguments to provide why i-deals have 'lost' the battle to job crafting. For instance, the concept of job crafting was translated into straightforward scales and measures, that could easily be used within existing frameworks and measurement models (e.g., job crafting can be easily fitted within the dominant moderated-mediation models, which are increasingly popular/dominant nowadays). Moreover, job crafting was also squeezed into the popular Job-Demands Resources Model (Tims & Bakker, 2010), through which it could both profit from an extensive body of literature (and thereby an enormous group of scholars) on the JDR-model, *and* enrich the JDR-model itself, which was running on empty for some years. While scales were developed for i-deal measurement (e.g., Bal & Vossaert, 2019; Rosen et al., 2013), they remained somewhat complex and lacked the possibility to obtain straightforward meaning and outcomes in empirical models.

Moreover, job crafting had two additional advantages over i-deals. First, the concept was so evidently symptomatic of the individualized nature of the employment relationship that it naturally 'outcompeted' i-deals for conceptual desirability among researchers (and practitioners). Job crafting is about self-initiated changes to makes one's own job better, or even perceptions of one's own job (which they call 'cognitive crafting', rather than cognitive dissonance). The job crafting literature offers only a very implicit understanding of the 'Other', be it the employer, manager, or coworker. Thereby, it fits perfectly with the individualistic nature of contemporary society, in the absence of a real other, and thus a self-centeredness of a concept that should be inherently relational (i.e., job crafting is either conducted collectively, or has effects on others). In contrast, the i-deals concept was by definition about the exchange, and thus the explicit acknowledgment and integration of the 'Other'. This Other is imperative, as it not only functions as an exchange partner (i.e., in i-deals, the person or party that one negotiates with), but also as an 'agent of appearance', or in other words, a controlling other, through which there are natural limits to one's feelings and behaviors, as there is always another person or party that is part of this exchange. The i-deals literature has always stood in the tradition of the psychological contract, whereby the primary focus is on the individual employee, but whereby there is always the Other (Guest, 1998). This other represents not just the organization, but is much more of a Father figure, an agent of appearances, that controls and dominates the individual employee. The absence of research on this Other in both psychological contract and i-deals literatures merely support the notion of the present, yet invisible Other, who in reality dictates the very notion of the contract or deal.

Job crafting, however, exemplifies this Lack of the Other, as there is only the worker herself, with no clear boundaries between oneself and one's environment. There is no limitation to job crafting, as conceptually or empirically there is no mentioning of the other party, and therefore, fits neatly with the individualized nature of contemporary society and workplaces (Greene, 2008). Hence, job crafting will never occur at the expense of the other, because there is no other in one's behavior at work. I-deals, however, have always been conceptualized, theorized, and limited to the extent that i-deals may be negotiated at the expense of others (see, e.g., the early conceptual work of Greenberg et al., 2004, on organizational justice and i-deals). There is always the coworker involvement in an i-deal (Rousseau, 2005), and researchers, unknowingly or knowingly neoliberal

(Bal & Dóci, 2018), prefer to project the workplace as a space consisting only of individuals (in line with Thatcher's 'There is no such thing as society').

Secondly, the term job crafting itself has a discursive advantage over i-deals. While i-deals always seemed to have the advantage of being understood as *ideal* (e.g., the ideal i-deal, or the ideal employment relationship; Van der Meij & Bal, 2013), it is the conceptual lack of what this ideal would consist of that perhaps offers another explanation for its relative failure vis-à-vis concepts such as job crafting and proactivity. What this ideal would look like is unknown, so both researchers and practitioners are left with a concept that does not yet give enough direction and postulates an ideal that is fundamentally unknown. One can explain the popularity of happiness in similar terms, as it is the perpetual striving toward happiness that motivates both research and practice, as the fulfillment of true happiness is never achievable (Cabanas & Illouz, 2019). Yet, happiness denotes a feeling that one *should* have, but actually will never truly have, therefore the eternal quest is what drives both research and practice (i.e., how one achieves happiness). Similarly, job crafting is presented as inherently desirable concept, as the notion of 'crafting' conveys an implicit message of being active, being in a state of improvement, and being self-initiated. It also even taps into the ideological desirable concept of craftsmanship (e.g., Sennett, 2008), as the deliberate, thoughtful, and reflective individual production process. Job crafting has this eternal search-element, where it is rather unclear what state one is actually striving for. However, the outcome is not what matters, as there is no outcome in the perpetual search for self-improvement, for bettering of one's job and life. This opens an understanding of job crafting as even more strongly anchored in neoliberal ideology (Bal, 2017a).

Notwithstanding this relative unpopularity of i-deals in comparison with job crafting, it still has received attention from a growing group of scholars worldwide. What is shared between i-deals and job crafting is the underlying philosophy of individualism (Bal & Hornung, 2019). As argued previously, individualism (which can be understood as the 'sociocultural beliefs and practices that encourage and legitimate the autonomy, equality and dignity of individuals'; Greene, 2008, p. 117) is not just a philosophy of the importance of the individual human being (as opposed to more collectivistic societies), but also taps into an important dimension of neoliberal capitalism (Bal & Dóci, 2018; Greene, 2008). It has to be understood, therefore, how i-deals are embedded both conceptually and empirically within the discourse of neoliberal capitalism. If individualism can be understood as the encouragement of the dignity of individuals, as stated above, one has to ask where the dignity of individuals is, when the world is confronted with the destructive effects of climate change, social inequalities, authoritarian populism, the rise of surveillance capitalism and so on (Bal, 2017a). If an ever smaller group of individuals who are primarily living in the West and somewhat spread out across the globe, are still profiting from income inequalities, and thereby have access to resources, what is the legitimacy of academics to continue researching such privileged groups? What does an i-deal mean to someone working in the Bangladeshi RMG-sector? The obsession of Western academics with privileged groups in global society continues to exist, thereby amplifying neocolonial practices, or in other words, the continued projection of Western hegemonic beliefs upon the rest of the world.

With such an attitude comes the implicit assumption of the workplace as being individualized, or a workplace where individuals are responsible themselves for their work and careers, and that such a perspective on individuals is not ideological, but a mere representation of 'how things are' (i.e., this is how critique is silenced—by defending research in WOP as non-ideological, a-political, and *scientific*; Bal & Dóci, 2018). While it can be seen that such beliefs are now dominant in the Western world, they are also currently exported worldwide, through academic research and publications which merely take such fundamental assumptions about humanity and the workplace for granted. If we zoom in into one particular manifestation of capitalism, inequality, we can observe the following relationship between i-deals and inequality.

First, inequality creates i-deals. One extreme of the political-economic spectrum dictates that inequalities should not exist (i.e., Communism), and as a result that everyone in society should have the same income and access to resources, notwithstanding one's job, effort, responsibilities and so on. While this has never been the case in recent history (e.g., the Soviet apparatchiks always has privileged access to resources during the Communist era), it is also for a variety of reasons impractical and undesirable. On the other extreme of the spectrum, we find unregulated capitalism, perhaps the kind that Hayek and Friedman dreamed about. In this vision, there is no government regulation whatsoever, and in this case, the 'invisible hand' of the market can provide 'fair' distribution of resources (Bal, 2017a). It is this extreme that Western countries are currently heading toward, with a notable exception, which is that government regulation fulfills an important role. For instance, when the 2007–2008 global economic crisis started, many governments in Western countries bailed out the banks and financial service organizations, thereby interfering with the free market, and offering trillions of dollars to financial firms. Nonetheless, this trend toward free-market thinking and the persistent belief in the 'invisible hand' of the market are not only inherent to contemporary capitalism, but are also responsible to a large extent for the rising inequality in societies globally. In the free market, there is a trend toward monopolies, who then start to control the entire market including government interference. For instance, the continued lowering of corporate taxes has been made possible by a combination of free-market ideology, as well as lobbying of the corporate sector for lower taxes. This has inevitably amplified inequalities worldwide.

I-deals, therefore, have to be understood in relation to growing inequality in the world. Such inequalities can be observed between countries (e.g., Global North vs. Global South), between sectors within countries (e.g., financial sector vs. educational sector), and within organizations (managers and high-potentials vs. precarious workers). I-deals will align with such inequalities, that i-deals will be more common in Western countries (i.e., the Global North), within sectors and organizations that have ample financial means (e.g., financial service sectors), and among workers who have a lot of human capital. Inequalities, therefore, create unequal access to i-deals, as those workers who are in privileged positions will be more likely to be granted i-deals. This was also corroborated in an earlier study (Bal, 2017b), which found that i-deal access and success were dependent upon employee status: employees who were more vulnerable (e.g., of easily losing their job due to the precarious nature of their employment) were also much more careful in negotiating and maintaining i-deals.

The possibility of getting i-deals in the broadest sense is therefore restricted depending on privilege and position. I-deals in this sense denote any favorable treatment, or access to special resources that matter, such as pay, development, flexibility, pensions, health care coverage, and more broadly any remuneration that enables one to live a 'dignified' life. Conversely, being in a state where one does not have privilege, the possibility of getting an i-deal is also somewhat ludicrous and absurd (like the possibility of a child working in a tin mine to obtain an i-deal). Such an example is not an exaggeration, but a true reflection of what is actually unfolding in the world; while it is known that the production of smartphones includes slave and child labor, it is also necessary to talk of such examples in relation to work psychology. In a broader sense, lack of privilege in whatever way, as discussed above, also ensures lack of access to i-deals. It is therefore of great importance to understand that inequalities shape the extent to which i-deals can be obtained, granted, and how they will look like.

Second, i-deals also create inequalities (Marescaux et al., 2019). However, this notion which has been established in the i-deals literature also needs to be explained in more detail. On the surface level, i-deals include special arrangements for workers, and thus, those workers who are able to obtain i-deals will have better and more access to resources. This amplifies existing differences with others in organizations, and thus the inequalities between those with i-deals and those without. This can also be empirically shown, and there are at least three studies showing that when workers obtain i-deals, coworkers who did not receive i-deals may react with feelings of injustice and ostracism, with complaints and requests for compensation (Marescaux et al., 2019; Ng, 2017), unless one is friends with the worker getting an i-deal and perceives a future opportunity to get one (Lai et al., 2009). However, this still adheres to some idea of i-deals being fairly distributed, and perpetuating the dream of getting an i-deal oneself.

It is not surprising that coworkers who are not getting i-deals are more lenient if they perceive a future opportunity to obtain special arrangements themselves in the future. This, of course, underpins the American Dream itself (Su, 2015), or the idea that if one works hard enough, that one will be rewarded in the future as well. However, this neglects that inequality in the first place was not created on the basis of meritocracy, but designed to favor those at the top and to remain the status quo in society (Harvey, 2005; Norris & Inglehart, 2019). We, therefore, observe an interesting relationship of i-deals with inequality. I-deals not only exemplify that contemporary society and workplaces are not driven by meritocracy but by structural inequalities determining access to resources, but they also contribute to deepening of structural inequalities.

Yet, the majority of research on i-deals still adheres to the 'social exchange' principles underpinning i-deals themselves. In other words, i-deals are theorized to always balance out in reality; Marescaux et al. (2019) showed how unfair i-deals may lead to complaints and requests for compensation. Such a perspective still neglects the very basis of i-deals as exploitation: while those who receive them may uphold perceptions of fairness and exchange, it is those who will never have access to i-deals, who are also suffering from exploitation, and whereby there *is* no exchange. It is therefore needed to ask whether social exchange principles truly underpin i-deals theory, or whether this perspective neglects more critical issues such as exploitation. Similarly, while a privileged elite may have benefitted from the disappearance of permanent contracts in the neoliberal era and have been able to negotiate lucrative self-employment contracts, it is insufficient to conclude on the basis of their experiences that it was actually a good thing to get rid of permanent contracts in the West. This would neglect the experiences of the majority of workers who were forced into precarious employment, without any job security, and health care or pension coverage. For i-deals, the same argument holds: while a privileged few will have benefitted from i-deals (e.g., most of the examples of Rousseau's seminal 2005 book on i-deals included privileged, white, white-collar workers), it is insufficient to state that i-deals have benefitted workers more generally.

It is important, therefore, to understand why there is a persistent belief in the 'promise' of i-deals, and thus the possibility of social engineering through research on i-deals. In their conceptual analysis of the scholarship of Work and Organizational Psychologists, Bal and Dóci (2018) identified social engineering as one of the most fundamental fantasies underpinning WOP-scholarship, or the idea that through technical interventions, workplaces can be created that ensure 'health, motivation and productivity' (Kooij, 2015). It can be stated that i-deal scholarship is underpinned by a similar fantasmatic logic (Glynos, 2008), whereby the interest in i-deals is spurred by the belief that organizations should implement the possibilities for individuals to negotiate special deals for themselves individually, such that they are thriving at work, thereby contributing to performance of the organization, while maintaining their well-being (so they are not burning out, and thus can remain loyal contributors to organizational performance). I-deals can therefore be used as 'technical' interventions in organizations that will help organizations to boost productivity and motivation of employees. Research in OB and HRM will thereby help to understand when and how i-deals lead to performance, and what the pitfalls are of suboptimal i-deal implementation or management.

However, such a technical and a-political perspective on i-deals neglects the more contested elements of i-deals, and the possibility that i-deals are not merely performative (i.e., aligning to dominant neoliberal discourse in society), but also have a meaning on their own. Hence, they become constative, or contributing to and shaping understandings of dominant discourses in society. Research on i-deals thus contributes to an understanding of the workplace as a 'special zone' where dreams are made possible, dreams of self-actualization, or entrepreneurship, dreams of following one's passion and so on. Literature on i-deals is hereby not any different from the main body of literature in work psychology, organizational behavior and HRM more widely. Most, if not all, literatures in these disciplines adhere to this notion, and contribute to the understanding of the workplace as that special place where people develop, are authentic, produce, find meaning, craft their lives and jobs, and are truly engaged. Research in WOP, OB, and HRM do not merely reflect the issues that are prevalent at work, but are contributing to the development of norms about workplace behavior. Academics are not merely expected to publish in scientific journals that are only read by academics (which would ensure that academic knowledge would remain with the academic sphere), but they are also expected to work with practitioners, governments, organizations, and therefore, to publish in magazines, newspapers, and to have a 'real' impact on the world. Such impact agendas (public engagement, or valorization) are by definition focused on the constative dimension of academic research for practice and society, and thus to convey the message that (a) workplaces are sanctified spaces for individual self-actualization, and (b) that workers have to be proactive and individually negotiate their special arrangements for self-actualization.

I-deals exemplify this process, as there is still this 'mythical' status of the i-deal as *ideal*. Idiosyncratic deals should be aligned to the point about sanctified workplaces for self-actualization, and create possibilities for the fulfillment of such ideals. However, most research on i-deals is stuck in the middle, overly focused on the mundane nature of everyday life, such as the quest for flexibility between work and private life, and the ongoing pressure of work on private life, which is sought to be resolved through an i-deal. This i-deal may seek some solution to the perpetual nature of the contemporary workplace as seeking the space that was once private, with the strict boundaries between work and private life, and the long lost protection of the 9–5 job. Hence, the mythical status of the i-deal as ideal is far from realized, as most research on i-deals show: there is hardly any research on i-deals that shows how i-deals are used for real meaning in life and work.

One of the first publications on i-deals (Rousseau, 2001) opens with the example of two high-potentials who got a year sabbatical to do underwater photography. Perhaps this example can be analyzed superficially as an example of an i-deal negotiated by two employees (i.e., high-potential, and thus indicative of their unequal status in the organization) trying to find meaning in their lives through underwater photography (of coral reef). Closer inspection, however, also elucidates the emptiness of such endeavor. Two high potential employees who 'follow their passion' through consumption and engaging in the experience-economy cannot serve as examples of true (ideology-free) meaning. Indicative is the absence of acknowledgment of the carbon foot print of such 'sabbaticals' (e.g., the air flights between the US and Australia), and thus the pollution that is created through such engagement in the experience-economy (a notion that is often silenced by academics, who prior to the COVID-19 crisis used to be notorious polluters with their global air travel for trips, conferences, and research visits). Moreover, most of the examples provided in Rousseau's work (2001, 2005) refer to either mundane arrangements (e.g., special working hours for young parents), or traditional capitalist arrangements (e.g., special pay arrangements or time off from work to conduct paid work somewhere else). This leaves i-deals research to be overly constrained within either the mundane level of everyday life without much possibility to 'theorize' such mundaneness into meaningfulness, or within the somewhat trite neoliberal capitalist dogma of growth, competition and freedom, underpinned by social Darwinist beliefs (Bal & Dóci, 2018).

The above discussion raises two fundamental issues: on the one hand, why such perspectives on i-deals have become hegemonic and why they are so persistent over time, and on the other hand, whether dignity offers a way out of the somewhat trite conceptualizations of i-deals so that they can play a more meaningful role in contemporary workplaces.

Ideology Underpinning I-deals

It has been argued elsewhere that research in WOP is/has become neoliberal (Bal & Dóci, 2018; Dóci & Bal, 2018). With the observation that WOP (and in extension OB, HRM and related disciplines) aligns with the dominant neoliberal capitalist discourse in society, it remains unclear why scholars persist in research and writing that ultimately maintains the status quo, and which does not fundamentally challenge existing structures in society and workplaces that inhibit i-deals to favor employees more generally rather than a privileged elite, which is usually the focus of study in the field. There are at least two main reasons for this: structural reasons (i.e., the need for reproduction of form), and the disavowal of the predicament of academia. First, there are structural constraints to freedom in neoliberal capitalist society, and in extension, academia. To be able to build an academic career, academics are nowadays forced to comply with the standards that are being set within academic fields. Academic careers are currently dependent on engagement in a range of activities (such as successful teaching, grant applications, and impact generation), but most of all journal output. Publication in top-tier journals is still the most relevant indicator of academic success and the chance to build an academic career. Standards set by top-tier journals are reproduced extensively across academic departments worldwide. Financial incentives to publish in top-tier journals are not uncommon in places like Australia, which means that academics have a lot of incentives to comply with these standards, both in terms of writing, methods, but more fundamentally, the ontologies underpinning such journals. It is noticeable how the large majority of i-deals research that is published in the better or top-tier journals utterly comply with such standards: they tend to be quantitative, using survey methods to test either predictors or outcomes of i-deal negotiation processes. Such studies are ultimately underpinned by the logic that i-deals contribute to both employee and organizationally relevant outcomes. Critical engagement with the i-deals literature is difficult to undertake and publish in mainstream, top-tier journals, and overall a risky business, as failure and rejection are much more likely than the pursuing of research that complies with standards set by the academic industry.

Such process, as crudely summarized as above, explains the current predicament of academia, which can be explained in terms of 'reproduction of form' (Yurchak, 2003, 2005). Reproduction of form was explained by Russian-born anthropologist Yurchak to understand late decades of the Soviet Union after the death of Stalin, and in particular the perfect replication of ideological texts within Communism. Reproduction of form ensured that the Soviet Union was both eternal and stagnating at the same time. We can observe a similar ideological 'reproduction of form' in contemporary academia, whereby the form is perfectly replicated over time (i.e., journal articles are perfectly crafted works of research), but whereby the content becomes more and more meaningless. This is noticeable particularly with the Journal of Applied Psychology, which represents the flagship journal of WOP, and which form is perfectly replicated over time (the highly dense writing, and uniform theory building sections leading to hypotheses, quantitative methods, results and discussion). However, the content of the journal becomes more and more meaningless, detached from reality of contemporary workplaces, also evidenced by the sentiment of many academics that they do not read the journal anymore, as it has become 'too boring'.

Reproduction of form is not innocent and, as shown by Yurchak (2005), provides the way through which ideology is maintained and strengthened over time. In fact, while the content seems to become more and more meaningless, the underlying ideological meaning remains intact and neatly conforms with neoliberal, capitalist ideology (i.e., of the competitive, instrumental and individualized workplace; Bal & Dóci, 2018). Nonetheless, as the structural constraints still favor compliance with the status quo (as academic careers are dependent upon reproduction of form), i-deals research is also largely stuck within such constraints.

However, this structural explanation is part of the narrative; it can also be observed how academics personally are engaged and involved in the maintenance of status quo, which explains the often hostile reactions toward critical voices in academia and academic research. The philosopher Žižek (1989) explains this attitude by 'disavowal' (i.e., denial): while we as academics know that what we do is meaningless reproduction of form in journals, we nonetheless still persist in doing it (see also Alvesson & Spicer, 2016). In other words, there is ideological investment and internalization of academics into the notion to pretend to do as if research is meaningful, even though we ultimately know that this is not true. This pretense is not merely superficial but deeply integrated into the beliefs of academics. Research on sustainable careers is a good example of such an attitude: while the concept of sustainable careers has little to do with sustainability of the planet, resources, and the people (Blühdorn, 2017), the concept itself is appealing in its pretense to contribute to sustainability, whereas its underpinnings are deeply ideologically neoliberal (Bal et al., 2020). At the same time, researchers remain invested in concepts that are only loosely connected to reality, or to any commitment to real social change and justice. This system is maintained through the disavowal of researchers of their role in reproduction of the system, and the internalized nature that contemporary research in

WOP can actually contribute to better workplaces. A similar observation could be made around research and literature on i-deals, whereby research tends to remain rather managerial, favoring elites over vulnerable people, favoring organizational interests over interests of dignity, and ultimately favoring maintenance of the status quo of neoliberal capitalism over transformation of society and workplaces toward real social justice, planetary conservation, and protection of the dignity of people, animals, and the planet.

Dignity and Idiosyncratic Deals

Greene (2008) noticed that individualism can be defined as the encouragement of the dignity of individuals. However, it remains less clear whose dignity is referred to, and whose dignity is neglected. Individualism in a Social Darwinist framework entails the notion of self-reliance, and hence the need for individuals to ensure their own dignity. This exposes the very limitation of dignity in individualism, as dignity has been conceptualized either within the framework of human rights (e.g., the Universal Declaration of Human Rights from 1948), or within the framework of philosopher Immanuel Kant, who emphasized the importance of duty toward the other in manifestation of dignity (Rosen, 2012). It is therefore important to emphasize the meaning of dignity in relation to i-deals, and the possibility for more radical reformulation of i-deals theory and research.

I-deals have been described as the opportunity for personalization or customization of work arrangements that provide people with jobs and careers that are suited within their abilities, needs, and wishes (Hornung et al., 2010; Rousseau, 2005). This positive view on how i-deals function in the workplace can be sustained through reinforcement of the individual dignity of the employee. It can be argued that because the employment relationship is individualized, employees are no longer treated as means to an end, that is, as resources that are employed by organizations in order to fulfill an organizational goal, such as survival or profit making. Hence, employees who negotiate i-deals no longer feel treated as a number, but rather as an individual human being, thereby enhancing their individual human dignity (Barresi, 2012). Human beings differ in their needs, capabilities, wishes, and personalities and when this is recognized by organizations, employees feel that their fundamental human needs are fulfilled (Taskin & Devos, 2005). In this sense, i-deals can indeed promote Kantian dignity: through i-deals people are no longer a nameless resource employed by the organization, but can maintain their dignity as a human being. Respect from the employer for the employee as a person is enhanced through the possibility to negotiate employment arrangements that are personalized to the situation of the employee. In other words, i-deals shape the possibility to add an ideological dimension to the employment relationship, through which employee commitment may be enhanced, and meaning of work is created (Bal & Vink, 2011).

Thus far, there has been no research on the underpinnings of i-deals, and the role of dignity in relation to i-deals. Future research may benefit from a relational perspective on i-deals (see, e.g., Anand et al., 2018; Bal, 2017a), focusing on the quality of the relationships between workers, their coworkers, leaders, and other stakeholders in managing i-deals. It has been argued that i-deals benefit relationships at work (e.g., Anand et al., 2018), and as such they could enact dignity at work. Dignity could therefore be an important dynamic and outcome of i-deals, and future research may focus in more depth when, how, and why i-deals are associated with greater dignity at work, and when i-deals lead to more dignity violations and denial of dignity. Management of i-deals in organizations is therefore inherently connected to the dignity of individuals in- and outside the organization.

In other words, organizational systems should take into account the dignity of the employee in its functioning. Hence, when strategic decisions are made as to how an organization should function, it no longer suffices to focus only on profitability of the firm, and with it shareholder value, as this might lead to severe violations of human dignity. In a similar vein, organizations that use i-deals to retain, attract, and reward employees should be aware that i-deals can be used to promote as well as to violate the dignity of employees (Lucas et al., 2013).

For i-deals researchers, it remains imperative to articulate the fundamental assumptions underpinning our research. Whereas discussion of ontology is generally absent in WOP-research as well as in i-deals research, it is necessary to break out of this implicitness, as it merely conceals ideological alliance with assumptions that researchers in reality rarely may agree with. Conversely, the explicit discussion of the purpose of i-deals research may shed light upon issues, including:

– Why i-deals researchers investigate i-deals in the workplace.
– Who the beneficiaries are or should be of i-deals research.

- Whether i-deals research have an emancipatory aim, including striving for greater social justice and equality.
- Whether and how i-deals can contribute to greater dignity of people, animals, and the planet.
- Whether distribution of and access to i-deals may be ensured in a way that benefits especially vulnerable people in the workplace.
- Whether i-deals have a real meaning beyond the privileged Western world.
- Whether the personal and professional academic values of researchers align with the research they conduct.

These are just some issues that are relevant for i-deals researchers to reflect upon in relation to the above discussion of the ideological underpinnings of i-deals research and practice. One of the key omitted debates in i-deals research concerns why academics engage in i-deals research, and what the contribution of i-deals can be in the workplace. As advocated by Bal (2017a), dignity manifests in the dialogue between individuals and through collective forms of dialogue (such as politics and labor unions). Human dignity concern the intrinsic worth of people, and in extension, workplace dignity concerns the intrinsic worth of all that is made part of workplaces, including animals, land, resources, and the planet itself. This intrinsic worth continues to be violated, when people are merely instrumental to organizational profit, and when animals, environmental resources, and the planet itself continue to be exploited within an economic model that is still dominant. The possibility of radical transformation toward a just society which protects dignity is far from evident. Nonetheless, integration of dignity into research, theory, and thinking around i-deals remains a necessity, as currently, i-deals research faces the predicament of meaninglessness, just as has happened with so many other topics of interest in WOP. It is to be hoped, therefore, that debate around the real meaning of i-deals in the workplace is continued, and that scholars become more aware of their professional responsibilities (see, e.g., Bal et al., 2019, for a manifesto of the responsibilities of WOP-academics).

References

Alvesson, M., & Spicer, A. (2016). (Un) conditional surrender? Why do professionals willingly comply with managerialism? *Journal of Organizational Change Management, 29*, 29–45.

Anand, S., Hu, J., Vidyarthi, P., & Liden, R. C. (2018). Leader-member exchange as a linking pin in the idiosyncratic deals-performance relationship in workgroups. *The Leadership Quarterly, 29*(6), 698–708.
Bal, P. M. (2017a). *Dignity in the workplace*. Palgrave MacMillan.
Bal, P. M. (2017b). Why do employees negotiate idiosyncratic deals? An exploration of the process of i-deal negotiation. *New Zealand Journal of Employment Relations, 42*, 2–18.
Bal, P. M., & Dóci, E. (2018). Neoliberal ideology in work and organizational psychology. *European Journal of Work and Organizational Psychology, 27*(5), 536–548.
Bal, P. M., Doci, E., Lub, X., Van Rossenberg, Y. G., Nijs, S., Achnak, S., Briner, R. B., Brookes, A., Chudzikowski, K., De Cooman, R., De Gieter, S., De Jong, J., De Jong, S. B., Dorenbosch, L., Galugahi, M. A. G., Hack-Polay, D., Hofmans, J., Hornung, S., Khuda, K., ... De Gieter, S. (2019). Manifesto for the future of work and organizational psychology. *European Journal of Work and Organizational Psychology, 28*(3), 289–299.
Bal, P. M., & Hornung, S. (2019). Individualization of work: From psychological contracts to ideological deals. In C. Cooper & Y. Griep (Eds.), *Handbook of research on the psychological contract at work*. Chapter 7. Edward Elgar.
Bal, P. M., & Lub, X. D. (2015). Individualization of work arrangements: A contextualized perspective on the rise and use of i-deals. In P. M. Bal & D. M. Rousseau (Eds.), *Idiosyncratic deals between employees and organizations: Conceptual issues, applications, and the role of coworkers* (pp. 9–23). Psychology Press.
Bal, P. M., Matthews, L., Doci, E., & McCarthy, L. (2020). An ideological analysis of sustainable careers: Identifying the role of fantasy and a way forward. *Paper under review*.
Bal, P. M., & Rousseau, D. M. (2015). *Idiosyncratic deals between employees and organizations: Conceptual issues, applications, and the role of coworkers*. Routledge.
Bal, P. M., & Vink, R. C. (2011). Ideological currency in psychological contracts: The role of team relationships in a reciprocity perspective. *The International Journal of Human Resource Management, 22*, 2794–2817.
Bal, P. M., & Vossaert, L. (2019). Development of an i-deals motivation and management measure. *Journal of Personnel Psychology, 18*, 201–215.
Barresi, J. (2012). On seeing our selves and others as persons. *New Ideas in Psychology, 30*(1), 120–130.
Blühdorn, I. (2017). Post-capitalism, post-growth, post-consumerism? Eco-political hopes beyond sustainability. *Global Discourse, 7*(1), 42–61.
Cabanas, E., & Illouz, E. (2019). *Manufacturing happy citizens: How the science and industry of happiness control our lives*. Wiley.

Dóci, E., & Bal, P. M. (2018). Ideology in work and organizational psychology: The responsibility of the researcher. *European Journal of Work and Organizational Psychology, 27*(5), 558–560.

Glynos, J. (2008). Ideological fantasy at work. *Journal of Political Ideologies, 13*(3), 275–296.

Greenberg, J., Roberge, M., Ho, V. T., & Rousseau, D. M. (2004). Fairness in idiosyncratic work arrangements: Justice as an i-deal. In J. J. Martocchio (Eds.), *Research in personnel and human resources management* (Vol. 23, pp. 1–34). Elsevier.

Greene, T. W. (2008). Three ideologies of individualism: Toward assimilating a theory of individualisms and their consequences. *Critical Sociology, 34*(1), 117–137.

Guest, D. E. (1998). Is the psychological contract worth taking seriously? *Journal of Organizational Behavior, 19*(S1), 649–664.

Harvey, D. (2005). *A brief history of neoliberalism*. Oxford University Press.

Hornung, S., & Höge, T. (2019). Humanizaton, rationalization or subjectification of work? Employee-oriented flexibility between i-deals and ideology in the neoliberal era. *Business & Management Studies: An International Journal, 7*(5), 3090–3119.

Hornung, S., Rousseau, D. M., Glaser, J., Angerer, P., & Weigl, M. (2010). Beyond top-down and bottom-up work redesign: Customizing job content through idiosyncratic deals. *Journal of Organizational Behavior, 31*(2–3), 187–215.

Kooij, D. T. (2015). Successful aging at work: The active role of employees. *Work, Aging and Retirement, 1*(4), 309–319.

Lai, L., Rousseau, D. M., & Chang, K. T. T. (2009). Idiosyncratic deals: Coworkers as interested third parties. *Journal of Applied Psychology, 94*(2), 547–556.

Liao, C., Wayne, S. J., & Rousseau, D. M. (2016). Idiosyncratic deals in contemporary organizations: A qualitative and meta-analytical review. *Journal of Organizational Behavior, 37*, S9–S29.

Lucas, K., Kang, D., & Li, Z. (2013). Workplace dignity in a total institution: Examining the experiences of Foxconn's migrant workforce. *Journal of Business Ethics, 114*(1), 91–106.

Marescaux, E., De Winne, S., & Sels, L. (2019). Idiosyncratic deals from a distributive justice perspective: Examining co-workers' voice behavior. *Journal of Business Ethics, 154*(1), 263–281.

Ng, T. W. (2017). Can idiosyncratic deals promote perceptions of competitive climate, felt ostracism, and turnover? *Journal of Vocational Behavior, 99*, 118–131.

Norris, P., & Inglehart, R. (2019). *Cultural backlash: Trump, Brexit, and authoritarian populism*. Cambridge University Press.

Rofcanin, Y., Berber, A., Koch, S., & Sevinc, L. (2016). Job crafting and i-deals: A study testing the nomological network of proactive behaviors. *The International Journal of Human Resource Management, 27*(22), 2695–2726.

Rosen, C. C., Slater, D. J., Chang, C. H., & Johnson, R. E. (2013). Let's make a deal: Development and validation of the ex post i-deals scale. *Journal of Management, 39*(3), 709–742.

Rosen, M. (2012). *Dignity: Its history and meaning.* Harvard University Press.

Rousseau, D. M. (2001). The idiosyncratic deal: Flexibility versus fairness? *Organizational Dynamics, 29*(4), 260–273.

Rousseau, D. M. (2005). *I-deals: Idiosyncratic deals employees bargain for themselves.* M. E. Sharpe.

Rousseau, D. M., Ho, V. T., & Greenberg, J. (2006). I-deals: Idiosyncratic terms in employment relationships. *Academy of Management Review, 31,* 977–994.

Rudolph, C. W., Katz, I. M., Lavigne, K. N., & Zacher, H. (2017). Job crafting: A meta-analysis of relationships with individual differences, job characteristics, and work outcomes. *Journal of Vocational Behavior, 102,* 112–138.

Santos, H. C., Varnum, M. E., & Grossmann, I. (2017). Global increases in individualism. *Psychological Science, 28*(9), 1228–1239.

Sennett, R. (2008). *The craftsman.* Yale University Press.

Su, J. (2015). Reality behind absurdity: The myth of American dream. *Sociology, 5*(11), 837–842.

Taskin, L., & Devos, V. (2005). Paradoxes from the individualization of human resource management: The case of telework. *Journal of Business Ethics, 62*(1), 13–24.

Tims, M., & Bakker, A. B. (2010). Job crafting: Towards a new model of individual job redesign. *SA Journal of Industrial Psychology, 36*(2), 1–9.

Van der Meij, K., & Bal, P. M. (2013). De ideale 'idiosyncratic-deal.' *Gedrag En Organisatie, 26*(2), 156–181.

Yurchak, A. (2003). Soviet hegemony of form: Everything was forever, until it was no more. *Comparative Studies in Society and History, 45*(3), 480–510.

Yurchak, A. (2005). *Everything was forever, until it was no More: The last Soviet generation.* Princeton University Press.

Zhao, H. A. O., Wayne, S. J., Glibkowski, B. C., & Bravo, J. (2007). The impact of psychological contract breach on work-related outcomes: A meta-analysis. *Personnel Psychology, 60*(3), 647–680.

Žižek, S. (1989). *The sublime object of ideology.* Verso.

Žižek, S. (2018). *Like a thief in broad daylight: Power in the era of post-humanity.* Penguin.

CHAPTER 9

The Dark Side of Individualization at Work: Idiosyncratic Deal Exploitation and the Creation of Elite Workers

Farooq Mughal, Siqi Wang, and Aneesa Zafar

The reality is plain and simple, as put by Nancy Fraser: whether we call it the hostile takeover of post-industrialization, neoliberalization or capitalization of our society, a new regime oriented to 'deregulation' and 'flexibilization' has emerged. As the Fordist model collapses and industries gear towards knowledge-based economies, a new form of political rationality underpins the restructuring of modern society: an avant-garde order which regulates affairs of everyday life to create alternate forms

F. Mughal (✉) · S. Wang
School of Management, University of Bath, Bath, UK
e-mail: f.mughal@bath.ac.uk

S. Wang
e-mail: sw783@bath.ac.uk

A. Zafar
Lancaster University Management School, Lancaster University, Lancaster, UK
e-mail: a.zafar2@lancaster.ac.uk

© The Author(s), under exclusive license to Springer Nature Switzerland AG 2022
S. Anand and Y. Rofcanin (eds.), *Idiosyncratic Deals at Work*,
https://doi.org/10.1007/978-3-030-88516-8_9

of governed reality (Jessop, 1995). This ordering, in principle, is driven by an economic-political rationale whose foundations are firmly rooted within the philosophy that privileges the individual over the collective (Harvey, 2005; Oyserman et al., 2002). Often labelled under neoliberalism, this ideology is prevalent in forcing a departure from the Fordist welfare state towards a desocialized competitive climate where individuals are given an illusion of autonomy to make rational (strategic) choices to maximize their benefits (Fraser, 2003; Sedlacek, 2011). Although the Fordist model was not unproblematic, creating political, social and economic fragmentation and giving rise to utilitarian forms of capitalism, it's guilty of dehumanizing workers and laying foundation to discourses of productivity and efficiency (Winsor, 1992). Alas, even in the post-Fordist era, the individual remains *subjected* to classifications based on their social, cultural, political and economic capital and *situated* within relations of power (Bowring, 2002; Hetrick & Boje, 1992).

Today, under the guise of neoliberalism, the rationalization of humanistic discourses of well-being, freedom and economic maximization constitute the basis of many beliefs that drive work and organizational behaviour (Bal & Dóci, 2018). For example, in the backdrop of a neoliberal landscape, where rising competition, labour market dynamism and changing individual attitudes underscore the reality of organizational life and society in general, individualized work arrangements are becoming a norm in the workplace (Rofcanin et al., 2017). The prevalence of neoliberal logics structuring everyday life has, in fact, put into motion the individualization of society where emphasis is on the individual to become self-reliant and responsible for their 'material and immaterial success' (Bal & Lub, 2015: 154). Those who take responsibility for themselves, as neoliberal agents *par excellence*, are likely to negotiate better work arrangements (e.g. Liao et al., 2016; Tyler, 2015). Akin to Nietzsche's 'will to power', this ideology draws parallels with the neo-Darwinian view of social struggle and survival of humanity (Newton, 1998: 438). The translation of these ideas into the work and organizational sphere, to a great extent, are neatly captured by Denise Rousseau in her seminal work on idiosyncratic deals or i-deals (Rousseau, 2001). She posits that i-deals are 'voluntary, personalized agreements of a non-standard nature negotiated between individual employees and their employers' (Rousseau, 2005: 23). They have emerged in response to the individualization of society and the transition of HRM towards individualized practices that benefit both the organization and the individual (Rousseau et al., 2009).

An overview of the literature on i-deals suggests a considerable theoretical expansion covering an array of issues from bargaining (Rousseau, 2005), leadership (Anand et al., 2018), careers (Brzykcy et al., 2019), commitment (Hornung et al., 2008) to citizenship behaviours (Anand et al., 2010), job satisfaction (Rosen et al., 2013), work-family interface (Las Heras et al., 2017) and so on. The reason for popularity could be attributed to the decline of collective bargaining (Farber & Western, 2001), prevalence of neoliberalism (Bal & Dóci, 2018), rise of the knowledge worker (Cullinane & Dundon, 2006) and a booming gig economy (Kuhn, 2016) among others. Recognizing the popularity of i-deals in the workplace (Bal & Lub, 2015) and its exponential growth in literature over the past decade and a half, this chapter aims to conduct a critical examination of the assumptions underpinning the notion of idiosyncratic deals in the workplace. In doing so, we employ the works of the French philosopher, Michel Foucault, to explore the implications of promoting individuality at work. By positioning individualized work arrangements as modes of neoliberal governmentality and a consequence of individualization of society, our chapter should be read as a critique of i-deals which produce discourses that portray the individual as agile and less recalcitrant (Fleming & Spicer, 2003). Our problematization of i-deals hinges on the idea that individualized arrangements at work create precarity, inequality, competition and alienation among workers. Therefore, this involves looking more closely at the operationality of i-deals, their underlying mechanisms and role in subjecting individuals to labour processes that (re)produce individuality, power-relations and dominance (Knights, 1990).

DIVIDE AND RULE: INDIVIDUATION AND INDIVIDUALIZATION AT WORK

Rising during the early 1900s and intensifying after World War II, most Western and socialist states witnessed austerity measures (Korpi & Palme, 2003). This resulted in deregulating state-run services such as education, healthcare, unemployment benefits, social housing and retirement schemes under the shadow of neoliberalism (Peck, 2010). Neoliberalism posits that resources should be distributed by the 'invisible hand' of the market instead of the state (Bal & Lub, 2015: 154). Scholars argue that neoliberalism is a pervasive ideology that permeates government policies and tickles down to shape our everyday practices and common-sensical understandings of reality (Harvey, 2005). Arguably, it influences our idiosyncrasies, tendencies and dispositions that constitute the very principle of our need to survive and thrive (Knights & Willmott, 1990). An underlying motive of neoliberalism is the explicit attempt to reduce the power of the collective, e.g. trade unions (Bal & Dóci, 2018: 538) and intensify the precarization of work (Herod & Lambert, 2016). This is problematic, insofar, that the individual as a rational agent is considered as responsible for acting strategically in a way to maximize their success as an interested party (Sedlacek, 2011). From this perspective, the labour-market decides the fate of individuals but those who possess more capital (e.g. human capital) are more likely to be successful.

What drives this market logic, as noted by Costea et al. (2012: 26), is the idea of 'potentiality': a philosophy that human subjects can become more than what they aspire, implying an elusive sense of self-entrepreneurism. They further note the affirmation of this entrepreneurial image is created through the bi-focal principles of potentiality, that is, (i) 'self as possessing the potential to be both innovative, creative; and (ii) self-expressive, as well as capable of calculative execution, maintenance and refinement of organisational routines' (ibid. p. 54). We argue that the interpenetration of these ideas in the workplace have destabilized traditional HRM practices and the standardization of employment contracts (Rousseau et al., 2006). Although free will of the individual agent appears to be a fallacy of neoliberalism, humans may have fallen victim to their own discourses of work, employment and society (Houghton, 2019). For instance, Bal and Lub (2015: 151) note a tendency among organizations in the uptake of individualized work arrangements due to the positive effects of i-deals and the societal preference for individualization.

To better understand how neoliberalism serves to individualize work and exert control over the labour processes, we turn our attention to the notion of individuation. While avoiding pitting the 'society against the individual' or the 'individual against the organization', we consider individualization as 'the process of progressive dissolution of traditional social milieus, which turn individuals back on themselves and provide them with more or less "risky" and "precarious freedoms"' (Weiskopf & Loacker, 2006: 396). The positioning of individualized work arrangements, such as, i-deals and flexi, temporary, part-time or reduced work, in relation to progressive dissolution renders the individual rational in choosing the best strategy for employment. For example, employees may choose to strike a deal with the employer prior to joining the organization (as *ex ante* i-deal) or after initiating employment (*ex post* i-deal) but the award of such deals is based on individuation (Rousseau et al., 2006). Individuation then becomes the criteria for differential awarding of i-deals, which is often based on employee characteristics which potentially differentiate individuals from others such as: good political skills, proactive personality or high emotional intelligence etc. (Hornung et al., 2008).

Aligning our intentions with those of the critics, we are, however, sceptical of these claims as individualization enhances precariousness of work, competition, job insecurity and inequality among workers (Burchell, 2009). In the earlier parts of this chapter, we reiterate the transition of human society from a regulated to somewhat deregulated state of being under neoliberalism. Taking a closer look at this transformation by drawing on the works of Michel Foucault (1977), we see this as the movement from a disciplinary to somewhat post-disciplinary society. Individualization in a disciplinary society is 'ascending' in nature where the power lies with those at the top of the social hierarchy, such as monarchies, with modified versions seen in Fredrick W. Taylor or Henry Ford's factory setup (see Weiskopf & Loacker, 2006: 399). In contrast, individualization in a post-disciplinary society is 'descending', which means 'power becomes more anonymous and more functional those on whom it is exercised tend to be more strongly individualized' (Foucault, 1977: 193).

Foucault (1977) identified three methods by which individuals can be distributed in a given (work/social)-space to retain control. This involves putting individuals in enclosures (creation of closed spaces like in the case of Ford company); partitioning (allocation of spaces to individuals to divide them); and finally ranking (hierarchical ordering of individuals based on ability/capital). The outcome of this process of dividing individuals is what Townley (1993) terms as individualization and individuation. She states that:

> The [individualization] effect denotes the process of making the individual more identifiable vis-a-vis other individuals or workers, that is, the process of identifying or differentiating individuals. The [individuation] effect refers to dividing practices that are internal to the individual, that is, those processes that attempt to identify components of individuality. (Townley, 1993: 535)

This is evident in how i-deals are awarded, that is, through the process of individuation—i.e. ranking individual qualities. Critically speaking, literature on i-deals suggests that a deal is brokered on the condition that it benefits both the organization and the focal employee (Bal & Lub, 2015). If it doesn't benefit the organization, it counts as favouritism or cronyism (Rousseau, 2005). By the very nature of engaging in an exchange relationship where individuals sell their knowledge, skills and abilities to benefit the organization in return for an individualized work arrangement, objectifies the individual. I-deals are, therefore, reductive in nature, having the tendency to reduce the individual to the closest net value, allowing the market to appropriate their economic commodification. Harvey (2005) terms this type of commodification as a consequence of neoliberalism. 'This entails the notion that every aspect of human life should be exchangeable on the market, as the market operates as an "ethic" in itself' (Bal & Dóci, 2018: 538). In conclusion, to this section, we posit that individualization at work is primed in ways which create competition and reduce the individual to the level of an object who is instrumental to profitability.

Locating the Subject: Individualism and Subjectivity

A key characteristic of the contemporary, neoliberal, society is deregulation and flexibilization in which adaptability rather than rigidity is the key to exerting control over individuals (Fraser, 2003). In this day and age, as put by Weiskopf and Loacker (2006), the 'loose coupling' of ideas (also see Weick, 1976) are not constraints but opportunities to 'thrive on chaos' (see Peters & Peters, 1987) and 'ride the waves of change' (see Morgan, 2013). This thinking marks a departure from the earlier labour process theory, a late Marxist philosophy, which rests upon the 'premise that capital constructs systems of control in order to secure the structurally necessary extraction of surplus value from labour' (O'Doherty & Willmott, 2001: 459). As Taylorism and Fordism dissipated and Braverman's thesis surfaced, labour process theory was critiqued under the premise that individuals are social creatures. The rigidity of the factory model and forcing individuals into enclosed spaces were no longer sustainable (Townley, 1998). Despite Braverman's labour analysis, it, however, marginalized and overlooked the role of individuals in reproducing relations of labour and capital or power (Storey, 1985).

Knights and Collinson (1987: 461) suggest that, in the post-Braverman era, the labour process literature mostly focused on different management strategies in the organization and control of labour. For example, they argue that during periods of economic recession and high unemployment in the labour market, individuals were subjected to 'responsible autonomy' which involved voluntary cooperation in the workplace without forgoing control. These late developments under (neo-)liberalism are indicative of a coordinated move away from HRM towards market mechanisms as the organizing principle in which individuals are responsible for adhering to the market logics. This new mode of (self-)regulation is elusive of individuals as agents of free will (Pereboom, 2006).

Before proceeding any further and discussing how i-deals as modes of neoliberal governmentality shape individual behaviour in the next section, it is important to delineate the theoretical underpinnings that provide impetus to the scholarship on work and organizational psychology (WOP). Individualism, as noted by Schatzki (2005: 466), has been a 'dominant ontological approach' in social sciences given its ability to quantify the individual through predicting or forecasting using 'mathematical model-building'. Individualists hold the view that 'social phenomena can be both decomposed into and explained by properties of individual people' (ibid.). Drawing parallels with the positivist paradigm of research, methodological individualism has penetrated scholarship on WOP as also noted by Bal and Dóci (2018). This approach has the tendency to depoliticize research, reinforce sociological positivism and legitimize the 'economic status quo' (Swanson, 2008: 56). Most WOP research struggles under this reductionist discourse and remains grounded in the belief that rational choice theory is the cornerstone of social sciences (Stein, 2017). Scott (2000) argues that rational choice theory maintains that individuals ought to anticipate the outcomes of an alternate course of action and calculate the best one for them. The outcome of actions is determined in terms of economic output and maximization of benefits using the principle of social exchange (Heath & Heath, 1976). Manifestation of individualism in scholarship on i-deals is not only prompted by societal transformations as discussed earlier but also due to the greater need for understanding the benefits of 'economic and social exchanges' in the workplace (Rofcanin et al., 2018).

For the sake of our argument, and assuming rational choice theory as ontological basis, the epistemic underpinnings for the production of knowledge on i-deals have been greatly influenced by social exchange theory (Anand et al., 2010; see also Blau, 1964). Although Rousseau did not explicitly draw on social exchange theory in her seminal works, this theoretical perspective has been predominantly used in WOP research from understanding employer-employee or leader-member relationships to explaining HRM practices and psychological contracts (e.g. Anand et al., 2011; Zhao et al., 2007 etc.). The central tenet of social exchange theory is the norm of reciprocity (Ng & Feldman, 2015). Reciprocity, in the context of i-deals, implies that the employee receiving individualized treatment by the employer will reciprocate in terms of benefits to the organization as part of their employment relationship (Anand et al., 2010). This relationship infers social (trust, loyalty, willingness) and economic (salary, bonus) exchange to take place for those who are deemed capable, entitled and valuable to the organization (Lai et al., 2009). What remains problematic in this relationship is the commodification of the individual and reduction to the value of its individual properties. As in the case of labour process theory (see Knights & Willmott, 1989), i-deals fail to recognize individual subjectivity and 'look beyond the political economy of capitalism to some existential self' (Thompson & Smith, 2000: 52).

In his book *Manufacturing Consent*, Michael Burawoy (1982) emphasized the significance of subjectivity in understanding the dynamics of capitalist institutions. Through his ethnographic study on shop-floor workers, Burawoy demonstrated the limits of labour relations theory in explaining the conditions which produce consent to work. He posits that workers are not empty vessels as purported by individualistic discourses but a product of both their existential and social needs. While criticizing Braverman for abandoning subjectivity in his thesis as limiting the objectivity to study work arrangements, Burawoy (1990: 35) positioned the individual (worker) as a product of social relations through what he referred to as 'political and ideological processes'. O'Doherty and Willmott (2001: 461) argue that Burawoy opens the problem of the 'missing subject' before falling short of exploring the struggles between labour and capital that shape subjectivity. Locating the subject (or subjectivity) in the workplace then opens up the historical, cultural and political dimensions that rational choice theory casts aside in favour of exchange and economic benefits. Subjectivity, as McCabe (2007: 245) states, 'is the culmination of various power relations and the reciprocal interpretations, reflexivity and actions of an individual at any given moment'. It is through the subjective 'self' that we understand ourselves and the world around us (Luckman & Berger, 1964). The notion of subjectivity is antithetical to individualism as it implies plurality and reflects the situated and constrained position of individuals within relations of power (e.g. gender, class, ethnicity etc.) (e.g. Reynaud, 1983).

As we proceed to the next section where we conduct a critical analysis to understand the contested nature of individuality in i-deals, our focus on subjectivity acts as a launching pad to illuminate neoliberal logics that regulate individual agency: that is, (mis)perceptions of autonomy, freedom and hope. Our attention has particularly been directed towards individual subjectivities that are 'manipulated through invoking a desire [by market mechanisms] to change one's self and to become something that one was not before' (Skinner, 2013: 906). Neoliberalism as a disciplinarian (governmental) apparatus, in Foucauldian terms, is thus capable of producing dispositions, tendencies or idiosyncrasies that are inclined towards individualization of society (Raffnsøe et al., 2016).To this end, we raise the question on whether subjectivity is the medium through which individuals fall victim to their idiosyncrasies. As in the words of O'Doherty and Willmott, we conclude this section by underlining this:

> ... question of subjectivity, the conceptual inheritance of 'system', 'structure', and 'objectivity', [which] can be de-reified in a way that enables us to better understand the enigmatic 'space' where capitalism both finds its source *and* gets reproduced and maintained. (O'Doherty & Willmott, 2001: 461)

IDIOSYNCRATIC EXPLOITATION: I-DEALS AS TECHNOLOGIES OF POWER AND THE SELF

Aligning the notion of i-deals, as mechanisms of individuation and individualization among workers, and with the help of literature on Foucauldian studies, we argue that the neoliberal gaze 'penetrates right to the very core of each [individual's] subjectivity' (Sewell & Wilkinson, 1992: 284). Reverting back, momentarily, to our earlier point about subjectivity as the medium of consuming dispositions produced by neoliberal (market) logics, we concur with Willmott (1993: 516–536, *emphasis added*) in asserting that organizations aim to 'win the *hearts* and *minds* of employees' not only to manage subjectivities but also to regulate their behaviour through what might be seen as a 'process of subjugation'. New discourses and dispositions are consumed and assimilated in everyday work routines to create new work regimes reflective of the wider societal order/market (du Gay, 1996). Although this line of thinking is missing from the WOP scholarship, we stress the need to identify mechanisms that predispose individual tendencies, dispositions and propensities towards individualized work arrangements and idiosyncratic deals. Denise Rousseau, in her book *I-Deals: Idiosyncratic Deals Employees Bargain for Themselves*, offers some insights to that effect. She writes:

> Idiosyncrasy in employment is found wherever individual workers change their job titles, draft their own job descriptions, revise the ones they started with, or otherwise customize their duties, work hours, and other conditions of work. Employees modify old roles and break in new ones to reflect their personal values, interests, and capabilities. (Rousseau, 2005: 22)

In this excerpt, Rousseau considers organizational-bound idiosyncrasies as reflective of individuals' everyday work (e.g. roles, tasks, etc.) and non-work (personal values, interests, etc.) lives. While positioned synonymously with 'eccentricity', Rousseau considers i-deals to signify 'one's particular bent or temperament and connotes strong individuality and independence of action' (ibid. p. 23). Idiosyncrasies arise as a result of what she calls 'incompleteness' which acts as a source of idiosyncrasy in employment (p. 23). Rousseau describes 'incompleteness' as something that organizations normally resolve unilaterally by providing resources or support to fulfil individuals needs and desires. However, those who are competitively (or extra-hierarchically) positioned have greater influence in overcoming this incompleteness at work. Researchers suggest that some individuals are likely to exert power by way of their social (e.g. relationship with supervisor/leader), human (knowledge, skills or experience) or gendered capital among others to achieve what they desire in the workplace (e.g. Ballout, 2007; Melamed, 1995; Seibert et al., 2001). Additionally, Rousseau (2005: 25) further comments that some employment contracts are deliberately kept incomplete out of the 'desire to protect [individual] freedom of action' and preserving work 'autonomy'. She further distinguishes employment from slavery labelling it as a 'voluntary agreement' (ibid. p. 25). As noted earlier, this view is closely aligned with neoclassicism, which we consider problematic as it overlooks the constrained position of the individual in a network of power relations (see also, Roemer, 1978).

This raises questions about freedom and autonomy for both, those who are in receipt of an i-deal (i.e. the focal employee) and the ones who aspire to acquire one (i.e. co-workers). In view of Beck and Beck-Gernsheim (2009: 13–25), such naive representations of autonomy are 'risky' and lead to 'precarious freedom'. Knights and Willmott (1989: 536) argue that the notion of freedom is often misunderstood as 'freedom from' rather than 'freedom to', rendering the illusion of flexibility to work. Moreover, Bal and Dóci (2018: 540) categorize this as 'freedom fantasy' which is also an underlying condition of neoliberalism: 'the importance of people's freedom to choose, and their ability to make decisions for themselves'. They argue that this thought of freedom is ensured by the free market and 'the liberation of the individual as entrepreneurs' (ibid. p. 540). However, this freedom is constrained by meritocracy and neo-Darwinian processes (Bal & Lub, 2015; Fraser, 2003; Newton, 1998). We argue that this sense of competitiveness underpins the notion of *incompleteness* as mentioned by Rousseau (2005). This enigmatic void deliberately left or created within employment relationships (by the market, employers or employees) is emblematic of a 'strategic' zone (space) in which individuals occupy an 'ambivalent position' (Weiskopf & Loacker, 2006: 403). We also argue that those suspended within these spaces are expected to find their own way out of ambivalence, and as a result intensify work in terms of becoming enterprising, innovative, creative, competitive and strategic in their actions (e.g. Neirotti, 2020).

In this sense, individualized work arrangements or i-deals are more likely to be awarded to those who demonstrate the need to fill the void, thus creating division among workers, rendering some workers visible (successful) and others invisible (unsuccessful) after evaluation (e.g. Foucault, 1973). Here, i-deals can be seen as a central tenet of individualization or acting as an individualizing technology. The subtle effect (gaze) of neoliberalism can be seen in operation as individuals are subjected to competitive processes which conform to logics of the labour market (Lemke, 2002). Aligning with Foucault, we are sceptical of positioning individuals as 'passive victims of power' or neoliberalization (Knights & Morgan, 1991: 269). We concur with Skinner (2013: 907) who considers individuals as 'less docile in the process of subject formation'. As also noted by Knights and McCabe (2000: 424), subjectivity is 'not something that is done to individuals; they participate in the constitution of their own subjectivity as they reflect on and reproduce the social world'. Employers involved in the process of granting i-deals to employees create conditions to regulate individual behaviour through new forms of work regimes in which certain practices act as technologies of power and lead to self-governance (Gane, 2012). According to Foucault (1988: 18), technologies of power 'determine the conduct of individuals and submit them to certain ends or domination'. Individuals are drawn towards 'mechanisms of power' (Foucault, 1978: 97), such as striving for ideal (individualized) employment contracts. In so doing, the individual becomes 'the principle of his own subjection' (Foucault, 1977: 203) as they compete and work on themselves to become successful and acquire i-deals - thus becoming a project of neoliberal capitalism.

In concluding this section, we would like to demonstrate how i-deals act as technologies of power to transform the self and lead towards idiosyncratic exploitation. To do so, we revisit Rousseau's (2005: 27) example of the hospital custodian:

> A custodian mopping hospital floors may personally define her housekeeping duties to include patient care and service, by offering support to a patient's bereaved family or by sensitively cleaning up after a patent has an embarrassing accident with the family present. (Rousseau, 2005: 27)

This example is reflective of Foucault's subject which is 'neither a passive being nor a dupe but, instead, someone "capable of knowing, analysing and ultimately altering reality"' (Foucault cited in Skinner, 2013: 918). For Foucault (2007), technologies of power dovetail with tecnologies of the self as individuals actively regulate (or exploit) themselves in their quest for achieving labour market success (e.g. enhancing their human or social capital etc.). He further argues that individuals:

> ... by their own means or with the help of others [perform] a certain number of operations on their own bodies and souls, thoughts, conduct, and way of being, so as to transform themselves in order to attain a certain state of happiness, purity, wisdom, perfection, or immortality. (Foucault, 1988: 18)

As evident from the excerpts above, technologies (like i-deals) enable and revolve around the 'principle of care of self' (e.g., Skinner, 2013: 908), that is, performed on one's self 'to attempt to transform oneself' (Foucault, 1984: 27). Each aspect of one's identity (e.g. as a custodian, housekeeping, carer, etc.) involves a certain level of 'self-crafting' (Weiskopf & Loacker, 2006: 408) which roughly translates into Rousseau's (2005: 27) understanding of informal 'job customization' or 'crafting'. The identity construction (or crafting) illustrates the ways individuals often resist/accept codified authority and power in organizations to present themselves as someone they are not (Deleuze, 1995). This moulding of the subject via technologies objectifies individuals in relation to dominant discourses (e.g. neoliberal ideology) or practices (of individuation), in pursuit of gratification. As a final point, it must be acknowledged that technologies operate through modes of governing at the macro-level (e.g. organizational culture; labour market mechanisms) and micro-level (mind; body) that provide a platform to the individual subject to actively (re)produce dominant discourses (see Fleming & Spicer, 2003).

Creation of Elite Workers: An (Un)Intended Consequence of I-deals

Literature on i-deals suggests that individualized or flexible work provisions often culminate in the form of 'uniquely negotiated arrangements between employees (i-dealers) and their supervisor' (Marescaux et al., 2021: 329). As Rousseau (2005) states, and considering the tenets of social exchange theory discussed previously, these arrangements are often designed in a way which benefits both the employee and the employer. Although i-deals are used to attract, retain and motivate employees (e.g. Liao et al., 2016), there are studies which also highlight the negative aspects of individualized work arrangements (Kong et al., 2020; Marescaux et al., 2019). I-deals have the tendency to 'single out' employees in the workplace, particularly those with better work deals (Marescaux et al., 2021: 330). I-deals are usually awarded to talented, competent and valued employees (*ex ante* or *ex post*) who possess certain forms of capital which act as resources for negotiating a deal (Rousseau et al., 2006). These can include, but not limited to, social capital (e.g. reputation) or human capital (e.g. knowledge and skills) etc. (see Ho & Tekleab, 2016). Rousseau et al. (2006) state that the power of bargaining is dependent on the labour market dynamics which dictate the value of capital possessed by an individual and the successful negotiation of a deal. Those who possess relevant forms of capital are more likely to succeed as compared to those who don't. In Bal and Lub's (2015: 154) view, this can be seen as an outcome of neoliberalization which differentiates between the 'winners and losers' in this competitive landscape. Some scholars argue that the incorporation of neoliberal logics through work and organizational cultures, particularly those that promote winners and losers, is grounded in the ideology of elitism (Evetts et al., 2006; see also Alvesson & Willmott, 2002).

Although i-deals are not (intentionally) designed to produce elite workers, the existence of i-deals, however, creates an environment to allow employees who have i-deals to feel privileged than the co-workers (or the co-workers may view them in a privileged position). As discussed above, employees' possession of capital is the prime reason for granting i-deals (Liao et al., 2016), and also, due to these characteristics, i-deals may unintendedly breed the perception of unfairness among employees which can contribute to the production of elite workers. Kulik and Ambrose (1992) argue that employees are likely to compare themselves with their colleagues in situations when they are in receipt of less/more desirable work benefits. According to social comparison theory, individuals compare and contrast themselves with others through a process of self-situational evaluation, mainly to make sense and reduce uncertainty (Brown et al., 2007). Like social exchange, the comparison theory also draws on economic benefits as the object of evaluation (Lockwood & Kunda, 1997). The defining features of social comparison theory include the availability of information and referent of comparison which determines the desirability of benefits (depending on their personal needs/wants). Self-evaluation is conducted through a cognitive appraisal of the situation which can trigger emotional responses such as frustration, anger, anxiety or guilt depending on the favourability of the i-deal granted to the i-dealer (Vidyarthi et al., 2016).

The elicitation of negative emotions or reactions from co-workers raises important questions in relation to the process of granting i-deals. As mentioned earlier, employers consider employees' characteristics (e.g. knowledge, skills or experience, etc.) as the reason to grant them i-deals. From a Foucauldian perspective, this idea of awarding or granting i-deals to facilitate star performers can result in 'othering': a process in which individuals are differentiated and distinctively positioned to others (Brewis, 2005; Johnson et al., 2004). Othering, according to Schwalbe et al. (2000), reproduces inequality and marginalizes those who are unable to secure a powerful position. This distinction can take the form of oppressive othering (elites dominate others), powerful othering (elites induce fear) and defensive othering (identity work performed by those seeking to become elites) (ibid.). Here, the role of supervisors or leaders as 'shadow elites', those who ensure the status quo remains intact, is also critical and requires further research (e.g. Reed, 2018: 303).

According to Rousseau et al. (2006), the apparent challenge of awarding i-deals is ensuring group fairness. Although i-deals are different from other preferential arrangements such as favouritism and cronyism, there exists a grey area between i-deals and favouritism (Rousseau et al., 2006). I-deals are designed to benefit both employees and employers (ibid.) but the expected ideal win–win situation cannot be guaranteed because of the bounded rationality of the grantor and grantee of i-deals. As an important part of i-deals, leaders decide the success of i-deals. Existing research finds that the relationship between leader and member (e.g. LMX) is positively related to the success of i-deals (Rosen et al., 2013). That means, employees who have a good relationship with their supervisor are more likely to obtain i-deals than others. Based on social exchange theory, leaders provide i-deals to certain workers who they believe can return the favour and benefit the organization in the long-term. Nonetheless, leaders can overestimate one's potential contributions and likewise underestimate other employees' potentiality, which could hamper perceptions of justice and fairness.

Resorting to Foucault's (1977) work, we find elitism as an inadvertent consequence of granting i-deals. Our attempts to delineate the negative effects of i-deals are not directed towards showing the inadequacy of individualized work arrangements for organizational success. Instead, we aim to problematize the notion of i-deals as a precursor of neoliberal rationalization of individualized work for purely economic benefits. From a Foucauldian perspective, elitism in this context has resulted in 'the constitution of a delinquent milieu' (e.g. Foucault, 1980: 195): that is, the entrapment of the individual (or the delinquent, in Foucauldian terms) within the individualization discourse to conceal the neoliberal, capitalist, reality of the labour market. Therefore, we conceptualize, i-deals to operate as a governmental mechanism of 'filtering, concentrating, professionalizing and circumscribing' an elitist culture that preserves the interest of the dominant class controlling the labour market (e.g. Foucault, 1980: 196).

Looking Ahead: The Future of I-deals

At the risk of sounding uncritical, our chapter highlights several implications for scholars and practitioners willing to employ i-deals as part of their work and organizational agendas. Our critique of i-deals as a source of idiosyncratic exploitation and creation of elite workers is indicative of the pervasiveness of neoliberalism which in turn favours the individualization of organizations and society. As we conclude this chapter, we highlight four key areas of concerns and encourage scholars/practitioners to think about these as shaping the future of i-deals:

First, there is a need to study the underlying structural mechanisms and work cultures which sustain and legitimize neoliberal work regimes. Overlooking the ways in which work is becoming precarious or intensified renders i-deals as conduits of neoliberal capitalism. This means scholars and practitioners need to focus on the subjective side of individualized work arrangements and identify the ways in which individual worker identities are shaped and moulded to conform to organizational interests. If the factory model was designed to shape human bodies, then individualized work arrangements (e.g. i-deals) are designed to shape human minds so that they are regulated by organizations in their own ways. The constant pressure of adaptability, having to renew the self to stay competitive is alarming as individuals become prisoners of their own self through the operation of (bio)-political technologies like i-deals.

Second, under different cultural contexts, i-deals will bring unwanted emotions and instability. As aforementioned, employees who are in possession of certain forms of capital (e.g. social capital) are more likely to obtain better deals than co-workers who don't. For instance, a good relationship between subordinate and the supervisor can result in valued social capital which in turn puts the individual in a better power position than others. However, to a certain extent, 'good relationships' with the right people could be seen as a factor for bias in the workplace— for example, the *guanxi* concept in the Chinese culture. Similar to LMX in the West, *guanxi* refers to the relationship quality between supervisors and subordinates mainly outside the work domain (Wei et al., 2010). In China, such supervisor-subordinate relationships can influence supervisor's decisions related to subordinates' tasks and promotion (Cheng et al., 2002). In terms of i-deals, subordinates who have a better *guanxi* with the supervisor are more likely to obtain i-deals. *Guanxi* has been criticized from a justice perspective since it discriminates against other employees who are outside the *guanxi* network and negatively related to perceived fairness (Chen et al., 2011; Dunfee & Warren, 2001). As the outside party, when co-workers perceive the allocation of i-deals as favourable outcomes of good *guanxi* with supervisors, they are more likely to express negative emotions (e.g. envy) which may hamper the effectiveness of i-deals (Marescaux et al., 2019). This goes to show that i-deals are not universally consistent across different cultural contexts, thus bringing to fore the implications of neoliberal globalization.

Third, individualized work arrangements like i-deals can intensify work and create precariousness among workers. The intensification of work can arise out of the fading work boundaries which the standardized employment offers (Bal & Lub, 2015; Weiskopf & Loacker, 2006). As individuals strike a deal, this could possibly set work schedules which suit them, thus leading them to work at odd-times and in different places (Las Heras et al., 2017). From a critical perspective, this can be seen as a form of work regulation where organizations retain control by altering the subjective preferences of individuals. Alvesson and Willmott (2002) view this as subjective regulation in which certain regimes of work are legitimized and promoted among workers. We consider this as the (bio)-colonization of worker minds and bodies. Fourth, the award of i-deals could stir up issues such as competition, fairness, transparency and injustice. This unequal distribution of resources among individuals is a hallmark of neoliberalism as it creates individualization at work. Employers can, however, try striking an ideal i-deal by reserving group-based resources to allow teams to self-select how work arrangements need to be organized among team members. These *responsible, shared* or *ethical i-deals* can allow the lateral flow of resources, unlike the vertical allocation as noted in the literature. This will enable equality and a consolidated effort by the group in responsibly using the flexibility provided by group-level i-deals, thus enhancing performance and satisfaction among members.

To conclude, this chapter has critically analysed the taken-for-granted assumptions underpinning the use of individualized work arrangements, i-deals, in the workplace. In so doing, it highlights the contested, subjected and situated nature of individuals performing work within neoliberally sanctioned power-relations and hierarchies, which regulate and intensify work. We believe the four areas, as future of i-deals/idiosyncratic research, are extremely critical and timely to address by scholars as we look to expand this literature.

References

Alvesson, M., & Robertson, M. (2006). The best and the brightest: The construction, significance and effects of elite identities in consulting firms. *Organization, 13*(2), 195–224.

Alvesson, M., & Willmott, H. (2002). Identity regulation as organizational control: Producing the appropriate individual. *Journal of Management Studies, 39*(5), 619–644.

Anand, S., Hu, J., Liden, R. C., & Vidyarthi, P. R. (2011). Leader-member exchange: Recent research findings and prospects for the future. In A. Bryman, D. Collinson, K. Grint, B. Jackson, & M. Uhl-Bien (Eds.), *The Sage handbook of leadership* (pp. 311–325). Sage.

Anand, S., Hu, J., Vidyarthi, P., & Liden, R. C. (2018). Leader-member exchange as a linking pin in the idiosyncratic deals-Performance relationship in workgroups. *Leadership Quarterly, 29*(6), 698–708.

Anand, S., Vidyarthi, P. R., Liden, R. C., & Rousseau, D. M. (2010). Good citizens in poor-quality relationships: Idiosyncratic deals as a substitute for relationship quality. *Academy of Management Journal, 53*(5), 970–988.

Bal, M., & Lub, X. D. (2015). Individualization of work arrangements. In M. Bal & D. M. Rousseau (Eds.), *Idiosyncratic deals between employees and organizations: Conceptual issues, applications and the role of co-workers* (pp. 9–23). Routledge.

Bal, P. M., & Dóci, E. (2018). Neoliberal ideology in work and organizational psychology. *European Journal of Work and Organizational Psychology, 27*(5), 536–548.

Ballout, H. I. (2007). Career success: The effects of human capital, person-environment fit and organizational support. *Journal of Managerial Psychology, 22*(8), 741–765.

Beck, U., & Beck-Gernsheim, E. (2009). Losing the traditional: Individualization and 'precarious freedoms.' In A. Elliott & P. du Gay (Eds.), *Identity in question* (pp. 13–36). Sage.

Blau, P. M. (1964). Social exchange theory. *Retrieved September, 3*(2007), 62.

Bourdieu, P. (1984). *Distinction: A social critique of the judgement of taste*. Harvard university press.

Bowring, F. (2002). Post-Fordism and the end of work. *Futures, 34*(2), 159–172.

Brewis, J. (2005). Othering organization theory: Marta Calás and Linda Smircich. *Sociological review, 53* (1_suppl), 80–94.

Brown, D. J., Ferris, D. L., Heller, D., & Keeping, L. M. (2007). Antecedents and consequences of the frequency of upward and downward social comparisons at work. *Organizational Behavior and Human Decision Processes, 102*(1), 59–75.

Brzykcy, A. Z., Boehm, S. A., & Baldridge, D. C. (2019). Fostering sustainable careers across the lifespan: The role of disability, idiosyncratic deals and perceived work ability. *Journal of Vocational Behavior, 112*, 185–198.

Burawoy, M. (1982). *Manufacturing consent: Changes in the labor process under monopoly capitalism.* University of Chicago Press.

Burawoy, M. (1990). *The politics of production* (p. 193). Verso.

Burchell, B. (2009). Flexicurity as a moderator of the relationship between job insecurity and psychological well-being. *Cambridge Journal of Regions, Economy and Society, 2*(3), 365–378.

Cheng, B. S., Farh, J., Chang, H., & Hsu, W. (2002). Guanxi, zhongcheng, competence and managerial behavior in Chinese context. *Journal of Chinese Psychology, 44*(2), 151–166.

Chen, Y., Friedman, R., Yu, E., & Sun, F. (2011). Examining the positive and negative effects of guanxi practices: A multi-level analysis of guanxi practices and procedural justice perceptions. *Asia Pacific Journal of Management, 28*(4), 715–735.

Costea, B., Amiridis, K., & Crump, N. (2012). Graduate employability and the principle of potentiality: An aspect of the ethics of HRM. *Journal of Business Ethics, 111*(1), 25–36.

Cullinane, N., & Dundon, T. (2006). The psychological contract: A critical review. *International Journal of Management Reviews, 8*(2), 113–129.

Deleuze, G. (1995). *Negotiations, 1972–1990.* Columbia University Press.

Du Gay, P. (1996). *Consumption and identity at work.* Sage.

Dunfee, T. W., & Warren, D. E. (2001). Is guanxi ethical? A normative analysis of doing business in China. *Journal of Business Ethics, 32*(3), 191–204.

Edwards, P. (2003). The employment relationship and the field of industrial relations. *Industrial Relations: Theory and Practice, 2*, 1–36.

Evetts, J., Mieg, H. A., & Felt, U. (2006). Professionalization, scientific expertise, and elitism: A sociological perspective. In K. A. Ericsson, R. R. Hoffman, A. Kozbelt & A .M. Williams (Eds.), *The Cambridge handbook of expertise and expert performance* (pp. 105–123). Cambridge University Press.

Farber, H. S., & Western, B. (2001). Accounting for the decline of unions in the private sector, 1973–1998. *Journal of Labor Research, 22*(3), 459–485.

Fleming, P., & Spicer, A. (2003). Working at a cynical distance: Implications for power, subjectivity and resistance. *Organization, 10*(1), 157–179.

Foucault, M. (1973). *Wahnsinn und Gesellschaft: Eine Geschichte des Wahns im Zeitalter der Vernunft.* Suhrkamp.

Foucault, M. (1975). *Surveiller Et Punir. Paris, 1*, 192–211.

Foucault, M. (1977). *Discipline and punish: The birth of the prison* (A. Sheridan, Trans.). Allen Lane.

Foucault, M. (1978 [1980]). The eye of power. In *Power/Knowledge: Selected Interviews and Other Writings 1972–1977*, In Colin Gordon et al. (Ed., Trans.) (pp. 146–165).
Foucault, M. (1984). *The use of pleasure: The history of sexuality* (Vol. 2). Penguin Books.
Foucault, M. (1988). *Technologies of the self: A seminar with Michel Foucault.* University of Massachusetts Press.
Foucault, M. (1980). *Power/knowledge: Selected interviews and other writings by Michel Foucault, 1972–77.* In C. Gordon (Ed.). Harvester.
Foucault, M. (2007). *Security, Territory and Population: Lectures at the Collège de France 1977–1978.* Basingstoke, UK: Palgrave Macmillan.
Fraser, N. (2003). From discipline to flexibilization? Rereading Foucault in the shadow of globalization. *Constellations, 10*(2), 160–171.
Gane, N. (2012). The governmentalities of neoliberalism: Panopticism, post-panopticism and beyond. *Sociological Review, 60*(4), 611–634.
Harvey, D. (2005). *A brief history of neoliberalism.* Oxford University Press.
Heath, A., & Heath, L. E. (1976). *Rational choice and social exchange: A critique of exchange theory.* CUP Archive.
Herod, A., & Lambert, R. (2016). Neoliberalism, precarious work and remaking the geography of global capitalism. In R. Lambert & A. Herod (Eds.), *Neoliberal capitalism and precarious work* (pp. 1–42). Edward Elgar Publishing.
Hetrick, W. P., & Boje, D. M. (1992). Organization and the body: Post-Fordist dimensions. *Journal of Organizational Change Management, 5*(1), 48–57.
Ho, V. T., & Tekleab, A. G. (2016). A model of idiosyncratic deal-making and attitudinal outcomes. *Journal of Managerial Psychology, 31*(3), 642–656.
Hornung, S., Rousseau, D. M., & Glaser, J. (2008). Creating flexible work arrangements through idiosyncratic deals. *Journal of Applied Psychology, 93*(3), 655.
Houghton, E. (2019). *Becoming a Neoliberal Subject. Ephemera, 19*(3), 615–626.
Jessop, B. (1995). The regulation approach, governance and post-Fordism: Alternative perspectives on economic and political change? *Economy and Society, 24*(3), 307–333.
Johnson, J. L., Bottorff, J. L., Browne, A. J., Grewal, S., Hilton, B. A., & Clarke, H. (2004). Othering and being othered in the context of health care services. *Health Communication, 16*(2), 255–271.
Knights, D. (1990). Subjectivity, power and the labour process. In D. Knights & H. Willmott (Eds.), *Labour process theory* (pp. 297–335). Palgrave Macmillan.
Knights, D., & Collinson, D. (1987). Disciplining the shopfloor: A comparison of the disciplinary effects of managerial psychology and financial accounting. *Accounting, Organizations and Society, 12*(5), 457–477.

Knights, D., & McCabe, D. (2000). Ain't misbehavin'? Opportunities for resistance under new forms of quality' management. *Sociology, 34*(3), 421–436.

Knights, D., & Morgan, G. (1991). Corporate strategy, organizations, and subjectivity: A critique. *Organization Studies, 12*(2), 251–273.

Knights, D., & Willmott, H. (1989). Power and subjectivity at work: From degradation to subjugation in social relations. *Sociology, 23*(4), 535–558.

Knights, D., & Willmott, H. (Eds.). (1990). *Labour Process Theory*. London: Macmillan.

Kong, D. T., Ho, V. T., & Garg, S. (2020). Employee and coworker idiosyncratic deals: Implications for emotional exhaustion and deviant behaviors. *Journal of Business Ethics, 164*(3), 593–609.

Korpi, W., & Palme, J. (2003). New politics and class politics in the context of austerity and globalization: Welfare state regress in 18 countries, 1975–95. *American Political Science Review, 97*(3), 425–446.

Kuhn, K. M. (2016). The rise of the "Gig Economy" and implications for understanding work and workers. *Industrial and Organizational Psychology, 9*(1), 157.

Kulik, C. T., & Ambrose, M. L. (1992). Personal and situational determinants of referent choice. *Academy of Management Review, 17*(2), 212–237.

Lai, L., Rousseau, D. M., & Chang, K. T. T. (2009). Idiosyncratic deals: Coworkers as interested third parties. *Journal of Applied Psychology, 94*(2), 547.

Las Heras, M., Rofcanin, Y., Matthijs Bal, P., & Stollberger, J. (2017). How do flexibility i-deals relate to work performance? Exploring the roles of family performance and organizational context. *Journal of Organizational Behavior, 38*(8), 1280–1294.

Lemke, T. (2002). Foucault, governmentality, and critique. *Rethinking Marxism, 14*(3), 49–64.

Liao, C., Wayne, S. J., & Rousseau, D. M. (2016). Idiosyncratic deals in contemporary organizations: A qualitative and meta-analytical review. *Journal of Organizational Behavior, 37*, S9–S29.

Lockwood, P., & Kunda, Z. (1997). Superstars and me: Predicting the impact of role models on the self. *Journal of Personality and Social Psychology, 73*(1), 91.

Luckmann, T., & Berger, P. (1964). Social mobility and personal identity. *European Journal of Sociology/archives Européennes De Sociologie/europäisches Archiv Für Soziologie, 5*(2), 331–344.

Marescaux, E., De Winne, S., & Rofcanin, Y. (2021). Co-worker reactions to i-deals through the lens of social comparison: The role of fairness and emotions. *Human Relations, 74*(3), 329–353.

Marescaux, E., De Winne, S., & Sels, L. (2019). Idiosyncratic deals from a distributive justice perspective: Examining co-workers' voice behavior. *Journal of Business Ethics, 154*(1), 263–281.
McCabe, D. (2007). Individualization at work? Subjectivity, team working and anti-unionism. *Organization, 14*(2), 243–266.
Melamed, T. (1995). Barriers to women's career success: Human capital, career choices, structural determinants, or simply sex discrimination. *Applied Psychology, 44*(4), 295–314.
Morgan, G. (2013). *Riding the waves of change*. Imaginization Inc.
Neirotti, P. (2020). Work intensification and employee involvement in lean production: New light on a classic dilemma. *The International Journal of Human Resource Management, 31*(15), 1958–1983.
Newton, T. (1998). Theorizing subjectivity in organizations: The failure of Foucauldian studies? *Organization Studies, 19*(3), 415–447.
Ng, T. W., & Feldman, D. C. (2015). Idiosyncratic deals and voice behavior. *Journal of Management, 41*(3), 893–928.
O'Doherty, D., & Willmott, H. (2001). Debating labour process theory: The issue of subjectivity and the relevance of poststructuralism. *Sociology, 35*(2), 457–476.
Oyserman, D., Coon, H. M., & Kemmelmeier, M. (2002). Rethinking individualism and collectivism: Evaluation of theoretical assumptions and meta-analyses. *Psychological Bulletin, 128*(1), 3.
Peck, J. (2010). *Constructions of neoliberal reason*. Oxford University Press.
Pereboom, D. (2006). *Living without free will*. Cambridge University Press.
Peters, T. J., & Peters, T. (1987). *Thriving on chaos: Handbook for a management revolution* (p. 561). Knopf.
Raffnsøe, S., Gudmand-Høyer, M., & Thaning, M. S. (2016). Foucault's dispositive: The perspicacity of dispositive analytics in organizational research. *Organization, 23*(2), 272–298.
Reed, M. I. (2018). Elites, professions, and the neoliberal state: Critical points of intersection and contention. *Journal of Professions and Organization, 5*(3), 297–312.
Reynaud, E. (1983). *Holy virility: The social construction of masculinity*. Pluto Press.
Roemer, J. E. (1978). Neoclassicism, marxism, and collective action. *Journal of Economic Issues, 12*(1), 147–161.
Rofcanin, Y., Las Heras, M., Bal, M., van der Heijden, B., & Erdogan, D. (2018). A trickle-down model of task and developmental I-deals. *Human Relations, 71*(11), 1508–1534.
Rofcanin, Y., Kiefer, T., & Strauss, K. (2017). What seals the I-deal? Exploring the role of employees' behaviours and managers' emotions. *Journal of Occupational and Organizational Psychology, 90*(2), 203–224.

Rosen, C. C., Slater, D. J., Chang, C. H., & Johnson, R. E. (2013). Let's make a deal: Development and validation of the ex post i-deals scale. *Journal of Management, 39*(3), 709–742.

Rousseau, D. (2001). Flexibility versus fairness? *Organizational Dynamics, 29*(4), 260–273.

Rousseau, D. M. (2005). *I-Deals: Idiosyncratic deals employees bargain for themselves.* M.E. Sharpe. Inc.

Rousseau, D. M., Ho, V. T., & Greenberg, J. (2006). I-deals: Idiosyncratic terms in employment relationships. *Academy of Management Review, 31*(4), 977–994.

Rousseau, D. M., Hornung, S., & Kim, T. G. (2009). Idiosyncratic deals: Testing propositions on timing, content, and the employment relationship. *Journal of Vocational Behavior, 74*(3), 338–348.

Schatzki, T. R. (2005). Peripheral vision: The sites of organizations. *Organization Studies, 26*(3), 465–484.

Schwalbe, M., Holden, D., Schrock, D., Godwin, S., Thompson, S., & Wolkomir, M. (2000). Generic processes in the reproduction of inequality: An interactionist analysis. *Social Forces, 79*(2), 419–452.

Scott, J. (2000). Rational choice theory. *Understanding Contemporary Society: Theories of the Present, 129,* 671–685.

Sedlacek, T. (2011). *Economics of good and evil: The quest for economic meaning from Gilgamesh to Wall Street.* Oxford University Press.

Seibert, S. E., Kraimer, M. L., & Liden, R. C. (2001). A social capital theory of career success. *Academy of Management Journal, 44*(2), 219–237.

Sewell, G., & Wilkinson, B. (1992). Someone to watch over me': Surveillance, discipline and the just-in-time labour process. *Sociology, 26*(2), 271–289.

Skinner, D. (2013). Foucault, subjectivity and ethics: Towards a self-forming subject. *Organization, 20*(6), 904–923.

Stein, J. G. (2017). The micro-foundations of international relations theory: Psychology and behavioral economics. *International Organization, 71,* (S1_Suppl.), S249–S263.

Storey, J. (1985). The means of management control. *Sociology, 19*(2), 193–211.

Swanson, J. (2008). Economic common sense and the depoliticization of the economic. *Political Research Quarterly, 61*(1), 56–67.

Thompson, P., & Smith, C. (2000). Follow the redbrick road: Reflections on pathways in and out of the labor process debate. *International Studies of Management & Organization, 30*(4), 40–67.

Townley, B. (1993). Foucault, power/knowledge, and its relevance for human resource management. *Academy of Management Review, 18*(3), 518–545.

Townley, B. (1998). Beyond good and evil: Depth and division in the management of human resources. In A. McKinlay & K. Starkey (Eds.), *Foucault, management and organization theory* (pp. 191–210). Sage.

Tyler, I. (2015). Classificatory struggles: Class, culture and inequality in neoliberal times. *The Sociological Review, 63*(2), 493–511.

Vidyarthi, P. R., Singh, S., Erdogan, B., Chaudhry, A., Posthuma, R., & Anand, S. (2016). Individual deals within teams: Investigating the role of relative i-deals for employee performance. *Journal of Applied Psychology, 101*(11), 1536.

Wei, L. Q., Liu, J., Chen, Y. Y., & Wu, L. Z. (2010). Political skill, supervisor-subordinate guanxi and career prospects in Chinese firms. *Journal of Management Studies, 47*(3), 437–454.

Weick, K. E. (1976). Educational organizations as loosely coupled systems. *Administrative Science Quarterly, 21*(1), 1–19.

Weiskopf, R., & Loacker, B. (2006). Snake's coils are even more intricate than a mole's burrow: Individualisation and subjectification in post-disciplinary regimes of work. *Management Revue, 17*(4), 395–419.

Willmott, H. (1993). Strength is ignorance; slavery is freedom: Managing culture in modern organizations. *Journal of Management Studies, 30*(4), 515–552.

Winsor, R. D. (1992). Talking the post-fordist talk... but Walking the post-industrial walk. *Journal of Organizational Change Management, 5*(2), 61–69.

Zhao, H., Wayne, S. J., Glibkowski, B. C., & Bravo, J. (2007). The impact of psychological contract breach on work-related outcomes: A meta-analysis. *Personnel Psychology, 60*, 647–680.

CHAPTER 10

I-deals: Not Ideal for Employee Diversity?

Sanjeewa Perera and *Yiqiong Li*

I-deals are defined as "voluntary, personalized agreements of a nonstandard nature negotiated between individual employees and their employers regarding terms that benefit each party." (Rousseau et al., 2006, p. 978). I-deals are different from standard human resource practices that usually address needs of a majority of the workforce. Unlike psychological contracts, i-deals are objective. They can be negotiated before an employment contract begins (i.e., recruitment phase, and ex ante) as well as after (i.e., during employment and ex post). Ex-post i-deals are more prevalent than ex ante i-deals (Rousseau et al., 2006). I-deals are sometimes also negotiated when an employee threatens to quit. Contents of i-deals can cover different elements of the employer–employee relationship relating to remuneration (e.g., performance incentives and bonuses), job content (e.g., reductions in workload and changes to job tasks), flexibility (e.g.,

S. Perera (✉)
University of South Australia, Adelaide, SA, Australia
e-mail: sanjee.perera@unisa.edu.au

Y. Li
University of Queensland, Brisbane, QLD, Australia
e-mail: yiqiong.li@business.uq.edu.au

© The Author(s), under exclusive license to Springer Nature Switzerland AG 2022
S. Anand and Y. Rofcanin (eds.), *Idiosyncratic Deals at Work*,
https://doi.org/10.1007/978-3-030-88516-8_10

flexibility in hours or place of work), and developmental opportunities (e.g., access to training and developmental opportunities) (Anand et al., 2010; Liao et al., 2016; Rousseau et al., 2016). Some researchers have categorized i-deals as soft and hard based on content (Bal et al., 2012). For example, flexibility i-deals are hard and measurable while developmental i-deals can be soft and subject to the quality of the relationship between the i-deal granter and the recipient.

Either an employee or a manager can initiate an i-deal, however, the employee is often pivotal in the i-deal negotiation process. The granter's (often the line manager) and the recipient's rationales for requesting or granting an i-deal can take different forms: as a reward for exceptional performance, an option for each employee to take a turn in accessing limited resources, an accommodation to address a non-work difficulty faced by the employee (Lai et al., 2009). The process of requesting and obtaining i-deals often include three stages: A pre-work stage where an employee gathers information and focuses on strengthening workplace relationships in order to build a strong case for an i-deal; a negotiation stage where the employee negotiates for an i-deal with an organizational representative, often their direct manager; and a final maintenance stage when an i-deal recipient takes efforts to ensure the i-deal's "legitimacy and fairness." (Rousseau, 2005). Gascoigne and Kelliher (2018) found that often there is another step in the pre-work stage where employees reflect on and weigh pros and cons of requesting an i-deal before moving to the negotiation stage.

BENEFITS OF I-DEALS

Unlike personalized arrangements like preferential treatment or nepotism, i-deals can benefit both employers and employees and often provide additional resources to employees. Individual employees who are fortunate to obtain i-deals can use them to achieve both objective and subjective career success (e.g., through developmental i-deals, Guerrero et al., 2016) and greater work-life balance (e.g., through flexibility i-deals). For example, Hornung et al. (2008) found that flexibility i-deals decreased unpaid overtime and work-life conflict.

I-deals enable organizations to motivate, engage and retain employees, particularly high-performing employees. Recipients of i-deals often report higher job satisfaction, higher affective commitment, enhanced leader-member exchange, and lower intentions to leave the organization (Anand et al., 2018; Ho & Tekleab, 2016; Hornung et al., 2008; Lemmon et al., 2016). Wang et al. (2018) illustrated how i-deals enhanced employee creativity. Social exchange theory-based research suggests that employees who are recipients of i-deals, will "pay back" the organization in terms of enhanced in-role work performance (Anand et al., 2018; Las Heras et al., 2017; Rofcanin et al., 2021) and/or discretionary behaviors such as organizational citizenship behaviors (Anand et al., 2010, 2018). I-deals can also have a buffering effect, ameliorating the effect certain negative events can have on the employee–employer relationship e.g., buffering the effect of psychological contract breach (Guerrero et al., 2014).

Benefits of I-deals in Promoting Diversity

Organizations often develop standard human resource practices taking the needs of a majority of their workforce into consideration (Arthur & Boyles, 2007). However, such standard policies and practices often do not consider the unique needs of employees who are from diverse backgrounds (Anand & Mitra, in press). Even when standard practices aim to support diverse employee groups, they can be "identity-blind" (Konrad & Linnehan, 1995, p. 789). Identity-blind practices use a "one-size-fits-all" approach and aim to treat all individual employees in the same manner based on principles of individual merit. These practices disregard unique attributes and challenges of employees from diverse backgrounds. Konrad and Linnehan (1995) in their seminal work argued that the needs of diverse employees are best addressed via "identity-conscious" practices (p. 780). These practices "formally" consider the experiences of diverse groups in the workplace and recognize that organizations need to give special considerations to the needs of these groups (e.g., "a special mentoring program for female mangers," Konrad & Linnehan, 1995, p. 817; "targeting older managerial and professional employees for training to update current job skills," Armstrong-Stassen & Ursel, 2009, p. 219).

Identity-conscious practices can address unique needs of diverse employees and provide greater support to these employees. However, identity-conscious practices are still formalized practices that treat each demographic group as homogenous (i.e., disregard within group differences). For example, the needs of a mature-age employee with elderly parents can be different from a mature-age employee who needs organizational support to manage age-related health declines. In contrast,

I-deals allow diverse employees access to work arrangements that suit their individual circumstances. Bal et al. (2015) demonstrated how older workers can benefit from individualized career paths. Employees from diverse groups can also use i-deals to correct inequalities in the workplace, for example, to bring their remuneration in line with other employees who are high performers (Bal, 2017). Thus, in theory, i-deals can provide diverse employees even greater benefit than identity-conscious practices. Our review of i-deals research suggests that i-deals can particularly benefit two groups of employees that we focus on in this chapter: women and mature-age workers.

Research on work-life practices indicates that i-deals can profoundly influence work experiences of women compared to men. For example, women with children who use flexible work arrangements especially teleworking feel less depressed compared to men or women without children (Kossek et al., 2006). Initiatives such as flexible scheduling, telecommuting, onsite childcare/elder care assistance, and tuition reimbursement have a more profound impact on women's aspiration for achieving a leadership position compared to men (Fritz & Van Knippenberg, 2018). Work–family conflicts increase the demand for accessing flexible work arrangements more for female managers than male managers because flexible work arrangements support female managers to perform their family roles with less interference from the work domain (Kim & Gong, 2017).

Older workers as a group are more heterogenous in terms of their work-related needs (e.g., rewards and work conditions) compared to younger workers because "with increasing age, people tend to become more heterogeneous from each other." (Bal et al., 2015, p. 425). Therefore, i-deals are a perfect solution for mature-age workers that allow them to negotiate work conditions aligned to their unique circumstances. Only a handful of studies have specifically examined the mature-age employee experience in negotiating and maintaining i-deals. Oostrom et al. (2016) reported how i-deals covering modifications to job tasks, work responsibilities, and work location increased mature-age workers' employability. Bal et al. (2012) investigated flexibility and developmental i-deals and found that flexibility i-deals increased motivation among older workers to continue working.

Rousseau et al. (2006) suggested that i-deals provide organizations an opportunity to strategically target diverse employee groups by addressing their unique needs that are often not addressed through standard human resource practices (e.g., law firms with low gender diversity may use i-deals to attract female lawyers). The negotiation process for an i-deal can be an information sharing process and an opportunity for a manager to identify the unique needs and resources needed by employees from diverse backgrounds. For example, Brzykcy and colleagues (2019) found that i-deals that provided accommodative resources needed by employees with disabilities, increased their work ability and in turn decreased these employees' intention to leave their employers. Flexibility and workload reduction i-deals can be used to support older workers who wish to ease into retirement (Rousseau et al., 2016). Overall, it is clear that access to i-deals can benefit employees from diverse backgrounds. I-deals are also an effective diversity management strategy for employers, creating a win–win strategy that is a cornerstone of an i-deal.

The Dark Side of I-deals

Research on i-deals report that outcomes of i-deals are not uniformly positive, in fact i-deals "have their dark sides" (Rousseau et al., 2006, p. 991). I-deals can lead to different outcomes based on their content (i.e., what is negotiated as part of an i-deal) and the timing (i.e., when an i-deal is negotiated) (Rousseau et al., 2016). Hornung et al. (2008) found that while flexibility i-deals decreased unpaid overtime and work-life conflict, developmental i-deals increased affective commitment but also increased work-life conflict. I-deals that focus on workload reductions can lead to employee–employer relationship transforming to a more transactional relationship (Rousseau et al., 2016). Employees granted ex ante i-deals have less incentive to reciprocate through enhanced performance as ex ante i-deals include more economic content (e.g., salary, incentives, promotion) compared to ex post i-deals and they may not necessarily attribute the receipt of the ex ante i-deals to employer "kindness, generosity, or appreciation of them." (Rousseau et al., 2016, p. 186).

Social comparisons that employees and co-workers make can influence whether employees view i-deals as beneficial. I-dealers judge their own i-deals within the context of group members' i-deals and such judgements might influence their performance. For example, when i-dealers compare their own i-deals with the average of their group members' i-deals and perceive they have a relatively poorer deal, this demotivates them and hinders their performance (Vidyarthi et al., 2016). Similarly, when i-dealers find their co-workers have more advantageous task i-deals, they experience greater emotional exhaustion and engage in deviant behaviors (Kong et al., 2020). Moreover, the target beneficiaries of i-deals may also have concerns about implications of i-deals on interpersonal relationships at the workplace. For example, recipients of developmental i-deals are likely to develop feelings of being envied, leading to feeling ostracized that can result in turnover (Ng, 2017).

Finally, i-deal recipients are impacted by manager responses and co-worker reactions during i-deal negotiation and maintenance. Managers often hold recipients of i-deals to higher performance standards (Hornung et al., 2008) and co-workers can resent recipients of i-deals (Ng, 2017). Managers can hold i-deal recipients to higher standards and impose additional demands as a way to "pay back" the organization. Managers often grant i-deals to employees they perceive as high performers (Atkinson & Sandiford, 2016; Kossek et al., 2016). Rofcanin et al.'s (2017) study of managers showed that managers felt more positive emotions toward i-deal recipients when these employees engaged in more socially connecting (e.g., helping co-workers, socializing with co-workers) behaviors. Managers were more likely to grant reduced workload i-deals to those who were willing to be flexible about family demands (i.e., prioritize work demands by changing personal commitments to suit work, e.g., checking emails on off days (Kossek et al., 2016). Additionally, managers can grant i-deals but fail to implement strategies that support the i-deal. For example, Gascoigne and Kelliher (2018) found that when employees were granted i-deals that reduced workload, the actual reduction of workload was often "a notable absence from many i-deal negotiations" (p. 71) leaving the responsibility for adopting strategies to reduce workload with the i-deal recipient. Participants in Gascoigne and Kelliher's (2018) study often redesigned their jobs in order to reduce their workloads as per the i-deal but did this by neglecting job tasks that are related to career progress (e.g., networking).

I-deals provide the most benefit to both recipients and their organizations when they are supported by co-workers: "An i-deal might be "win–win" to the focal worker and the employer, but its ultimate effectiveness can depend on coworkers' acceptance of it." (Lai et al., 2009., p. 547). Co-workers are more likely to accept i-deals, when these i-deals do not present a threat to their instrumental outcomes. For example, co-worker acceptance of others' i-deal is positively related to their belief in the chance of accessing comparable i-deals in future (Lai et al., 2009; Lemmon et al., 2016; Rousseau et al., 2006).

Co-workers, especially non or less-targeted beneficiaries of i-deals, can react negatively to i-deals based on their perceptions of injustice and concerns about increased workload (Marescaux et al., 2021). When i-deals primarily prioritize the needs of working parents and carers, the potential for "backlash" from non- or less-targeted beneficiaries is very likely as these employees view i-deals as a threat to their own instrumental outcomes. Co-workers who witness others receive developmental i-deals (e.g., access to special training opportunities) may become envious, due to the perceived lower chances of their own work success and perceived lower outcome-input ratio compared to their co-workers (Ng, 2017). Flexibility i-deals in particular can be resented by co-workers who are concerned about having to adjust their own work to accommodate the i-deal (Rousseau et al., 2016). Non-beneficiaries of job content i-deals may be concerned with increased work burden because beneficiaries reduce work hours or workload (Beauregard, 2014; Marescaux et al., 2019). The non-beneficiaries particularly perceive more distributive injustice toward financial i-deals (e.g., a bonus) compared with i-deals concerning work-hour flexibility and workload reduction (Marescaux et al., 2019). These perceptions of injustice can be aggravated when financial i-deals are secret (Rousseau et al., 2016). Finally, co-workers often react negatively to i-deals employees obtain as a result of threats to quit the organization (Rousseau et al., 2016). Non-beneficiaries' negative perceptions can motivate them to complain, resulting in negative consequences for both the organization (e.g., co-workers also demanding i-deals thereby increasing costs) and the focal employee (e.g., i-deal loses its salience and therefore its motivating power) (Marescaux et al., 2019).

Instrumentality is not the only factor that influences co-worker and manager reactions to recipients of i-deals. Employees are likely to scrutinize the rationale for why i-deals are granted (Lai et al., 2009; Marescaux et al., 2019; Wilkinson et al., 2018). Allocation of i-deals can be based on *merit* (e.g., i-deals are used to reward high performance), *equity* (an equity perception arises if an i-deal can balance the ratio of work inputs and outputs of an i-dealer in comparison to other employees), *need* (i-deals are given to those who have the greatest need to accommodate personal or family difficulties), and *equality* (every individual receives equal opportunity to access to i-deals; for example, take turns to attend training). Research on i-deals indicates that the merit/equity principle seems to be the predominant rule in organizational setting, while the need principle is attracting growing attention. For example, a national survey shows that co-workers who perceive an i-deal to be equitable in terms of performance or effort are more likely to judge the i-deal as distributively fair. Moreover, the need principle is perceived as equally important as the equity principle (Marescaux & De Winne, 2016). Research has not so far accumulated comprehensive evidence as to which rationale or justification is more favored by co-workers and managers (Liao et al., 2016). Nevertheless, research does show that it is not only "being able to take up i-deals or not" that influences employees' attitudes, but also "how i-deals are allocated and communicated." Often secrecy about compensation leads employees to overestimate their deprivation (Belogolovsky, & Bamberger, 2014). Employees who were not thoroughly or honestly informed regarding the availability of i-deal arrangements and how decisions were made regarding i-deals allocation, are likely to sustain unfairness perceptions that can consequently trigger counterproductive behaviors (Beauregard, 2014).

I-deal recipients recognize the importance of co-worker and managers responses in maintaining i-deals and are keen to avoid negative outcomes. Therefore, the target beneficiaries of i-deals or i-dealers may not necessarily perceive i-deals favorably. For example, employees with partners and/or dependent children are found to view i-deals less favorably than childfree and single employees (de Janasz et al., 2013). Another excellent example is highlighted in the attitudes of beneficiaries toward flexibility stigma—a belief that employees who use flexible work arrangements are less productive and less committed. Early and developing career employees are particularly concerned with the likely negative career impact of these i-deals because availing i-deals may signal that they are less committed to work (Darcy et al., 2012). Men are more reluctant to take up flexible work arrangements due to perceived negative impacts on career progression (Burnett et al., 2012).

Overall, research on i-deals suggests that i-deals are not always beneficial to the i-deal recipient or the employer (win–win) (Vidyarthi et al., 2014). I-deals could also end up being win-lose or lose-lose work arrangements. I-deals have the potential to deliver a win–win, but this depends on the content and timing of the i-deal as well as the process involved in negotiating and communicating about i-deals. On paper, i-deals appear to be a win–win solution that levels the playing field for diverse employees. However, there are several reasons that i-deals may not benefit diverse employees. Only a few studies have examined women's (Gascoigne, & Kelliher, 2018) and mature-age workers' (Atkinson & Sandiford, 2016; Bal et al., 2015; Oostrom et al., 2016) experience with i-deals. We draw on these few studies and supplement them with broader research on workforce diversity in the next section to examine specific challenges that employees from diverse backgrounds can face when negotiating and maintaining i-deals.

I-deals not Ideal for Employee Diversity?

Our review suggests that whether a diverse i-deal recipient and his/her organization benefits from an i-deal will depend on several factors: the content and the timing of i-deal, i-deal negotiation process and its context. It also suggests that the benefits may differ across employees from different demographic groups.

I-deals Can Activate Stereotypes

I-deals are individualized employment agreements that are provided only to selected employees. Recipients of i-deals are likely to stand out among their co-workers and the content of an i-deal can draw attention to how the recipient is different or has different needs compared to other employees. Societal stereotypes often remain dormant in workplaces, but i-deals can activate them and make them more salient to employees and their co-workers. Demographic information (e.g., age, gender, and race/ethnicity) is "immediately recognizable" and such information triggers "stereotypes rapidly" (Davison & Burke, 2000: 227). Decision-making based on stereotypes is more likely when managers or other decision makers deal with employees who are a numerical minority in their workplace (Banchefsky & Park, 2018; Tsui & O'Reilly, 1989). Older worker related stereotypes portray them as less competent, less trainable, less able to learn, and resistant to change (Posthuma & Campion, 2009); gender stereotypes often depict women as caring and interdependent but less suitable for management/leadership roles (Rudman & Phelan, 2008; Schein, 2007). Women and older workers who access i-deals can be quickly seen as different with *special needs* that need to be *accommodated*. For example, "Flexible, especially part-time, working can be perceived as an alternative, 'female way' to work" (Gascoigne & Kelliher, 2018, p. 71). This situation can be exacerbated when organizations make i-deals available only to certain groups of employees, "such as 'women' or even more ambivalent, 'working mothers'," (Kossek et al., 2016, p. 155). Atkinson and Sandiford (2016) reiterated how managers granted flexibility i-deals to mature-age employees as accommodations that helped them cope with "having a senior moment" (page 21). Their study also found that decisions to grant or deny i-deals were often based on gender stereotypes, raising the "spectre of gender discrimination" (p. 21). Activation of gender and age-based stereotypes via i-deal access can lead to several outcomes in relation how these employees negotiate and maintain i-deals.

First, concerns about these stereotypes can trigger stereotype threat (i.e., perception that their group identity is not valued by co-workers and managers, Lamont et al., 2015; Steele, 1997) among women and mature-age workers. Worried about confirming and reiterating stereotypes, women and older workers can be reluctant to negotiate i-deals. Do these employees (e.g., women in male dominated industries or occupations, mature-age workers) negotiate fewer i-deals? Our review of previous research does not provide sufficient evidence to answer this question fully as most research on i-deals exclusively focus on i-deals that are successfully negotiated (Liao et al., 2016).

Second, rationales provided to co-workers about i-deals and attributions manager make about i-deals can activate stereotypes and may lead to biased decision-making. I-deals can lead to perceptions of injustice, favoritism and etc., unless there is an explanation provided to co-workers of the recipient (Marescaux et al., 2021). But this very explanation then can draw attention to the group and group member differences. Rationales provided to co-workers to support i-deals can highlight the business case (e.g., retention of valued employees) or the need to accommodate diverse employee needs (e.g., employee need for flexible work arrangements to accommodate their caregiving responsibilities). While co-workers may see i-deals given to employees who are different as fair and just (Bal & Boehm, 2019), highlighting of differences and the need for accommodation can also have negative effects. Michielsens et al. (2014) reported that when a business case attribution is prioritized by managers, flexible work arrangements did not promote inclusivity. Accommodation attributions may lead to managers viewing i-deals as *remedial* and i-deal recipient as having a "deficit that needs correcting" (Tharenou & Kulik, 2020, p. 1170). Such interpretations can color the perceptions of co-workers and managers toward the i-deal recipient. For example, Bal et al. (2012) reported that developmental i-deals only encouraged older workers to continue working when their work unit had a low accommodative climate but a high developmental climate. Similarly, managers are more likely to grant and support the maintenance of i-deals, when they think that the employee is using the i-deal to try to be more productive at work as opposed to accommodate a personal need (Rousseau et al., 2016).

Third, when women and mature-age workers negotiate and maintain i-deals, their success may be impacted by the decisions of their managers. Managers' stereotypes can influence their decision-making about granting as well as supporting an i-deal. Majority of studies on i-deals examine successful i-deals (i.e., i-deals that are requested and granted), however we have a limited understanding of the negotiation process involved in i-deals (e.g., i-deals that are denied) (Liao et al., 2016). I-deals are not guided by standard human resource policies or practices and are critically shaped by individual manager decisions. For example, career customization i-deals lead to higher levels of job engagement among middle-aged and older workers only when they receive high levels of manager support (Bal et al., 2015). When managers have a high amount of discretionary power to provide or deny requests for i-deals, women can be more disadvantaged compared to men (Chasserio & Legault, 2010). Women and mature-age workers who negotiate i-deals may find it harder to prove that they are "worthy" of i-deals compared to other employees. Despite research that shows i-deals no longer as the prerogative of star performers (Rousseau et al., 2006), both employees and managers often consider i-deals as the privilege of high performers. Managers often require that the employee accumulate sufficient "idiosyncrasy credits" (Rousseau et al., 2006, p. 979) by demonstrating "rare or highly rated skills or knowledge, a good reputation, or a relationship with the manager" (Gascoigne & Kelliher, 2018, p. 71; see also Atkinson & Sandiford, 2016). So, employees often feel they that they need to "earn" i-deals with high performance; higher compared to similar others in the workplace, before they make a request (Bal, 2017). Often manager perceptions of a "high performer" can be based on the physical presence and the availability of employees (Elsbach et al., 2010; Hornung et al., 2008; O'Connor & Cech, 2018). Women and older workers are more likely to desire access to flexibility i-deals (Pitt-Catsouphes & Matz-Costa, 2008; Rudolph & Baltes, 2017). However, negotiating flexibility i-deals can signal to managers that the employee is less committed to their work, organization or career, impacting their perceptions of the employee as a "high performer." A strong body of research has documented how manager perceptions of flexible work arrangements have career consequences for employees who use these arrangements (e.g., Leslie et al., 2012). I-deal recipients can also be in a vulnerable position at times of layoffs. For example, Bal (2017) illustrated how a female employee who had negotiated a flexibility i-deal was a ready target of a layoff "because of her special arrangements." (p. 14).

Based on previous research on flexible work arrangements, we can assume that it is likely that employees from diverse backgrounds are aware of these potential drawbacks of negotiating i-deals. Women, especially mothers are more likely to believe those who work flexibly have fewer promotion opportunities (Chung, 2018). Gascoigne and Kelliher (2018) found that their participants progressed through a "secret stage" where they considered the impact of requesting flexibility i-deals could have on their career and their status in the organization before actually making the i-deal request.

Gender and Age Impact I-deal Negotiations

Successfully accessing i-deals depend on an employee's ability to negotiate. When women and mature-age workers negotiate i-deals, they may be differentially successful. Negotiation research suggests that the process of i-deal negotiation can be particularly challenging for women. The few studies that have examined the women's flexible work negotiations suggest i-deal negotiations are likely to be gender stereotypical. Compared with men, women are more likely to use a bending strategy (i.e., request for individual exceptional accommodation that may be deviate from organizational norms or standard organizational practice) in work-life negotiation, partially in response to more resistance they encounter when they ask for standard accommodation (Bowles et al., 2019). However, women who initiate negotiations are viewed as more demanding and less likable (Bowles et al., 2007). Ho and Tekleab (2016) found that even though overall gender did not moderate the association between requests and receipts of i-deal, men were more likely to succeed at obtaining financial i-deals compared to women. Ho and Tekleab (2016) argue that gender differences in their study may be due to the fact that women are more likely to negotiate only when they can be sure of success and expect little backlash. Women who perceive the organization as lacking a culture of work-life support are less likely to confidently and collaboratively engage in negotiation for i-deals (Greenberg & Landry, 2011).

Employees gain "credit" to successfully negotiate ex post i-deals through high performance and social capital built on trusted workplace relationships (Rousseau et al., 2006). Mature-age employees may have an advantage in demonstrating worthiness and successfully negotiating i-deals. Mature-age workers have a deeper understanding of their resource needs and how to use these resources in the workplace (Rudolph & Baltes, 2017) which can give them an advantage in negotiating for specific resources and providing a rationale for their efficacy. As employees age, they often reduce the emphasis on financial motivators (Stynen et al., 2014) and organizations are less likely to offer financial i-deals to older workers (Ho & Tekleab, 2016). Therefore, mature-age workers might find it easier to align their needs to employee benefits offered by their organizations and get to a win-win i-deal. Age can indicate social status (Lawrence, 1988) giving mature-age workers an advantage in their i-deal negotiations. Mature-age employees are also likely to have long-tenure in their organizations having had the opportunity to develop deep relationships with the organization, their line managers, and co-workers. They may benefit as some organizations offer i-deals as a reward for "loyalty" and "an extended track record" (Rosseau et al., 2006, p. 984). Guerrero and Jeanblanc (2017) found that networking skills were positively related to obtaining developmental i-deals. Mature-age employees may be especially able to leverage workplace relationships to negotiate developmental i-deals (Cabrera & Thomas-Hunt, 2007).

I-deals Can Increase Inequity

Despite evidence that there can be negative co-worker reactions when i-deals are not clearly communicated (Rousseau et al., 2006), employees are often discouraged from discussing the content of i-deals with other employees, specially i-deals that involve compensation (Bal, 2017). Secrecy or lack of transparency in relation to i-deals could have an impact on workplace equity, particularly in relation to gender pay gap at both individual and organizational levels. Gender pay gap is an equity issue that is enduring, an issue that is prevalent in most organizations, in most countries (World Economic Forum, 2020). Research suggests that pay transparency motivates women to negotiate for compensation which can reduce the gender pay gap (Bowles et al., 2005). Research also suggests that pay transparency at the organizational level is critical to closing the gender pay gap (Bennedsen et al., 2019; Kulik, 2020). Therefore, i-deals related to compensation (which are often kept secret) have the potential to exacerbate disparities in compensation between men and women.

In conclusion, i-deals can disadvantage recipients from diverse backgrounds compared to others. However, these effects are critically shaped by organizational contextual factors: organizational structure and power differences, the existence of formal human resource policies and programs, and the prevalence of i-deals.

Organizational Contexts and I-deal Access

I-deals place a disproportionate amount of responsibility on individual employees, who are responsible for negotiating i-deals. In these negotiations, the power imbalance between the employee and the organization can play a critical role and "hierarchical structures and authoritarian" managers can hinder an employee's ability to negotiate i-deals (Hornung et al., 2010). Thus i-deals can thrive in organizational contexts with "symmetric power" (Rousseau et al., 2006, p. 979). These factors are likely to have greater impact on employee groups who lack power and social status compared to other employees (e.g., women compared to men). Women are more likely to find such organizational contexts challenging for i-deal negotiations (Berdahl, 2007). Bal (2017) highlighted how young women in hierarchical organizations where top decisionmakers were mostly men, lacked the power and confidence to request i-deals.

Rousseau et al. (2016) argued that i-deals are more likely to be available in start-ups and small businesses where standard human resource practices often do not exist. However, studies on flexible work arrangement negotiations suggest that formal human resource practices may boost employees' confidence to negotiate i-deals. For example, in an investigation of women's experiences with negotiating flexible work arrangements, Greenberg and Landry (2011) highlighted the critical role of structural work-life support (i.e., formal organizational policies or practices supportive of employees' management of work-life issues) in influencing women's access to flexible work arrangements. They found that when structural work-life support does not exist, access to flexible work arrangements can be seen as a privilege offered to those women who perceive themselves as having more power. However, when structural work-life support exists, women are more likely to have access to flexible work arrangements, especially those who perceive as having low levels of power in their organizations. These results reiterate Konrad and Linnehan's (1995) argument that "formalized HRM structures can alter power relations in organizations" (p. 795).

Employees from diverse backgrounds can draw attention to their differences and unique needs by utilizing i-deals. Use of i-deals by these employees is likely to become more distinct when such i-deals counter organizational norms. If i-deals are prevalent in an organization and are seen generally as acceptable, women and mature-age i-deal recipients will be able to blend in. For example, Hornung et al. (2008) found that work structures promoting idiosyncrasy (measured as introduction of a telecommuting program, part-time work and fieldwork) were positively associated with negotiation of i-deals related to part-time work and telecommuting programs.

Suggestions for Future Research

In this chapter, we incorporated research on i-deals with broader research on workforce diversity to examine the experiences of women and mature-age workers in negotiating and maintaining i-deals. Research evidence to date shows that i-deals have the potential to address unique needs of diverse employees. I-deals can also be an excellent strategy for organizations that are keen to create inclusive workplaces. The benefits of i-deals to women and mature-age employees and their employers will depend on the content and timing of i-deals. Unfortunately, only a handful of studies have examined diverse employees' experience with i-deals: women (Gascoigne, & Kelliher, 2018); mature-age workers (Atkinson & Sandiford, 2016; Bal et al., 2015; Oostrom et al., 2016); and employees with disabilities (Brzykcy et al., 2019); young, educated employees (Ng, 2017). These studies suggest that benefits of i-deals to these groups can differ based on i-deal content (e.g., mature-age workers benefiting more from developmental i-deals) and i-deal timing (e.g., mature-age workers may have advantages in negotiating ex post i-deals). Given potential advantages and disadvantages i-deals can provide to employees from diverse backgrounds and the increases in workforce diversity globally, more research is needed for us to fully understand how i-deals impact diverse employees and organizations where they work.

Research on the process of i-deal negotiation is limited (Liao et al., 2016) and we did not find any studies that specifically examined how women and older workers negotiated i-deals. However, research suggests that demographics differences can shape i-deal negotiation process. For example, Rousseau et al. (2016) demonstrated how broader cultural differences can manifest in i-deal negotiation with evidence showing "…that younger employees are more likely to ask for and obtain i-deals in Western cultures, while women may be more reluctant to ask for or be granted i-deals in Eastern cultures" (page 195; see also Liao et al., 2016). Negotiation research suggests that the i-deal negotiation process can be an additional challenge for some employees (e.g., women) but maybe advantageous for some (e.g., mature-age workers). However, it is not clear whether what we know about how gender impacts negotiation processes can be directly applied to i-deal negotiations. More research on how employees from diverse backgrounds negotiate i-deals is needed for us to understand how and when employees from these groups can successfully navigate the i-deal negotiation process.

Most i-deals research examines outcomes of i-deals for i-dealers and their organizations and focuses less on the maintenance phase and how non-recipient reactions can influence that stage. Co-worker reactions and manager responses to i-deal recipients can critically shape employees' experience post negotiation. Liao et al.'s (2016) meta-analysis shows that i-deal research on co-worker reactions focuses primarily on factors that can increase co-worker acceptance but fails to examine rationales provided to employees. As we describe above, i-deal maintenance phase can be critical for women and mature-age workers as i-deals can activate and draw attention to gender and age-based stereotypes. Organizational rationales provided to co-workers are a key variable that can shape manager and co-worker reactions and possibly reduce stigma associated with i-deal use. The rationales provided when women are granted i-deals and how co-workers and managers react to these are likely to be different to the rationales provided when mature-age employees are granted i-deals. For example, co-workers will react differently when told that a female manager is granted a flexibility i-deal to accommodate her caring responsibilities in comparison to when they are told that an older worker is granted a flexibility i-deal as a reward for his/her long and loyal tenure. We urge researchers to examine this critical phase of i-deal process with an exclusive focus on employees who are demographically diverse and we encourage researchers to focus on different aspects of demographic diversity in their studies of i-deal communication. Such studies will also need to incorporate perspectives of multiple stakeholders, i-deal recipient, i-deal granter, and third-party employees e.g., i-deal recipients' co-workers. Most research on i-deal to date are cross-sectional and predominately use quantitative approaches (Liao et al., 2016). Given the limited evidence on this topic and the need to capture multiple stakeholder perspectives, exploratory qualitative research methods and longitudinal research designs will be most appropriate in examining these topics.

Practical Implications

I-deals provide organizations and managers an excellent opportunity to support diverse employees. For women and mature-age employees who can often be a minority in their workplaces, i-deals can be a lifeline. However, benefits of i-deals to i-deal recipients and their employers will depend on the content and timing of i-deals, how the i-deals are negotiated and how they are communicated to non-recipients. It is important that organizations and employees recognize both the potential and the drawbacks of i-deals and work to mitigate the drawbacks.

I-deals are an excellent strategy for organizations to address unique needs of diverse employees. However, research suggests that diverse employees also benefit from formal human resource practices in their i-deal negotiations. For example, these practices provide a boost of confidence to women encouraging them in i-deal negotiation process. This would suggest that "i-deals are good supplements, but not necessarily always the best substitutes for standard organizational practices" (Rousseau et al., 2016, p. 195). Identity-blind and identity-conscious practices together can support diverse employees and lead to inclusion climates (Kulik et al., 2016; Li et al., 2019). This would suggest that organizations interested in supporting workforce diversity should invest in both formal human resource practices as well as i-deals. Formal human resources practices in the form of identity-blind and identity-conscious practices can address unique needs of certain demographic groups. However, these programs aim to address needs of all employees or needs of each employee group and do not necessarily take individual employee needs into consideration. I-deals allow organizations the opportunity to consider the needs of each individual employee. We encourage organizations to *supplement* their identity-blind and identity-conscious human resources practices with i-deals.

I-deals provide individualized work arrangement to only a select group of employees and therefore can trigger perceptions of injustice, subsequently "eroding trust and cooperation in the organization" (Rousseau et al., 2006, p. 978). I-deals also have the potential to activate stereotypes based on demographic differences. Research on unconscious bias and its effect on decision-making suggests that organizations can disrupt biased decision-making processes most effectively by disrupting the link between activated stereotypes and decision-making (Kawakami et al., 2005) in contrast to unconscious bias training that attempts to disrupt the activation of stereotypes. This body of research suggests that how i-deals are framed and communicated to i-deal recipients and other employees is likely to be the key in disrupting the association between gender and age-based stereotypes that are activated and decision-making. Similar to formal human resource practices, i-deal can be signals from the employer to employees communicating what behaviors are valued and rewarded (Bowen & Ostroff, 2004; Rousseau et al., 2006). Clear and transparent communication about i-deals and the rationale underpinning granting of i-deals can influence how non-recipients react to i-deals. When employees are provided with limited information about i-deals, they are more likely to judge them as unfair (Rousseau et al., 2006). For example, to improve fairness perception of i-deals, organizations might benefit from framing i-deals to be a more inclusive arrangement for all employees, instead of accommodating the needs of those who have a family (Wilkinson et al., 2018) which can reinforce the misalignment between gender-based stereotypes and work roles (e.g., leadership roles). Such communication could specifically target line managers. Requests for i-deals from diverse employees can make their demographic differences more salient for their managers and could potentially lead to biased decision-making with immediate (e.g., manager denying the i-deal request) and long-term (e.g., manager views the employee as less committed to work) career consequences for i-deal recipients.

As granters of i-deals, line managers play a critical role in the i-deal process, as they can prevent employee access to i-deals (Kossek et al., 2016) or support employees to access and maintain i-deals by championing them (Paustian-Underdahl, & Halbesleben, 2014). Organizations that are keen to support workforce diversity should train line managers in managing the i-deal process. For example, they can train line managers in listening and negotiation skills so that line managers can fully understand the unique needs of employees and are able to offer i-deals that are beneficial to the employee as well as the organization. Line managers also play a key role as sense-givers shaping how employees interpret organizational practices (Maitlis, 2005). Organizations can use line managers as essential connectors in their communications to employees about i-deals and clearly explain the i-deals and the rationale for i-deals to line managers first. This would mean that line managers would clearly communicate the rationale behind i-deals to their team members. Consequently, line managers can be the key to managing how non-recipients perceive and react to i-deals granted to employees from diverse backgrounds.

Conclusion

I-deals have the potential to benefit both employees and organizations in particular employees from diverse demographic groups. I-deals provide these employees an opportunity to access work arrangements that suit their individual circumstances. I-deals can also be a key strategic tool that organizations can utilize in managing workforce diversity. In this chapter, we considered benefits of i-deals for two groups of employees: women and mature-age workers. Integrating research on i-deals with research on diversity management, we identified challenges that women and mature-age workers may face in requesting, negotiating, and maintaining i-deals. Our review also revealed how i-deals have the potential to benefit women and mature-age workers specially when their organizations manage the process of granting and communicating i-deals taking into consideration the specific implications for employees from diverse demographic groups. However, there is sparse research evidence that has specifically examined i-deals and their impact for diverse demographic groups. We strongly encourage further research that can extend our understanding of this important topic.

References

Anand, S., Hu, J., Vidyarthi, P., & Liden, R. C. (2018). Leader-member exchange as a linking pin in the idiosyncratic deals-Performance relationship in workgroups. *The Leadership Quarterly, 29*(6), 698–708.

Anand, S. & Mitra, A. (In press). No family left behind: Flexibility i-deals for employees with stigmatized family identities. *Human Relations*.

Anand, S., Vidyarthi, P. R., Liden, R. C., & Rousseau, D. M. (2010). Good citizens in poor-quality relationships: Idiosyncratic deals as a substitute for relationship quality. *Academy of Management Journal, 53*(5), 970–988.

Armstrong-Stassen, M., & Ursel, N. D. (2009). Perceived organizational support, career satisfaction, and the retention of older workers. *Journal of Occupational and Organizational Psychology, 82*(1), 201–220.

Atkinson, C., & Sandiford, P. (2016). An exploration of older worker flexible working arrangements in smaller firms. *Human Resource Management Journal, 26*(1), 12–28.

Arthur, J. B., & Boyles, T. (2007). Validating the human resource system structure: A levels- based strategic HRM approach. *Human Resource Management Review, 17*(1), 77–92.

Bal, P. M. (2017). Why do employees negotiate idiosyncratic deals? An exploration of the process of i-deal negotiation. *New Zealand Journal of Employment Relations, 42*(1), 2–18.

Bal, P. M., & Boehm, S. A. (2019). How do i-deals influence client satisfaction? The role of exhaustion, collective commitment, and age diversity. *Journal of Management, 45*(4), 1461–1487.

Bal, P. M., De Jong, S. B., Jansen, P. G., & Bakker, A. B. (2012). Motivating employees to work beyond retirement: A multi-level study of the role of I-deals and unit climate. *Journal of Management Studies, 49*(2), 306–331.

Bal, P. M., Van Kleef, M., & Jansen, P. G. (2015). The impact of career customization on work outcomes: Boundary conditions of manager support and employee age. *Journal of Organizational Behavior, 36*(3), 421–440.

Banchefsky, S., & Park, B. (2018). Negative gender ideologies and gender-science stereotypes are more pervasive in male-dominated academic disciplines. *Social Sciences, 7*(27), 1–21.

Beauregard, T. A. (2014). Fairness perceptions of work—Life balance initiatives: Effects on counterproductive work behaviour. *British Journal of Management, 25*(4), 772–789.

Belogolovsky, E., & Bamberger, P. A. (2014). Signaling in secret: Pay for performance and the incentive and sorting effects of pay secrecy. *Academy of Management Journal, 57*(6), 1706–1733.

Bennedsen, M., Simintzi, E., Tsoutsoura, M., & Wolfenzon, D. (2019). Research: Gender pay gaps shrink when companies are required to disclose them. *Harvard Business Review*, Available at https://hbr.org/2019/01/research-gender-pay-gaps-shrink-when-companies-are-required-to-disclose-them

Berdahl, J. L. (2007). Harassment based on sex: Protecting social status in the context of gender hierarchy. *Academy of Management Review, 32*(2), 641–658.

Bowen, D. E., & Ostroff, C. (2004). Understanding HRM–firm performance linkages: The role of the "strength" of the HRM system. *Academy of Management Review, 29*(2), 203–221.

Bowles, H. R., Babcock, L., & Lai, L. (2007). Social incentives for gender differences in the propensity to initiate negotiations: Sometimes it does hurt to ask. *Organizational Behavior and Human Decision Processes, 103*, 84–103.

Bowles, H. R., Babcock, L., & McGinn, K. L. (2005). Constraints and triggers: Situational mechanics of gender in negotiation. *Journal of Personality and Social Psychology, 89*, 951–965.

Bowles, H. R., Thomason, B., & Bear, J. B. (2019). Reconceptualizing what and how women negotiate for career advancement. *Academy of Management Journal, 62*(6), 1645–1671.

Brzykcy, A. Z., Boehm, S. A., & Baldridge, D. C. (2019). Fostering sustainable careers across the lifespan: The role of disability, idiosyncratic deals and perceived work ability. *Journal of Vocational Behavior, 112*, 185–198.

Burnett, S. B., Gatrell, C. J., Cooper, C. L., & Sparrow, P. (2012). Fathers at work: A ghost in the organizational machine. *Gender, Work & Organization, 20*(6), 632–646.

Cabrera, S. F., & Thomas-Hunt, M. C. (2007). Street cred and the executive woman: The effects of gender differences in social networks on career advancement. In S. J. Correll (Ed.), *Social psychology of gender* (Vol .24, pp. 123–147). Elsevier Science.

Chasserio, S., & Legault, M. J. (2010). Discretionary power of project managers in knowledge-intensive firms and gender issues. *Canadian Journal of Administrative Sciences/revue Canadienne Des Sciences De L'administration, 27*(3), 236–248.

Chung, H. (2018). Gender, flexibility stigma and the perceived negative consequences of flexible working in the UK. *Social Indicators Research, 151*, 521–545.

Darcy, C., McCarthy, A., Hill, J., & Grady, G. (2012). Work–life balance: One size fits all? An exploratory analysis of the differential effects of career stage. *European Management Journal, 30*(2), 111–120.

Davison, H. K., & Burke, M. J. (2000). Sex discrimination in simulated employment contexts: A meta-analytic investigation. *Journal of Vocational Behavior, 56*(2), 225–248.

de Janasz, S., Forret, M., Haack, D., & Jonsen, K. (2013). Family status and work attitudes: An investigation in a professional services firm. *British Journal of Management, 24*(2), 191–210.

Elsbach, K. D., Cable, D. M., & Sherman, J. W. (2010). How passive 'face time' affects perceptions of employees: Evidence of spontaneous trait inference. *Human Relations, 63*(6), 735–760.

Fritz, C., & Van Knippenberg, D. (2018). Gender and leadership aspiration: The impact of work–life initiatives. *Human Resource Management, 57*(4), 855–868.

Gascoigne, C., & Kelliher, C. (2018). The transition to part-time: How professionals negotiate 'reduced time and workload' i-deals and craft their jobs. *Human Relations, 71*(1), 103–125.

Greenberg, D., & Landry, E. M. (2011). Negotiating a flexible work arrangement: How women navigate the influence of power and organizational context. *Journal of Organizational Behavior, 32*(8), 1163–1188.

Guerrero, S., Bentein, K., & Lapalme, M. È. (2014). Idiosyncratic deals and high performers' organizational commitment. *Journal of Business and Psychology, 29*(2), 323–334.

Guerrero, S., & Jeanblanc, H. C. (2017). Networking and development idiosyncratic deals. *Career Development International, 22*(7), 816–828.

Guerrero, S., Jeanblanc, H., & Veilleux, M. (2016). Development idiosyncratic deals and career success. *Career Development International, 21*(1), 19–30.

Ho, V. T., & Tekleab, A. G. (2016). A model of idiosyncratic deal-making and attitudinal outcomes. *Journal of Managerial Psychology, 31*(3), 642–656.

Hornung, S., Rousseau, D. M., & Glaser, J. (2008). Creating flexible work arrangements through idiosyncratic deals. *Journal of Applied Psychology, 93*(3), 655–664.

Hornung, S., Rousseau, D. M., Glaser, J., Angerer, P., & Weigl, M. (2010). Beyond top-down and bottom-up work redesign: Customizing job content through idiosyncratic deals. *Journal of Organizational Behavior, 31*(2–3), 187–215.

Kawakami, K., Dovidio, J. F., & van Kamp, S. (2005). Kicking the habit: Effects of nonstereotypic association training and correction processes on hiring decisions. *Journal of Experimental Social Psychology, 41*(1), 68–75.

Kim, H., & Gong, Y. (2017). Effects of work–family and family–work conflicts on flexible work arrangements demand: A gender role perspective. *The International Journal of Human Resource Management, 28*(20), 2936–2956.

Kong, D. T., Ho, V. T., & Garg, S. (2020). Employee and coworker idiosyncratic deals: Implications for emotional exhaustion and deviant behaviors. *Journal of Business Ethics, 164*(3), 593–609.

Konrad, A. M., & Linnehan, F. (1995). Formalized HRM structures: Coordinating equal employment opportunity or concealing organizational practices? *Academy of Management Journal, 38*(3), 787–820.

Kossek, E. E., Lautsch, B. A., & Eaton, S. C. (2006). Telecommuting, control, and boundary management: Correlates of policy use and practice, job control, and work-family effectiveness. *Journal of Vocational Behavior, 68*, 347–367.

Kossek, E. E., Ollier-Malaterre, A., Lee, M. D., Pichler, S., & Hall, D. T. (2016). Line managers' rationales for professionals' reduced-load work in embracing and ambivalent organizations. *Human Resource Management*, 55(1), 143–171.

Kulik, C. T. (2020). 2019 Presidential address—Management scholars, end users, and the power of thinking small. *Academy of Management Review*, 45(2), 273–279.

Kulik, C. T., Perera, S., & Cregan, C. (2016). Engage me: The mature-age worker and stereotype threat. *Academy of Management Journal*, 59(6), 2132–2156.

Lai, L., Rousseau, D. M., & Chang, K. T. T. (2009). Idiosyncratic deals: Coworkers as interested third parties. *Journal of Applied Psychology*, 94(2), 547–556.

Lamont, R. A., Swift, H. J., & Abrams, D. (2015). A review and meta-analysis of age-based stereotype threat: Negative stereotypes, not facts, do the damage. *Psychology and Aging*, 30, 180–193.

Las Heras, M., Rofcanin, Y., Matthijs Bal, P., & Stollberger, J. (2017). How do flexibility i-deals relate to work performance? Exploring the roles of family performance and organizational context. *Journal of Organizational Behavior*, 38(8), 1280–1294.

Lawrence, B. S. (1988). New wrinkles in the theory of age: Demography, norms, and performance ratings. *Academy of Management Journal*, 31, 309–337.

Lemmon, G., Westring, A., Michel, E. J., Wilson, M. S., & Glibkowski, B. C. (2016). A cross-domain exploration of performance benefits and costs of idiosyncratic deals. *Journal of Leadership & Organizational Studies*, 23(4), 440–455.

Leslie, L. M., Manchester, C. F., Park, T. Y., & Mehng, S. A. (2012). Flexible work practices: A source of career premiums or penalties? *Academy of Management Journal*, 55(6), 1407–1428.

Li, Y., Perera, S., Kulik, C. T., & Metz, I. (2019). Inclusion climate: A multilevel investigation of its antecedents and consequences. *Human Resource Management*, 58(4), 353–369.

Liao, C., Wayne, S. J., & Rousseau, D. M. (2016). Idiosyncratic deals in contemporary organizations: A qualitative and meta-analytical review. *Journal of Organizational Behavior*, 37, S9–S29.

Marescaux, E., & De Winne, S. (2016). Equity versus need: How do coworkers judge the distributive fairness of i-deals? In M. Bal & D. M. Rousseau (Eds.), *Idiosyncratic deals between employees and organizations: Conceptual issues, applications and the role of co-workers* (pp. 107–121). Psychology Press.

Marescaux, E., De Winne, S., & Rofcanin, Y. (2021). Co-worker reactions to i-deals through the lens of social comparison: The role of fairness and emotions. *Human Relations*, 74(3), 329–353.

Marescaux, E., De Winne, S., & Sels, L. (2019). Idiosyncratic deals from a distributive justice perspective: Examining co-workers' voice behavior. *Journal of Business Ethics, 154*(1), 263–281.

Maitlis, S. (2005). The social processes of organizational sensemaking. *Academy of Management Journal, 48*(1), 21–49.

Michielsens, E., Bingham, C., & Clarke, L. (2014). Managing diversity through flexible work arrangements: Management perspectives. *Employee Relations, 36*(1), 49–69.

Ng, T. W. (2017). Can idiosyncratic deals promote perceptions of competitive climate, felt ostracism, and turnover? *Journal of Vocational Behavior, 99*, 118–131.

O'Connor, L. T., & Cech, E. A. (2018). Not just a mothers' problem: The consequences of perceived workplace flexibility bias for all workers. *Sociological Perspectives, 61*(5), 808–829.

Oostrom, J. K., Pennings, M., & Bal, P. M. (2016). How do idiosyncratic deals contribute to the employability of older workers? *Career Development International, 21*(2), 176–192.

Paustian-Underdahl, S. C., & Halbesleben, J. R. (2014). Examining the influence of climate, supervisor guidance, and behavioral integrity on work–family conflict: A demands and resources approach. *Journal of Organizational Behavior, 35*(4), 447–463.

Pitt-Catsouphes, M., & Matz-Costa, C. (2008). The multigenerational workforce: Workplace flexibility and engagement. *Community Work & Family, 11*, 215–229.

Posthuma, R. A., & Campion, M. A. (2009). Age stereotypes in the workplace: Common stereotypes, moderators, and future research directions. *Journal of Management, 35*(1), 158–188.

Rofcanin, Y., Kiefer, T., & Strauss, K. (2017). What seals the I-deal? Exploring the role of employees' behaviours and managers' emotions. *Journal of Occupational and Organizational Psychology, 90*(2), 203–224.

Rofcanin, Y., Las Heras, M., Jose Bosch, M., Stollberger, J., & Mayer, M. (2021). How do weekly obtained task i-deals improve work performance? The role of relational context and structural job resources. *European Journal of Work and Organizational Psychology, 30*(4), 555–565.

Rousseau, D. M. (2005). *I-deals: Idiosyncratic deals employees bargain for themselves*. ME Sharp. Inc.

Rousseau, D. M., Ho, V. T., & Greenberg, J. (2006). I-deals: Idiosyncratic terms in employment relationships. *Academy of Management Review, 31*(4), 977–994.

Rousseau, D. M., Tomprou, M., & Simosi, M. (2016). Negotiating flexible and fair idiosyncratic deals (i-deals). *Organizational Dynamics, 45*(3), 185–196.

Rudman, L. A., & Phelan, J. E. (2008). Backlash effects for disconfirming gender stereotypes in organizations. *Research in Organizational Behavior, 28*, 61–79.

Rudolph, C. W., & Baltes, B. B. (2017). Age and health jointly moderate the influence of flexible work arrangements on work engagement: Evidence from two empirical studies. *Journal of Occupational Health Psychology, 22*(1), 40–58.

Schein, V. E. (2007). Women in management: Reflections and projections. *Women in Management Review, 22*(1), 6–18.

Steele, C. M. (1997). A threat in the air: How stereotypes shape intellectual identity and performance. *The American Psychologist, 52*, 613–629.

Stynen, D., Forrier, A., & Sels, L. (2014). The relationship between motivation to work and workers' pay flexibility: The moderation of age. *Career Development International, 19*(2), 183–203.

Tharenou, P., & Kulik, C. T. (2020). Skilled migrants employed in developed, mature economies: From newcomers to organizational insiders. *Journal of Management, 46*(6), 1156–1181.

Tsui, A. S., & O'reilly, C. A., III. (1989). Beyond simple demographic effects: The importance of relational demography in superior-subordinate dyads. *Academy of Management Journal, 32*(2), 402–423.

Vidyarthi, P. R., Chaudhry, A., Anand, S., & Liden, R. C. (2014). Flexibility i-deals: How much is ideal? *Journal of Managerial Psychology, 29*, 246–265.

Vidyarthi, P. R., Singh, S., Erdogan, B., Chaudhry, A., Posthuma, R., & Anand, S. (2016). Individual deals within teams: Investigating the role of relative i-deals for employee performance. *Journal of Applied Psychology, 101*(11), 1536–1552.

Wang, S., Liu, Y., & Shalley, C. E. (2018). Idiosyncratic deals and employee creativity: The mediating role of creative self-efficacy. *Human Resource Management, 57*(6), 1443–1453.

Wilkinson, K., Tomlinson, J., & Gardiner, J. (2018). The perceived fairness of work–life balance policies: A UK case study of solo-living managers and professionals without children. *Human Resource Management Journal, 28*(2), 325–339.

World Economic Forum [WEF]. (2020). *Mind the 100 year gap*. World Economic Forum, Available at https://www.weforum.org/reports/gender-gap-2020-report-100-years-pay-equality

CHAPTER 11

I-deals and Employee Well-Being: Examining I-deals from JD-R Perspective

Arnold B. Bakker and *Can Ererdi*

Introduction

Change is constant, and the world is now changing at a very rapid pace. This change in the fundamental mechanisms of the world not only encompasses nations, sectors and industries, but organizations and people within them as well (Nye Wille et al., 2021). Thus, it is fair to say that people working within organizations are not immune to changes within the external environment. This change brings about certain expectations, both on the part of the organizations and on part of the employees. While the modern organizations demand certain elements from the employees such as agility, adaptability and preciseness, the employees in turn have

A. B. Bakker
Erasmus University Rotterdam, Lingnan University Hong Kong, University of Johannesburg, Johannesburg, South Africa
e-mail: bakker@essb.eur.nl

C. Ererdi (✉)
University of Reading, Reading, UK
e-mail: c.ererdi@henley.ac.uk

© The Author(s), under exclusive license to Springer Nature Switzerland AG 2022
S. Anand and Y. Rofcanin (eds.), *Idiosyncratic Deals at Work*,
https://doi.org/10.1007/978-3-030-88516-8_11

their own demands from organizations in the form of individualized practices, especially revolving around human resource management processes (Rousseau et al., 2009). In relation to these dyadic expectations from organizations and employees, and with the increasing expectations of the employees (especially with millennials entering the workforce) Bal and Rousseau (2015) have argued for individualized human needs and values to be placed at the centre of human resource practices. Building on the tenets of i-deals theory (Rousseau et al., 2006), scholars have explored the reciprocal exchange between individual work needs and preferences of employees and the mechanisms through which organizations respond to these needs and preferences, referred as idiosyncratic deals. I-deals[1] research shows that granting of such arrangements results in positive outcomes on part of the emloyee such as productivity and desirable work behaviours and attitudes (see Liao et al., 2016 for a review).

The core aim of this chapter is to understand and examine the transformation of the view on i-deals from a reciprocity-based view to a resource-based view. Exploration of this transition is important because modern employees aim to expand or change their boundaries and aim to be more proactive compared to previous generations (Basile & Beauregard, 2016). In regard to this exploration, we integrate a well-being perspective and explore this transformation on the view on i-deals from a well-being point of view. In doing so, we provide future research questions which could be addressed in regard to i-deals and well-being.

In this chapter, first, we will examine the dominant theoretical perspectives on i-deals. The most popular theoretical framework in examining i-deals, social exchange theory (SET), conceptualizes the i-deal negotiation process as a set of social exchanges among employee, employer and co-workers (Blau, 1964). Additionally, SET argues that the end goal of granting i-deals is creating reciprocity, which refers to a context where employees with i-deals are apt to feel obligated to reciprocate through positive work attitudes and behaviours that ultimately benefit the employer (Anand et al., 2018). Further on, the psychological contract approach to i-deals will be examined, again touching on the aspect of

---

[1] Research to date on i-deals has conceptualized different types of such deals: namely flexibility, task and development i-deals. We adopt a generic perspective on i-deals and do not discuss the differences between such deals. Some theoretical perspectives in this chapter will be more relevant for specific types of i-deals but this is not the core goal of this chapter. In our investigation of i-deals, we adopt a more generic and general view.

reciprocity, but focusing on the difference between i-deals and psychological contracts. The third dominant theory on i-deals, signalling theory, incorporates the aspect of emotional signals within the i-deals negotiation process. After these dominant theories, this chapter will focus on a resource-based view, where i-deals are conceptualized as desired and beneficial resources for the employee. Finally, this chapter will examine the role of person-organization fit in relation to how a central motive for negotiating (employee) and granting (supervisor) i-deals is to create a better fit between the person and the job/organization.

This chapter contributes to recent debates on the importance of person-organization fit, which could be the link between i-deals and their conceptualization as resources within the job demands-resources theory (JD-R; Bakker & Demerouti, 2017; Demerouti et al., 2001). We maintain that extant research falls short in capturing exactly how i-deals arrive at their positive outcomes, or how they could be used as tools to improve employee compatibility with organizations. Hence, the first aim of this chapter is to apply JD-R theory to understand how i-deals could be used as mechanisms for employees and organizations in improving person-organization fit. In this context, we argue that a central motive for negotiating and granting i-deals is to create a better fit between the person and the job/organization. Building on JD-R theory, we conceptualize i-deals as mechanisms in which employees create job resources through individualized arrangements with the organization, as a response to job demands, by increasing person-organization and person-job fit.

Our arguments and review of i-deals literature offer a fresh perspective of how i-deals research can evolve from a reciprocity-based view to a resource-based view. This is in line with the genesis of i-deals (Rousseau, 2005) wherein individual arrangements between the employee and the organization may improve employee attitudes such as fit with their jobs and organizations. While in this chapter we offer a general perspective of i-deals, two types of such deals are prevalent in the literature: flexibility i-deals and developmental i-deals. Flexibility i-deals refer to one-off deals between employees and the organization, where certain aspects such as working times and schedules are negotiated (Tang & Hornung, 2015). On the other hand, development i-deals are concerned with enrichment of one's job structure, expanding the scope of the job within the boundaries of the work domain. Building on this angle, while majority of the previous studies have mainly drawn on reciprocity or signalling perspectives to drive work performance (e.g. Anand et al., 2010; Liao et al., 2016), we point out that i-deals should be conceptualized as strategies to accumulate certain personal resources which employees can use to counter the strain caused by job demands and to improve their fit with their organizations.

Dominant Theoretical Perspectives on I-deals

Reciprocity Based Perspectives on I-deals

Social Exchange Theory

Since the initial conceptualization of i-deals by Rousseau (2005), the dominant perspective on i-deals has been social exchange theory. With regard to their triangular nature (Lai et al., 2009), which involves the employee, the employer and the co-workers, i-deals could be conceptualized as social exchanges, in which actors and observers exchange behaviour and information, with the end aim of fulfilling unique needs of the deal seeking employees. According to Blau (1964), social exchange refers to voluntary actions of individuals that are motivated by the returns they are expected to bring from the exchange partners. The position on i-deals from a social exchange perspective starts at the idea that i-deals by their nature are exchanges between employer and employees. By granting personalized work arrangements to employees, organizations generate a basis for reciprocity with their employees (Rousseau, 2005). The main motivation in granting i-deals on part of the organization is the idea that these work arrangements are actually responses to specific employee needs. The recipients of such deals are likely to reciprocate with the grantor through constructive behaviours (Anand et al., 2010). Indeed, empirical studies reveal that i-deals are positively associated with organizational commitment (Rosen et al., 2013), constructive voice (Ng & Feldman, 2012) and organizational citizenship behaviours (Anand et al., 2010).

Eisenberger, Armeli, Rexwinkel and Lynch (2001) argue that employees should strengthen their ties with their organizations through long-term and prolonged social exchanges, which then would increase perceived organizational support, and finally in role performance of the focal employee. Conceptualizing granting of i-deals as successful social exchanges between employer and employee then would make the employee feel as a valued member of the organization. Moreover, i-deals represent the organization signalling interest in the development and personal growth of the employee (Liu et al., 2013). Furthermore, Hornung et al. (2008) argue that employees who enjoy these social exchanges with their employers tend to be more motivated. Social exchange and reciprocity have thus been used to establish positive outcomes of i-deals. In addition, scholars have also utilized social exchange theory to show the impact of supervisor and subordinate relationship quality on successful negotiation of i-deals (Rosen et al., 2013).

Although social exchange theory has been the dominating theoretical framework in analyzing i-deals, Liao et al. (2016) argue that it is insufficient in explaining the process as a whole. The central tenet in this argument is that i-deals don't necessarily generate reciprocity, and that these mechanisms and their consequences are dependent on the type of the i-deal itself. Thus, further in this chapter, we will explore other theoretical perspectives through which i-deals could be examined.

FUTURE RESEARCH DIRECTIONS ON SOCIAL EXCHANGE THEORY PERSPECTIVE ON I-DEALS IN RELATION TO EMPLOYEE WELL-BEING

The research path that we propose is again related to the reciprocity approach of social exchange practices. Investigating i-deals from a social exchange perspective tells us that positive outcomes of the i-deal granting process are a result of reciprocity; the employee feels obliged to react positively to successful granting of i-deal. Also, we have seen that reciprocity is a discretionary behaviour, where the employee doesn't have to react positively, even if the negotiation is successful.

Psychological Contract Perspective on I-deals

While the relationship between employees and organizations have usually been conceptualized as an exchange relationship (i.e. social exchange), psychological contracts provide a different conceptualization to this relationship, albeit still building the theory on an exchange perspective. Rousseau (1989) defines the psychological contract as the depiction of the exchange relationship between the individual employee and the organization. Psychological contacts comprise a summary of subjective individual beliefs regarding the 'terms and conditions of a reciprocal exchange agreement between that focal person and another party' (Robinson & Rousseau, 1994), which include judgments about own contributions and the employer/organization's reciprocal obligations. Further studies on psychological contracts within organizational settings looked at i-deals as mechanisms in shaping the psychological contract between employee and employer, and as tools to improve employee engagement in times of austerity (Davis & van der Heijden, 2018). A more recent study investigated the effects of psychological contract breach by subordinates in relation to the weekly emotional exhaustion of supervisors (De Jong et al., 2020). Guerrero et al. (2014) on the other hand investigated the relationship between idiosyncratic deals and high performers organizational commitment through the lens of psychological contracts. While person-organization exchange relationships are at the core of organizational behaviour, we can assume psychological contract as the control through which this mechanism is audited.

Looking at i-deals from a psychological contract perspective requires us to refer back to social exchange theory and the concept of reciprocity. Davis and Van der Heijden (2018) argue that not everyone may be motivated by social exchange and expecting the obligation to be reciprocated in cognitive/behavioural ways is not always applicable, since these responses are discretionary. Accordingly, we can argue that i-deals are related to, but different from psychological contracts. While i-deals are actual treatments that result in resources granted by the organization to the employee, psychological contracts are expectations of employees from their organizations or promises and obligations of organizations to their employees (Guest & Conway, 2002). Employee pursuit of an i-deal can thus be dependent on whether the employee perceives the organization to have obligations towards them as a result of their efforts. We note that this relationship is reciprocal, as the outcome of i-deal negotiation process can change some elements (e.g. new obligations or expectations) or the nature (e.g. relational to transactional) of the psychological contract between the employee and the organization.

Future Research Directions on Psychological Contract Perspective on I-deals in Relation to Employee Well-Being

Looking at i-deals through the lens of psychological contracts requires another perspective: although the i-deal itself is not a psychological contract, the expectations of such i-deals from the organization can be conceptualized as the psychological contract itself. Future researchers may conceptualize employee and employer expectations of an i-deal as the content of the psychological contract. The fulfilment of this expectation within the psychological contract framework would then lead to different well-being outcomes. The relationship between the breach of a psychological contract and negative employee consequences in the form of anger, disappointment, betrayal and intentions to quit are already examined within the literature (Robinson & Rousseau, 1994). Drawing on and extending this research, future researchers may investigate i-deals as expectations from one party of the psychological contract, and how the response from the organization, either in the shape of fulfilment of this expectation or its disregard, affects employee well-being within organizations.

Signalling Function Based Perspectives of I-deals

The third dominant framework in analysing i-deals is signalling theory (Spence, 1978). Signalling theory encompasses communications by and within organizations (Guest, Sanders, Rodrigues & Oliveira, 2021). According to signalling theory, the effectiveness of signalling depends on whether the message is interpreted in a manner consistent with the actual intention of the signaller (Spence, 2002). According to this framework, the granting of i-deals to employees by the organization signals good-will and supportive intentions on part of the organization. This framework is built on the idea that employees are valuable members of organizations and in turn, granting i-deals to the valuable members of the organization signals the good intent of the organization towards its employees. Referring to signalling theory from the perspective of an employee receiving an i-deal, the successful negotiation of an i-deal may be perceived as a signal of recognition from the organization. Moreover, the signaller (employer) conveys certain messages to the receiver (employee) in the hope of eliciting positive behaviours favourable to both parties (Belogolovsky & Bamberger, 2014). The effectiveness of the signalling process depends on both the signaller who has to be consistent in their actions (Bergh et al., 2014), and the receiver who has to accurately interpret the signal.

The perspective of signalling theory on i-deals is aligned with the aspect of emotional signals within the i-deals negotiation process. Individuals' emotions have two purposes within the i-deals process: first, they act as a reflector of one's inner state, and second they convey information about the intentions of the individual who is at the receiving end of these emotions. Relating this dual tenet of signalling theory to i-deals, research has shown that positive emotions facilitate the realization of a negotiated deal (Rofcanin et al., 2017). Thus, we posit that employees who persist in receiving i-deals convey positive emotional responses as a result of the successful i-deal process. While Kong et al. (2020) have shown that employee and co-worker idiosyncratic deals had implications for decrease in the emotional exhaustion of employees, Marescaux, de Winne and Rofcanin (2021) have supported the argument that i-deals have positive emotional consequences by looking at such deals from a social comparison perspective.

Future Research Directions on Signalling Perspective on I-deals in Relation to Employee Well-Being

If the i-deal granting process is examined under the signalling theory lens, the intentions and messages of both parties in the process should be clear and concise enough to not create any information discrepancies. In the event where one party of the i-deal granting process doesn't adhere to these standards, information discrepancy can occur and negatively impact employee well-being. On the other hand, if both parties are clear in the messages they want to signal, employee well-being will not be negatively impacted. Furthermore, future researchers may look at the signals conveyed by both parties in the i-deal process and examine the conditions under which discrepancies occur. We posit that investigating the signals and examining which scenarios lead to changes in employee well-being would be a welcome expansion of the i-deals literature.

Resource-Based Perspectives of I-deals in Relation to Job Demands-Resources Theory

JD-R theory (Bakker & Demerouti, 2014; Demerouti et al., 2001) defines job demands as job aspects that require physical and psychological effort, and thus are associated with certain physiological and psychological costs on part of the employee. On the flip side of the coin, job resources refer to those aspects of the job which are: (a) functional in achieving work goals, (b) reduce job demands and the associated physiological and psychological costs, and (c) stimulate personal growth, learning, and development (Bakker et al., 2014; Crawford et al., 2010). These tenets of job resources are not only beneficial in responding to the job demands but are beneficial in their own right as well. Linking job resources to the tenet of conservation of resources theory (Hobfoll, 2001), where the prime motivation of humans is maintaining and accumulating certain resources, we can see that job resources are not only important as a tool in responding to job demands, but also are tools in reaching other resources in the environment. JD-R framework provides researchers with the ability of conceptualizing each work environment irrespective of the actual demands and resources of the job. Substantial research has utilized this framework to explore the impact of job characteristics on employee well-being (For a review see Bakker & Demerouti, 2017). Looking at job characteristics from a JD-R theory perspective, scholars have argued that job demands such as high work pressure, emotional demands and role ambiguity can lead to negative well-being outcomes for employees. On the other hand, job resources such as social support, performance feedback and autonomy are related to positive employee outcomes.

Investigating i-deals from a JD-R theory perspective, it is argued that in creating job demands, and as a result, job strain, certain characteristics of jobs inadvertently lead to depletion of employees' mental and physical resources (Bakker & Demerouti, 2007). This depletion of resources, according to Hockey, Hockey, Gaillard and Burov (2003), happens through several different patterns of indirect degradation. Of these degradations, compensatory costs refer to an increase in activity or effort, strategy adjustments refer to narrowing of attention and increased selectivity in task attainment, and finally fatigue-after-effects, which refer to risky choices and fatigue (Bakker & Demerouti, 2007). While the direct effects of job demands and job resources are certainly important in understanding the impact of job characteristics on employees' physiological and psychological well-being, the interaction of job demands and resources are also important in understanding these effects. Bakker et al. (2003) propose that job resources can be effectively used as tools in buffering the impact of job demands on job strain. It is important to note that although i-deals have been scrutinized through different theoretical lenses within the literature (e.g. reciprocity-based and signalling-based), limited attention has been given to integrating with JD-R theory. We believe this integration will contribute substantially to i-deals literature since the issue of job demands and the resulting job strain continues to be an important challenge for organizations, and i-deals may offer concrete resources for countering strain.

On the other side of the coin, there are job resources, which are motivational in nature. This motivational aspect of job resources then leads to positive outcomes on part of the employee such as engagement and performance. The intrinsic motivational role of job resources arises from the idea that job resources are in fact tools to foster employee growth and development. The extrinsic motivational aspect of job resources arises because they can be helpful in attaining certain work goals. This extrinsic aspect of job resources can further be strengthened through effort-recovery model, which argues that certain job aspects provide employees with the resources to improve their dedication and effort towards the task in hand. As the content of an i-deal is the resource it involves (Rousseau et al., 2009), it makes sense to examine i-deals from JD-R lens.

Future Research Directions on Resource-Based Perspective on I-deals in Relation to Employee Well-Being

Researchers working on i-deals from a resource-based perspective in relation to employee well-being can conceptualize i-deals as job resources to counter the unwanted strain caused by job demands. In this context, conceptualizing the granting of i-deals as resources within the environment is crucial: researchers and HR professionals alike can use i-deals as a countermeasure in buffering the strain created by job demands. The operationalization of i-deals as resources to counter job-stress has been under-studied. We believe applying a resource-based view on i-deals and measuring how well they work as buffering resources in contrast to job demands and strain will be a fruitful future research endeavour.

Person-Organization Fit Perspective in Linking I-deals and JD-R Theory

Broadly defined, Person-Organization fit refers to the compatibility between individuals and organizations (Kristof, 1996). But this idea of compatibility is the differentiator in the context of P-O fit. Supplementary compatibility refers to characteristics possessed by individuals that are similar to others in the environment. On the other hand, complementary fit refers to characteristics that make whole or fill what is missing in the environment (Muchinsky & Monahan, 1987). Further, there are two perspectives to understand fit: needs-supplies and demands-abilities. The needs-supply perspective on P-O Fit explores the organization satisfying employee needs. On the other hand, demands-abilities perspective looks at the match between employee abilities and organization's expectations or demands (Kristof, 1996). Overall, it is possible to discuss four different operationalizations of P-O fit: value congruence, goal congruence, individual preferences and personality congruence.

Based on value and/or goal congruence individuals are selected into organizations, improving the organizational homogeneity over time (Schneider et al., 2001; Vroom, 1966). The second operationalization of P-O fit happens at the individual personality level: P-O fit is measured as the match between individuals' characteristics and personality and the organizational climate (or organizational personality). The final operationalization refers to the match between the needs or preferences of the individual and the organizational systems and structures in place (Cable & Judge, 1994). In this context, it is possible to see the similarities between person-job fit and person-organization fit. Individuals who have certain needs from their jobs will feel fulfilled if those needs are satisfied by their jobs. Person-job fit is defined by Edwards (1991) as the fit between the abilities of a person and the demands of a job (demands-abilities) or the desires of a person and the attributes of a job (needs-supplies). It is not uncommon to see people choosing jobs based on the congruence with their own personal characteristics.

In this chapter, particular attention is given to person-organization fit theories, and especially person-job fit in explaining the link between i-deals and JD-R theory. The definition of a job by Kristof (1996) is very relevant to how we conceptualize person-organization or person-job fit: the tasks a person is expected to accomplish in exchange for employment, as well as the characteristics of the task. We propose and recommend future studies to use person-job fit, especially demands-abilities and needs-supplies fit in explaining how i-deals can serve as a mechanism to improve person-organization fit. Further delving into the needs-supplies perspective, individual desires or needs can be defined as goals, psychological needs, interests and values (Hoffman & Woehr, 2006; Kristof-Brown et al., 2005). On the other hand, organizational supplies or resources include general characteristics of the occupation, pay and other job attributes. We integrate needs-supplies fit with job demands and resources theory (Bakker & Demerouti, 2007), arguing that the central motivation for negotiation and granting of i-deals is to create a better fit between the person and the job. Relating this argument to the idea that i-deals can be made for concrete job resources and can fulfil job demands, we posit needs-supplies as demands and responses within the workplace. In organizations, through i-deals, job characteristics or work environment can be optimized for the individual employee's needs and skills. A natural conclusion is that the whole process of negotiation and granting of i-deals has the aim of improving person-job fit, especially on the needs and supplies aspect of the concept. Overall, we argue that in responding to employees' needs of individualized HRM practices by the process of negotiating and granting i-deals, the main aim of organizations is to create a better person-job fit. Moreover, looking at the demands-abilities aspect of person-job fit, the demands can be defined as the set of requirements for carrying out job tasks, while abilities represent what the individual has (e.g. knowledge and skills) that can be used to meet the job requirements (Caldwell & O'Reilly, 1990; Rounds et al., 1987). Looking at demands-abilities fit through the lens of JD-R and i-deals, we argue that i-deals are not only made regarding certain job resources but also job demands.

Future Research Directions on P-O Fit perspective on I-deals in Relation to Employee Well-Being

The relationship between person-organization fit and employee well-being has been previously tested in the literature: Park et al. (2011) investigated how core self-evaluations and person-organization fit affects the relationship between person-job fit, employees' self-esteem and subjective well-being. They have shown that employees with high P-O fit displayed increases in happiness compared to employees with low P-O fit as P-J fit increased. Further, Roczniewska et al. (2018) illustrate that fit creates perceptions of organizational justice that in turn lead to employee well-being. The have found that the more organizational characteristics matched individual promotion and prevention focus of the employees, the more the employees perceived their workplace as just. Other research has shown that lack of fit creates detrimental outcomes for employees. For example, Bakker and Costa (2014) argue that a misfit between the person and the organization can lead to burnout as a result of exposure to job demands which are not attainable by the skillset of the employee. Burnout can also result when employees perceive unfairness as a consequence of non-fit with their organizations (Roczniewska et al., 2018). Referring back to the JD-R model (Demerouti et al., 2001), burnout is related to a combination of physical exhaustion and mental disengagement, which can lead to lower employee well-being. We argue that the relationship between P-O fit and employee well-being revolves around burnout, and especially the physical consequences of exhaustion leading to a decline in employee well-being.

We therefore offer two interesting research paths related to P-O fit, i-deals and employee well-being. The first research stream conceptualizes i-deals as tools to improve P-O fit. Future researchers may investigate how the i-deal process can impact employee well-being by either leading to or decreasing burnout. Since it is argued that improved P-O fit decreases burnout by creating perceptions of justice, we believe it will be fruitful to explore how i-deals, with their delicate links to issues of fairness, can in fact improve P-O fit and employee well-being. The second stream of research that we propose is related to P-O mismatch: future researchers should investigate how co-workers react to the granting of i-deals in the workplace, and how these perceptions impact P-O fit and resulting employee well-being.

Discussion and Conclusion

One of the aims of this chapter is to understand and investigate the dominant theoretical frameworks through which i-deals are examined in the literature. In doing so, we first looked at social exchange theory as a framework, which argues for a set of exchanges between employee and employer with the end goal of creating reciprocity, and thus positive outcomes for both parties. We argue that social exchange theory is not comprehensive enough in that it does not consider situations that do not generate reciprocity, which is discretionary in nature and cannot be demanded or forced. Next, we examined i-deals through the lens of psychological contract theory. Psychological contracts and i-deals are similar in that they are both agreements between the employee and the employer; however, psychological contracts are expected contributions and reciprocal obligations, whereas i-deals are concrete resources to improve employee outcomes in the organization.

Signalling theory on the other hand relates to emotional responses of the contractual parties in the i-deals negotiation process. Key takeaways from this perspective on i-deals are that i-deals may serve as signals from the employer, effectiveness of the signalling process depends on consistency and accuracy of signals and can invoke emotional responses. Finally, from a resource-based perspective, i-deals can serve as resources to address strain created by job demands. In contrast to the previously mentioned theoretical frameworks through which i-deals have been scrutinized, JD-R theory has certain distinctions and advantages (Bakker & Demerouti, 2017). Perhaps the most important is the idea that i-deals can improve P-O fit and provide concrete resources to tackle job demands. This focus on i-deals as resources is a novel addition to the literature. Additionally, understanding this aspect of i-deals is important for supervisors who are committed to improving cohesion and compatibility between their employees and the organization. Supervisors can use negotiation and granting of i-deals as an organizational resource in order to (1) alleviate the strain created by job demands on employees, and (2) create a better fit between the person and the job/organization.

Finally, the last aim of this chapter is to provide different research paths for future researchers to benefit from, especially regarding the relationship between i-deals and employee well-being, under different theoretical frameworks. In doing so, we have included pathways for social exchange theory, psychological contract theory, signalling theory, resource-based view and person-organization fit. For social exchange, we believe a re-evaluation of the perspective in looking at i-deals as simple social exchanges is necessary, especially on the aspect of reciprocity where positive behaviour is expected as a response. On part of psychological contracts, we argued that future researchers may examine i-deals as expectations on part of employees, and how fulfilment or breach of these expectations can lead to different well-being outcomes. For signalling, we argued that clarity and consistency of the message is really important, and investigating the relationship between the quality of signals during the i-deal negotiation and implementation process and employee well-being is important. From a resource-based view on i-deals and employee well-being, future research should examine how i-deals can act as buffers in responding to job demands from the organization, and how this can in turn affect employee well-being. Finally, from a person-organization fit perspective, we argue that future research endeavours explore the association between i-deals, P-O fit and resulting employee well-being.

This chapter investigates reciprocity and signalling-based perspectives on i-deals. We argue that these perspectives make assumptions about employee reciprocity and assign a more active role to the organization. Finally, we argue that the dynamic conceptualization of employees in the resource-based perspective offers better understanding of employee behaviours within the i-deals granting process. We hope this discussion will ignite future research adopting a resource-based view (Table 11.1).

Table 11.1 Summary and recommendations for future research

Theoretical perspective	*Insights*
Social exchange theory perspective	• I-deals generate feelings of reciprocity in the recipients (employees) of such deals
	• Employees likely pay back the grantor (organization or supervisor) through positive outcomes due to feelings of indebtedness and expectations
	Future Research Pathways
	• Can i-deals simply be conceptualized as social exchanges between employers and employees?
	• Does the reciprocity angle of social exchange offer a complete perspective on the i-deal negotiation process?
	• What other mechanisms besides social exchange can offer positive well-being consequences as a result of the i-deals negotiation process?
Psychological contract perspective	• Implicit mutual expectations between the organization and the employee
	• While i-deals are actual treatment or resources granted by the organization to the employee (Davis & van der Heijden, 2018), psychological contracts reflect reciprocal expectations and obligations between employees and organizations (Rousseau, 1989)
	Future Research Pathways
	• Can employee expectations of i-deals from the organization be conceptualized as the content of the psychological contract?
	• If so, what are the effects of fulfilment or breach of the i-deal negotiation process on employee well-being?

(continued)

Table 11.1 (continued)

Theoretical perspective	Insights
Signalling theory perspective	• I-deals generate signals; employees as recipients of such deals receive, interpret and make use of these signals • The signals conveyed by the organization within the i-deals granting process should be clear, consistent and transparent to all stakeholders *Future Research Pathways* • What is the relationship between clarity and consistency of signals on part of the organization and the well-being of employees? • What is the impact of signal discrepancy within the i-deal negotiation process on the well-being of employees? • What types of HR policies can create positive well-being outcomes for employees?
Job demands—Resources theory perspective	• Job demands are defined as job aspects that require physical and psychological effort, and thus are associated with certain physiological and psychological costs for employees • Job resources refer to certain aspects of the job which are functional in achieving work goals, stimulate personal growth, learning and development (Bakker & Demerouti, 2007), and reduce job demands and the associated physiological and psychological costs *Future Research Pathways* • How can i-deals be conceptualized as job resources to buffer the strain created by job demands? • How can i-deals be used as motivational tools by HR departments to foster well-being in employees?
Person-organization fit perspective	• Person-Organization fit refers to the compatibility between individuals and organizations (Kristof, 1996) • The central motivation for negotiation and granting of i-deals is to create a better fit between the person and the job • Looking at demands-abilities fit through the lens of JD-R and i-deals, we argue that i-deals are not only made regarding certain job resources but also job demands *Future Research Pathways* • How can i-deals be used as tools to improve Person-Organization fit, and as a result, improve employee well-being through its impact on burnout? • What are the effects of i-deals on fit, fairness, and as a result, employee well-being?

REFERENCES

Anand, S., Hu, J., Vidyarthi, P., & Liden, R. C. (2018). Leader-member exchange as a linking pin in the idiosyncratic deals-performance relationship in workgroups. *The Leadership Quarterly, 29*(6), 698–708.

Anand, S., Vidyarthi, P. R., Liden, R. C., & Rousseau, D. M. (2010). Good citizens in poor-quality relationships: Idiosyncratic deals as a substitute for relationship quality. *Academy of Management Journal, 53*(5), 970–988.

Bakker, A. B., & Costa, P. L. (2014). Chronic job burnout and daily functioning: A theoretical analysis. *Burnout Research, 1*(3), 112–119.

Bakker, A. B., & Demerouti, E. (2007). The job demands-resources model: State of the art. *Journal of Managerial Psychology, 22*(3), 309–328.

Bakker, A. B., & Demerouti, E. (2014). Job Demands–Resources theory. In C. Cooper & P. Chen (Eds.), *Wellbeing: A complete reference guide* (pp. 37–64). Wiley-Blackwell.

Bakker, A. B., & Demerouti, E. (2017). Job demands–resources theory: Taking stock and looking forward. *Journal of Occupational Health Psychology, 22*(3), 273–285.

Bakker, A. B., Demerouti, E., & Sanz-Vergel, A. I. (2014). Burnout and work engagement: The JD-R approach. *Annual Review of Organizational Psychology and Organizational Behavior, 1*, 389–411.

Bakker, A. B., Demerouti, E., De Boer, E., & Schaufeli, W. B. (2003). Job demands and job resources as predictors of absence duration and frequency. *Journal of Vocational Behavior, 62*(2), 341–356.

Bal, M., & Rousseau, D. M. (Eds.). (2015). *Idiosyncratic deals between employees and organizations: Conceptual issues, applications and the role of co-workers*. Routledge.

Basile, K. A., & Beauregard, T. A. (2016). Strategies for successful telework: How effective employees manage work/home boundaries. *Strategic HR Review*.

Belogolovsky, E., & Bamberger, P. A. (2014). Signaling in secret: Pay for performance and the incentive and sorting effects of pay secrecy. *Academy of Management Journal, 57*(6), 1706–1733.

Bergh, D. D., Connelly, B. L., Ketchen, D. J., Jr., & Shannon, L. M. (2014). Signalling theory and equilibrium in strategic management research: An assessment and a research agenda. *Journal of Management Studies, 51*(8), 1334–1360.

Blau, P. M. (1964). Social exchange theory. *Retrieved September, 3*(2007), 62.

Cable, D. M., & Judge, T. A. (1994). Pay preferences and job search decisions: A person-organization fit perspective. *Personnel Psychology, 47*(2), 317–348.

Caldwell, D. F., & O'Reilly, C. A., III. (1990). Measuring person-job fit with a profile-comparison process. *Journal of Applied Psychology, 75*(6), 648.

Crawford, E. R., Lepine, J. A., & Rich, B. L. (2010). Linking job demands and resources to employee engagement and burnout: A theoretical extension and meta-analytic test. *Journal of Applied Psychology, 95*, 834–848.

Davis, A. S., & Van der Heijden, B. I. (2018). Reciprocity matters: Idiosyncratic deals to shape the psychological contract and foster employee engagement in times of austerity. *Human Resource Development Quarterly, 29*(4), 329–355.

Demerouti, E., Bakker, A. B., Nachreiner, F., & Schaufeli, W. B. (2001). The job demands-resources model of burnout. *Journal of Applied Psychology, 86*(3), 499–512.

De Jong, J., Clinton, M., Bal, M., & Van Der Heijden, B. (2020). Caught in the middle: How and when psychological contract breach by subordinates relates to weekly emotional exhaustion of supervisors. *Frontiers in Psychology, 11*, 3906.

Edwards, J. R. (1991). *Person-job fit: A conceptual integration, literature review, and methodological critique*. John Wiley & Sons.

Eisenberger, R., Armeli, S., Rexwinkel, B., Lynch, P. D., & Rhoades, L. (2001). Reciprocation of perceived organizational support. *Journal of Applied Psychology, 86*(1), 42.

Guerrero, S., Bentein, K., & Lapalme, M. È. (2014). Idiosyncratic deals and high performers' organizational commitment. *Journal of Business and Psychology, 29*(2), 323–334.

Guest, D. E., & Conway, N. (2002). Communicating the psychological contract: An employer perspective. *Human Resource Management Journal, 12*(2), 22–38.

Guest, D. E., Sanders, K., Rodrigues, R., & Oliveira, T. (2021). Signalling theory as a framework for analysing human resource management processes and integrating human resource attribution theories: A conceptual analysis and empirical exploration. *Human Resource Management Journal*, 31, 796–818. https://doi.org/10.1111/1748-8583.12326.

Hobfoll, S. E. (2001). The influence of culture, community, and the nested-self in the stress process: Advancing conservation of resources theory. *Applied Psychology, 50*, 337–370.

Hockey, G. R. J., Hockey, R., Gaillard, A. W., & Burov, O. (Eds.). (2003). *Operator functional state: The assessment and prediction of human performance degradation in complex tasks* (Vol. 355). IOS Press.

Hoffman, B. J., & Woehr, D. J. (2006). A quantitative review of the relationship between person–organization fit and behavioral outcomes. *Journal of Vocational Behavior, 68*(3), 389–399.

Hornung, S., Rousseau, D. M., & Glaser, J. (2008). Creating flexible work arrangements through idiosyncratic deals. *Journal of Applied Psychology, 93*(3), 655.

Kristof, A. L. (1996). Person-organization fit: An integrative review of its conceptualizations, measurement, and implications. *Personnel Psychology, 49*(1), 1–49.

Kristof-Brown, A. L., Zimmerman, R. D., & Johnson, E. C. (2005). Consequences of individuals fit at work: A meta-analysis OF person–job, person–organization, person–group, and person–supervisor fit. *Personnel Psychology, 58*(2), 281–342.

Kong, D. T., Ho, V. T., & Garg, S. (2020). Employee and coworker idiosyncratic deals: Implications for emotional exhaustion and deviant behaviors. *Journal of Business Ethics, 164*(3), 593–609.

Lai, L., Rousseau, D. M., & Chang, K. T. T. (2009). Idiosyncratic deals: Coworkers as interested third parties. *Journal of Applied Psychology, 94*(2), 547.

Liao, C., Wayne, S. J., & Rousseau, D. M. (2016). Idiosyncratic deals in contemporary organizations: A qualitative and meta-analytical review. *Journal of Organizational Behavior, 37,* S9–S29.

Liu, J., Lee, C., Hui, C., Kwan, H. K., & Wu, L. Z. (2013). Idiosyncratic deals and employee outcomes: The mediating roles of social exchange and self-enhancement and the moderating role of individualism. *Journal of Applied Psychology, 98*(5), 832.

Marescaux, E., De Winne, S., & Rofcanin, Y. (2021). Co-worker reactions to i-deals through the lens of social comparison: The role of fairness and emotions. *Human Relations, 74*(3), 329–353.

Muchinsky, P. M., & Monahan, C. J. (1987). What is person-environment congruence? Supplementary versus complementary models of fit. *Journal of Vocational Behavior, 31*(3), 268–277.

Ng, T. W., & Feldman, D. C. (2012). Employee voice behavior: A meta-analytic test of the conservation of resources framework. *Journal of Organizational Behavior, 33*(2), 216–234.

Nye, C. D., Wille, B., Amory, J., & De Fruyt, F. (2021). Are work activities related to interest change over time? A 22-year longitudinal study. *Journal of Personality and Social Psychology, 121*(4), 865–893.

Park, H. I., Monnot, M. J., Jacob, A. C., & Wagner, S. H. (2011). Moderators of the relationship between person-job fit and subjective well-being among Asian employees. *International Journal of Stress Management, 18*(1), 67.

Robinson, S. L., & Rousseau, D. M. (1994). Violating the psychological contract: Not the exception but the norm. *Journal of Organizational Behavior, 15*(3), 245–259.

Roczniewska, M., Retowski, S., & Higgins, E. T. (2018). How person-organization fit impacts employees' perceptions of justice and well-being. *Frontiers in Psychology, 8,* 2318.

Rofcanin, Y., Kiefer, T., & Strauss, K. (2017). What seals the I-deal? Exploring the role of employees' behaviours and managers' emotions. *Journal of Occupational and Organizational Psychology, 90*(2), 203–224.

Rosen, C. C., Slater, D. J., Chang, C. H., & Johnson, R. E. (2013). Let's make a deal: Development and validation of the ex post i-deals scale. *Journal of Management, 39*(3), 709–742.

Rounds, J. B., Dawis, R., & Lofquist, L. H. (1987). Measurement of person-environment fit and prediction of satisfaction in the theory of work adjustment. *Journal of Vocational Behavior, 31*(3), 297–318.

Rousseau, D. M. (1989). Psychological and implied contracts in organizations. *Employee Responsibilities and Rights Journal, 2,* 121–139.

Rousseau, D. M. (2005). *I-deals: Idiosyncratic deals employees Bargain for themselves.* ME Sharpe.

Rousseau, D. M., Ho, V. T., & Greenberg, J. (2006). I-deals: Idiosyncratic terms in employment relationships. *Academy of Management Review, 31*(4), 977–994.

Rousseau, D. M., Hornung, S., & Kim, T. G. (2009). Idiosyncratic deals: Testing propositions on timing, content, and the employment relationship. *Journal of Vocational Behavior, 74*(3), 338–348.

Schneider, B., Smith, D. B., & Paul, M. C. (2001). P-E fit and the attraction-selection-attrition model of organizational functioning: Introduction and overview. In M. Erez, U. Kleinbeck, & H. Thierry (Eds.), *Work motivation in the context of a globalizing economy* (pp. 231–246). Lawrence Erlbaum Associates Publishers.

Spence, M. (1978). Job market signaling. In *Uncertainty in economics* (pp. 281–306). Academic Press.

Spence, M. (2002). Signaling in retrospect and the informational structure of markets. *American Economic Review, 92*(3), 434–459.

Tang, Y., & Hornung, S. (2015). Work-family enrichment through I-Deals: Evidence from Chinese employees. *Journal of Managerial Psychology.*

Vroom, V. H. (1966). Organizational choice: A study of pre- and post-decision processes. *Organizational Behavior and Human Performance, 1*(2), 212–225.

CHAPTER 12

I-Deals in Context: A Summary and Critical Review of I-Deals Literature Around the Globe

S. Arzu Wasti, Nevra Cem Ersoy, and Berrin Erdogan

Idiosyncratic deals, or i-deals, are voluntary and individualized arrangements that are negotiated between an employee and an employer (Rousseau et al., 2006). These deals are customized to meet employees' specific needs and are intended to be beneficial for the organization as

S. A. Wasti (✉)
Sabancı University, Istanbul, Turkey
e-mail: awasti@sabanciuniv.edu

N. C. Ersoy
Izmir University of Economics, İzmir, Turkey
e-mail: nevra.ersoy@ieu.edu.tr

B. Erdogan
Portland State University, Portland, OR, USA
e-mail: berrine@pdx.edu

University of Exeter, Exeter, UK

© The Author(s), under exclusive license to Springer Nature Switzerland AG 2022
S. Anand and Y. Rofcanin (eds.), *Idiosyncratic Deals at Work*, https://doi.org/10.1007/978-3-030-88516-8_12

well, by allowing an organization to attract, retain, and motivate talent that would otherwise have been unavailable. The prevalence of i-deals suggests that employment terms are no longer standard and generic, but are differentiated across the organization at least in certain contexts. Mainstream research shows that supervisors believe i-deals would motivate the individual and result in higher performance, help them achieve higher levels of work-life balance, and can be a way of fulfilling otherwise unfulfilled obligations of the organization to the employee (Anand, 2010, 2018; Hornung et al., 2009). Further, i-deals may provide organizations with an expanded pool of highly qualified employees, as in the case of allowing employees to work beyond retirement (Bal et al., 2012).

Understanding the full implications of i-deals for employees, work groups, and organizations requires explicit consideration of the context in which they are granted and implemented. The legal, cultural, and economic context in which i-deals are negotiated will affect their prevalence, motivational value, and the potential backlash that may emerge through coworker reactions. Specifically, the very concept of i-deals assumes that employment relationships are negotiable. Rousseau (2001) referred to this idea as the "zone of negotiability". She observed that in countries like the United States (US), United Kingdom (UK), and New Zealand, very few aspects of employment conditions are legally prescribed, allowing organizations and individuals significant leeway in negotiating the terms and conditions of employment. In contrast, she noted that France and Belgium constitute the other end of the spectrum, where many aspects of employment has less flexibility and less room for negotiation, and countries such as India and Mexico show characteristics in between. Government regulations, industry norms about employment, and prevalence of unions constitute some of the reasons why there may be constraints on i-deal use at a country level. Similarly, societal culture may facilitate or hinder how acceptable and common i-deals are likely to be. For example, it is plausible that in collectivistic cultures where in-group harmony is given priority over individual achievement, employees will experience more discomfort with the idea of differentiated work arrangements, and prefer more uniform treatment of employees (e.g., Anand et al., 2010). Despite the importance of these country- or societal-level constraints or affordances, research on i-deals has tended to focus on individual and group-level influences, neglecting an explicit study and discussion of the macro-context-related factors in relation to the meaning, prevalence, and implications of i-deals for employees and organizations.

In this chapter, we critically review the empirical literature on i-deals with an eye toward country- or societal-level contextual factors that are likely to vary across national borders. The management/organizational behavior research emerging from the US has been repeatedly criticized for being non-contextual, i.e., for failing to explicate the implications of the cultural and institutional context in which the investigated organizations are embedded (e.g., Rousseau & Fried, 2001). Moreover, much of the management/organizational behavior research originating outside of the US is reflective of a "pseudo etic" approach, which refers to the treatment of US theories, constructs, and measures to be etic (universal), and to their unquestioning application in other societal contexts (Kim, 2001). While this approach can facilitate the identification of universals guiding human behavior and the comparison of such universals, there is increasing criticism that a pseudo etic approach limits researchers to Western constructs of uncertain cross-cultural relevance and hinders the study of important emic (culture-specific) constructs (e.g., Katigbak et al., 2002). These concerns have resulted in calls for indigenization of research pertaining to human behavior to make them contextually appropriate (Tsui, 2004).

In sum, research traditions across the board have not encouraged a greater appreciation or investigation of the cultural and institutional context that is crucial for a complete understanding of i-deals. Therefore, the main purpose of this systematic review is to assess the extent of contextualization in the i-deals research and to summarize the insights gleaned from the relatively more contextualized studies. We are particularly interested in pointing out possible country- or societal-level influences such as the societal culture, labor market characteristics, labor laws, and the economic prosperity over emerging findings. In the following section, we present the sample of studies that constituted our review and the coding scheme that was developed to assess the issues outlined above. Next, we present the results of our evaluation and conclude with recommendations for future work on i-deals.

Method

Sample

The search, which covered the period till November 2020, was restricted to English-language journals currently indexed in the Social Sciences Citation Index (SSCI) and Emerging Sources Citation Index (ESCI) using the keywords idiosyncratic deals and i-deals. This criterion allowed a conservative evaluation of methodological rigor and broad selection of journals. Given our focus, theoretical studies and literature reviews were eliminated from the sample, which resulted in a total of 74 articles, one of which was a meta-analysis.

Article Coding

All articles were initially coded for their reference information as well as whether they were single-country, multi-country (data collected from different countries but not comparatively analyzed), comparative, or mixed (combination of different countries) sample studies, which countries were investigated, and their substantive i-deals research topic (the construct itself, antecedents, and/or outcomes).

To evaluate the extent of contextualization in the articles, we focused on issues pertaining to research design, sampling, and instrumentation (Wasti & Önder, 2009). In terms of research design, we evaluated whether and to what extent any national or societal-level variables (e.g., societal culture, labor market, labor laws, and economic prosperity) were incorporated to the theorization of the study. It should be noted that the context, operationalized as such, can inform the research questions or the measures of single-country studies as well. In terms of sampling, we assessed if the sampling was convenience based or purposive, i.e., whether the studied countries were justified on substantive grounds in a theory-guided fashion (van de Vijver & Leung, 1997). Finally, our assessment regarding instrumentation pertained to studies that used a scale developed in another country context. The use of imported scales raises concerns about construct bias, as they may not be covering all aspects relevant to the construct in the new culture (Cheung & Leung, 1998). Yet, there are often practical reasons to use an existing instrument. Hence, in addition to assessing whether there were attempts to develop contextually sensitive scales, we evaluated whether imported instruments were tested in terms of their cross-cultural validity.

The specific codes that were applied are presented below. We also took extensive notes for each coding dimension as well as for an overall evaluation.

Approach to cross-cultural research design. All articles were examined to see whether the (national/cultural) context of the study setting was explicitly incorporated to the research questions or design. Specifically, articles were classified into one of the following five categories: Low contextualization articles were studies with no or passing mention of the national or societal-level characteristics of the study setting (e.g., societal culture, labor market, labor laws, economic prosperity), studies that simply mentioned that the study context is different than mainstream research, or those that only noted the findings may not be generalizable, without elaborating in what ways. Generalizability articles were studies with no explicit hypotheses based on national or societal-level characteristics of the study setting, but with an explicit aim to test generalizability or studies with ex post facto incorporation of national or societal-level characteristics of the study setting to interpret findings. Qualitative studies that identified national or societal characteristics in their findings were also categorized in this group. Theory-driven articles advanced hypotheses based on the national or societal-level characteristics of the study setting. Derived etic articles were studies that adapted imported theories or measures to better suit the local context by incorporating culture/context-specific theories or measures. Finally, high contextualization studies were articles that explicitly problematized the national or societal-level characteristics of the study setting for a better understanding of the phenomenon.

Sampling of culture/country. If an article explicitly justified the choice of the sample on the basis of cross-cultural theory or institutional characteristics, or explained that the sample constituted a meaningful test of generalizability, the sampling of culture/country was coded as purposive. Otherwise, it was coded as convenience sampling.

Instrumentation. All articles were first inspected to see whether satisfactory or acceptable reliability information was provided regarding the i-deals scale. Comparative studies were assessed in terms of whether they included covariance structure analysis, or some surrogate for it as a means for ascertaining conceptual equivalence across samples. Single-country articles were coded for the validation information they contained on the i-deals scale. Possible coding options for articles using imported scales were that there was no information, reference was provided for validation in the original source language, reference was provided for validation in the local language, or that validation analyses were conducted and satisfactorily reported.

Results

The Appendix presents all the articles and a summary of their associated codes. Before presenting the results of our analysis, some general observations are worthy of reporting. Only two studies were comparative with purposive sampling (Hornung et al., 2010; Ng & Feldman, 2015). Bal and Vossaert's (2019) scale development article had three studies with Dutch samples and a final study combining UK, US, European, and Asian samples. Kelly et al. (2020) combined samples from Chile and Columbia; Gascoigne and Kelliher (2018) combined Dutch and British interviewees in their qualitative study. Secondly, the samples represented a wide variety of countries from around the world, namely Australia, Belgium, Canada, Chile, China, Columbia, El Salvador, France, Germany, Greece, Hong Kong, India, Italy, Kenya, Netherlands, Philippines, South Korea, Switzerland, Taiwan, Turkey, UK, US, and Vietnam. The majority of the samples were from China, Germany, Netherlands, US, and Vietnam. Finally, of the 74 studies that were examined, one was a meta-analysis, one was an experimental vignette, eight were interview studies, and the remaining vast majority were survey-based studies.

Table 12.1 presents a summary of the articles in terms of their approach to contextualization. The findings with respect to research design indicate that about half of the articles (51%) are "Low contextualization" articles that do not incorporate national or societal-level variables at all, despite the availability and increased awareness of cultural theories, and calls for more contextualized research (e.g., Gelfand et al., 2017; Rousseau & Fried, 2001). Note that this approach is not limited to research emanating from white, educated, industrialized, rich, and democratic (WEIRD; Henrich et al., 2010) countries (e.g., Germany, Netherlands, US). Studies from countries like China, India, Kenya, and Vietnam have also derived their research questions, models, and measures from the mainstream literature, without explicating their significance to their own setting. As a case in point, Wang et al.'s (2018) study of Chinese employees begins by discussing the popularity of i-deals in the US without

Table 12.1 Approach to cross-cultural research design

	Low contextualization	Generalizability	Theory-driven	Derived etic	High contextualization
Comparative	0	1	1	0	0
Mixed	1	1	0	0	0
Multi-country	0	1	0	0	0
Single-country	36	22	3	2	5
Total	37 (51%)	25 (34%)	4 (5%)	2 (3%)	5 (7%)

Note The numbers represent the number of articles and the percentages are provided in parentheses. The meta-analytic study by Liao et al. (2014) is not included in the calculations
Low contextualization: Studies with no or passing mention of the national or societal-level characteristics of the study setting (e.g., societal culture, labor market, labor laws, economic prosperity); studies that simply note the study context is different than mainstream research; studies that note the findings may not be generalizable
Generalizability: Studies with no explicit hypotheses based on national or societal-level characteristics of the study setting, but with an explicit aim to test generalizability; studies with ex post facto incorporation of national or societal-level characteristics of the study setting to interpret findings; qualitative studies that identify the relevance of national or societal-level characteristics of the study setting
Theory-driven: Studies advancing theoretical hypotheses based on national or societal-level characteristics of the study setting
Derived etic: Studies adapting imported theories and methods to better suit the local context by incorporating culture/context-specific or culture/context-salient theories or measures
High contextualization: Studies that problematize the national or societal-level characteristics of the study setting for a better understanding of the phenomenon

a reference to their relevance in the Chinese context. In many of these studies, a passing mention is made to the study context, sometimes only in the methods section.

Table 12.1 shows that 36% of all articles were generalizability studies, which refer to studies that note that the study context is different (culturally, institutionally, or economically) than those covered in the mainstream literature or speculate on the role of their study context ex post, but do not advance hypotheses as to how these differences may play out. The generalizability studies covered a wide range of countries (including Australia, Belgium, China, El Salvador, France, Germany, Greece, India, Italy, Kenya, Netherlands, Philippines, South Korea, Switzerland, Vietnam, Turkey, UK, and US).

A few of these studies simply noted that the study context is different than the mainstream literature, and cautioned for generalizability. However, most were more cognizant about context. For instance, some studies in the generalizability group noted the specific characteristics of their study context to be relevant to their research question by reference to the extant literature. For instance, Rofcanin et al. (2018) proposed and found that servant leadership, which they argued was more prevalent in Southeast Asia, contributed to managers' using their i-deals for their subordinates' benefits in the Philippines. They also noted that their findings from the high in-group collectivist and uncertainty avoidant Philippines may not generalize to other contexts. Similarly, Las Heras, van der Heijden, et al. (2017) mentioned that El Salvador was an appropriate setting to study caregiving responsibilities and schedule i-deals, as it is characterized by collectivism and segregated gender roles. Likewise, Luu's (2017) study from Vietnam explored i-deals in public organizations noting that public organizations have greater organizational constraints, such as centralization and bureaucracy compared with private organizations, and that this was more the case in Vietnam, whose shift from central planning to market orientation is incomplete.

Several generalizability studies interpreted their findings in light of the study context. For example, Lee, Bachrach, and Rousseau (2015) argued that their study conducted in South Korea represents a conservative test of i-deals initiation as collectivism may act as a constraint due to employees' concern for group-level outcomes. Similarly, Anand and her colleagues (2018) also noted that the effects of i-deals on LMX and subsequently on citizenship behaviors may be attenuated in India, where individualized work arrangements run counter to collectivistic norms. Rofcanin et al. (2017) discussed that in their study context, namely Turkey, paternalism was the dominant leadership style, which may have facilitated employees' approaching their managers for i-deals. As a final example, Guerrero and Challiol-Jeanblanc (2016) argued that employee relations are less individualized in France, which in turn may contribute to greater organization-based self-esteem (OBSE) when one receives i-deals.

Some studies introduced context-specific speculations ex post facto, typically to explain unsupported hypotheses or unexpected findings. For example, Marescaux et al. (2019) noted that the strong collective bargaining tradition in Belgium may have constrained individual negotiations for i-deals but amplified complaints in response to coworker i-deals. Across US and German samples, Hornung and colleagues (2010) found that LMX influenced negotiation of task i-deals similarly in both countries. However, factors related to hierarchy (e.g., job level) were only significant in Germany, which led the authors to propose that the high level of power distance in Germany vis-à-vis the US, that is the higher degree to which unequal distribution of power is normalized may hinder bottom-up negotiation of task ideals.

Finally, in the only meta-analytic study in this review, Liao and colleagues (2016) combined US, Dutch, and German samples as Western, and Chinese, Indian, and South Korean samples as Eastern to assess the cross-cultural generalizability of i-deals antecedents and outcomes. Their findings showed that i-deals had similar relations to leader-member exchange (LMX), perceived organizational support (POS), job satisfaction, and proactive personality in both regions, and neither tenure nor education was significant in either region. However, they observed a strong relation to commitment and turnover in the Eastern sample, whereas i-deals did not predict commitment in the Western sample. In addition, while no relation was observed between age and i-deals in the Eastern sample, it was negatively related in the Western sample. In contrast, being female had no relation to i-deals in the Western sample, but a negative relation in the Eastern sample. It should be noted that the meta-analysis was based on a small number of studies (e.g., two studies on turnover intentions); yet, it is suggestive regarding the role of cultural or institutional factors.

Table 12.1 also shows that the percentage of theory-driven studies which develop a priori hypotheses with respect to national or societal-level characteristics of the study setting is rather low (5%). Nonetheless, these studies have investigated i-deals in contexts that provide an informative contrast to North America (namely China and Vietnam) and question the boundary conditions of mainstream findings by drawing on constructs such as collectivism-individualism, paternalism, and Confucianism. Specifically, Luu and Djurkovic (2019) found that paternalistic leadership has a stronger influence on the i-deals of employees in Confucian societies such as Vietnam. Ng and Feldman's (2015) comparative study showed that reciprocity norms were a stronger mediator between i-deals and voice behavior in collectivist China than individualist US. Lee and Hui (2011) showed that Chinese employees who endorsed individualism to a greater extent were more likely to strike *ex ante* i-deals, despite cultural norms that may render this timing less appropriate compared to *ex post* i-deals. Finally, Liu et al. (2013) found that organization-based self-esteem was a stronger mediator between i-deals and employee outcomes for employees who endorsed higher levels of individualism. In contrast, for employees with low levels of individualism, the mediating role of POS was stronger.

Our review also indicated that only two studies (3%) were derived etic studies, meaning that they had adapted mainstream i-deals theory to their particular setting. Both of these studies were conducted in China and evoked in-group collectivism and Chinese traditionalism for a better understanding of i-deals in the Chinese context. Specifically, Tang and Hornung (2015) noted that i-deals, as work role adjustments, are entangled with family life in the Chinese context. In particular, they observed that work time has priority over personal and even family time, but primarily because a successful career brings honor and prosperity to the family (Redding, 1990). Huo et al. (2015) showed that i-deals elicited the highest level of organizational citizenship behaviors (OCB) from Chinese employees with low traditionality and high perceived visibility of i-deals with the expectation that they would also earn i-deals. In contrast, high traditionalists facing the same circumstances exhibited lower levels of OCB.

Finally, five studies (7%) were coded as high contextualization studies in that the research question was explicitly context-driven and explored the influence of the national or societal-level characteristics on i-deals. These studies were from Australia, Netherlands, UK, and US. All these studies were very much couched in their local i.e., WEIRD circumstances, with reference to societal trends of increasing individualism, declining role of trade unions, and aging populations. For instance, with reference to the UK context, Atkinson and Sandiford (2016) noted the lack of research on flexible work arrangements specific to older workers vis-à-vis working parents. In particular, they proposed that older workers may benefit from arrangements with respect to their work role, such as taking up less demanding roles. Similar concerns regarding how to attract older workers through individualized HRM were also expressed by Bal and Dorenbosch (2014) with respect to the Netherlands. Interestingly, none of these studies focused on understanding the implications of societal culture from an indigenous perspective. It should also be noted that more than half (60%) of these studies were qualitative, which no doubt contributed to the richness of contextual information.

We also examined the articles with respect to sampling and instrumentation. Although many studies were not particularly informative regarding the role of cultural or the institutional context, they were contributory in terms of providing further validation evidence for mainstream scales, in particular those by Hornung et al. (2008), Rosen et al. (2013), and Rousseau and Kim (2006). The reported reliability and validity information was largely satisfactory, although there were a few instances where the reliability was lower than 0.70, often due to use of fewer items (Hornung et al., 2009; Lee & Hui, 2011; Ng & Feldman, 2015; Wang et al., 2019). Most of the articles conceptualized i-deals as development opportunities and flexibility regarding time and work location. Finally, mirroring the large percentage of low contextualization studies, the sampling strategy used in the reviewed studies was predominantly convenience sampling. In fact, only 27% of the studies used purposive sampling, meaning they associated the characteristics of their study context to their research question (e.g., Las Heras, Rofcanin, et al., 2017; Luu & Djurkovic, 2019).

Discussion

On the occasion of the centennial issue of the Journal of Applied Psychology, Gelfand et al. (2017) traced the development of cross-cultural research in industrial and organizational psychology/behavior by noting the advances over time. The studies that equated culture with nation and were exploratory in terms of how, why, and when culture might play a role in explaining organizational outcomes were described as representing an earlier, currently outdated phase of cross-cultural organizational psychology/behavior. It seems that the cross-cultural i-deals research is still in the very early phases, with a strong need to conduct additional research in this area. We see this as an important omission

Table 12.2 Summary ideas for future research

Topic	Ideas
Measurement	• Do the currently used measures do an adequate job of capturing the entire domain of i-deals in different contexts? • Do the measures of i-deals show measurement equivalence in different cultural contexts? • Are there emic dimensions of i-deals that have been neglected in the extant literature?
Antecedents	• What makes employees worthy of i-deals in different contexts? • What cultural, economic, or legal factors affect the initiation or the prevalence of i-deals? • How do societal or demographic trends affect different types of i-deals that are negotiated?
Outcomes	• What cultural, economic, or legal influences shape employee reactions to i-deals? • Does culture shape the mechanisms by which i-deals affect employee attitudes and behaviors? • Do i-deals similarly affect organizational outcomes in different cultural or institutional contexts? • Does culture influence how and why employees react to how their i-deals compare to those of their coworkers?
Coworker reactions	• How does culture affect how coworkers react to others' i-deals? • Are i-deals perceived to be differentially fair depending on cultural variation?

and a missed opportunity. In this section, we will share our observations regarding the treatment of macro-context variables in studies of i-deals and identify themes for future research. We summarize some of these ideas in Table 12.2.

Meaning of I-Deals Around the World

An important concern in cultural research is to explore universal (i.e., etic) as well as culturally embedded (i.e., emic) constructs (Gelfand et al., 2017). Perhaps one of the main conclusions of our review is that even though the overarching context did not play a key role in study design and methodology, the fact that researchers were able to study i-deals in diverse settings and show that it was related to important outcomes of interests suggests that i-deals may be a meaningful construct of interest, and a potentially useful practice across countries. In other words, there seem to be notable similarities in how managers and employees construe and react to i-deals across the world.

That said, future research may nonetheless benefit from an exploration as to whether i-deals manifest emic or culture-specific operationalizations as well. Although our review provides strong evidence for the usefulness of the mainstream i-deals scales, there is always the possibility that an imported instrument is "underinclusive" even if it yields a structure identical to that found in the original culture (van de Vijver & Leung, 2001). Future research can challenge the meaning or construal of i-deals in various contexts. In particular, in many countries around the world, employees have to negotiate for things that WEIRD countries take for granted (Rousseau, 2005). For instance, in countries with relatively less munificent social benefits or suboptimal infrastructure, employees may negotiate for i-deals relevant to basic livelihood or family support. Along the same lines, in high power distance cultural contexts, employees may seek i-deals that may increase their access to top management or involvement in strategic decisions.

Furthermore, what makes employees "worthy" of i-deals is likely to be context-specific (Rousseau, 2005). For instance, neotraditional countries (e.g., ex-communist or developing countries; Pearce et al., 2000) tend to be low trust contexts, which may encourage the provision of i-deals to foster loyalty, rather than performance. Relatedly, collectivist cultures tend to uphold loyalty over fairness or individual performance (e.g., Doney et al., 1998; Haidt & Kesebir, 2010), which again may generate i-deals geared toward empowering trustworthy in-group members. Finally, as noted by Rousseau (2005), contexts characterized by lack of formal performance appraisal or systematic employee development makes it difficult to keep legitimate i-deals distinct from favoritism. Considering that neotraditional countries or emerging economies typically have weak human resources management systems, the question as to what makes an i-deal legitimate or shady as a function of the context emerges as an important dilemma. Thus, a potentially fruitful venue for future i-deals research involves an in-depth exploration of the construct across contexts.

National Context May Shape the Prevalence of I-Deals

It is particularly important to pay explicit attention to some of the fundamental assumptions underlying i-deals in order to recognize that there may be variation across societies in the receptiveness to i-deals and therefore prevalence of i-deals. Bal and Lub (2016) underlined that i-deals are based on the assumption that individuals have bargaining power in the employment relationship, the terms of the employment relationship are negotiable, and that they have the potential to distinguish themselves from others. We agree with these observations and contend that these assumptions may not always be meaningful, requiring researchers to develop models more suitable to the context.

The notion that employment terms are individually negotiable may be more valid in some contexts than others. Parker et al. (2017) predicted that i-deals would be more common in contexts where unions are disappearing, because i-deals may provide to individuals what unions may be providing in different contexts. By the same token, we may expect to see a larger percentage of employees who are able to successfully negotiate i-deals or even attempt to negotiate an i-deal in countries where unions are more precarious and less prevalent. Similarly, the absence of i-deals may simply indicate that those benefits are already available to everyone in that particular context. As a case in point, Conway and Coyle-Shapiro (2016) noted that flexibility i-deals may not be so important in countries such as the UK where part-time work is already a legally guaranteed entitlement.

As with the observation regarding the decline of the unions, much of the i-deals research is fueled by the societal changes experienced in WEIRD countries (e.g., aging, telecommuting). It seems that a parallel analysis can be offered for other country contexts, which may be experiencing other societal or economic imperatives that might necessitate the provision of i-deals. Rousseau (2005) has argued that i-deals are sometimes created in response to past distributive injustices such as budget cuts that halt a promotion or an educational opportunity. It is possible that emerging economies are chronically inclined to renege on such promises and are more inclined to devise remedial i-deals. Emerging economy contexts also have difficulty developing and retaining human capital (Ready et al., 2008). In such contexts, talent management and retention may be highly contingent on the provision of i-deals. A nation's business context with respect to mix of industries and employment concentration across sectors further influences employer responsiveness to worker requests (Rousseau, 2005). Countries with high levels of government employment or staid industries can be expected to be less responsive to individual bargaining than countries with a more dynamic private sector or a greater percentage of entrepreneurial ventures.

In addition to economic circumstances or institutional constraints, our review suggests that cultural values and norms, as reflected in leadership styles or organizational cultures, may influence the prevalence of i-deals. Specifically, Rofcanin and his colleagues (2017, 2018) have argued that servant or paternalist leadership styles, which are more common in collectivist cultures, may be conducive to the negotiation of i-deals. Likewise, individualist cultures may also offer greater opportunity for such negotiations (e.g., Wang & Long, 2018). More generally, future research may advance our understanding of i-deals by incorporating cultural variables such as performance orientation, uncertainty avoidance, gender egalitarianism (House et al., 2004), and tightness-looseness, which is defined as the strength of social norms and the degree of sanctioning within societies (Gelfand et al., 2011). For instance, looser as opposed to tighter societies may be more likely to condone variance in employment contracts. In addition to prevalence, what is perhaps more interesting to explore is the different circumstances that influence the initiation of i-deals as well as the different motivations that inform their negotiation across cultural contexts. For instance, employees in high power distance cultures may be less likely to broach such possibilities to their supervisors out of a concern to observe norms regarding respect for authority. On the other hand, when a society's norms promote equality and downplay differences, employees may be similarly reluctant to initiate i-deals (Rousseau, 2005).

National Context May Shape How Employees React to I-Deals

There is reason to expect that the degree to which i-deals contribute to employee motivation, retention, and commitment may show variation depending on cultural or other macro influences. As a case in point, Liao et al.'s (2016) meta-analysis suggested that the relationship between i-deals, commitment, and turnover was significant only in Eastern cultures (China, India, and S. Korea) as opposed to Western cultures (US, Germany, and the Netherlands). This may be because the successful negotiation of i-deals may generate different psychological mechanisms in different contexts. For example, Liu et al. (2013) showed that for employees high in collectivism, i-deals triggered social exchange mechanisms, whereas among individualistic employees, it was associated with self-enhancement. In fact, in different cultural contexts, employees may interpret i-deals differently. In high power distance cultures, employees may particularly appreciate i-deals as signs of their high-quality relationship with their supervisors (Anand et al., 2018). In collectivistic cultures, employees may interpret an i-deal as a signal that the organization cares about the needs of the employee, which may engender social exchange processes resulting in higher levels of commitment to the organization and higher desire for reciprocation. In contrast, in individualistic cultures, employees may regard the i-deals as the organization needing them and as a signal of their market value, which may have weaker effects on commitment and the desire for reciprocation.

Even when the effects of i-deals on employee attitudes and behaviors are comparable, the specific mechanisms shaping employee reactions to i-deals may vary. For example, in collectivistic cultures, i-deals may facilitate higher levels of performance and retention by nurturing employees' sense of belongingness, whereas in individualistic cultures they may aid performance and retention by contributing to employees' sense of status and esteem. In other words, even when i-deals are equally effective across cultures, the reason for their effectiveness may show cultural variation, suggesting that an exploration of the mediating mechanisms across different cultural contexts is warranted.

National culture may also have implications for how employees react to the different distributions of i-deals in their work groups. Vidyarthi et al. (2016) examined the implications of relative i-deals or employees' within group standing with respect to i-deals. Their study showed that having a higher level of i-deals relative to the average person on the team was advantageous for employee performance. At the same time, the positive effects of relative status were more positive in organizations with cultures characterized by low levels of team orientation. We might expect similar effects for cultures that are individualistic. Specifically, having i-deals that are better or more favorable to the individual may serve the individual more in cultures high in individualism, whereas such favorable standing relative to one's team members may attract backlash in cultures high in collectivism. In other words, national culture may shape the implications of i-deals configurations for individuals and groups.

National Context May Shape How Coworkers React to I-Deals

An important future theme for research is an examination of how coworkers and observers react to i-deals negotiated by others. The effectiveness of i-deals depends on whether the individual benefits received from the i-deals are greater than the costs experienced through factors such as coworker backlash. For example, to the degree to which coworkers withhold help and support as a result of the focal employee's receipt of i-deals, the net benefit to the individual and organization may be minimal. Further, to the degree to which coworker backlash results in reduced benefits at the group level such as loss of group cohesion, the provision of i-deals may be highly problematic for individuals, groups, and organizations.

Research conducted in Western settings suggests that i-deals may have some benefits for coworker relationships. For example, Guerrero and Challiol-Jeanblanc (2016) showed that individuals who received i-deals perceived higher levels of OBSE and reciprocated by helping their coworkers. However, these results are likely to be context bound, and they may be different in contexts where differentiation represents the exception rather than the norm. In contexts where egalitarian norms are more powerful, focal employees may experience higher levels of embarrassment as opposed to pride, which may result in withdrawing from their interactions with coworkers (Rousseau, 2005). Similarly, in collectivist cultures, employees may find it difficult to be the recipient of special treatment at their peers' expense (Anand et al., 2010). These prevailing norms may also have implications as to how to measure i-deals. For instance, Anand et al. (2010) opted to measure i-deals by asking the managers rather than the employees themselves, as they were concerned that Indian employees might downplay i-deals. As a result, the cultural context is likely to matter a great deal in understanding and studying how i-deals affect interpersonal relationship dynamics.

Garg and Fulmer (2017) have theorized that coworker reactions to i-deals held by others should depend on the personal impact of such deals on themselves, and on whether they believe that the i-deal is deserved by the recipient. Their model explicitly recognizes the role of organizational norms around differentiation, with norms disallowing differentiation predicted to make i-deals less acceptable to coworkers. It is possible to make similar predictions with respect to the role of national culture. For example, collectivism is associated with an endorsement of the equality norm (Leung & Iwawaki, 1988), suggesting that in collectivistic cultures, coworkers may demonstrate more negative reactions to i-deals when they find out about them.

Because reactions to coworker i-deals are likely to depend on how individuals conceptualize what is fair, cultural values, and norms regarding definitions of fairness will play a role in understanding coworker reactions to i-deals. Research on cultural differences suggests that how individuals define what is fair depends on cultural values. For example, research shows that distributing rewards based on age may be regarded as more fair in Japan as opposed to Australia (Kashima et al., 1988). Hence, coworkers may have less negative reactions and show less tendency for backlash when i-deals are awarded to older and perhaps more senior members of their group, as opposed to a high potential employee who is new to the organization.

National Context May Shape Organization-Level Benefits of I-Deals

Research linking i-deals to firm-level outcomes are sparse. Still, it is important to consider labor market and other country-level influences when examining the nature of the relationship between i-deals and organization-level outcomes. For example, Bal and Dorenbosch (2014) showed in a study of over 5,000 organizations in Netherlands that firm-level availability and use of i-deals were related to firm-level outcomes. They also showed that these results were moderated by the percentage of older workers in the organization such that, in firms with a larger percentage of older workers, the use of flexibility i-deals were more strongly and negatively related to sickness absence. These findings may be extrapolated to country-level effects such that in countries with an aging population, flexibility i-deals may become more impactful for firm-level outcomes.

Conclusions

As the i-deals literature develops a greater sensitivity toward context, it is important to benefit from discussions in the broader fields of cultural psychology and organizational behavior with respect to sound methodology. For instance, with respect to comparative studies, there are many useful guidelines as to how to build multilevel models that incorporate nation- or culture-level variation to account for societal differences in organizational practices and employee attitudes (e.g., Fischer, 2009; Gelfand et al., 2008). For single-country studies, the recent calls for high-quality indigenous research have been complemented with sound recommendations regarding how to conduct context-embedded or context-specific research (e.g., Tsui, 2004).

The greater interest in culture-sensitive research has also alerted scholars to the empirical evidence that shows substantial within-nation or intraregional divergence in cultural values due to differences like geographic and climactic patterns, immigration history, or differential rates of economic development (e.g., Dheer et al., 2014). Accordingly, equating culture with nationality is being increasingly questioned. Finally, with growing intercultural contact and recognition that culture is not only a national-level variable, it has been argued that it may be more accurate to treat individuals as cultural mosaics, who are comprised of many different cultural references (e.g., nationality, profession, gender, exposure to different cultures) and retrieve these references according to the situation (e.g., Chao & Moon, 2005). Compared to traditional approaches, these dynamic views of culture have served better with respect to explicating the behaviors of biculturals, expatriates, and immigrants (Leung & Morris, 2015). As workplaces around the world become increasingly multicultural, we anticipate that the i-deals research will naturally evolve to reflect these concerns.

Appendix

Journal	Author(s) & year	Title of the article	Sample(s)	Research method	Ideals scale	Reliability evidence	Validity evidence	Sampling of culture	Cultural approach	Cultural/ Contextual Dimensions Invoked
Journal of Management	Bal, P. M., & Boehm, S. A. (2019)	How do i-Deals influence client satisfaction? The role of exhaustion, collective commitment, and age diversity	Germany	Survey	Hornung et al. (2008)	Satisfactory	Not reported	Convenience	Low contextualization	None
Journal of Management Studies	Bal, P. M., De Jong, S. B. Jansen, P. G. W. & Bakker, A. B. (2012)	Motivating employees to work beyond retirement: A multilevel study of the role of i-deals and unit climate	Netherlands	Survey	Hornung et al. (2008)	Satisfactory	Reported	Convenience	Low contextualization	None
Academy of Management Journal	Broschak, J. P., & Davis-Blake, A. (2006)	Mixing standard work and non-standard deals scale: The consequences of heterogeneity in employment arrangements	US	Survey	Employment arrangement heterogeneity was assessed by Blau's index (1977)	NA	NA	Convenience	Low contextualization	None

(continued)

(continued)

Journal	Author(s) & year	Title of the article	Sample(s)	Research method	Ideals scale	Reliability evidence	Validity evidence	Sampling of culture	Cultural approach	Cultural/ Contextual Dimensions Invoked
Istanbul Business Research	Calışkan, E., & Torun, A (2019)	Individualized HR practices and idiosyncratic deals (I-deals) and the expected positive individual and organizational outcomes	Turkey	Interview	–	–	–	Convenience	Low contextualization	None
Human Resource Management	De Menezes, L. M. & Kelliher, C. (2016)	Flexible working, individual performance, and employee attitudes: Comparing formal and informal arrangements	UK	Survey	Single item	NA	NA	Convenience	Low contextualization	None
Human Resource Management	De Vos, A., & Cambré, B. (2016)	Career management in high-performing organizations: A set-theoretic approach	Belgium	Survey	Bal et al. (2012)	NA	NA	Convenience	Low contextualization	None

(continued)

(continued)

Journal	Author(s) & year	Title of the article	Sample(s)	Research method	Ideals scale	Reliability evidence	Validity evidence	Sampling of culture	Cultural approach	Cultural/ Contextual Dimensions Invoked
Review of Managerial Science	Ding, C. G. & Chang, Y. W. (2019)	Effects of task and work responsibilities idiosyncratic deals on perceived insider status and the moderating roles of perceived overall justice and coworker support	Taiwan	Survey	Rosen et al. (2013)	Satisfactory	Reported	Convenience	Low contextualization	None
Personnel Psychology	Gajendran, Harrison & Delaney-Klinger (2015)	Are telecommuters remotely good citizens? Unpacking telecommuting's effects on performance via i-deals and job resources	US	Survey	One item i-deals as Tele-commuting (Thatcher & Zhu, 2006) telecommuting intensity (Golden & Veiga, 2005)	NA	NA	Convenience	Low contextualization	None
Journal of Business and Psychology	Guerrero, S., Bentein, K., & Lapalme, M. E. (2014)	Idiosyncratic deals and high performers' organizational commitment	Canada	Survey	Rousseau and Kim (2006)	Satisfactory	Reported	Convenience	Low contextualization	None

(continued)

(continued)

Journal	Author(s) & year	Title of the article	Sample(s)	Research method	Ideals scale	Reliability evidence	Validity evidence	Sampling of culture	Cultural approach	Cultural/ Contextual Dimensions Invoked
Personnel Review	Guerrero, S., & Challiol-Jeanblanc, H (2017a)	Ex ante i-deals, perceived external prestige and turnover intentions	France	Survey	Rousseau et al. (2009)	Satisfactory	Reported	Convenience	Low contextualization	None
Career Development International	Guerrero, S., Challiol-Jeanblanc, H., & Veilleux, M. (2016)	Development idiosyncratic deals and career success	France	Survey	Hornung et al. (2008)	Satisfactory	Reported	Convenience	Low contextualization	None
Career Development International	Guerrero, S., & Challiol-Jeanblanc, H. C. (2017)	Networking and development idiosyncratic deals	France	Survey	Hornung et al. (2008)	Satisfactory	Reported	Convenience	Low contextualization	None
Psychological Reports	Hornung, S., Glaser, J., Rousseau, D. M., Angerer, P., & Weigl, M. (2011)	Employee-oriented leadership and quality of working life: Mediating roles of idiosyncratic deals	Germany	Survey	Hornung et al. (2008)	Satisfactory	Reported	Convenience	Low contextualization	None
Journal of Applied Psychology	Hornung, S., Rousseau, D. M., & Glaser, J. (2008)	Creating flexible work arrangements through idiosyncratic deals	Germany	Survey	Rousseau and Kim (2006)	Satisfactory	Reported	Convenience	Low contextualization	None

(continued)

(continued)

Journal	Author(s) & year	Title of the article	Sample(s)	Research method	Ideals scale	Reliability evidence	Validity evidence	Sampling of culture	Cultural approach	Cultural/Contextual Dimensions Invoked
Journal of Managerial Psychology	Hornung, S., Rousseau, D. M., & Glaser, J. (2009)	Why supervisors make idiosyncratic deals: antecedents and outcomes of i-deals from a managerial perspective	Germany	Survey	Rousseau and Kim (2006)	Acceptable	Reported	Convenience	Low contextualization	None
European Journal of Work and Organizational Psychology	Hornung, S., Rousseau, D. M., Weigl, M., Müller, A., & Glaser, J. (2014)	Redesigning work through idiosyncratic deals	Germany	Survey	Hornung et al. (2010)	Satisfactory	Reported	Convenience	Low contextualization	None
Journal of Vocational Behavior	Kelly, C., Rofcanin, Y., Las Heras, M., Ogbonnaya, C., Marescaux, E., & Jose Bosch, M. (2020)	Seeking an "i-deal" balance: Schedule-flexibility i-deals as mediating mechanisms between supervisor emotional support and employee work and home performance	Chile and Colombia	Survey	Rosen et al. (2013)	Satisfactory	Reported	Convenience	Low contextualization	None

(continued)

(continued)

Journal	Author(s) & year	Title of the article	Sample(s)	Research method	Ideals scale	Reliability evidence	Validity evidence	Sampling of culture	Cultural approach	Cultural/ Contextual Dimensions Invoked
Journal of Business Ethics	Kong, D. T., Ho, V. T., & Garg, S. (2020)	Employee and coworker idiosyncratic deals: Implications for emotional exhaustion and deviant behaviors	US	Survey	Rosen et al. (2013)	Satisfactory	Reported	Convenience	Low contextualization	None
Journal of Applied Psychology	Lai, L., Rousseau, D. M., & Chang, K. T. T. (2009)	Idiosyncratic deals: Coworkers as interested third parties	US	Survey	Lai et al. (2009)	Satisfactory	Reported	Convenience	Low contextualization	None
Human Resource Management	Lee, B. Y., Kim, T. Y., Gong, Y., Zheng, X., & Liu, X. (2020)	Employee well-being attribution and job change intentions: The moderating effect of task idiosyncratic deals	China	Survey	Rosen et al. (2013)	Satisfactory	Reported	Convenience	Low contextualization	None
Journal of Leadership and Organizational Studies	Lemmon, G., Westring, A., Michel, E. J., Wilson, M. S., & Glibkowski, B. C. (2016)	A cross-domain exploration of performance benefits and costs of idiosyncratic deals	US	Survey	Rousseau (2005)	Satisfactory	Not reported	Convenience	Low contextualization	None

(continued)

(continued)

Journal	Author(s) & year	Title of the article	Sample(s)	Research method	Ideals scale	Reliability evidence	Validity evidence	Sampling of culture	Cultural approach	Cultural/ Contextual Dimensions Invoked
Leadership Quarterly	Liao, C., Wayne, S. J., Liden, R. C., & Meuser, J. D. (2017)	Idiosyncratic deals and individual effectiveness: The moderating role of leader-member exchange differentiation	US	Survey	Hornung et al. (2014)	Satisfactory	Reported	Convenience	Low contextualization	None
R&D Management	Liu, F., & Zhou, K (2020)	Idiosyncratic deals and creative deviance: The mediating role of psychological entitlement	China	Survey	Rosen et al. (2013)	Satisfactory	Reported	Convenience	Low contextualization	None
Journal of Organizational Behavior	Luksyte & Spitzmueller (2015)	When are overqualified employees creative? It depends on contextual factors	US	Survey	Hornung et al. (2008)	Satisfactory	Not reported	Convenience	Low contextualization	None
Journal of Business Ethics	Luu, T. L. (2016)	Organizational ambidexterity, entrepreneurial orientation, and I-deals: The moderating role of CSR	Vietnam	Survey	Rosen et al. (2013)	Satisfactory	Reported	Convenience	Low contextualization	None

(continued)

(continued)

Journal	Author(s) & year	Title of the article	Sample(s)	Research method	Ideals scale	Reliability evidence	Validity evidence	Sampling of culture	Cultural approach	Cultural/ Contextual Dimensions Invoked
Human Resource Management Journal	Morf, M., Bakker, A., & Feierabend, A. (2019)	Bankers closing idiosyncratic deals: Implications for organizational cynicism	Switzerland	Survey	Hornung et al. (2010)	Satisfactory	Reported	Convenience	Low contextualization	None
Journal of Vocational Behavior	Ng, T. W. H., & Feldman, D. C. (2010)	Idiosyncratic deals and organizational commitment	US	Survey	Rousseau et al. (2009)	Satisfactory	Reported	Convenience	Low contextualization	None
Human Relations	Ng, T. W. H., & Feldman, D. C. (2012)	Breaches of past promises, current job alternatives, and promises of future idiosyncratic deals: Three-way interaction effects on organizational commitment	US	Survey	Ng and Feldman (2010)	Satisfactory	Reported	Convenience	Low contextualization	None
Journal of Organizational Behavior	Ng, T. W. H., & Lucianetti, L. (2016)	Goal striving, idiosyncratic deals, and job behavior	Italy	Survey	Hornung et al. (2008)	Satisfactory	Reported	Convenience	Low contextualization	None

(continued)

(continued)

Journal	Author(s) & year	Title of the article	Sample(s)	Research method	Ideals scale	Reliability evidence	Validity evidence	Sampling of culture	Cultural approach	Cultural/ Contextual Dimensions Invoked
Journal of Vocational Behavior	Ng, T. W. H. (2017)	Can idiosyncratic deals promote perceptions of competitive climate, felt ostracism, and turnover?	Hong Kong	Survey	Hornung et al. (2008)	Satisfactory	Reported	Convenience	Low contextualization	None
Journal of Management	Rosen, C. C., Slater, D. J., Chang, C-H., & Johnson, R. E. (2011)	Let's make a deal: Development and validation of the ex post i-deals scale	US	Survey	Rosen et al. (2013)	Satisfactory	Reported	Convenience	Low contextualization	None
Journal of Vocational Behavior	Rousseau, D.M., Hornung, S., & Kim, T. G. (2009)	Idiosyncratic deals: Testing propositions on timing, content, and the employment relationship	US	Survey	Rousseau et al. (2009)	Satisfactory	Reported	Convenience	Low contextualization	None
Personnel Review	Luu, T. L., & Rowley, C. (2015)	From value-based human resource practices to i-deals: Software companies in Vietnam	Vietnam	Survey	Rosen et al. (2013)	Satisfactory	Reported	Convenience	Low contextualization	None

(continued)

(continued)

Journal	Author(s) & year	Title of the article	Sample(s)	Research method	Ideals scale	Reliability evidence	Validity evidence	Sampling of culture	Cultural approach	Cultural/Contextual Dimensions Invoked
Journal of Managerial Psychology	Vidyarthi, P., Chaudhry, A., Anand, S., & Liden, R. C. (2014)	Flexibility i-deals: How much is ideal?	India	Survey	Rousseau and Kim (2006)	Satisfactory	Reported	Convenience	Low contextualization	None
Journal of Applied Psychology	Vidyarthi, P. R., Singh, S., & Erdogan, B., Chaudhry, A., Posthuma, R., & Anand, S. (2016)	Individual deals within teams: Investigating the role of relative i-deals for employee performance	India	Survey	Rousseau and Kim (2006)	Satisfactory	Reported	Convenience	Low contextualization	None
Social Behavior and Personality: An International Journal	Wang, L. L., & Long, L. R. (2018)	Idiosyncratic deals and taking charge: The roles of psychological empowerment and organizational tenure	China	Survey	Ng and Feldman (2010)	Satisfactory	Reported	Convenience	Low contextualization	None
Human Resource Management	Wang, S. H., Liu, Y., Shalley, C. E. (2018)	Idiosyncratic deals and employee creativity: The mediating role of creative self-efficacy	China	Survey	Rousseau and Kim (2006)	Satisfactory	Reported	Convenience	Low contextualization	None

(continued)

(continued)

Journal	Author(s) & year	Title of the article	Sample(s)	Research method	Ideals scale	Reliability evidence	Validity evidence	Sampling of culture	Cultural approach	Cultural/ Contextual Dimensions Invoked
Leadership Quarterly	Anand, S. Hu, J., Vidyarthi, P. & Liden, R. C. (2018)	Leader-member exchange as a linking pin in the idiosyncratic deals: Performance relationship in workgroups	India	Survey	Hornung et al. (2008)	Satisfactory	Reported	Convenience	Generalizability	Collectivism
Academy of Management Journal	Anand, S., Vidyarthi, P., Liden, R. C., & Rousseau, D. M. (2010)	Good citizens in poor-quality relationships: Idiosyncratic deals as a substitute for relationship quality	India	Survey	Rousseau and Kim (2006)	Satisfactory	Reported	Convenience	Generalizability	Collectivism
New Zealand Journal of Employment Relations	Bal, M. (2017)	Why do employees negotiate idiosyncratic deals? An exploration of the process of i-deal negotiation	Netherlands	Interview	NA	NA	NA	Convenience	Generalizability	Legislation, labor agreements
Journal of Personnel Psychology	Bal, M., & Vossaert, L. (2019)	Development of an ideals motivation and management measure	Netherlands, UK, US, Europe, and Asia samples	Scale development study	Bal & Vossaert (2019)	Satisfactory	Reported	Convenience	Generalizability	None

(continued)

(continued)

Journal	Author(s) & year	Title of the article	Sample(s)	Research method	Ideals scale	Reliability evidence	Validity evidence	Sampling of culture	Cultural approach	Cultural/ Contextual Dimensions Invoked
International Journal of Human Resource Management	Bayazit, Z. E., & Bayazit, M. (2019)	How do flexible work arrangements alleviate work-family-conflict? The roles of flexibility i-deals and family-supportive cultures	Turkey	Survey	Hornung et al. (2009)	Satisfactory	Reported	Purposive	Generalizability	Collectivism, performance orientation, institutional collectivism, uncertainty avoidance
Journal of Vocational Behavior	Brzykcya, A. Z., & Stephan A., Boehma, D. & Baldridgeb, C. (2019)	Fostering sustainable careers across the lifespan: The role of disability, idiosyncratic deals, and perceived work ability	Germany	Survey	Rousseau and Kim (2006)	Satisfactory	Reported	Purposive	Generalizability	Legislation
Human Relations	Gascoigne, C. & Kelliher, C, (2018)	The transition to part-time: How professionals negotiate "reduced time and workload" i-deals and craft their jobs	Netherlands and UK	Interview	NA	NA	NA	Convenience	Generalizability	Legislation

(continued)

(continued)

Journal	Author(s) & year	Title of the article	Sample(s)	Research method	Ideals scale	Reliability evidence	Validity evidence	Sampling of culture	Cultural approach	Cultural/ Contextual Dimensions Invoked
Journal of Business and Psychology	Guerrero & Challiol-Jeanblanc, H. (2016)	Idiosyncratic deals and helping behavior: The moderating role of i-deal opportunity for coworkers	France	Survey	Hornung et al. (2008)	Satisfactory	Reported	Convenience	Generalizability	Less individualized nature of work relations
Journal of Organizational Behavior	Hornung, S., Rousseau, D. M., Glaser, J., Angerer, P. & Weigl, M. (2010)	Beyond top-down and bottom-up work redesign: Customizing job content through idiosyncratic deals	Germany and US	Survey	Hornung et al. (2008)	Satisfactory	Reported	Convenience	Generalizability	Power distance
International Human Resource Management	Katou, A. A, Budhwar, P. S., & Patel, C (2020)	Idiosyncratic deals in less competitive labor markets: Testing career i-deals in the Greek context of high uncertainties	Greece	Survey	Rousseau et al. (2009), Hornung et al. (2014)	Satisfactory	Reported	Purposive	Generalizability	High uncertainty (economic crisis)

(continued)

(continued)

Journal	Author(s) & year	Title of the article	Sample(s)	Research method	I-deals scale	Reliability evidence	Validity evidence	Sampling of culture	Cultural approach	Cultural/Contextual Dimensions Invoked
Personnel Review	Katou, A. A., Budhwar, P. S., & Dhiman, M. C. (2020)	The moderating effects of transformational leadership and self-worth in the idiosyncratic deals—Employee reactions relationship A study of Indian hospitality industry	India	Survey	Rousseau et al. (2009), Hornung et al. (2014)	Satisfactory	Reported	Purposive	Generalizability	National differences in zone of negotiability
International Journal of Innovation Science	Kimwolo, A. A., & Cheruiyot, T. (2019)	Intrinsically motivating idiosyncratic deals and innovative work behavior	Kenya	Survey	Rosen et al. (2013)	Satisfactory	Reported	Convenience	Generalizability	Importance of family values, rareness of labor specialization
Human Resource Management	Kossek, E., Ollier-Malaterre, A., Lee, M., Pichler, S., & Hall, D. (2016)	Line managers' rationales for professionals' reduced load work in embracing and ambivalent organizations	US and Canada	Interview	NA	NA	NA	Convenience	Generalizability	Norms and public policy systems regarding career flexibility

(continued)

(continued)

Journal	Author(s) & year	Title of the article	Sample(s)	Research method	Ideals scale	Reliability evidence	Validity evidence	Sampling of culture	Cultural approach	Cultural/ Contextual Dimensions Invoked
Journal of Organizational Behavior	Las Heras, M., Rofcanin, Y., Bal, P. M., & Stollberger, J. (2017)	How do flexibility i-deals relate to work performance? Exploring the roles of family performance and organizational context	El Salvador	Survey	Rosen et al. (2013)	Satisfactory	Reported	Purposive	Generalizability	None
Human Resource Management Journal	Las Heras, M., Van der Heijden, B., De Jong, J., & Rofcanin, Y. (2017)	"Handle with care": The mediating role of schedule i-deals in the relationship between supervisors' own caregiving responsibilities and employee outcomes	El Salvador	Survey	Rosen et al. (2013)	Satisfactory	Reported	Purposive	Generalizability	Collectivism and segregated gender roles
Organization Science	Lee, J. Y., Bachrach, D. G., & Rousseau, D. M. (2015)	Internal labor markets, firm-specific human capital, and heterogeneity antecedents of employee idiosyncratic deal requests	S. Korea	Survey	Lee et al. (2015)	Satisfactory	Reported	Purposive	Generalizability	Collectivism

(continued)

(continued)

Journal	Author(s) & year	Title of the article	Sample(s)	Research method	Ideals scale	Reliability evidence	Validity evidence	Sampling of culture	Cultural approach	Cultural/ Contextual Dimensions Invoked
Journal of Organizational Behavior	Liao, C., Wayne, S., & Rousseau, D. M. (2014)	Idiosyncratic deals in contemporary organizations: A qualitative and meta-analytic review	US, Germany, Netherlands (West) and China, India, S. Korea (East)	Meta analytical review	Reviewed all the scales	NA	NA	Convenience	Generalizability	East versus West comparison
International Public Management Journal	Luu, T. L. (2017)	Administrative error control the role of value-based HR practices, i-deals, and organizational politics	Vietnam	Survey	Rosen et al. (2013)	Satisfactory	Reported	Purposive	Generalizability	Transition from a centrally-planned economy
Journal of Business Ethics	Marescaux, E., De Winne, S., & Sels, L. (2019)	Idiosyncratic deals from a distributive justice perspective: Examining coworkers' voice behavior	Belgium	Experimental vignette study	NA	NA	NA	Convenience	Generalizability	Strong collective bargaining tradition

(continued)

(continued)

Journal	Author(s) & year	Title of the article	Sample(s)	Research method	Ideals scale	Reliability evidence	Validity evidence	Sampling of culture	Cultural approach	Cultural/ Contextual Dimensions Invoked
New Technology, Work and Employment	Neirotti, P., Raguseo, E., & Gastaldi, L. (2019)	Designing flexible work practices for job satisfaction: The relationship between job characteristics and work disaggregation in different types of work arrangements	Italy	Survey	Golden and Veiga (2005)	Satisfactory	Not reported	Convenience	Generalizability	Individualism-collectivism
International Journal of Human Resource Management	Roficanin, Y., Berber, A., Koch, S., & Sevinc, L. (2016)	Job crafting and I-deals: A study testing the nomological network of proactive behaviors	Turkey	Survey	Rosen et al. (2013)	Satisfactory	Reported	Purposive	Generalizability	Power distance, high uncertainty avoidance; non-Western context, emerging economy
Human Relations	Roficanin, Y., Las Heras, M., Bal, M., van der Heijden, B. & Erdogan, D. (2018)	A trickle-down model of task and development i-deals	Philippines	Survey	Rosen et al. (2013)	Satisfactory	Reported	Purposive	Generalizability	In-group collectivism, uncertainty avoidance

(continued)

Journal	Author(s) & year	Title of the article	Sample(s)	Research method	Ideals scale	Reliability evidence	Validity evidence	Sampling of culture	Cultural approach	Cultural/ Contextual Dimensions Invoked
European Journal of Work and Organizational Psychology	Rofcanin, Y., Las Heras, M., Bosch, M. J., Stollberger, J., & Mayer, M. (2020)	How do weekly obtained task i-deals improve work performance? The role of relational context and structural job resources	Turkey	Survey	Rosen et al. (2013)	Satisfactory	Reported	Convenience	Generalizability	Paternalism
Journal of Occupational and Organizational Psychology	Rofcanin, Y., Kiefer, T., & Strauss, K. (2017)	What seals the I-deal? Exploring the role of employees' behaviors and managers' emotions	Turkey	Survey	Rosen et al. (2013)	Satisfactory	Reported	Purposive	Generalizability	Paternalism
International Journal of Organizational Analysis	Luu, T. L., & Rowley, C. (2016)	The relationship between cultural intelligence and i-deals: Trust as a mediator and HR localization as a moderator	Vietnam	Survey	Rosen et al. (2013)	Satisfactory	Reported	Convenience	Generalizability	Emerging economy, collectivism

(continued)

(continued)

Journal	Author(s) & year	Title of the article	Sample(s)	Research method	Ideals scale	Reliability evidence	Validity evidence	Sampling of culture	Cultural approach	Cultural/ Contextual Dimensions Invoked
Human Resource Management Journal	Wang, P., Wang, S., Yao, X., Hsu, I.-C., & Lawler, J. (2019)	Idiosyncratic deals and work to family conflict and enrichment: The mediating roles of fit perceptions and efficacy beliefs	China	Survey	Rousseau and Kim (2006)	Acceptable	Reported	Convenience	Generalizability	Collectivism
Frontiers of Business Research in China	Lee, C., & Hui, C. (2011)	Antecedents and consequences of idiosyncratic deals: A frame of resource exchange	China	Survey	Rousseau and Kim (2006)	Unsatisfactory	Reported	Convenience	Theory-driven	Individualism
Journal of Applied Psychology	Liu, J., Lee, C., Hui, C., Kwan, H. K., & Wu, L. Z. (2013)	Idiosyncratic deals and employee outcomes: The mediating roles of social exchange and self-enhancement and the moderating role of individualism	China	Survey	Rousseau and Kim (2006)	Satisfactory	Reported	Convenience	Theory-driven	Individualism

(continued)

(continued)

Journal	Author(s) & year	Title of the article	Sample(s)	Research method	Ideals scale	Reliability evidence	Validity evidence	Sampling of culture	Cultural approach	Cultural/ Contextual Dimensions Invoked
Journal of Management	Ng, T. W. H., & Feldman, D. C. (2015)	Idiosyncratic deals and voice behavior	China and US	Survey	Hornung et al. (2008)	Acceptable	Reported	Purposive	Theory-driven	Individualism-collectivism
International Human Resource Management	Huo, W. W., Luo, J. L., & Tam, K. L. (2015)	Idiosyncratic deals and good citizens in China: The role of traditionality for recipients and their coworkers	China	Survey	Rousseau and Kim (2006)	Satisfactory	Reported	Purposive	Derived etic	Chinese traditionalism
Management Decision	Lau, T. T., & Djurkovic, N. (2019)	Paternalistic leadership and idiosyncratic deals in a healthcare context	Vietnam	Survey	Rosen et al. (2013)	Satisfactory	Reported	Purposive	Derived etic	Paternalism
Journal of Managerial Psychology	Tang, Y. P., & Hornung, S. (2015)	Work-family enrichment through I-Deals: Evidence from Chinese employees	China	Survey	Hornung et al. (2008)	Satisfactory	Reported	Purposive	Derived etic	In-group collectivism
Human Resource Management Journal	Atkinson, C., & Sandiford, P. (2016)	An exploration of older worker flexible working arrangements in smaller firms	UK	Interview	NA	NA	NA	Purposive	High contextualization	National trends regarding aging

(continued)

(continued)

Journal	Author(s) & year	Title of the article	Sample(s)	Research method	Ideals scale	Reliability evidence	Validity evidence	Sampling of culture	Cultural approach	Cultural/ Contextual Dimensions Invoked
Human Resource Management Journal	Bal, P. M., & Dorenbosch, L. (2014)	Age-related differences in the relations between individualized HRM and organizational performance: A large-scale employer survey	Netherlands	Survey	Single item	NA	NA	Purposive	High contextualization	National trends regarding aging
Human Resource Development Quarterly	Davis, A. S., & Van der Heijden, B. I. J. M. (2018)	Reciprocity matters: Idiosyncratic deals to shape the psychological contract and foster employee engagement in times of austerity	UK	Interview	NA	NA	NA	Purposive	High contextualization	National public sector funding cuts
Career Development International	Oostrom, J. K., Pennings, M., & Bal, P. M. (2016)	How do idiosyncratic deals contribute to the employability of older workers?	Netherlands	Survey	Rosen et al. (2013)	Satisfactory	Reported	Purposive	High contextualization	National trends regarding aging

(continued)

(continued)

Journal	Author(s) & year	Title of the article	Sample(s)	Research method	Ideals scale	Reliability evidence	Validity evidence	Sampling of culture	Cultural approach	Cultural/ Contextual Dimensions Invoked
International Journal of Human Resource Management	Townsend, K., McDonald, P., & Cathcart, A. (2017)	Managing flexible work arrangements in small not-for-profit firms: The influence of organizational size, financial constraints, and workforce characteristics	Australia	Interview	NA	NA	NA	Purposive	High contextualization	Small non-profit organizations in the national regulatory context

References

Anand, S., Hu, J., Vidyarthi, P., & Liden, R. C. (2018). Leader-member exchange as a linking pin in the idiosyncratic deals—Performance relationship in workgroups. *Leadership Quarterly, 29*, 698–708.

Anand, S., Vidyarthi, P., Liden, R. C., & Rousseau, D. M. (2010). Good citizens in poor-quality relationships: Idiosyncratic deals as a substitute for relationship quality. *Academy of Management Journal, 53*, 970–988. https://doi.org/10.5465/amj.2010.54533176

Atkinson, C., & Sandiford, P. (2016). An exploration of older worker flexible working arrangements in smaller firms. *Human Resource Management Journal, 26*, 12–28. https://doi.org/10.1111/1748-8583.12074

*Bal, P. M. (2017). Why do employees negotiate idiosyncratic deals? An exploration of the process of i-deal negotiation. *New Zealand Journal of Employment Relations, 42*, 2–18.

*Bal, P. M., & Boehm S. A. (2019). How do I-deals influence client satisfaction? The role of exhaustion, collective commitment, and age diversity. *Journal of Management, 45*, 1461–1487. https://doi.org/10.1177/0149206317710722

*Bal, P. M., De Jong, S. B., Jansen, P. G. W. & Bakker, A. B. (2012). Motivating employees to work beyond retirement: A multi-level study of the role of i-deals and unit climate. *Journal of Management Studies, 49*, 306–331. https://doi.org/10.1111/j.1467-6486.2011.01026.x

Bal, P. M., & Dorenbosch, L. (2014). Age-related differences in the relations between individualised HRM and organisational performance: A large-scale employer survey. *Human Resource Management Journal, 25*, 41–61. https://doi.org/10.1111/1748-8583.12058

Bal, M., & Lub, X. D. (2016). Individualization of work arrangements: A contextualized perspective on the rise and use of i-deals. In M. Bal & D. M. Rousseau (Eds.), *Current issues in work and organizational psychology: Idiosyncratic deals between employees and organizations: Conceptual issues, applications and the role of co-workers* (pp. 9–23). Routledge/Taylor & Francis Group.

Bal, M., & Vossaert, L. (2019). Development of an i-deals motivation and management measure. *Journal of Personnel Psychology 18*, 201–215. https://doi.org/10.1027/18665888/a000236

*Broschak, J. P., & Davis-Blake, A. (2006). Mixing standard work and nonstandard deals: The consequences of heterogeneity in employment arrangements. *Academy of Management Journal, 49*, 371–393. https://doi.org/10.5465/AMJ.2006.20786085

Brzykcy, A., Boehm, S., & Baldridge, D. (2019). Fostering sustainable careers across the lifespan: The role of disability, idiosyncratic deals and perceived work ability. *Journal of Vocational Behavior, 112*, 185–198. https://doi.org/10.1016/j.jvb.2019.02.001

*Çalışkan, E., & Torun, A. (2019). Individualized HR practices and idiosyncratic deals (I Deals) and the expected positive individual and organizational outcomes. *Istanbul Business Research, 48*, 36–63. https://doi.org/10.26650/ibr.2019.48.0016

Chao, G. T., & Moon, H. (2005). The cultural mosaic: A meta-theory for understanding the complexity culture. *Journal of Applied Psychology, 90*, 1128–1140. https://doi.org/10.1037/0021-9010.90.6.1128

Cheung, F. M., & Leung, K. (1998). Indigenous personality measures: Chinese examples. *Journal of Cross-Cultural Psychology, 29*, 233–248. https://doi.org/10.1177/0022022198291012

Conway, N., & Coyle-Shapiro, J. A.-M. (2016). Not so i-deal: A critical review of idiosyncratic-deals theory and research. In: M. Bal & D. M. Rousseau (Eds.), *Idiosyncratic deals between employees and organizations: Conceptual issues, applications and the role of co-workers* (pp. 36–64). Routledge.

*Davis, A. S., & Van der Heijden, B. I. J. M. (2018). Reciprocity matters: Idiosyncratic deals to shape the psychological contract and foster employee engagement in times of austerity. *Human Resource Development Quarterly, 29*, 329–355. https://doi.org/10.1002/hrdq.21327

*De Menezes, L. M. & Kelliher, C. (2016). Flexible working, individual performance, and employee attitudes: Comparing formal and informal arrangements. *Human Resource Management, 56*, 1051–1070. https://doi.org/10.1002/hrm.21822

*De Vos, A., & Cambré, B. (2016). Career management in high-performing organizations: A set theoretic approach. *Human Resource Management, 56*, 501–518.

Dheer, R., Lenartowicz, T., Peterson, M. F., & Petrescu, M. (2014). Cultural regions of Canada and United States: Implications for international management research. *International Journal of Cross Cultural Management, 14*, 343–384. https://doi.org/10.1177/1470595814543706

*Ding, C. G., & Chang, Y. W. (2019). Effects of task and work responsibilities idiosyncratic deals on perceived insider status and the moderating roles of perceived overall justice and coworker support. *Review of Managerial Science, 14*, 1341–1361. https://doi.org/10.1007/s11846-01900335-6. https://doi.org/10.1007/s11846-01900335-6

Doney, P. M., Cannon, J. P., & Mullen, M. R. (1998). Understanding the influence of national culture on the development of trust. *The Academy of Management Review, 23*, 601–620. https://doi.org/10.2307/259297

Fischer, R. (2009). Where is culture in cross cultural research? An outline of a multilevel research process for measuring culture as a shared meaning system. *International Journal of Cross Cultural Management, 9*, 25–49.

*Gajendran, R. S., Harrison, D. A., & Delaney-Klinger, K. (2015). Are telecommuters remotely good citizens? Unpacking telecommuting's effects on performance via i-deals and job resources. *Personnel Psychology, 68*, 353–393. https://doi.org/10.1111/peps.12082

Garg, S., & Fulmer, I. (2017). Ideal or an ordeal for organizations?: The spectrum of co-worker reactions to idiosyncratic deals. *Organizational Psychology Review, 7*, 281–305. https://doi.org/10.1177/2041386617733136

*Gascoigne, C., & Kelliher, C. (2018). The transition to part-time: How professionals negotiate 'reduced time and workload' i-deals and craft their jobs. *Human Relations, 71*, 103–125. https://doi.org/10.1177/0018726717722394

Gelfand, M. J., Aycan, Z., Erez, M., & Leung, K. (2017). Cross-cultural industrial organizational psychology and organizational behavior: A hundred-year journey. *Journal of Applied Psychology, 102*, 514–529. https://doi.org/10.1037/apl0000186

Gelfand, M. J., Leslie, L. M., & Fehr, R. (2008). To prosper, organizational psychology should... adopt a global perspective. *Journal of Organizational Behavior, 29*, 493–517.

Gelfand, M. J., Raver, J. L., Nishii, L., Leslie, L. M., Lun, J., Lim, B. C., Duan, L., Almaliach, A., Ang, S., Arnadottir, J., ZAycan, Z., Boehnke, K., Boski, P., Cabecinhs, R., Chan, D., Chhokar, J., D'Amato, A., Ferrer, M., Fischlmar, I. C., ... Aycan, Z. (2011). Differences between tight and loose cultures: A 33-nation study. *Science, 332*, 1100–1104. https://doi.org/10.1126/science.1197754

Guerrero, S., Bentein, K., & Lapalme, M. E. (2017). Idiosyncratic deals and high performers' organizational commitment. *Journal of Business and Psychology, 29*, 323–334. https://doi.org/10.1007/s10869-013-9316-7

Guerrero, S., & Challiol-Jeanblanc, H. C. (2016). Idiosyncratic deals and helping behavior: The moderating role of i-deal opportunity for co-workers. *Journal of Business and Psychology, 31*, 433–443. https://doi.org/10.1007/s10869-015-9421-x

*Guerrero, S., & Challiol-Jeanblanc, H. C. (2017a). Ex ante i-deals, perceived external prestige and turnover intentions. *Personnel Review, 46*, 1199–1212. https://dois.org/1108/PR-10-2015-0271. https://doi.org/10.1108/CDI-08-2015-0115

*Guerrero, S., & Challiol-Jeanblanc, H. C. (2017b). Networking and development idiosyncratic deals. *Career Development International, 22*, 816–828. https://doi.org/10.1108/CDI-012017-0017" https://doi.org/10.1108/CDI-012017-0017

*Guerrero, S., & Challiol-Jeanblanc, H. C., Veilleux, M. (2016). Development idiosyncratic deals and career success. *Career Development International, 21*, 19–30.

Haidt, J., & Kesebir, S. (2010). Morality. In S. T. Fiske, D. T. Gilbert, & G. Lindzey (Eds.), *Handbook of social psychology* (p. 797–832). Wiley. https://doi.org/10.1002/9780470561119.socpsy002022

Henrich, J., Heine, S. J., & Norenzayan, A. (2010). The weirdest people in the world? *Behavioral and Brain Sciences, 33*, 61–83. https://doi.org/10.1017/S0140525X0999152X

Hornung, S., Rousseau, D. M., & Glaser, J. (2008). Creating flexible work arrangements through idiosyncratic deals. *Journal of Applied Psychology, 93*, 655–664. https://doi.org/10.1037/0021-9010.93.3.655

Hornung, S., Rousseau, D. M., & Glaser, J. (2009). Why supervisors make idiosyncratic deals: Antecedents and outcomes of i-deals from a managerial perspective. *Journal of Managerial Psychology, 24*, 738–764. https://doi.org/10.1108/02683940910996770

Hornung, S., Rousseau, D. M., Glaser, J., Angerer, P. & Weigl, M. (2010). Beyond top-down and bottom-up work redesign: Customizing job content through idiosyncratic deals. *Journal of Organizational Behavior, 31*, 187–215. https://doi.org/10.1002/job.625

*Hornung, S., Rousseau, D. M., Weigl, M., Müller, A., & Glaser, J. (2014). Redesigning work through idiosyncratic deals. *European Journal of Work and Organizational Psychology, 23*, 608–626. https://doi.org/10.1080/1359432X.2012.740171

House, R. J., Hanges, P. J., Javidan, M., Dorfman, P. W., & Gupta, V. (2004). *Culture, leadership and organizations: The GLOBE Study of 62 Societies.* Sage.

Huo, W. W., Luo, J. L., & Tam, K. L. (2015). Idiosyncratic deals and good citizens in China: The role of traditionality for recipients and their coworkers. *The International Journal of Human Resource Management, 25*, 3157–3177. https://doi.org/10.1080/09585192.2014.919949

Kashima, Y., Siegal, M., Tanaka, K., & Isaka, H. (1988). Universalism in lay conceptions of distributive justice: A cross-cultural examination. *International Journal of Psychology, 23*, 51–64. https://doi.org/10.1080/00207598808247752

Katigbak, M. S., Church, A. T., Guanzon-Lapeña, M. A., Carlota, A. J., & del Pilar, G. H. (2002). Are indigenous personality dimensions culture specific? Philippine inventories and the five-factor model. *Journal of Personality and Social Psychology, 82*, 89–101. https://doi.org/10.1037/0022-3514.82.1.89

*Katou, A. A., Budhwar, P. S., & Dhiman, M. C. (2020). The moderating effects of transformational leadership and self-worth in the idiosyncratic deals—Employee reactions relationship: A study of Indian hospitality industry. *Personnel Review, 49*(7), 1399–1418. https://doi.org/10.1108/PR-11-2019-0596

*Katou, A. A., Budhwar, P. S., & Patel, C. (2020). Idiosyncratic deals in less competitive labor markets: testing career i-deals in the Greek context of high uncertainties. *The International Journal of Human Resource Management*, 1–28. https://doi.org/10.1080/09585192.2020.1759672

Kelly, C., Rofcanin, Y., Las Heras, M., Ogbonnaya, C., Marescaux, E., & Jose Bosch, M. (2020). Seeking an "i-deal" balance: Schedule-flexibility i-deals as mediating mechanisms between supervisor emotional support and employee work and home performance. *Journal of Vocational Behavior*, *118*. https://doi.org/10.1016/j.jvb.2019.103369

Kim, U. (2001). Culture, science and indigenous psychologies: An integrated analysis. In D. Matsumoto (Ed.), *Handbook of culture and psychology* (pp. 51–76). Oxford University Press.

Kimwolo, A., & Cheruiyot, T. (2019). Intrinsically motivating idiosyncratic deals and innovative work behaviour. *International Journal of Innovation Science*, *11*, 31–47. https://doi.org/10.1108/IJIS-05-2017-0038

*Kong, D. T., Ho, V. T. & Garg, S. (2020).Employee and coworker idiosyncratic deals: Implications for emotional exhaustion and deviant behaviors. *Journal of Business Ethics*, *164*, 593–609. https://doi.org/10.1007/s10551-018-4033-9

*Kossek, E., Ollier-Malaterre, A., Lee, M., Pichler, S., & Hall, D. (2016). Line managers' rationales for professionals' reduced-load work in embracing and ambivalent organizations. *Human Resource Management*, *55*, 143–171. https://doi.org/10.1002/hrm.21722

*Lai, L., Rousseau, D. M., & Chang, K. T. T. (2009). Idiosyncratic deals: Coworkers as interested third parties. *Journal of Applied Psychology*, *94*, 547–556. https://doi.org/10.1037/a0013506

Las Heras, M., Rofcanin, Y., Bal, P. M., & Stollberger, J. (2017). How do flexibility ideals relate to work performance? Exploring the roles of family performance and organizational context. *Journal of Organizational Behavior*, *38*, 1280–1294. https://doi.org/10.1002/job.2203

Las Heras, M., Van der Heijden, B., De Jong, J., & Rofcanin, Y. (2017). '': The mediating role of i-deals in the relationship between supervisors' caregiving responsibilities and employee outcomes. *Human Resource Management Journal*, *27*, 335–349. https://doi.org/10.1111/1748-8583.12160

*Lee, B.-Y., Kim, T.-Y., Gong, Y., Zheng, X., & Liu, X. (2020). Employee well-being attribution and job change intentions: The moderating effect of task idiosyncratic deals. *Human Resources Management*, *59*, 327–338. https://doi.org/10.1002/hrm.21998

Lee, C., & Hui, C. (2011). Antecedents and consequences of idiosyncratic deals: A frame of resource exchange. *Frontiers of Business Research in China*, *5*(3), 380–401. https://doi.org/10.1007/s11782-011-0136-1

Lee, J. Y., Bachrach, D. G., & Rousseau, D. M. (2015). Internal labor markets, firm-specific human capital, and heterogeneity antecedents of employee idiosyncratic deal requests. *Organization Science, 26,* 794–810. https://doi.org/10.1287/2014.0955

Lemmon, G., Westring, A., Michel, E. J., Wilson, M. S., & Glibkowski, B. C. (2016). A cross-domain exploration of performance benefits and costs of idiosyncratic deals. *Journal of Leadership and Organizational Studies, 23,* 440–455. https://doi.org/10.1177/1548051816645748

Leung, K., & Iwawaki, S. (1988). Cultural collectivism and distributive behavior. *Journal of Cross-Cultural Psychology, 19,* 35–49. https://doi.org/10.1177/0022002188019001003

Leung, K., & Morris, M. W. (2015). Values, schemas, and norms in the culture-behavior nexus: A situated dynamics framework. *Journal of International Business Studies, 46,* 1–23. https://doi.org/10.1057/jibs.2014.66

*Liao, C., Wayne, S., & Rousseau, D. M. (2014). Idiosyncratic deals in contemporary organizations: A qualitative and meta-analytical review. *Journal of Organizational Behavior, 37,* 9–29.

*Liao, C., Wayne, S. J., Liden, R. C., & Meuser, J. D. (2017). Idiosyncratic deals and individual effectiveness: The moderating role of leader-member exchange differentiation. *The Leadership Quarterly, 28,* 438–450. https://doi.org/10.1016/j.leaqua.2016.10.014

Liao, C., Wayne, S., & Rousseau, D. M. (2016). Idiosyncratic deals in contemporary organizations: A qualitative and meta-analytical review. *Journal of Organizational Behavior, 37,* 9–29. https://doi.org/10.1002/job.1959

*Liu, F., & Zhou, K. (2020). Idiosyncratic deals and creative deviance: The mediating role of psychological entitlement. *R&D Management,* 1–14. https://doi.org/10.1111/radm.12430

Liu, J., Lee, C., Hui, C., Kwan, H. K., & Wu, L. Z. (2013). Idiosyncratic deals and employee outcomes: The mediating roles of social exchange and self-enhancement and the moderating role of individualism. *Journal of Applied Psychology, 98,* 832–40. https://doi.org/10.1037/a0032571

*Luksyte, A., & Spitzmueller, C. (2016). When are overqualified employees creative? It depends on contextual factors. *Journal of Organizational Behavior, 37,* 635–653. https://doi.org/10.1002/job.2054. https://doi.org/10.1002/job.2054

*Luu, L. T. (2016). Organizational ambidexterity, entrepreneurial orientation, and i-deals: The moderating role of CSR. *Journal of Business Ethics, 135,* 145–159. https://doi.org/10.1007/s10551-014-2476-1

Luu, L. T. (2017). Administrative error control: The role of value-based HR practices, i-deals and organizational politics. *International Public Management Journal, 20,* 648–674. https://doi.org/10.1080/10967494.2016.1269858

Luu, L. T., & Djurkovic, N. (2019). Paternalistic leadership and idiosyncratic deals in a healthcare context. *Management Decision, 57*, 621–648. https://doi.org/10.1108/MD-06-2017-0595

*Luu, L. T., & Rowley, C. (2015). From value-based human resource practices to i-deals: software companies in Vietnam. *Personnel Review, 44*(1), 39–68. https://doi.org/10.1108/PR-08-2013-0151

*Luu, L. T., & Rowley, C. (2016). The relationship between cultural intelligence and I ideals: Trust as a mediator and HR localization as a moderator. *International Journal of Organizational Analysis, 24*, 908–931. https://doi.org/10.1108/IJOA-03-2015-0848

Marescaux, E., De Winne, S., & Sels, L. (2019). Idiosyncratic deals from a distributive justice perspective: Examining co-workers' voice behavior. *Journal of Business Ethics, 154*, 263–281. https://doi.org/10.1007/s10551-016-3400-7

*Morf, M., Bakker, A., & Feierabend, A. (2019). Bankers closing idiosyncratic deals Implications for organisational cynicism. *Human Resource Management Journal, 29*, 585–599. https://doi.org/10.1111/1748-8583.12245

*Neirotti, P., Raguseo, E., & Gastaldi, L. (2019). Designing flexible work practices for job satisfaction: the relationship between job characteristics and work disaggregation in different types of work arrangements. *New Technology, Work and Employment, 34*, 116–138. https://doi.org/10.1111/ntwe.12141

Ng, T. W. H. (2017). Can idiosyncratic deals promote perceptions of competitive climate, felt ostracism, and turnover? *Journal of Vocational Behavior, 99*, 118–131. https://doi.org/10.1016/j.jvb.2017.01.004

Ng, T. W. H., & Feldman, D. C. (2010). Idiosyncratic deals and organizational commitment. *Journal of Vocational Behavior, 76*, 419–427. https://doi.org/10.1016/j.jvb.2009.10.006

Ng, T. W., & Feldman, D. C. (2012). Breaches of past promises, current job alternatives, and promises of future idiosyncratic deals: Three-way interaction effects on organizational commitment. *Human Relations, 65*, 1463–1486. https://doi.org/10.1177/0018726712453472

Ng, T. W. H., & Feldman, D. C. (2015). Idiosyncratic deals and voice behavior. *Journal of Management, 41*, 893–928. https://doi.org/10.1177/0149206312457824

Ng, T. W. H., & Lucianetti, L. (2016). Goal striving, idiosyncratic deals, and job behavior. *Journal of Organizational Behavior, 37*, 41–60. https://doi.org/10.1002/job.2023

Oostrom, J. K., Pennings, M., & Bal, P. M. (2016). How do idiosyncratic deals contribute to the employability of older workers? *Career Development International, 21*(2), 176–192. https://doi.org/10.1108/CDI-08-2015-0112

Parker, S. K., Van den Broeck, A., & Holman, D. (2017). Work design influences: A synthesis of multilevel factors that affect the design of jobs. *Academy of Management Annals, 11,* 267–308. https://doi.org/10.5465/annals.2014.0054

Pearce, J. L., Branyiczki, I., & Bigley, G. A. (2000). Insufficient bureaucracy: Trust and commitment in particularistic organizations. *Organization Science, 11,* 148–162.

Ready, D. A., Hill, L. A., & Conger, J. A. (2008). Winning the race for talent in emerging markets. *Harvard Business Review, 86*(11), 62–70. https://doi.org/10.1287/orsc.11.2.148.12508

Redding, S. G. M. (1990). An empirical study of overseas Chinese managerial ideology. *International Journal of Intercultural Relations, 25,* 629–641. https://doi.org/10.1080/00207599008247917

*Rofcanin, Y., Berber, A., Koch, S., & Sevinc, L. (2016). Job crafting and i-deals: A study testing the nomological network of proactive behaviors. *The International Journal of Human Resource Management, 27*(22), 2695–2726. https://doi.org/10.1080/09585192.2015.1091370

Rofcanin, Y., Kiefer, T., & Strauss, K. (2017). What seals the i-deal? Exploring the role of employees' behaviours and managers' emotions. *Journal of Occupational and Organizational Psychology, 90,* 203–224. https://doi.org/10.1111/joop.12168

Rofcanin, Y., Las Heras, M., Bal, M., van der Heijden, B. & Erdogan, D. (2018). A trickle-down model of task and development i-deals. *Human Relations, 71,* 1508–1534. https://doi.org/10.1177/0018726717751613

*Rofcanin, Y., Las Heras, M., Jose Bosch, M., Stollberger, J., & Mayer, M. (2020). How do weekly obtained task i-deals improve work performance? The role of relational context and structural job resources. *European Journal of Work and Organizational Psychology.* https://doi.org/10.1080/1359432X.2020.1833858

*Rosen, C. C., Slater, D. J., Chang, C. H., & Johnson, R. E. (2013). Let's make a deal: Development and validation of the ex post i-deals scale. *Journal of Management, 39,* 709–742. https://doi.org/10.1177/0149206310394865

Rousseau, D. M. (2001). Idiosyncratic deals: Flexibility versus fairness. *Organizational Dynamics, 29,* 260–273. https://doi.org/10.1016/S0090-2616(01)00032-8

Rousseau, D. M. (2005). *I-deals, idiosyncratic deals employees bargain for themselves.* ME Sharpe.

Rousseau, D. M., & Fried, A. Y. (2001). Location, location, location: Contextualizing organizational research. *Journal of Organizational Behavior, 11,* 1–13. https://doi.org/10.1002/job.78

Rousseau, D. M., Hornung, S., & Kim, T. G. (2009). Idiosyncratic deals: Testing propositions on timing, content, and the employment relationship. *Journal of Vocational Behavior, 74*(3), 338–348. https://doi.org/10.1016/j.jvb.2009.02.004

Rousseau, D. M., Ho, V. T., & Greenberg, J. (2006). I-deals: Idiosyncratic terms in employment relationships. *Academy of Management Review, 31*, 977–994. https://doi.org/102307/20159261

Rousseau, D. M., & Kim, T. (2006). *Idiosyncratic deals: How negotiating their own employment conditions affects workers' relationships with an employer.* Paper presented at the annual meeting of the British Academy of Management, Oxford, UK.

Tang, Y. P., & Hornung, S. (2015). Work-family enrichment through I-deals: Evidence from Chinese employees. *Journal of Managerial Psychology, 30*, 940–954. https://doi.org/10.1108/JMP-02-2013-0064

*Townsend, K., McDonald, P., & Cathcart, A. (2017). Managing flexible work arrangements in small not-for-profit firms: The influence of organisational size, financial constraints and workforce characteristics. *The International Journal of Human Resource Management, 14*, 2085–2107. https://doi.org/10.1080/09585192.2015.1136671

Tsui, A. S. (2004). Contributing to global management knowledge: A case for high quality indigenous research. *Asia Pacific Journal of Management, 21*, 491–513. https://doi.org/10.1023/B:APJM.0000048715.35108.a7

van de Vijver, F. J. R., & Leung, K. (1997). *Methods and data analysis for cross-cultural research.* Sage.

van de Vijver, F. J. R., & Leung, K. (2001). Personality in cultural context: Methodological issues. *Journal of Personality, 69*, 1007–1031. https://doi.org/10.1111/1467-6494.696173

*Vidyarthi, P., Chaudhry, A., Anand, S., & Liden, R. C. (2014). Flexibility i-deals: how much is ideal? *Journal of Managerial Psychology, 29*, 246–265. https://doi.org/10.1108/JMP-07-2012-0225

Vidyarthi, P. R., Singh, S., Erdogan, B., Chaudhry, A., Posthuma, R., & Anand, S. (2016). Individual deals within teams: Investigating the role of relative i-deals for employee performance. *Journal of Applied Psychology, 101*, 1536–1552. https://doi.org/10.1037/apl0000145

Wang, L. L., & Long, L. R. (2018). Idiosyncratic deals and taking charge: The roles of psychological empowerment and organizational tenure. *Social Behavior and Personality, 46*, 1437–1448. https://doi.org/10.2224/sbp.7084

Wang, P., Wang, S., Yao, X., & Hsu, I., & Lawler, J. (2019). Idiosyncratic deals and work to family conflict and enrichment: The mediating roles of fit perceptions and efficacy beliefs. *Human Resource Management Journal, 29*, 600–619. https://doi.org/10.1111/1748-8583.12246

Wang, S. H., Liu, Y., & Shalley, C. E. (2018). Idiosyncratic deals and employee creativity: The mediating role of creative self-efficacy. *Human Resource Management, 57*, 1443–1453. https://doi.org/10.1002/hrm.21917

Wasti, S. A., & Önder, Ç. (2009). Commitment across cultures: Progress, pitfalls, and propositions. In H. Klein, T. E., Becker, & J. P. Meyer (Eds.), *Commitment in organizations: Accumulated wisdom and new directions.* (pp. 309–343). Routledge Academic.

CHAPTER 13

I-deals and the Future of Work: A Research Agenda for the Post-pandemic Age

Smriti Anand and Yasin Rofcanin

In an era defined by pandemic, work is going to change in fundamental ways. The impact of COVID-19 on the nature of work, the employees, and the workplace will persist even after the pandemic subsides. Ongoing research on the impact of COVID-19 demonstrates that the interruptions to work caused by the pandemic will be larger than had been estimated, especially for the lowest-paid, least educated, and most vulnerable workers (Shockley et al., 2021). Trends accelerated by COVID-19 include: (a) remote work, such that 20–25% of employees in advanced economies are likely to work at least three days from a destination other than the office, (b) digitalization of work, which underscores the increasing reliance on information and communication technologies to do business,

---

S. Anand (✉)
Stuart School of Business, Illinois Institute of Technology, Chicago, IL, USA
e-mail: smriti.Anand@stuart.iit.edu; sanand12@stuart.iit.edu

Y. Rofcanin
University of Bath, Bath, UK
e-mail: Y.Rofcanin@bath.ac.uk; yr308@bath.ac.uk

© The Author(s), under exclusive license to Springer Nature Switzerland AG 2022
S. Anand and Y. Rofcanin (eds.), *Idiosyncratic Deals at Work*,
https://doi.org/10.1007/978-3-030-88516-8_13

and (c) individualization of work, which is reflected in the way employees seek personalized treatment at work (McKinsey Global Institute Report, 2021). In the context of the ongoing pandemic and drawing from the various themes delineated in this book, we relate i-deals to the future of work in this concluding chapter. We begin by reflecting on the current state of i-deals research as depicted in the previous chapters. After explicating the insights from these chapters, we critique extant methods in i-deals research and make recommendations for future scholars. We end this chapter with a discussion of key trends that will shape the future of work in relation to i-deals.

STATE OF I-DEALS RESEARCH

This book is divided into three parts. The first part describes the motivations of i-deal seekers and grantors, and also introduces the idea that the process of i-deals negotiation has stakeholders from both work and non-work domains. Two of the most commonly studied forms of idiosyncratic work arrangements are development and flexibility i-deals that employees negotiate to customize career growth opportunities, and work schedule and/or location (Liao et al., 2016). Thus, the first two chapters by Guerrero and Bentein, and Afacan Findikli and her colleagues focus on development and flexibility i-deals, respectively. Chapter 1 aims to understand why employees request development i-deals from their organizations, and what are the underlying mechanisms in the i-deal granting process. The chapter also examines inactive employees who don't request or receive such deals. Noting the trend of putting the responsibility of career management on individual employees rather than the organization (e.g., Arthur, 2014; Greenhaus & Kossek, 2014), the authors emphasize the role of development i-deals as a career shaping device. Guerrero and Bentein review the extant i-deals literature to identify factors underlying i-deal requests, and their success or failure. Further, they discuss the outcomes of the negotiation process in 3 prominent scenarios: (1) no i-deal is sought, (2) an i-deal is sought and granted, and (3) an i-deal is sought and refused. This discussion lies in contrast to bulk of the i-deals research that equates seeking to obtainment, and ignores the possibility of failed negotiations, or promised deals failing to materialize (See Rofcanin et al., 2017 for an exception). Altogether this chapter stresses the need for future research to disentangle the i-deals negotiation and obtainment process by exploring unique antecedents and consequences of both successful and failed negotiations.

The next chapter explores flexibility i-deals negotiation process and outlines the role of stakeholders from non-work domain. Afacan Findkli and her colleagues argue that research has largely ignored the non-work domain and treated only the employee, the leader, and the co-workers as the relevant parties to i-deals (Rousseau et al., 2006). Flexibility i-deals are becoming common devices for employees to achieve balance between work and non-work domains (e.g., Las Heras et al., 2017), which makes it important to understand how each domain shapes these deals. Further, today's work settings, especially in the times of COVID-19, have made work and family live inseparable, so adopting a holistic perspective on i-deals is critical to advancing this field of research. The authors maintain that spouses, family members, and friends provide socio-emotional resources and play a key role in i-deals negotiation process. This chapter introduces new concepts such as family and leisure i-deals and calls on scholars to empirically validate and test those to understand the relationship between flexibility i-deals and non-work domains.

Chapter 3 argues that managerial decision-making processes have received scant attention despite the key role of managers in negotiating and implementing i-deals noted in i-deals theory (Rousseau et al., 2006). Sharma and her colleagues emphasize that most manager-employee interactions including those related to i-deals take place in situations where one party is more informed than the other regarding some payoff-relevant variables, and the information asymmetry may encourage the informed party to behave in a self-serving manner that may hurt the objectives of the other. To explicate managerial decision-making, the authors assume that i-deal seeking employees have private information about their skills, working habits, and/or intent to exert effort, while the manager is the less informed party who has to decide whether to grant or continue an i-deal. Applying the economic concepts of adverse selection and moral hazard, this chapter illustrates the challenges in designing and implementing effective i-deals in that managers may not have either full information about employees' performance potential or the ability to monitor/assess all of their actions. The authors recommend signaling and screening mechanisms to mitigate information asymmetry and associated issues. The discussion in this chapter illustrates various managerial decision-making pitfalls arising from information asymmetry and invites scholars to investigate the conditions that promote or deter these issues while creating new i-deals or continuing existing i-deals.

The final chapter in this part of the book stands in contrast to its predecessors in that it challenges the prevalent assumption in i-deals literature of employees being the sole initiators of i-deal negotiations. Meuser and Cao explore what can happen if and when leaders initiate i-deals for their subordinates. Leaders operate from a position of power that adds complexity to how their offered deals are perceived and used by the followers. Drawing on theories of servant and exploitative leadership, Meuser and Cao argue that i-deals granted by servant leaders are likely meant to grow, develop, and support followers, whereas those granted by exploitative leaders may be a manipulation tactic. The authors theorize that leader's offer of an i-deal triggers an appraisal process in the follower such that acceptance of the offered deal is based on whether it is seen as servant or exploitative leadership. Moreover, the appraisal process is shaped by individual and workgroup factors such as the follower's attachment style and social information from colleagues. The discussion in this chapter stresses the need to develop and test a model of the entire i-deal negotiation process, including all stakeholders, and without assuming who initiates an i-deal. For example, i-deals initiated by either party may not be accepted in the end because new information (e.g., details on daily implementation of the work arrangement) emerged during negotiation to dissuade the follower.

The second part of the book focuses on the dilemma at the heart of i-deals: The customization designed to benefit individuals can hurt collective effectiveness (Anand et al., in press). The three chapters in this part expound on i-deals negotiation and implementation process and discuss issues pertaining to fairness of these differentiated work arrangements. Reviewing societal and organizational trends favoring individualization of work, the authors also recommend best practices for institutionalizing i-deals as a strategic human resource management device. First, Vidyarthi and his colleagues draw on theories of social comparison and organizational justice to address the dynamic process of i-deals negotiation and implementation in the context of workgroups. The authors argue that i-deals unfold in a team context wherein employees engage in a social comparison process of evaluating what they have relative to the others, and this comparison shapes the i-deals negotiation process and subsequent outcomes. Their assertion is based on past research in that employees use i-deals to evaluate their standing and worth to the organization (Vidyarthi et al., 2016) and enhance their outputs by modifying the terms of their work arrangement via an i-deal. Integrating theories of social comparison and justice Vidyarthi et al. conceptualize a 4-stage framework to explain the lifecycle of i-deals as follows: (1) recognition of potential i-deals, where the employee identifies unmet needs, (2) negotiation of i-deals, where the employee bargains with the supervisor or another organizational agent, (3) execution of agreed-upon i-deals, where the granted terms are implemented, and (4) renegotiation of i-deals, where the deal may end or continue with same or modified terms depending on employee needs. Their model stresses the importance of understanding the entire lifecycle of i-deals and invites future researchers to empirically validate the different stages of i-deals process and investigate the reactions and outcomes of both employees and co-workers at each stage.

The next chapter also looks beyond the individual seekers and the granting organizations to focus on co-workers, who observe and may get affected by the differentiation engendered by i-deals (Rousseau et al., 2006). Rofcanin and his colleagues argue that research on i-deals negotiation process has largely focused on benefits to their recipients and grantors and ignored the co-workers' outcomes. This chapter starts by examining the drivers of individualism at the organizational and societal levels, and then delves into the role of co-workers in the i-deals process, especially from an emotional perspective. Limited research on co-worker and manager reactions to focal's i-deals shows a range of emotions from sympathy and acceptance to malicious envy and contempt (e.g., Marescaux et al., 2021). The authors maintain that these reactions are shaped by: (a) the quality of relationships between i-dealers and the others, (b) the nature of the employment relationship, (c) perceptions of workplace justice, and (d) organizational climate for collaboration. This discussion encourages future researchers to explore the different conditions that lead to positive or negative emotions around i-deals to generate benefits or harm relationships with an i-dealer's co-workers. In addition, new theoretical perspectives such as emotions as social information and emotional contagion are suggested to investigate team level emotions and trickle-down effects to other domains.

Finally, Chapter 7 contends that fairness issues surrounding i-deals can be addressed by establishing appropriate HR policies to guide their negotiation and implementation processes. Integrating extant HR literature with theories of fairness, Varma and his colleagues outline how organizations can effectively institutionalize i-deals as a HR differentiation device for effective talent management. In terms of HR policies critical to maintaining fair i-deals, Varma et al. advocate consistent criteria for awarding individualized arrangements, and clear terms of the arrangements that can be changed as and when required. Further, transparent communication with the entire team is advised to create a supportive climate for successful institutionalization of i-deals. Moreover, since contemporary organizations increasingly operate in a global context, it is important to account for local/societal culture in implementing any i-deals. Altogether this chapter urges future scholars to explore i-deals as a strategic HR management practice and investigates antecedents and consequences of their entire range including denied, granted but failed to materialize, granted and implemented, suspended, and renegotiated deals.

The third and final part of the book offers a critique of extant i-deals research and suggests several new pathways for growth of this area. The authors question why despite the increasing relevance of individualization of work and individualism in contemporary society (Bal & Dóci, 2018) growth in i-deals research lags behind that in job crafting and other conceptually similar areas. In addition to criticizing instruments for assessing i-deals, the chapters probe an implicit assumption in i-deals literature that individualization is available and beneficial to everyone. Scrutinizing i-deals through the lens of social justice these chapters argue that individualization of work arises from and further perpetuates social inequality. This part begins with Bal's assertion that i-deals, a device designed to create inequality among workers, must be understood in the context of growing social inequalities globally. Bal points to research findings that show linkages between employee's privileged status and i-deal receipts and explains the ideological and practical risks in assuming egalitarian bases for i-deals. To address these issues, he introduces a relational perspective on i-deals in that customization of work arrangements to fulfill an individual employee's unique needs is a sign of respect from the employer that promotes employee dignity as a human being. However, employee dignity is at risk when employers or organizations merely focus on profit maximization. The ideas in this chapter challenge future researchers to question the core assumptions underlying i-deals research and analyze the conditions under which i-deals promote, violate, or deny dignity, and provide real meaning in life and work.

In a similar vein, the next chapter draws on Foucault's works to critically examine the core assumptions underlying the concept of individualization of work. Mughal et al. observe that individualization of work shifts the responsibility of employee welfare from the organization to the employees and serves as a device to objectify individuals who sell their knowledge, skills, and abilities to benefit the organization in return for i-deals designed to fulfill their unique needs. In this view, i-deals serve only those who have the ability to express their needs and have something to bargain with. Further, by virtue of being special arrangements, i-deals may bestow elite status on their recipients, which in turn can promote perceptions of unfairness and alienation in the co-workers. The criticism in this chapter is meant to showcase the potential downside of promoting individualization of work for purely economic benefits and motivate future scholars to explore the subjective side of i-deals to learn how they shape individual worker identities to conform to organizational interests. Future studies should apply Focault's perspectives to understand the emotions generated by i-deals in different organizational/societal cultures, intensification of work in relation to i-deals, and issues of justice and transparency in the i-deal negotiation and implementation process.

Next, Chapter 10 extends the critique of i-deals by questioning their benefits for employees from diverse backgrounds. The review of i-deals research by Perera and Li points to an important gap: Empirical studies have largely ignored the challenges faced by diverse employees in negotiating and maintaining i-deals. Few scholars have theorized that i-deals provide employers with avenues to support diverse employees through work arrangements customized to fulfill their unique needs that lay beyond the standard HR policies (Anand & Mitra, in press). However, i-deals can also activate stereotypes based on their recipients' social identities, and negatively influence managerial decision-making and co-worker reactions. Perera and Li argue that the potential for stereotyping may dissuade diverse employees from expressing their needs and obtaining i-deals. The discussion in this chapter invites future studies to understand how women and mature-age employees strike i-deals. Interesting future studies may include: Do diverse individuals face unique challenges in making i-deals, and if so, how can the organization address these challenges? Under what conditions i-deals benefit employees from diverse backgrounds? How can i-deals be used to augment both identity blind and identity-conscious HR practices?

The last two chapters in this part of the book review various theoretical perspectives such as social exchange and signaling used in i-deals research and highlight the need to incorporate new theoretical approaches to grow and enrich this literature. First, Bakker and Ererdi in Chapter 11 argue that i-deals are resources that can be utilized to tackle work demands and thus should be explored through the job demands-resources (JD-R) lens. The integration of JD-R with i-deals theory invites future scholars to test how and when i-deals may provide resources to enhance employee well-being and performance. Then, Chapter 12 emphasizes the lack of attention toward societal/cultural context in i-deals research. Wasti and her colleagues argue that i-deal negotiation and associated processes may unfold uniquely across different cultural contexts, and understanding cross-cultural differences is critical to the growth of i-deals literature. These scholars urge future researchers to pursue questions such as the meaning of i-deals around the world, the effect of national context on prevalence of i-deals, employee, and co-worker reactions to i-deals in different societal contexts, and other effects of labor market characteristics, economic prosperity, and labor laws.

Critique of I-deals Research and Recommendations for Future

I-deals theory has been around for close to two decades and continues to draw significant attention from scholars and practitioners alike. Despite a large number of empirical studies devoted to this area, a number of issues are yet to be resolved. In the following, we discuss the following broad categories of issues: approaches to measurement of i-deals, research design problems, and lack of attention to the dynamic nature of i-deals.

Measurement Issues

The most commonly utilized scales in i-deals research are developed by Rousseau and her colleagues (Hornung et al., 2010; Rousseau et al., 2009), and Rosen et al. (2013). These scales capture different types of i-deals such as developmental opportunities, work schedule and location flexibility, reduced work hours, work and task responsibilities, and financial incentives. By focusing on what is negotiated these scales allow scholars to examine differential antecedents and consequences of various types of i-deals. For instance, i-deals made prior to organizational entry are more likely to comprise concrete resources such as work hours or bonus, whereas post-entry i-deals are more likely to include particularistic resources such as challenging job assignments (Rousseau et al., 2009). In terms of consequences, flexibility i-deals reduce employee's work-family conflict, whereas developmental i-deals are associated with increased organizational commitment (Hornung et al., 2008). Despite these benefits, the content-specific measurement approach poses certain limitations to research on i-deals (Anand et al., in press).

I-deals usually occur in the context of a workgroup, wherein one group member may negotiate reduced work hours while another may negotiate work location flexibility, and yet another may negotiate career development opportunities. By definition, i-deals create within group heterogeneity because employees negotiate what they need, and that makes comparing effects of different deals across the group a challenge. For instance, not all employees care to negotiate location flexibility i-deal, so using that scale to assess i-deals will not capture the entire variability in the workgroup. Developing a broader understanding of i-deals operating in workgroups thus requires scholars to assess and compare myriad types of i-deals from all group members, which may create survey fatigue in the respondents and adversely affect the research.

We therefore argue that i-deals should be conceptualized and assessed in general rather than content-specific terms. While the content of each employee's i-deal is different, their essence is same: All of these arrangements are personalized to meet the unique needs and preferences of the negotiating employees. I-deals should therefore be defined and measured in a broad way as personalized arrangements. This will allow researchers to capture various types of variability in employment arrangements across group members and make meaningful comparisons across individuals and workgroups without being mired in the various content-specific forms of i-deals. In support of our argument, the meta-analytic review by Liao et al. (2016) underlines "There is good reason to treat different i-deals contents as distinct variables, just as there is support for examining i-deals as a single general concept. The appropriateness of each approach depends on the nature of the research question." A global measure is needed to pursue research questions focused on the interpersonal processes surrounding i-deals in group settings. One such measure has been created by Anand and her colleagues (in press) to study antecedents and consequences of i-deals at individual, meso, and group levels. This measure also facilitates investigations of social comparison-driven consequences of within group i-deals distribution on group level outcomes. We recommend future research to utilize this measure to advance multi-level theorizing on i-deals.

Self-Ratings of I-deals

Research has so far relied on assessing i-deals from the recipient perspective, whereby employees are asked to rate the extent to which they have successfully negotiated i-deals with their employers. We note several problems with this measurement approach in addition to those deliberated in the previous chapters. First, the i-deals recipients may feel that they are entitled to special treatment and thus underreport their receipts. Second, employees may not realize the extent to which their arrangements differ from those of the other workgroup members and end up under or over reporting their i-deals. Lastly, the group context (e.g., highly cohesive group) may push employees to fit in and under report any work arrangements that are distinct from what the others have. We therefore recommend future studies to focus on objective measurements of i-deals.

In line with the recommendations of prior research (e.g., Anand et al., 2010; Rofcanin et al., 2019), managers, along with HR representatives, may develop transparent procedures explaining who have been granted i-deals, what is the content and the level of customization of the deals, and what are the criteria for granting the deals. This approach may set a reference point against which existing and future i-deals may be compared (e.g., inventory of employee i-deals). Consequently, social desirability and entitlement biases emanating from self-assessment of i-deals may be reduced.

A further avenue of future research is the measurement of i-deals from co-workers' perspective. I-deals are unique to each individual, and thus their implementation can potentially raise issues of fairness. Future studies may rely on co-worker evaluations of a focal employee's i-deals to address these issues. For instance, imagine a professor who put substantial effort without any compensation during summer break to design a new course for Fall semester. Later on, after successful negotiations, she gets a course load reduction in spring, which may be seen as an "unfair deal" by the co-workers. Evaluation of a focal employee's i-deals from co-worker perspective will help investigate unfairness concerns among employees in a workgroup setting, and the effects of differentiation on group dynamics and effectiveness.

The Dynamic Nature of I-deals

In the initial conceptualization of i-deals, Rousseau (2005) noted that these arrangements might be renegotiated over relatively short periods, hinting at their dynamic nature and underlining the potential for repeated bargaining. Despite this early recognition, most studies on i-deals have treated these arrangements with a static approach, assuming that employees may negotiate over relatively long periods. This is surprising given research in similar fields (e.g., job crafting, initiative taking) has demonstrated that employee-driven approaches to job design tend to be dynamic and change across shorter periods of time (e.g., Wang et al., 2016). We recommend future studies to explore the possibility of i-deals being negotiated over shorter periods of time such as weekly (e.g., Rofcanin, Las Heras, Bosch, Stollberger, & Mayer, in press) or daily. Capturing within-person and dynamic nature of i-deals will help researchers explore an array of exciting research questions: Can i-deals be re-bargained? Do employees renegotiate the terms and conditions they once obtained? What is the process of re-bargaining? Do i-deals have to involve drastic changes to one's work design, or can these deals involve small and incremental adjustments to one's work conditions? Most importantly, we recommend future studies to disentangle the within-person variability of different types of i-deals and compare the impact they have on employee and organizational outcomes. For example, flexibility i-deals may show more variation (e.g., daily or weekly changes in work hours or location) in comparison to task and development i-deals. A focus on the dynamic nature of i-deals and adoption of a scale to tap into within-person changes may open up a new stream of research.

Research Design Issues

Our overview of latest i-deals research has shown the major strides taken by researchers to enhance the scientific rigor in this field. Scholars have started developing research designs that have one or more of the following features: (a) other rated evaluations of work outcomes (usually collected from the focal employee's supervisor), (b) time lagged or longitudinal assessments (e.g., usually ranging between one to six months), and (c) multi-level assessments (e.g., moderators are conceptualized at team or organizational level). However, very few studies combine all these features to rigorously test and advance i-deals theory. We highlight an opportunity to develop i-deals research in a direction where researchers can design and implement multi-level studies to capture temporal changes in i-deals and their outcomes. We urge future scholars to utilize intact workgroup samples to pursue questions pertaining to social comparison and other interpersonal dynamics pertaining to i-deals (Anand & Vidyarthi, 2015). This is because i-deals are negotiated, implemented, evaluated, and reacted to in the shadow of all the other interactions in the workgroup (Vidyarthi et al., 2016). As noted in previous research, while i-deals represent an individual level phenomenon, their implications are significant for teams and organizations (Anand et al., in press; Bal & Boehm, 2019).

We also call on scholars to design studies including multiple types of i-deals and investigate their differential effects. For instance, i-deals such as financial incentives or promotion involve fixed resources whose allocation is likely competitive, whereas others such as training may be broadly available and offer benefits for the entire team in an integrative manner. I-deals that are seen as scarce resources are likely to affect group dynamics and outcomes (e.g., performance) in a manner vastly different from those that are seen as widely available.

Another area of future research is to employ experimental designs to ascertain causal direction of relationships between i-deals and their antecedents and consequences. It behooves scholars to conduct field experiments to study the impact of i-deals on employee outcomes such as well-being and productivity. While other fields of job design-oriented research such as job crafting, strength use, and work engagement have adopted an intervention approach (see Veenhoven et al., 2019 for an overview of interventions in job crafting research), surprisingly no research exists on designing and implementing i-deal interventions. Exploring this opportunity may be an exciting avenue for i-deals research, as it outlines the possibility of (a) offering a toolkit to HR practitioners to see if i-deals are indeed effective and useful tools to improve employee motivation and productivity, and (b) addressing some of the concerns about causality inherent in cross-sectional designs.

Post-pandemic Agenda for I-deals Research

In the context of the ongoing pandemic, i-deals are well suited to address the unique needs and preferences of employees and employers alike. With the aim of linking i-deals to the future of work, below we discuss possible trends that are likely to impact the growth and direction of this exciting field of research.

The Nature and Relevance of I-deals

The defining feature of i-deals is that they are person-specific arrangements designed to meet the unique work needs and goals of individual employees (Rousseau, 2005; Rousseau et al., 2006). Customization based on the preferences of a focal employee sets these work arrangements apart from what the rest of the co-workers have (Rofcanin et al., in press). One employee may seek customization of the when, where, and how of doing the work, while another may ask for individualized rewards associated with the work, and yet another may wish to tailor the opportunities for growth in the workplace. For almost two decades, i-deals scholars have explored these ways of work individualization; however, because of the pandemic the meaning of i-deals may have changed.

COVID-19 pandemic has dramatically changed the way we live and work. For instance, working from home and/or with a flexible work schedule has become the new reality. It is estimated that globally more than 50% employees across an array of industries desire to continue working from home post-pandemic, and in response organizations are seeking ways to create policies and practices to develop flexi-spaces for their employees (Trougakos et al., in press). Given the emergence of these new work trends, future scholars must explore the boundaries between flexible work and flexibility i-deals to investigate the extent of i-deals negotiation for addressing individual needs of work schedule and location flexibility. For example, under split shifts, policy employees are divided in two groups such that one group works in the office on Monday/Wednesday/Friday one week and on Tuesday/Thursday the next, and this pattern keeps alternating between the groups. While this policy provides work location flexibility, many employees may still need i-deals to customize their work start and end times, or the days they can be present at work.

We assert that i-deals are going to remain relevant and important in the post-pandemic world; however, their nature may change. Empirical studies are needed to understand what defines an i-deal in the presence of increased flexible work policies. Scholars maintain that i-deals are more likely to be granted if the organization has some flexible work structures (Hornung et al., 2008), but this relationship may have boundaries. Split shifts, for example, pose a conundrum to both the employee and the employer in that granting an individualized schedule requires more planning and coordination in the presence of overall flexibility. Future research needs to address these questions pertaining to the fundamentals of i-deals. Moreover, it is possible that in the presence of widespread flexible work i-deals no longer have the well-touted positive effects such as enhanced perceptions of organization-based self-esteem and citizenship behaviors. These advantages rooted in reciprocity, competence need satisfaction, and self-enhancement motives (Anand et al., 2010; Ho & Kong, 2015; Liu et al., 2013) may not hold if employees start taking customized arrangements for granted. Assuming i-deals will continue to benefit employees and employers alike in the post-pandemic world maybe a folly; scholars must investigate how the content and extent of i-deals shape employee attitudes and behaviors.

Pre- Versus Post-Recruitment I-deals

The initial theorization on i-deals discussed that employees can strike idiosyncratic deals either before they take up their new jobs, or following their recruitment (ex-ante and ex-post i-deals, respectively; Rousseau et al., 2006). Indeed, bulk of the empirical evidence on the topic suggests that employees are more likely to negotiate i-deals post-recruitment (Liao et al., 2016; Rousseau et al., 2009). This is based on the assumption that following recruitment, employees get opportunities to show their performance, develop better relationships with their supervisors, and hence feel at ease to seek i-deals. Put differently, the employees' skills and abilities, and their potential benefits to their employers become more salient and observable post-recruitment. However, this trend is likely to be reversed during and post-pandemic. Latest research conducted across countries, occupations, and age groups demonstrates that employees' choices of firms they would like to work for will be heavily shaped by the flexible-work package offer. According to the Future of Work Report (2021) by the McKinsey Global Institute, more than half of the employees surveyed reported that flexibility offers of the employer matter when they make job decisions. In a context where big multinational companies like Dell and Sodexo have formalized their flexibility policies to develop supportive cultures (Greatplacetowork, 2021), it is no surprise that employees are likely to evaluate organizations in light of their flexibility offers, and engage in i-deal negotiations during recruitment process with their employers.

We urge future scholars to explore whether (and if so, why) ex-ante i-deals are more prevalent and important than ex-post i-deals in post-pandemic organizations. Further, rather than assuming ex-ante i-deals will focus on concrete resources such as bonus while ex-post i-deals will focus on particularistic resources such as developmental training (Rousseau et al., 2009), scholars should conduct empirical studies to understand if and how the content differs between these two types of i-deals. In addition, research should explore the differential effects of ex-ante and ex-post i-deals.

Skill Transitions and I-deals

The COVID-19 pandemic has decimated certain industries and jobs while creating new ones, thus accelerating demand for employees across occupations. Employees are likely to face greater challenges in equipping themselves with new skillsets to find jobs in emerging new occupations and to manage their transition successfully. A transition usually occurs when an employee is displaced from a job by automation (e.g., computer-aided manufacturing), technological change (e.g., e-commerce), or another trend, and no other jobs in the same occupation are available because demand for that occupation has declined. This new trend is likely to have implications for research on i-deals.

Over the last two decades, research on i-deals has identified developmental i-deals (Anand et al., 2010), and task and work responsibility i-deals (Rosen et al., 2013), which emphasize the importance of investing in one's career, allocating resources for career progression, and obtaining resources for training and development. A shared feature among these different types of i-deals is that those are intended to improve employee's skills and capabilities so they can better adapt to changing and demanding work conditions. In this respect, the types of i-deals that are focused on career and self-development can be seen as tools to help employees' transition to new occupations, jobs, or areas of expertise. This is an important avenue for future research as globally the workforce is getting older, and individuals are changing careers/jobs more often (Catalyst, 2021). Future studies on i-deals should explore what types of deals (e.g., development vs. flexibility) are being negotiated more. Research is also needed on how employees and employers alike can adapt the existing i-deals to ensure that the recipients of such deals utilize the benefits in a new career field or occupation.

Hybrid Ways of Working and I-deals

As the pandemic has been unfolding, the need for an allocated space to work from home has gained recognition and importance. According to a recent report by Mercer (2021), the tipping point for remote work seems to have arrived: Over 70% of companies globally plan to examine remote and/or flexible work as a workforce priority in the next three to six months (2021, Mercer COVID-19 survey live results). In this study, only a minority of managers (8%) revealed that they will expect their employees to return to work physically. Since one stream of i-deals literature focuses on work schedule and location flexibility, these findings have implications for future research. We expect post-pandemic hybrid ways of working will have a significant impact on i-deals research. First, a new type of i-deals is likely to emerge. As the need for office space has been diminishing, in a parallel fashion, the need for office space at home has been rising. Employers have realized the importance of providing comfortable office space and place for employees who conduct their work remotely. Reliable remote work technology (e.g., computer and internet connection) and communication equipment (e.g., microphone and headphones), standing desk, ergonomic chair, and other office furniture will likely constitute elements of idiosyncratic work arrangement negotiations in the future research. Future studies are recommended to integrate access to and use of personal home office and associated furniture as potential mechanisms and boundary conditions to understand how these new types of i-deals generate positive outcomes for employees and organizations.

Second, office design and space allocation to employees will also become i-deals. Before the coronavirus pandemic erupted, workspace designers and executives often aimed to create high-touch, collaborative, open space work environments that afforded opportunities for frequent impromptu social interactions among employees. An underlying idea of collaborative office spaces has been to create an open and transparent workspace wherein employees can see each other on a usual basis and feel part of a big family. In such settings, personal offices are avoided for those may create feeling of alienation and status differences. However, in the post-pandemic, world organizations are expected to opt for some degree of social distancing and virtual interaction rather than a face-to-face work environment with an open layout. Employees upon their return to the office will engage in a new hybrid workspace which will bring new challenges of communication and status signaling functions. To accommodate safe and secure distancing among employees, most organizations will see the return of the cubicle or workstation pod—but with hard, cleanable surfaces instead of foam and fabric. Plexiglas barriers may also be installed in certain areas. Questions such as who will be entitled to a large (or small) office, who is required to be physically present at work, and who is allowed to work from home or even from another city or country imply that the definition of i-deals will change.

In hybrid work settings, many i-deals such as work from home or being away for training may not be apparent to the recipients' co-workers, which might change the within group dynamics. I-deals literature recognizes the potential for perceptions of unfairness arising from within group heterogeneity created by individualization of work (Marescaux et al., 2021; Rousseau et al., 2006). These issues may worsen as the absence of social cues may lead co-workers to overestimate how many group members have i-deals, and to what degree they are able to customize their work arrangements. New issues may also arise based on who gets the new desired ways to work and why. I-deal researchers need to be prepared to tackle these questions by integrating better with theories on remote and flexible work.

Employee Well-Being and I-deals

Another area that is going to gain importance in i-deals research is employee well-being. As the pandemic has been unfolding over the last two years, concerns for employee well-being have become more salient and significant than ever. While the potential gains of i-deals have been widely studied for employee attitudes and behaviors (see Liao et al., 2016 for an extensive review), relatively limited research exists on how i-deals contribute to employee well-being (Chapter 11). This is problematic, but at the same time, poses an opportunity for future research where scholars may develop i-deal interventions and study their effects on various aspects of employee well-being. To illustrate the importance of this topic, we draw a parallel to research on job crafting (another bottom-up employee-driven approach to address employee work needs and preferences), which has evolved in the direction of developing and studying interventions. A large number of studies have demonstrated that job crafting interventions benefit both employees and employers by enhancing employee well-being (see Veenhoven et al., 2019 for an overview).

In considering the implications of i-deal interventions for employee well-being, scholars may focus on work schedule and location flexibility.

Work flexibility has long been proposed as a tool to achieve work-life balance; however, these practices never fully took off largely due to the out-of-sight-out-of-mind phenomenon. A big deterrent against flex work is the fear that employers may not acknowledge accomplishments of employees who are not present in the office during standard hours. This is because employers recognize the potential for moral hazard in flex work, that is, employees may not put their full effort when they are not being monitored (Chapter 3). Nevertheless, attitudes toward flex work have shifted during the pandemic. Social distancing requirements forced a natural experiment whereby most employers had to adopt work schedule and location flexibility. Employers have come to appreciate the benefits of flex work, which has made these practices more acceptable (Mercer, 2021). At the same time, having tasted the joys of flex work most employees are unwilling to go back to the old ways of work on a standard schedule in the office (Trougakos et al., in press).

Schedule and location flexibility can be used as a tool to achieve work-life balance; however, these can also lead to work-life imbalance (Mazmanian et al., 2013). With the increase in flex work during the pandemic, employees have reported increasing extent of work intensification and exhaustion emanating from stress related to work demands (Shockley et al., 2021). This may be because employees working from home or working on a flexible schedule feel obligated to be available round the clock and end up putting in more hours. This potential for employees conforming to unreasonable standards in return for i-deals has been noted by scholars (Chapters 8 and 9). We therefore urge future scholars to examine the efficacy of flexibility i-deals in different contexts in promoting employee well-being. Moreover, research should explore new types of i-deals that may emerge with a focus on minimizing overwork, during times of flex work, and achieving work-life balance. For instance, employees may negotiate unplugged time wherein they will not be expected to check work emails or other messages, or productivity measurement in terms of outcomes rather than the hours worked. Scholars should also investigate the differential effects of various types of i-deals on employee well-being. In addition to flexibility, employees may benefit from task, development, and other types of i-deals that fulfill their unique needs for autonomy, control, and growth. Findings of such research will inform practicing managers and HR directors to collaborate in developing and implementing i-deal interventions to foster a positive and cohesive work environment, supportive of employee well-being.

Widening Divide Between Blue and White-Collar Employees and I-deals

I-deals literature tacitly assumes individualization of work is available to all employees to tailor work to their individual situations (Chapters 8 and 10). However, empirical studies have mostly relied on samples of white-collar employees at mid to higher ranks in their organizations. Only a few studies have included employees at lower hierarchical levels (e.g., Bal & Boehm, 2019; Collins et al., 2013). Questions of power and privilege fundamental to the concept of i-deals thus remain unanswered. Empirical evidence (e.g., Anand et al., 2010; Hornung et al., 2008) supports that i-deals are likely to be observed among employees working in both for-profit (e.g., software development) and non-profit sectors (e.g., government agencies). In terms of gender differences, female employees are more likely to seek flexibility i-deals, as they tend to value schedule and location flexibility more than their male counterparts (Blau & Kahn, 2006). Developmental i-deals are more likely to be obtained by men, especially those in managerial positions (Rofcanin, 2016). Barring noteworthy exceptions (See Chapter 10 for a review), research has not explicitly addressed the question of whether the obtainment of i-deals, regardless of their content, is more likely for those who have some type of power or privilege in the institutions of society.

In a world defined by pandemic, the questions of power and privilege are going to be more salient than before: Shifts in demand post-pandemic are likely to impact the most vulnerable workers. The trends accelerated by the pandemic indicate that more than half of low-wage workers in declining occupations may need to shift to occupations in higher wage brackets that require different skills (CIPD, 2020). Most strikingly, women, people with less education, employees coming from Black and ethnic minority (BAME) backgrounds, and the young may face a higher need to switch occupations, which will require help in the form of individualized interventions such as training. The polarization in employment markets is also expected to widen: Individuals at the upper echelons of organizations will continue to gain power and money while those in the lower ranks will further lose both income and importance, with middle ranks disappearing across the globe (Economic Policy Institute, 2021). This trend is partly due to automation and globalization expedited by the pandemic. What remains to be tackled by future studies in i-deals is to understand and advocate for the participation of women, employees with less education, employees working in blue-collar jobs, and most importantly employees coming from BAME backgrounds. In so doing, i-deal scholars will be able to bridge the ever-widening gap between academic scholarship and management practice (Rynes, 2007) by making recommendations for improving worker lives. I-deals research can create a workplace where all employees have equal opportunities, with a level playing field for everyone who seeks i-deals and who can benefit from their receipt. To this end, i-deal scholars need to reframe HR policies and interventions to help under-represented group of employees enjoy similar opportunities and career development benefits as their counterparts from well-represented groups.

Can Individual Deals Benefit the Society Overall?

By definition, i-deals represent a phenomenon that relates to individual gains such as an employee seeking and receiving individualized training and developmental opportunities to advance her career. Employers likely grant these deals to get benefits for the company, such as increased performance or more cohesive teamwork (e.g., Hornung et al., 2009; Anand et al., in press). These defining features of i-deals theory have been supported by empirical evidence. Research to date has shown that i-deals lead to myriad benefits for both the grantors and the recipients (e.g., Anand et al., 2010; Liu et al., 2013; Rofcanin et al., in press).

A possible meaningful extension of this research is to explore whether and how i-deals can spur benefits to the various stakeholders in the local community and the society at large. Many small and medium-sized companies (SMEs), start-ups, or local independent stores (e.g., coffee places, grocery shops) have had their business drastically cut by the pandemic. Many industries such as tourism, hospitality, and restaurant have been adversely impacted and pushed to the brink of permanent closure. In the wake of the pandemic and the changing landscape of work, i-deals can be seen as a tool for advancement of the local community and the wider society. Such an approach will give rise to interesting and theoretically important questions such as: how do different types of i-deals benefit the communities surrounding a business, are there ways of generating sustainable spillover effects and bridging the individualized gains of i-deals to the benefit of local industries, and who will be the ultimate recipient of i-deal gain chains. To illustrate this new conceptualization of i-deals in a context, imagine a business school professor whose university grants i-deals in the form of tuition and support (e.g., teaching load reduction or schedule flexibility) for completing an online degree on entrepreneurial start-up success and marketing strategies so she can design and teach new courses on those topics. The i-deals allow the employee to update her skillset and gain knowledge in a new field of expertise, and thus create a win–win situation for both parties. The benefits of these i-deals are likely to amplify if shared with local businesses, and other stakeholders in the local community (e.g., local high school). The professor may mentor high school students so they can dream of creating new entrepreneurial ventures. The professor may lecture at the local library and guide local community members trying to launch or run small businesses. The professor may also serve as an expert for the community members when they need information and advice. The professor's i-deals in this manner can improve the community, augment the grantor university's linkages with the community, and elevate the university's reputation.

Organizations do not operate in a vacuum; their success and survival both are dependent on the interactions and resource exchanges with the context in which they are situated (Starbuck, 1976). Considering the benefits of i-deals for the surrounding communities will evoke important theoretical angles such as crossover and spillover and inspire multi-level theorizing in the future. This will also allow scholars to bridge the gap between research and practice (Rynes, 2007).

Conclusion

COVID-19 pandemic has significantly impacted the way we work now and the way we will in the future. A challenging future of work is emerging in which i-deals are positioned to play a strategic role in addressing employees' unique work needs and preferences by enabling employers to adapt to these requests and new forms of working, such as hybrid and flexible work. In this chapter, we discussed key trends that are likely to emerge in the field of i-deals and underscored some of the concerns about the extant research methods. The future trends coupled with the improvements in i-deals research methods will continue to make this field of inquiry exciting and important. An important direction of this research stream is to reconsider the impact of the ongoing pandemic and adapt the defining features of i-deals theory.

REFERENCES

Anand, S., Meuser, J. D., Vidyarthi, P. R., Liden, R. C., Rousseau, D. M., & Ekkirala, S. (in press). A multi-level model of i-deals in workgroups: Employee and coworker perceptions of leader fairness, i-deals and group performance. *Journal of Management Studies*.

Anand, S., & Mitra, A. (In press). No family left behind: Flexibility i-deals for employees with stigmatized family identities. *Human Relations*.

Anand, S., & Vidyarthi, P. (2015). Idiosyncratic deals in the context of workgroups. In P. M. Bal & D. M. Rousseau (Eds.), *Idiosyncratic deals between employees and organizations: Conceptual issues, applications, and the role of coworkers* (pp. 92–106). Routledge-Taylor & Francis Group.

Anand, S., Vidyarthi, P. R., Liden, R. C., & Rousseau, D. M. (2010). Good citizens in poor-quality relationships: Idiosyncratic deals as a substitute for relationship quality. *Academy of Management Journal*, 53, 970–988.

Arthur, M. B. (2014). The boundaryless career at 20: Where do we stand and where can we go? *Career Development International*, 19, 627–640.

Bal, P. M., & Boehm, S. A. (2019). How do i-deals influence client satisfaction? The role of exhaustion, collective commitment, and age diversity. *Journal of Management*, 45, 1461–1487.

Bal, P. M., & Dóci, E. (2018). Neoliberal ideology in work and organizational psychology. *European Journal of Work and Organizational Psychology*, 27, 536–548.

Blau, F. D., & Kahn, L. M. (2006). The U.S. gender pay gap in the 1990s: Slowing convergence. *Industrial & Labor Relations Review*, 60, 45–66.

Catalyst. (2021). *Generations—Demographic trends in population and workforce: Quick Take*. https://www.catalyst.org/research/generations-demographic-trends-in-population-and-workforce/ (Accessed May 24, 2021).

CIPD. (2020). *Coronavirus (COVID-19): Flexible working during the pandemic and beyond*. Available on-line at: https://www.cipd.co.uk/knowledge/fundamentals/relations/flexible-working/during-COVID-19-and-beyond

Collins, A. M., Cartwright, S., & Hislop, D. (2013). Homeworking: Negotiating the psychological contract. *Human Resource Management Journal*, 23, 211–225.

Economic Policy Institute. (2021). *Preliminary data show CEO pay jumped nearly 16% in 2020, while average worker compensation rose 1.8%*. Available online at: https://www.epi.org/blog/preliminary-data-show-ceo-pay-jumped-nearly-16-in-2020-while-average-worker-compensation-rose-1-8/ (Accessed May 24, 2021).

Greatplacetowork. (2021). https://www.greatplacetowork.com/resources/blog/q-a-how-dell-technologies-is-using-an-outcome-based-work-culture-to-create-flexibility-in-the-workplace (Accessed May 30, 2021).

Greenhaus, J. H., & Kossek, E. E. (2014). The contemporary career: A work–home perspective. *Annual Review of Organizational Psychology and Organizational Behavior, 1,* 361–388.

Ho, V. T., & Kong, D. T. (2015). Exploring the signaling function of idiosyncratic deals and their interaction. *Organizational Behavior and Human Decision Processes, 131,* 149–161.

Hornung, S., Rousseau, D. M., & Glaser, J. (2008). Creating flexible work arrangements through idiosyncratic deals. *Journal of Applied Psychology, 93,* 655–664.

Hornung, S., Rousseau, D., & Glaser, J. (2009). Why supervisors make idiosyncratic deals: Antecedents and outcomes of i-deals from a managerial perspective. *Journal of Managerial Psychology, 24,* 738–764.

Hornung, S., Rousseau, D. M., Glaser, J., Angerer, P., & Weigl, M. (2010). Beyond top-down and bottom-up work redesign: Customizing job content through idiosyncratic deals. *Journal of Organizational Behavior, 31,* 187–215.

Las Heras, M., Rofcanin, Y., Matthijs Bal, P., & Strollberg, J. (2017). How do flexibility i-deals relate to work performance? Exploring the roles of family performance and organizational context. *Journal of Organizational Behavior, 38,* 1280–1294.

Liao, C., Wayne, S. J., & Rousseau, D. M. (2016). Idiosyncratic deals in contemporary organizations: A qualitative and meta-analytical review. *Journal of Organizational Behavior, 37,* S9–S29.

Liu, J., Lee, C., Hui, C., Kwan, H. K., & Wu, L. Z. (2013). Idiosyncratic deals and employee outcomes: The mediating roles of social exchange and self-enhancement and the moderating role of individualism. *Journal of Applied Psychology, 98,* 832–840.

Marescaux, E., De Winne, S., & Rofcanin, Y. (2021). Co-worker reactions to i-deals through the lens of social comparison: The role of fairness and emotions. *Human Relations, 74,* 329–353.

Mazmanian, M., Orlikowski, W. J., & Yates, J. (2013). The autonomy paradox: The implications of mobile email devices for knowledge professionals. *Organization Science, 24,* 1337–1357.

McKinsey Global Institute. (2021). *Future of Work after COVID-19.* On-line at: https://www.mckinsey.com/featured-insights/future-of-work/the-future-of-work-after-covid-19 (Accessed April 10, 2021).

Mercer. (2021). *The new shape of work is flexibility for all.* Available on-line at: https://www.mercer.com/our-thinking/career/the-new-shape-of-work-is-flexibility-for-all-global.html (Accessed June 12, 2021).

Rofcanin, Y. (2016). *R differentiation: A double-edged sword?* Unpublished PhD dissertation. University of Warwick, Coventry.

Rofcanin, Y., Berber, A., Marescaux, E., Bal, P., Mughal, F., & Afacan Findikli, M. (2019). Human resource differentiation: A theoretical paper integrating co-workers' perspective and context. *Human Resource Management Journal, 29*, 270–286.

Rofcanin, Y., Kiefer, T., & Strauss, K. (2017). What seals the I-deal? Exploring the role of employees' behaviours and managers' emotions. *Journal of Occupational and Organizational Psychology, 90*(2), 203–224.

Rofcanin, Y., Las Heras, M., Bosch, M.J., Stollberger, J., & Mayer, M. (in press). How do weekly obtained task i-deals improve work performance? The role of relational context and structural job resources. *European Journal of Work and Organizational Psychology.* https://doi.org/10.1080/1359432X.2020.1833858

Rosen, C. C., Slater, D. J., Chang, C. H., & Johnson, R. E. (2013). Let's make a deal: Development and validation of the ex post I-deals scale. *Journal of Management, 39*, 709–742.

Rousseau, D. M. (2005). *I-deals: Idiosyncratic deals employees bargain for themselves.* M.E. Sharpe.

Rousseau, D. M., Ho, V. T., & Greenberg, J. (2006). I-deals: Idiosyncratic terms in employment relationships. *Academy of Management Review, 31*, 977–994.

Rousseau, D. M., Hornung, S., & Kim, T. G. (2009). Idiosyncratic deals: Testing propositions on timing, content, and the employment relationship. *Journal of Vocational Behavior, 74*, 338–348.

Rynes, S. L. (2007). Editor's afterword—Let's create a tipping point: What academics and practitioners can do, alone and together. *Academy of Management Journal, 50*, 1046–1054.

Shockley, K. M., Clark, M. A., Dodd, H., & King, E. B. (2021). Work-family strategies during COVID-19: Examining gender dynamics among dual-earner couples with young children. *Journal of Applied Psychology, 106*(1), 15–28.

Starbuck, W. H. (1976). Organizations and their environments. In M. D. Dunnette (Ed.), *Handbook of industrial and organizational psychology* (pp. 1069–1123). Rand McNally.

Trougakos, J. P., Chawla, N., & McCarthy, J. M. (In press). Working in a pandemic: Exploring the impact of COVID-19 health anxiety on work, family, and health outcomes. *Journal of Applied Psychology.* Advance online publication. https://doi.org/10.1037/apl0000739

Veenhoven, R., Bakker, A. B., Burger, M., Van Haren, P., & Oerlemans, W. (2019). Effect on happiness of happiness self-monitoring and comparison with others: Using the Happiness Indicator. In L. VanZyl & S. Rothmann (Eds.), *Positive psychology interventions: Theories, methodologies and applications within multi-cultural contexts* (pp. 1–23). Springer International.

Vidyarthi, P. R., Singh, S., Erdogan, B., Chaudhry, A., Posthuma, R., & Anand, S. (2016). Individual deals within teams: Investigating the role of relative i-deals for employee performance. *Journal of Applied Psychology, 101,* 1536–1552.

Wang, H.J., Demerouti, E., & Bakker, A.B. (2016). *A review of job crafting research: The role of leader behaviors in cultivating successful job crafters.* In S. K. Parker & U. K. Bindl (Eds.), *Proactivity at work.* Routledge.

Index

A
Adverse selection, 49–51, 53, 54, 58, 63, 65–67
Affective commitment, 144
Agency, 195
Agile, 23
Appraisal, 77
Asymmetric information, 48, 49, 53, 54, 58
Attachment style, 74, 79
Avoidant attachment, 78

B
Bargaining, 54
Behavioral responses, 242
Burnout, 249, 252

C
Capitalism, 171–173, 180
Career goals, 3, 15
Career i-deals, 32, 38
Career inertia, 5
Career management practices, 10

Career regrets, 15
Career success, 2, 8, 9, 13–15
Cognitive responses, 242
Collaboration tactics, 75
Collectivism, 264, 266, 271–273
Compensation, 47, 51–62
Compensation design, 55, 60, 61
Context, 36, 49, 98, 100, 105, 119–122, 124, 125, 127, 130, 132–138, 310, 312, 314, 316–318, 320, 322, 326, 328, 329
Contract, 46–49, 55–57, 61, 62, 64, 65
Contract design, 57, 66
Coping, 135
COVID-19, 143, 158, 177, 309, 311, 321, 323, 324, 329
Coworkers, 99, 100, 102, 105–109, 111, 112
Coworker support, 278
Creativity, 27
Critique, 189, 310, 314, 315
Cross-cultural, 259–261, 265, 267

Crossover, 36, 329
Culture, 200–202, 258–261, 267, 269, 271–273, 275
Customized employment terms, 151

D

Decision, 46, 48, 49, 51–53, 55, 65
Demands-abilities fit, 248, 252
Development i-deals, 1–4, 7–14
Dialogue, 182
Dignity, 168, 171, 172, 177, 180–182
Dual-earner family, 24
Dynamic nature, 96, 316, 319

E

Elite workers, 199, 200
Emerging economies, 269, 270
Emotional support, 26, 28, 29
Emotion regulation, 135, 136
Emotions, 126–129, 131, 133–137
Employee creativity, 144
Employee differentiation, 147, 148, 152
Employee engagement, 242, 296
Employee outcomes, 144, 145
Employee performances, 8
Employee well-being, 241, 243–246, 248, 249, 325
Etic versus emic, 268
Ex-ante i-deals, 65, 66, 146, 158, 211, 323
Exchange, 96–99, 101, 106–108
Exchange tactics, 75
Expatriate assignments, 157
Exploitative leadership, 73, 74, 82, 312
Ex-post i-deals, 65, 66, 322, 323

F

Fairness, 102, 105, 109–112, 114, 120, 121, 125, 127
Flexibility, 22, 24
Flexibility i-deals, 144, 145, 147, 149, 150, 152, 153, 155, 158
Follower-initiated, 74, 83, 85
Foucault, Michel, 189, 191, 197, 198, 201
Future of work, 310, 320, 322, 329
Future work selves, 13

G

Generalizability, 261, 263–265
Group context, 96–100, 106, 107, 113

H

Hidden-action Principal-agent model, 49, 50, 57
Hidden-information Principal-agent model, 49, 50, 53, 65
HR differentiation, 314
HR practices, 10, 120, 121, 137, 138, 145, 146, 148, 149, 151, 152, 155, 158, 159, 315
Humanism, 188
Human resource philosophy, 160
Hybrid work, 325

I

Ideal, 171, 176
i-deal interventions, 320, 325, 326
i-deals lifecycle, 96, 97, 101, 103, 109, 112–114
i-deals negotiation, 97, 101, 104–106
Ideology, 171, 173, 179
Idiosyncratic deals request, 7
Incentives, 49, 50, 60
Indigenous, 267, 274

INDEX 337

Individualism, 193, 195, 266, 272
Individualization, 168, 169, 188–192, 195, 197, 198, 201, 202
Individualization of work, 65, 310, 312, 314, 315, 325, 327
Individuation, 190–192, 195, 199
Inequality, 172–174
Influence tactics, 75
Information asymmetry, 45, 47–52, 61–63, 311, 312
Institutional context, 259, 267
Instrumental support, 27, 28
Intergroup contact, 155

J
Job crafting, 31, 37, 169–171, 314, 319, 320, 325
Job demands, 239, 240, 245, 246, 248–251
Job demands-resources (J-DR) theory, 239, 245–247, 250
Job design, 319, 320
Job resources, 239, 245, 246, 248, 252
Job strain, 245, 246
Justice, 126

K
Knowledge and appraisal personality architecture (KAPA), 77–83, 85

L
Labour process, 189, 190, 192–194
Leader-follower relationships, 64, 66
Leader-member exchange (LMX), 72, 73, 80, 88
Leadership, 72, 73, 75, 76, 79, 80, 82–85
Leadership prototypes, 74
Leader-subordinate relationship, 145

Lifecycle framework, 100, 101, 112–114

M
Managerial decision-making, 311, 315
Managers, 97, 100, 107, 108, 110–113
Managers' perceptions, 7
Mature-age employees, 220, 223, 225–227
Measurement of i-deals, 316, 318
Meso-level, 96, 99–101, 112–114
Mood regulation, 135
Moral hazard, 49, 50, 54–58, 63–67
Motives, 3, 4
Multi-level, 99, 100, 113, 114
Multi-level theorizing, 318, 329

N
Needs, 3, 4, 8, 10, 12–14
Negotiation of idiosyncratic deals, 27, 104, 114, 225, 241, 243, 271, 313
Negotiations, 54
Neoliberalism, 188–193, 195, 197, 202, 203

O
Operationalization, 269
Organizational citizenship behavior, 145, 155
Organizational climate, 132
Organizational culture, 10, 29, 66, 112, 199, 200, 271
Organizational effectiveness, 144
Organizational justice, 96, 98, 100, 102–114
Organizational support, 22, 29, 32
Othering, 200

P

Person-job fit, 239, 247, 248
Person-organization fit, 239, 247, 248, 250–252
Perspective taking, 151, 154, 155, 159
Power distance, 265, 269, 271
Power relations, 194, 196
Precarity, 189
Principal-agent model, 48
Private information, 46–49, 53, 58, 59, 61–63
Privilege, 75, 121, 173, 188, 221, 224, 327
Proactive behavior, 144
Psychological contract, 167, 169, 170, 238, 241–243, 249–251

R

Rational-actor model, 48
Reciprocity, 194
Renegotiation, 96, 98, 107, 110–114
Reproduction of form, 178, 179
Research design, 316, 319
Resource-based view on idiosyncratic deals, 246

S

Screening, 49–51, 61–64, 66
Screening model, 61
Secure attachment, 79
Self-concepts, 6
Servant leadership, 73, 74, 76, 82, 264, 271, 312
Signaling, 49–51, 58–60, 62, 64
Signaling model, 58
Signal jamming, 60
Signalling theory, 252

Skills and abilities, 8, 9
Skill transitions, 323
Social-cognitive, 81
Social comparison, 96–107, 109–114
Social exchange, 144, 149
Social exchange theory (SET), 238, 240–242, 249, 251
Societal context, 259
Spillover, 328, 329
Spousal support, 33
Stereotypes, 219–221, 228
Subjective age, 34
Subjectivity, 194, 195, 197
Suspended i-deals, 148, 152

T

Task i-deals, 32, 38
Teams, 86–88, 131, 132, 137, 150, 203, 320
Technologies of power, 198
Technologies of the Self, 195
Tightness-looseness, 271
Time-spatial job crafting, 37
Trust propensity, 74, 79

V

Values, 6

W

Within-person change, 319
Women, 214, 219–222, 224–227, 229
Workgroups, 96–107, 109, 111–114
Work-life balance, 24, 25
Work/non-work interface, 23
Work stressors, 144
Work trends, 321

Printed in the United States
by Baker & Taylor Publisher Services